TRANSACTIONS OF THE
ROYAL HISTORICAL SOCIETY

FIFTH SERIES

VOLUME 25

LONDON
OFFICES OF THE ROYAL HISTORICAL SOCIETY
UNIVERSITY COLLEGE LONDON, GOWER ST., W.C.1
1975

ISBN 0 901050 26 1

Made and Printed in Great Britain by Butler & Tanner Ltd, Frome and London

CONTENTS

ELIE HALÉVY AND
THE BIRTH OF METHODISM

By J. D. Walsh, M.A., Ph.D.

READ 8 FEBRUARY 1974

PROBABLY the most famous passages in Halévy's work are those attributing England's immunity from revolution after 1789 to the influence of Methodism. The 'Halévy thesis' encouraged, though it did not begin, a debate which still fizzes, jumps and occasionally explodes. Little attention has been given to Halévy's first essay in Methodist history, 'The Birth of Methodism in England', which appeared in *La Révue de Paris* in 1906, even though one of its central themes prefigured his famous thesis. After decades of neglect, this has been disinterred, translated and excellently introduced by Bernard Semmel.[1] Compared with Halévy's major writings it is thin and slightly documented, for much of the primary research on which it was based was crowded into a few weeks in the Bodleian Library, after which he seems to have been discouraged by the misleading news that his subject had been pre-empted.[2] The essay remained a rather slender piece, sweepingly written, which found its outlet in a cultural periodical rather than a learned journal. But it is something of a *tour de force*.

In this brief paper I do not intend to assess the place of the essay in Halévy's evolution as historian, nor offer a coherent alternative model for the genesis of Methodism, but merely to examine some of Halévy's answers to the problem he posed himself: why did the Methodist movement break out in 1738-39 and what was its character at that time?

Before Halévy—and long afterwards—the birth of Methodism was for the most part treated incidentally through biographies of its leaders, especially John Wesley, which did much to illuminate the

[1] E. Halévy, *The Birth of Methodism in England*, transl. with introduction by B. Semmel (Chicago, 1971).

[2] 'Alain' (E. A. Chartier), *Correspondance avec E. et F. Halévy* (8e édn, Paris, 1958), pp. 331-32.

interplay of events and personalities as well as the inner religious aspirations of the Holy Club members who helped to launch the Revival. However, the earlier biographers took little account of the social, or indeed the wider theological setting of the 1730s and 1740s, viewing the arrival of Methodism (as Halévy complained) as an act of providential immediacy, a virtual creation *ex nihilo*. In the last few years Methodist history has swerved away into more secular directions as studies of its demography, geography and sociology have begun to open up vistas scarcely glimpsed by Halévy. We now know more about the distribution, social and spatial, of Methodism, and the environments conducive to its growth— outsize parishes in upland or forest areas, 'open' or freehold parishes, squatter settlements, out-townships, rapidly expanding industrial villages.[3] However, this valuable work is of only partial use in solving Halévy's chosen problem: it does not get us much closer to the specific location of Methodism's birth in the years 1738–39. Some of the conditions for the spread of Methodism (such as the growth of extra-parochial industrial settlements like the collieries round Kingswood) had existed for decades, others (like the large parishes with dispersed settlement in the West Riding) for centuries. A movement resembling Methodism might perhaps have been launched well before 1738; witness the success, on a small scale, of Richard Davis, Independent minister of Rothwell in Northampton-shire, from whose revival-minded chapel in the 1690s lay preachers went out to create sister meetings in other villages, almost fore-shadowing the Methodist connexional system.[4] But it was not until the late 1730s that the peculiar conjunction of forces occurred to make the large-scale movement of Methodism possible. Fruitfully, Halévy set out to fit together some of the short-term, biographical and 'accidental' trigger-causes precipitating Methodism, with some of the structural conditions for its nurture and growth.

His argument may be summarised thus. In the early eighteenth century among the English people there was a deep but latent Protestant fervour, the inheritance of decades of Puritan indoctrina-tion. Before it could be made effective, this half-dormant piety needed to be revitalized. The orthodox Dissenters were unequal to

[3] See A. M. Everitt, *The Pattern of Rural Dissent: the Nineteenth Century* (Leicester, 1972); R. Currie, 'A Micro-theory of Methodist Growth', *Proceedings of the Wesley Historical Society*, xxxvi (1967), pp. 65–73. Also the important unpublished theses by B. Greaves, 'Methodism in Yorkshire 1740–1851' (Liverpool University Ph.D., 1968), D. M. Thompson, 'The Churches and Society in Leicestershire 1851–1881' (Cambridge University Ph.D., 1969), A. D. Gilbert, 'The Growth and Decline of Nonconformity in England and Wales' (Oxford University D.Phil., 1973).

[4] T. Coleman, *Memorials of the Independent Churches in Northamptonshire* (London, 1853), pp. 54 ff.

the task, declining in numbers and racked by controversy. Nor was
the Church of England apparently much better equipped. Certainly,
it contained some vital 'seeds of religious renovation', notably in its
great voluntary societies like the S.P.C.K., the S.P.G. and, above
all, the small devotional groups known as the 'Religious Societies',
but these cells of associational piety could seldom reproduce themselves effectively, being tinged with High Church, even Jacobite
views, which cut them off from the Protestantism of the masses.

Yet, remarkably, from this Anglican piety sprang the Revival.
From one of the societies, the Oxford Holy Club, came leaders like
the Wesleys and Whitefield; from the Religious Societies in Bristol,
London and elsewhere, came many of the earliest converts. How
had the transformation come about? From two exogenous influences
which radically altered the existing religious compound. First was
the ferment of ideas brought by Protestant refugees and visitors to
this country, above all by the Moravian Brethren whose simple,
emotional doctrine of justification by faith helped convert John
Wesley, 'teaching him what he must preach in order to capture
hearers'. The second influence came from Wales. Rightly recogniz-
ing that the Revival in Wales antedated that in England, Halévy
produced evidence to suggest that techniques of field-preaching
which turned Methodism into a truly popular movement, were
copied by Whitefield from the Welsh evangelists.

But why did a movement which had made 'only slow progress in
Pembrokeshire and Cardiganshire, suddenly create such a sensation
in Gloucestershire, and Somerset, and soon all over England?'
Because in 1739 England was passing through a period of unusual
turbulence, agitated by the political crisis which led to the fall of
Walpole in 1742, and shaken by a 'crisis of industrial overproduction
of extreme gravity' which in particular threatened the woollen
industry and, exacerbated by bad harvests, brought the labouring
classes to the brink of general revolt. Was it not natural that the
'Christian enthusiasm' of the newly converted Methodist leaders
should 'endeavour to turn this popular ferment to its own profit?'
Alarmed contemporaries feared that the evangelicals would give the
lower orders a revolutionary ideology and leadership. They need not
have worried. Wesley and Whitefield, representative bourgeois
conservatives, took care to bend the popular excitement 'to the form
which most favoured the respect for . . . existing institutions.'

Halévy's first major premise, that Methodism 'revived what was
left of the Puritan religious sense in the national consciousness'
commands respect. Halévy saw the main signs of the continuity of
Puritanism in the characteristics of melancholy which were regarded—especially by foreigners—as pronounced traits of English

national character: the 'hyp', the spleen, the vapours, the proclivity to suicide widely discussed at this time. These symptoms, he held, exactly matched the anxieties and guilt feelings which were the prelude to the classical evangelical conversion experience; they were the legacy of the Puritan sense of sin. 'A melancholy people are a religious people.' But while interest in the 'English Malady' seems to have peaked towards the middle of the eighteenth century it is impossible to determine whether its polymorphous signs were an index of vestigial Puritanism, or of the hypochondria and *ennui* of a bored leisure class, or the invention of fashionable doctors, or a sequence in a long literary tradition stretching at least from Elizabethans to Romantics, or merely a perennial malaise of the human condition. Contemporaries were apt to blame it on diet, weather and the baneful effects of 'luxury'.[5] Nor is Halévy's second example of submerged Protestant-Puritan fervour—the persistence of anti-Roman Catholic hysteria—to be treated as more than a highly negative form of religiosity, shared as it was by Deists and a conspicuously non-churchgoing 'Church rabble.'

Though a wide range of religious, social and psychological explanations have been put forward for the phenomena of religious anxiety, Halévy's argument needs more examination. It will not be an easy enquiry, for Puritanism, notoriously hard to define in the seventeenth century, is far harder to identify in the eighteenth, when much of its spirit is said to be secularized and traceable indirectly in expressions as far apart as the funeral elegy and the gospel of work. Even in a religious context it is difficult to isolate specifically Puritan attitudes from others. Anglican High Church-manship often possessed a strongly ascetical outlook; Nonjurors in particular took a stance on questions like the Sabbath, the stage or the redemption of time which was barely distinguishable from the Puritan. Halévy never grappled with a paradox implicit in his own essay: why Methodism drew in so many High Churchmen like the Wesleys or the members of the Anglican Religious Societies, whose 'Anglo-Catholic' spirituality (he believed) was not only un-Puritan, but virtually 'an altogether different religion.' He ignored the congruity in moral aspiration, though not in its theological basis, between the two types of religion.[6]

But it would be unwise to dismiss Halévy's belief that years of Puritan indoctrination had deeply scored the English character.

---

[5] See C. A. Moore, *Backgrounds of English Literature 1700–1760* (Minneapolis, 1953), pp. 179–235.

[6] See J. D. Walsh, 'Origins of the Evangelical Revival', in *Essays in Modern English Church History*, ed. G. V. Bennett and J. D. Walsh (London, 1966), pp. 138–48.

Puritanism in its plenitude of power was only two generations away. Its literature, if sometimes used as wrapping paper in shops, or rudely exposed on second-hand barrows, still survived to awaken or solace future Methodists who found that works like *Grace Abounding* still spoke immediately to their spiritual condition. How many families were there, now strongly Anglican, which possessed parents like the Wesleys of Epworth or the Cennicks of Reading, raised in stern Puritan Nonconformity? How many energetic Anglican moralists like Sir John Philipps, patron of the S.P.C.K., or Sir John Barnard, reforming Lord Mayor of London, had been nurtured in Puritan homes?[7] Puritanism has a habit of transmitting its sense of moral duty and feeling of sin more effectively than its doctrines of grace. The conversion experiences of the first Methodists show many anxiety-producing factors—spiritual yearning, religious doubt, sexual difficulty, social and geographical mobility, pain, bereavement—but the tensions which derived from a strictly moralistic upbringing accentuated many of them. Early eighteenth-century England looked to the seventeenth century for most of its ethical precepts or stereotypes of good and evil. It may be that in England, as in the American colonies, the jeremiads on vice, luxury and irreligion which poured out in the early decades of the eighteenth century epitomized the bewilderment of men whose moral norms had been formed in an age of Puritan morality and economic scarcity and could not be applied without strain under conditions of greater prosperity and growing religious latitude.[8] The themes of death, judgment, providence, the imminence of eternity, the need for personal salvation, were only just below the surface of men's minds; it needed only an earth-tremor, even a violent thunderstorm, to awaken them. Events like the South Sea Bubble or the '45 were widely and easily interpreted as judgments on a wicked nation. The appeal of Methodism lay partly in its ability to arouse and direct beliefs of this kind.

Halévy would have stood on firmer ground had he examined the patent rather than the latent vestiges of Puritanism; the piety of orthodox Dissenters, self-professed 'offspring of the Puritans', or the forlorn Calvinists who survived in an almost totally Arminian Church of England. Both were diminishing in numbers, especially the Anglicans, who had (as one complained bitterly) been obliged

[7] T. Shankland, 'Sir John Philipps; the S.P.C.K. and the Charity-School Movement in Wales 1699–1737', *Transactions of the Honourable Society of Cymmrodorion* (1904–5), pp. 74 ff; *Memoirs of Sir J. Barnard* (repr. London, 1885), pp. 2–12.

[8] See J. P. Greene, 'Search for Identity: an Interpretation of the Meaning of Selected Patterns of Social Response in Eighteenth Century America', *Journal of Social History*, iii (1970), pp. 195–99.

'to betake themselves into corners and obscurity'.[9] Halévy sketched the state of the Dissenting Interest, especially the fierce internal disputes, over new Arian and Arminian ideas. These conflicts—he noted—frequently had a class-dimension, since the liberals tended to be the chapel elite of pastors and well-to-do, educated members, the conservatives, the poorer element who expressed their resentment by heresy hunts and schisms. Orthodox pastors felt powerless to stop the decline and seize hold of the rising generation.

Examining Dissent in order to show why it did not generate the Evangelical Revival—an important question—Halévy missed the positive, symbiotic relationship between declining Nonconformity and rising Methodism. Over the century Methodism gave Dissent more than it took: (methods, pastors, members, whole congregations), but at first it probably took more than it gave, absorbing a considerable, though unknown, number of Nonconformists into its societies. There was much to attract the grandsons of the Puritans in the new movement. The Calvinistic Methodism of Whitefield, in particular, though tinged with 'enthusiasm', sounded to many appreciative connoisseurs like *Puritanismus redivivus*.[10] The Methodists claimed to represent the pure, untainted, 'plain old religion' of the English Reformation. Pressing home their claim by *catenae* of quotations from the Articles, Homilies, divines like Jewel or Davenant, they touched the guilt feelings of some who had lapsed from, or at least compromised their traditional beliefs. Methodism profited from the normative conflict engendered by a period of unusually rapid theological transition. It gathered in Dissenters who were uneasy at their failure to produce, in a cooler religious climate, the classic marks of regeneration demanded of them by Puritan doctrine and Puritan forebears, but managed to achieve them in an emotional New Birth at a fervent Methodist society meeting. Among Anglicans, Methodist apologetic exploited the dangerously wide gap which had opened up between the plain sense of the 39 Articles, and the glosses put on them by rationalistic theologians in the eighteenth century; its appeal to Reformation orthodoxy disturbed many clerical consciences and won many lay converts. Methodism was a potent blend of traditionalism and novelty; its content appealed to atavistic longings for the 'old religion', while its form—emotional, vivid, simple—pleased those who wearied of conventional Nonconformist preaching, ossified in a seventeenth-century idiom which now appeared archaic, stylized and unduly metaphysical.

There were obstacles in the way of the Dissenter who contem-

[9] (R. Seagrave), *A Letter to the People of England* (2nd edn, London, ? 1735), p. 20.
[10] *George Whitefield's Journals* (London, 1961), p. 461.

plated turning Methodist—tradition, hostility from his own pastor, inbred suspicion of clergymen dressed in gowns and bands, especially if they were Arminians like the brothers Wesley. But the journals of the Methodist leaders show them garnering a crop of Nonconformist converts and even inducing some of them to undergo Anglican baptism.[11] A number of these were individuals disturbed by the 'Arian blight' gaining ground in their congregations at the expense of the old divinity. Occasionally, evangelicalism profited by larger secessions from heterodox chapels, as in Bolton and Leeds.[12] In Newcastle, where Wesley had opened his Orphan House chapel, a Nonjuror reported in 1743, 'one Presbyterian meeting is quite deserted and others of them very much thinned'.[13] In London, where some admiring Dissenters had helped to pay for Whitefield's Tabernacle, another complained that Methodism had 'devoured' some meetings, leaving 'but a mere skeleton of a church and congregation'.[14] Even the saintly, orthodox and successful Doddridge lost members to the Moravians at Northampton.[15] Rural patterns are less clear. The shrinking of Dissent often posed more problems in the country than in the town, for small country causes with scattered membership fell more easily than urban ones below the critical number needed to support a pastor and chapel; as meetings closed, piety became more dispersed, focused on family hearth rather than meeting house. But here too was an opportunity for Methodism. One or two surviving Moravian membership lists suggest that the early itinerants, scouring the country, picked up some of these scattered folk, gathered them into societies or little cottage meetings, and gave them the heartening pastoral oversight they lacked.[16] Field preaching, helped by the enormous publicity given to early Methodism, called old Puritanism out of its 'corners and obscurity', and gave it new heart. Whitefield observed the process in his own itinerancy: 'I find there are some thousands of secret ones yet living amongst us who have not bowed the knee to Baal; and this public way of acting brings them out'.[17] Wesley noted how his preachers, searching for flagrant sinners, unexpectedly

[11] E.g. *The Journal of the Rev. C. Wesley*, ed. T. Jackson (London, 1849), i, pp. 192, 234, 358, 430, 441; ii, p. 81.

[12] W. H. Davison, *Centenary Memorials of Duke's Alley Chapel, Bolton* (Bolton, 1854), p. 49; R. Burdsall, *Memoirs* (2nd edn, York, 1811), p. 139.

[13] H. Broxap, *The Later Nonjurors* (Cambridge, 1924), p. 214.

[14] *The Causes and Reasons of the Present Declension among the Congregational Churches* (London, 1766), p. 9; L. Tyerman, *The Life of the Rev. G. Whitefield* (2nd edn, London, 1890), i, pp. 484–86.

[15] *The Northampton Group of Moravian Chapels* (London, 1886), p. 10.

[16] See John Rylands Library, Eng. MS 1076 (24).

[17] *Whitefield's Journals*, p. 275.

picked up many devout folk.[18] The rise of Methodism owed much to its ability not only to create religious zeal where none existed before, but to recharge and articulate existing cells of piety. Its growth was not only frontal—by recruitment from the unchurched, but lateral—from committed church members, Anglican and Nonconformist. Halévy was right: the Revival was not simply a creation *ex nihilo*.

How can one account for the irony that this quasi-Puritan revival was launched by men who a few years earlier had been strict High Churchmen in cloistered Oxford? Halévy pointed to the first of the three historical 'accidents' which transformed the religious situation in England; the influence of the German-speaking Moravian Brethren, who converted the 'Catholic' John Wesley to Protestantism, enabling him 'to discover religious feelings that he had not previously known, feelings that could be translated into action'. The Moravian influence on Methodism is incontrovertible, and has been often retailed, not least in the pages of Wesley's *Journal*. Here indeed was a new departure, as the emotional, experiential pietism of the Germans was grafted onto the sterner stock of English High Churchmanship. Yet Halévy's analytical scheme is a little too tidy and coherent and leaves some intractable loose ends. If the Moravians—notably Peter Böhler—led the brothers Wesley and other early Methodists to the threshold of evangelicalism, there were many other contemporary Methodist leaders, like Whitefield, or the early Welsh 'Methodists', who had no relations with the Brethren at the time of their conversions. The same holds good for most of the founding fathers of what became the distinctively Anglican Evangelical wing of the Revival. The genesis of the evangelical movement as a whole remains more obscure and complex than Halévy's neatly drawn miniature suggests.

Halévy's second 'accident', the meeting of English Methodists with Welsh revivalists, put forward a more original but more conjectural thesis. Picturing the Welsh as a half-civilized nation, 'barely emerging from savagery', darkly Celtic and given to violent emotion, he suggested that the primitive, unrestrained enthusiasm of their evangelical revival 'leaping over the border' to nearby Bristol, inspired the staider English Methodists to copy the passionate methods of Welsh oratory and the cavalier techniques of field preaching used so successfully by Harris and Rowland. Certainly, it was soon after Whitefield had been in fraternal correspondence with the fiery and leather-lunged Harris that he 'broke the ice' and began his life-long career as outdoor preacher by addressing the

---

[18] *The Letters of the Rev. J. Wesley*, ed. J. Telford (London, 1931), ii, p. 271.

Kingswood colliers from Hanham Mount on 17 February 1739. Halévy's claim for Welsh example may well be right; Whitefield's latest biographer would side with him.[19] Yet the evidence is inferential and not conclusive. Whitefield himself attributed his debut as field preacher to his banishment from the Bristol churches, and if external influences are still thought necessary to explain this step, it is clear that he was aware not only of the work in Wales but of an example far closer to home, that of William Morgan, a Cotswold clergyman—soon to turn Quaker—who had addressed the colliers from the same spot only months before.[20] Nor can it be proved that literary links with Celts induced Whitefield to make his own preaching more fiery and plebeian; he was already a popular preacher of extraordinary magnetism, whose presence could fill London churches to overflowing and leave his hearers 'like persons struck with pointed arrows, or mourning for a firstborn child'.[21] Halévy was shrewd to emphasize the critical importance of 17 February 1739, the point at which Methodism, hitherto largely a church-based movement, reached out to the unchurched. Curiously, however, he barely mentioned the other organizational innovations which turned Methodism into a popular movement; pastoral itinerancy, for instance, and the enlistment of lay helpers. These may have been copied from Wales, but their use by seventeenth-century sects and in the American Great Awakening reinforces the impression that they developed spontaneously. Without its army of lay preachers, crude but fervent, Methodism could hardly have spanned the gap between the polite culture of the clergy and the popular culture of colliers and fishermen. Without its itinerant ministry, it could never have stretched its manpower resources to reach beyond the normal limits of pastoral activity to touch some of those on the fringes of organized society, colliery villages, army garrisons, refugee settlements like those of the Palatine German *diaspora* in Ireland, integrating each flock, however isolated, in the wider life of the connexion.

We come to the crux of Halévy's argument, the 'great accident', the economic depression of the late 'thirties which, in a 'crisis of overproduction of extreme gravity, reduced the lower orders of the manufactories to poverty and made them accessible to all forms of collective emotion'. This is not the place to criticize Halévy's economic history (some of which needs radical revision) since there is no doubt of his premise, that the years 1739–41 were harsh and bitter. The lowered sales of cloth overseas, accentuated by the

[19] A. A. Dallimore, *George Whitefield* (London, 1970), i, p. 233 ff.
[20] *The Works of the Rev. G. Whitefield* (London, 1771–72), i, p. 30; *Procs. Wesley Hist. Soc.*, vi (1907), pp. 102–03, 124–27.   [21] *Whitefield's Journals*, p. 89.

stoppages of war in 1739, depressed the textile industry; the great frosts, which began at the end of 1739 and continued till 1741, led to soaring food prices and encouraged the ravages of epidemics; there was a disastrous murrain among cattle.[22] In the early months of 1740 there were violent grain riots from Salisbury to Edinburgh.

How could this be related to the birth of Methodism? Halévy put forward two hypotheses. First, that acute economic distress rendered the masses of the industrial poor susceptible to Methodist preaching. The atmosphere of anger and riot which smouldered in the South West and North East in 1738–40 provided 'favourable circumstances for the demonstration of religious enthusiasm'. Halévy never explored the psychological mechanisms by which this transition was made, resting content with the claim that industrial disturbances and Methodist preaching erupted almost simultaneously and in the same areas; Bristol, Wiltshire, the West Riding, Newcastle. He may be right, but the thesis cannot be satisfactorily proved either way since virtually no evidence survives from these years to indicate the names or occupations of the earliest members. There might seem to be a strong *prima facie* likelihood for Halévy's supposition, for it was a truism of evangelical pastoral theology that suffering, physical or mental, was high among the means by which God awakened sinners; man's extremity was God's opportunity. Yet though there are very clear links between epidemics (whether of humans or livestock) and revivals, the connexion between economic depression and revivals is far harder to establish. Boom, moderate boom, economic stability, moderate depression, acute depression; each has been claimed as a favourable environment for collective religious emotion. If instances from America and Australia appear to point to links between economic slump and religious growth in general, the statistics of nineteenth-century English Methodism do not, and seem strongly to confirm the impression from other sources that ordinary recruitment, at least, fluctuated with, rather than against, the trade cycle.[23] Why there should be apparent differentials in the religious response to suffering is an unexplored problem. Was it because some

---

[22] See T. S. Ashton, *Economic Fluctuations in the Eighteenth Century* (Oxford, 1959), pp. 76, 146–47; A. H. John, 'The Course of Agricultural Change', in *Studies in the Industrial Revolution*, ed. L. S. Pressnell (London, 1960); J. de L. Mann, *The Cloth Industry in the West of England from 1640 to 1880* (Oxford, 1971), pp. 37 ff, 89 ff; C. Creighton, *A History of Epidemics in Britain* (2nd edn, London, 1965), i, p. 27; ii, p. 80.

[23] See W. R. Cross, *The Burned-over District* (New York, 1950), p. 75; T. L. Smith, *Revivalism and Social Reform in Mid Nineteenth Century America* (New York, 1957), pp. 63–64; R. B. Walker, 'The Growth and Typology of the Wesleyan Methodist Church in New South Wales 1812–1901', *Journal of Religious History*, vi (1971), pp. 337–39. I am indebted to Dr Robert Currie for the information about English Methodist membership.

forms of distress (visitations of typhus for instance) represented a threat apparently beyond human causation and control, and so focussed attention on problems of theodicy and eternity, while others (lowered wages, heightened food prices) could be laid at the door of identifiable human agents like employers or landlords? Perhaps acute economic suffering does foster unease and anxiety which can be directed towards religion, but it may have the opposite effect; the struggle to avoid destitution may displace other less urgent requirements in the hierarchy of human needs, religion among them. In an atmosphere of total crisis, even the minimal demands of a weekly subscription to the class-meeting, or respectable dress for chapel attendance, might be seen as an unnecessary and dispensable cost.

Halévy exaggerated the impression which Methodism made on the industrial poor in its early years. Methodism did not 'inundate the nation' in 1739. Though the publicity given to it by press and pulpit attracted some huge crowds, little of this passing interest was translated into the commitment of membership, and even if it had been, the handful of preachers available could hardly have reaped the harvest or given the pastoral oversight necessary to prevent backsliding. Halévy's picture of Methodism spreading rapidly 'through the entire industrial area of Somersetshire, Gloucestershire and Wiltshire' cannot be substantiated. True, in Bristol, second city of the realm, with a population of over 20,000, Methodism made impressive gains (Wesley's societies held 700 in 1743 and Whitefield's 134 by 1744) but it is not clear that this growth derived from the 'despair of the working classes'. A high proportion of the earliest members in 1738–39 probably came from the respectable Religious Societies, which did not usually contain many representatives of the abjectly poor.[24] The first Kingswood preaching drew thousands of hearers, but by 1746, though Wesley had over 300 members in the Forest, he admitted that the majority of those who had once listened eagerly to Methodism were now 'nearly as they were . . . not much better or worse'.[25] The Calvinistic Methodist societies and preaching stations in Gloucestershire and Wiltshire were quite numerous, but seem to have been very small, for in 1741 Whitefield claimed only 300 Wiltshire members.[26] Nor is there much proof of a bumper harvest in the woollen towns

---

[24] *The Journal of the Rev. J. Wesley*, ed. N. Curnock (London, 1938), iii, pp. 97, 181; Tyerman, *Life of Whitefield*, ii, p. 109. For an attempt to identify the age and occupation of those named on a fragmentary list surviving from Bristol in 1741, see W. A. Goss, 'Early Methodism in Bristol', (unpublished M.A. thesis, Bristol University, 1932), pp. 69–81.

[25] *Letters of J. Wesley*, ii, p. 271.   [26] Whitefield, *Works*, i, p. 325.

which were the centre of the rioting in 1738, and should, on Halévy's thesis, have been swept by Methodism. A circuit list drawn up in 1757 after nearly two decades of Methodist effort, showed only 18 members in Trowbridge, 38 in Frome (where it struggled for bare existence) though a respectable 118 in Bradford on Avon.[27] It was much the same story in Taunton and Devizes, in Exeter and in North Devon towns and perhaps for the same reason; orthodox Dissent was here too well entrenched to allow Methodism an easy entry.[28] In the West Riding, later to become *terra sancta* for Methodism, the Revival had similarly small beginnings. In 1738–48 Benjamin Ingham built up a flourishing group of societies with over 800 members round his home town of Ossett and far beyond, though he lost most of them not long after.[29] But Halévy's picture of John Wesley traversing the 'whole of Yorkshire' after his arrival in the North in 1741 creates a misleading picture of superhuman activity and success, for a decade later his societies in the whole of Yorkshire claimed only 3,000 members.[30] Even when allowances are made for the effects of preaching on mere 'hearers', as distinct from members, or for the likelihood of a rapid membership turnover, it is highly improbable that infant Methodism was strong enough to have much overall effect as an emollient to industrial disturbance, let alone prevent a 'general revolt'. Halévy's image of England in 1739 underestimated the regionalization of society, economy and politics in the early eighteenth century. Riots, excitements and economic dislocations were far more localized than he suggests: so too was Methodism, still a tiny operation, whose leaders were experimenting gingerly with new ideas, techniques and organizational forms, and only slowly probing into the missionary *terra incognita* which stretched beyond them.

While revivals and other expressions of intense group emotion played some part in eighteenth-century Methodism (though far more after the 1790s), the patterns of its growth were normally less dramatic than Halévy's essay might imply. Wesley delighted in revivals, but his movement owed more to careful institutionalization than to oscillations of popular feeling; he enjoyed comparing the meteoric rise and fall of 'awakenings' like those in Jonathan Edwards's New England with the steady growth of his own con-

---

[27] S. Tuck, *Wesleyan Methodism in Frome* (Frome, 1837), pp. 32–34.

[28] J. Toulmin, *The History of Taunton*, 2nd edn enlarged by J. Savage (Taunton, 1822), pp. 192–93; M. Dunsford, *Historical Memoirs of Tiverton* (Exeter, 1790), pp. 232–35; (anon.), *A History of the Devizes* (Devizes, 1859), pp. 380–90; A. Brockett, *Nonconformity in Exeter 1650–1875* (Manchester, 1962), pp. 121 ff.

[29] MS Inghamite notebook, Colne Public Library.

[30] *Letters of J. Wesley*, iii, p. 85.

nexion.[31] The long-term appeal of Methodism to industrial workers cannot be explained simply by reference to the short-run effects of a slump, and we now have a choice of other hypotheses, though none of them has more than limited explanatory value. Did Methodism, like Puritanism, appeal to the 'industrious sort of people' by its asceticism, its gospel of work, its glorification of thrift?[32] Or because such social groups tended to be comparatively free of the pre-scriptive controls of gentry and clergy, 'more in a state of independ-ence' (as one eighteenth-century itinerant put it) 'and less subject to the influence of superiors, who may be hostile to itinerant preach-ing, than (in) those counties which depend wholly upon agri-culture'?[33] Or because industrialization, in its early and most disruptive phases, heightened the desire for forms of group associa-tion, of surrogate, voluntaristic community, to replace the traditional communities now lost?[34] In the case of isolated settlements like those of Kingswood colliers or Cornish tinners, was it the result of social marginality and spiritual, moral and educational deprivation; a yearning by disadvantaged outlanders to partake of cultural privileges enjoyed by more integrated communities, though in forms which did not do violence to the particular demands of popular culture? If Methodism was pushed by aggressive evangelism it was also often pulled by eager demand, as with the Renton colliers who chided Wesley and his preachers for being 'too long a-coming'.[35]

The second plank of Halévy's argument was that the economic crisis of 1738–39, by drawing fresh attention to the 'bestial state' of the poor, their irreligion, their threat to the social order, excited the ardour of Christian philanthropists long muzzled by Walpole's policy of moral and religious scepticism. Sensing a heaven-sent opportunity, the Methodist leaders hurried to the areas where the industrial crisis raged most strongly, and 'bent the popular impulse to the form the bourgeoisie wanted to give it; a religious and conservative form'.

Halévy squarely raised the problem of motivation behind the Methodist mission to the poor. It is quite possible that the economic crisis influenced the Methodist leaders. The unusual series of riots between 1736 and 1740—the Porteous, gin and turnpike riots, still more the grain riots and the risings by colliers and weavers—may have fed that feeling of moral declension and social disintegration

[31] *Ibid.*, vii, p. 352.
[32] C. Hill, *Society and Puritanism in Pre-Revolutionary England* (London, 1964), pp. 131–34.
[33] *The Baptist Annual Register*, ed. J. Rippon (London, 1790–1802), ii, p. 461.
[34] *E.g.* M. Walzer, *The Revolution of the Saints* (London, 1966), pp. 199 ff.
[35] *Journal of J. Wesley*, iii, p. 288.

which was a prominent feature of the psychic economy of the 1730s and which certainly affected the Wesleys and Whitefield. The riots of 1738–40 focussed attention on the plight of the poor and the cause and cure of poverty, as in the debate which followed the publication in the *Gloucester Journal* and elsewhere of the 'Essay on Riots' which dissected the disturbances in the Wiltshire clothing areas.[36] But it would be unwise to view Methodism as no more than an agency either of temporal philanthropy or social control. If the Methodist leaders were concerned with anything it was with the salvation first of their own souls and then the souls of others. The Wesleys, after all, had begun their mission not to the dangerous classes in England but to settlers and Indians in the American wilderness. Yet in 1739 their perspectives seem to have changed as they dedicated themselves self-consciously to an apostolate at large among the English poor. Wesley's first text as outdoor preacher was significant: 'the Spirit of the Lord is upon me . . . to preach the Gospel to the poor'.[37] In his *Farther Appeal* (1745) he told the clergy, 'the rich, the honourable, the great, we are thoroughly willing . . . to leave to you. Only let us alone among the poor.'[38] But why? Field preaching to the poor was by no means a necessary corollary of conversion, however much the experience excited the impulse to proselytise; plenty of converted clergymen contented themselves with a conventional parish ministry.

No easy answer suggests itself. Sensitivity to the plight of the poor had been forced on the Holy Club by its philanthropic work in Oxford, and Wesley had been shaken by what he saw; it was then that he formulated his radical ethic of charity, telling himself 'everything about thee which cost more than Christian duty required thee to lay out is the blood of the poor'.[39] Before he began field-preaching at Kingswood he had emphasized in his Oxford University sermon of 11 June 1738, that the poor 'have a peculiar right to have the gospel preached unto them'.[40] The plight of the unchurched poor, 'outcasts of men', 'the forlorn ones', apparently as disadvantaged in the redemptive order as in the human economy, excited pity. Whitefield went out to Kingswood because its inhabitants were 'sheep having no shepherd'; Wesley made a detour to visit the Plessey colliers, noting 'I felt great compassion for these poor creatures . . . and the more because all men seemed to despair of them'.[41] What made this campaign doubly attractive was its

---

[36] See Mann, *The Cloth Industry in the West of England*, pp. 109–12.
[37] *Journal of J. Wesley*, ii, p. 173.
[38] *The Works of the Rev. J. Wesley*, ed. T. Jackson (3rd edn, London, 1872), viii, p. 239.   [39] *Ibid.*, vii, p. 21.   [40] *Ibid.*, v, p. 15.
[41] *Whitefield's Journals*, p. 216; *Journal of J. Wesley*, iii, p. 73.

astonishing success. At a time when the revival seemed to be slowing down, gains from the urban Religious Societies had passed their peak, the hierarchy was beginning to show its teeth and counter-attack and city churches were increasingly closed to Methodist preaching, the Methodist leaders discovered an almost untapped, apparently limitless market for the Gospel. Here was an audience receptive to a degree, 'child-like, artless, teachable,' almost a pastoral *tabula rasa*.[42] Many miners having 'never in their lives pretended to any religion of any kind,' noted Wesley, '. . . were the more ready to cry to God for . . . redemption'.[43] The spectacular results of field preaching possessed a further attraction: they strengthened those whose faith in the authenticity of the New Testament and the reality of the Holy Spirit had been buffeted by the propaganda of Deists. The striking conversion of hardened sin-ners recalled the world of the *Acts of the Apostles*; God, it seemed, was not the *Deus absconditus* of the freethinkers, remote from a world governed by the inexorable mechanics of natural law, but the living God of Christian theology.[44]

Whitefield's arrival in Bristol in 1739 was probably not motivated —as Halévy believed—by a desire to cash in on industrial unrest (he was visiting his sister before leaving for America), nor was Benjamin Ingham's activity in the textile villages round Osset (which was, after all, his home town round which he was busily preaching more than two years before the riots there in 1740). The motive of social control was not absent from Methodist preaching, however. The reformation of manners was an insistent, if subordin-ate, theme. Wesley shared the widespread pessimism of moralists at the 'dreadful degeneracy of the age' and dedicated himself to 'a reformation of vice in every kind'.[45] Explicitly, the Methodist leaders expressed their hope that in the transformation of evangelical conversion lay a way of internalizing moral norms, and of achieving that reformation which external, legal sanctions had signally failed to effect. As Whitefield observed in his Journal in 1739, 'that reformation which is brought about by a coercive power will only be outward and superficial; but that which is done by the force of God's Word, will be inward and lasting'.[46] The first target of Methodist itinerancy was 'the most flagrant, hardened, desperate sinner'.[47] If, as a Christian moralist, Wesley viewed vice more in religious terms as sin than in secular terms as a threat to social order, he nevertheless took delight in making the turbulent poor clean, industrious and sober. Reflecting on the relative peace which

---

[42] *Ibid.*, ii, p. 216.
[44] *Ibid.*, ii, p. 202.
[46] *Whitefield's Journals*, p. 241.

[43] *Ibid.*, iii, p. 74.
[45] *Letters of J. Wesley*, vi, p. 61.
[47] *Letters of J. Wesley*, ii, p. 271.

Methodism had brought to some Kingswood families, he rejoiced at the way it had made them 'mild, gentle and easy to be entreated'.[48] Halévy's belief in the essential conservatism of Methodist teaching has a good deal to recommend it. John Wesley had a deep and religious respect for magistracy and obedience; Charles in his hymns portrayed the model Methodist as meek, long-suffering and hardworking and took pride in the relectance of Methodist colliers to join a corn riot in 1740.[49] Though (in Halévy's words) Methodist organization combined 'the hierarchical and egalitarian principles in equal proportions', the discipline of its classes and societies was in many ways highly authoritarian.

Yet, as Halévy noted rather uneasily, there were undertones in early Methodism of a very different kind, especially in its determination to recapture the spirit and practice of the early church. 'There is in the Gospels,' he observed, 'too pronounced a messianic element for the governing classes not to be truly alarmed whenever Christian sects advocate a return to primitive Christianity.' This ebullient primitivism was stronger than Halévy realized and pushed Methodists into social attitudes at odds with their social theories. The outbreak of Methodism released an uprush of religious enthusiasm and millennial expectation which echoed, if more faintly, the early Quaker feeling of a 'primitive Christianity' revived in the 'last days'.[50]

The mysterious suddenness of the Revival, breaking out almost simultaneously in America, Wales, England and Scotland, the scenes of group excitement, the striking conversions, convinced some Methodist leaders that this was an outpouring of the Spriti unparalleled since Pentecost; not surprisingly, some were led to expect, even lay claim to, quasi-apostolic powers: direct 'impressions' from God, the power of 'discerning spirits', prophesying, exorcizing, performing miraculous cures. Brooding over the practice of the primitive Christians who 'had all things in common' and 'gave their goods to all men, as every man had need', a few evangelicals revived the interest in the community of goods held by radical sects— Anabaptists, Diggers, French Prophets—before them. Halévy noticed how Ingham was accused of preaching the common ownership of property; he did not know that John Wesley, whom he regarded as a thorough-going conservative, was contemplating in 1744 a scheme of voluntary Christian communism by which society members, irrespective of their incomes, would put their weekly earnings into a common box, drawing out no more than was needed

---

[48] *Journal of J. Wesley*, ii, p. 323.
[49] *Journal of C. Wesley*, i, p. 249.
[50] H. Barbour, *The Quakers in Puritan England* (New Haven, 1964), p. 189.

to maintain themselves and their families and distributing the remainder to the poor in the manner of *Acts* 11, 44–5.[51] Communitarian ideas—as Halévy observed—also circulated, finding fulfilment in the Moravian settlements like Fulneck, with its workshops, bakehouses, schools and residential 'choir-houses' and in Howell Harris's religious commune, the Trevecka 'Family', about 120 strong at one time, which ran a woollen manufactory and a printing press of its own.[52]

The congruities between Methodism and sectarian Puritanism did not go unnoticed. Field-preaching, lay preaching, notions of inner-light and perfectibility, all roused traumatic recollections of the Commonwealth. Early Methodism was regarded as a potentially revolutionary rather than a conservative force. Those who feared popular Puritanism and Jacobitism were alarmed at the way in which educated Methodist leaders, 'men of figure' whose motives were obscure, marshalled the poor into disciplined cadres. If inflated by paranoia, these anxieties were explicable. Especially in its early, most enthusiastic phase, Methodism was in some ways a disruptive and anti-establishmentarian movement whose rhetoric held resonances of seventeenth-century religious radicalism. Though for the most part professedly Anglican, its spokesmen often gave vent to bitter anticlericalism, few more than the ordained Whitefield, who told the London crowds in 1739 'our clergy . . . are only seeking after preferment . . . either to spend on the pleasures of life, or to gratify their sensual appetites, while the poor of their flock are forgotten; nay, worse, they are scorned, hated and disdained'.[53] He dismissed the much admired Latitudinarian Archbishop Tillotson as one who knew no more of true Christianity than Mahomet.[54] Another ordained Methodist, Jacob Rogers, preaching to great Yorkshire crowds in 1739 from the anticlerical text of 'Beware of dogs', lashed the clergy who 'preached false doctrine that they may fill their coffers with money and preach your souls to the devil' and soon afterwards renounced his orders to be a Baptist.[55] William Seward pronounced the Scarlet Whore of Babylon to be not more corrupt than the Church of England.[56] One of the earliest lay preachers, David Taylor, 'seeing the clergy in those parts to be enemies of the truth' refused to be married by any of them, considering himself wed by a simple but solemn declaration before friends—

[51] *Procs. Wesley Hist. Soc.* xiv (1924), pp. 29–30.
[52] See M. H. Jones, *The Trevecka Letters* (Caernarvon, 1932), pp. 185–206.
[53] Whitefield, *Works*, vi, p. 231.
[54] *Three Letters from the Rev. Mr. G. Whitefield* (Philadelphia, 1740), p. 2.
[55] *The Weekly Miscellany*, 26 July 1740.
[56] W. Seward, *Journal of a Voyage from Savannah* (London, 1740), p. 45.

an act of defiance which aligned him with Commonwealth radicals, Elizabethan Familists and Lollards.[57]

The morals of aristocracy, gentry and large merchants were held up for similar obloquy in front of the attentive poor. Howell Harris took particular delight in 'humbling the pride' of the 'polite world'. Mounted provocatively on a table before Monmouth town hall, where a party of noblemen was dining after the races, he bore loud testimony 'against their balls, assemblies, horseraces, whoredom and drunkenness, etc.'[58] Whitefield's early sermons should be studied by those content merely to stress the bromide qualities of the evangelical movement. Playing deliberately on themes of class-conflict, he compared the godliness of his hearers with the selfishness and irreligion of the rich who 'indulge themselves in the follies of life, and had much rather spend their estates in lusts and pleasures while the poor all around them are not thought worthy to be set with the dogs'.[59] The poor were not only ignored and despised, they were actively hated by the frivolous, uncaring, 'polite' or 'fashionable ones' who did not deem them 'fit for company and conversation'.[60] In early Methodist hands the gospel of work sounded often more like an aggressive vindication of the dignity of labour than a justification for the social *status quo*. Attacking idleness, Whitefield cried, 'I would have rich men to work as well as poor'.[61] The Methodists dissented from the theory that riches were a mark of divine favour. 'Learn, ye godly poor', said Whitefield, 'that poverty and temptations are no mark of your being cast off by God'.[62] Wesley's praise of industriousness did not carry with it the conventional inference that idleness was the ubiquitous cause of the poverty of the poor; he attacked as 'wickedly, devilishly false . . . that common objection "they are poor only because they are idle" '.[63]

The glorification of the 'godly poor' and its obverse, denunciation of the ungodly rich, was a prominent early Methodist theme. Charles Wesley harped continually on both in his hymns.

> The rich and great in every age
> Conspire to persecute their God.[64]

[57] Methodist Archives, MS Copies of Original Letters collected by L. Tyerman, iii, pp. 301–02.
[58] *A Brief Account of Howell Harris* (Trevecka, 1791), p. 45.
[59] Whitefield, *Works*, vi, pp. 237–38.
[60] *Ibid.*, vi, p. 238.
[61] *Ibid.*, v, p. 133.   [62] *Ibid.*, v, p. 272.
[63] *Journal of J. Wesley*, iv, p. 52.
[64] *The Poetical Works of J. and C. Wesley*, ed. G. Osborn (London, 1868–71) p. 301.

> Our Saviour by the rich unknown
> Is worshipped by the poor alone.[65]

> A rich man saved. It cannot be
> But by a more abundant grace.[66]

With apocalyptic relish he anticipated the fate which would be meted out to the exponents of spiritual wickedness in high places:

> Go, thou sharp, iron-flail of God
> And thresh the loftiest of mankind.[67]

John Wesley, maintaining that 'the poor are the Christians', extrapolated from his own pastoral experience to advance the claim that all religious movements for reform began among the poor, moving slowly up the social ladder until finally, in the millennial day, they touched the nobility; conversely, scepticism and Deism began among the great and filtered downwards.[68] The Methodist itinerants, in their campaign to purify a fallen Church of England, were liable to end up furiously bandying texts with some enraged parish clergyman whose ministry they had condemned as carnal and unregenerate; though they enjoined obedience to magistrates, they found themselves calling down providential judgments on alarmed and astonished country gentry who threatened them with prosecution under the Toleration or Conventicle Acts. In a variety of ways Methodism was an active solvent of patriarchal deference. There was a wide gap between its political theory and the situational reality of continual collision with the representatives of the established order. What gave the conflict an added, generational dimension was the belligerent youth of many converts and, indeed, preachers (Whitefield himself was only 24 in 1739); they were a pack of 'insolent boys' complained Bishop Chandler.[69] Methodism was certainly not a revolutionary movement, but in the context of Walpole's England it was hardly a consistently conservative one.

It is a pity that Halévy did not pursue his suggestion that Methodism represented a moral reaction to the cynicism and scepticism of the Walpolean order. Concentrating heavily on the effects of a 'crisis of overproduction' he ignored the catalytic effect of other crises more immediately germane to the religious mood of the 1730s; the Deist attack on priestcraft and the Bible, the parliamentary attack of the erastian, anticlerical Old Whigs on the prerogatives

---

[65] *Ibid.*, xi, p. 411.   [66] *Ibid.*, x, p. 327.   [67] *Ibid.*, ix, p. 411.
[68] *Letters of J. Wesley*, vii, p. 343; J. Wesley, *Works*, vi, p. 283.
[69] *Procs. Wesley Hist. Soc.*, xxviii (1951–52), p. 49; J. Wesley, *Works*, xi, pp. 183–84.

of the established Church, the repercussions of the political assault on the corruption of Walpole's regime by the *Craftsman* and other Tory or 'Patriot' publicists, which intensified fears that England was fast glissading, like post-Antonine Rome, into an abyss of selfishness and profligacy.[70] Here lie some neglected clues to Methodist motivation in the critical years of 1738–39. Yet *The Birth of Methodism* remains a remarkably fertile piece, not least for the many questions which Halévy shot out in a few pages, directly, or by implication. What was the link between Puritanism and Methodism? Why was Methodism born not among Dissenters who had preserved the Reformed tradition but in an Arminian Church which had virtually abandoned it? Do religious revivals burgeon out of economic distress? What motives, patent or latent, prompted the Methodism mission to the poor? Was Methodism a conservative, stabilizing force in mid-eighteenth-century society? For the most part, his questions hang unanswered in the air.

Jesus College, Oxford

[70] See Walsh, 'Origins of the Evangelical Revival', pp. 140–41; T. F. J. Kendrick, 'Sir Robert Walpole, the Old Whigs and the Bishops, 1733–1736', *The Historical Journal*, xi (1968), pp. 421–45; I Kramnick, *Bolingbroke and his Circle* (Cambridge. Mass., 1968).

THE SOCIAL HISTORY OF CONFESSION
IN THE AGE OF THE REFORMATION

By John Bossy, M.A., Ph.D., F.R.Hist.S.

READ 8 MARCH 1974

WHEN I offered to read a paper on this subject, I had a particular hypothesis in mind. I thought—perhaps it would be more honest to say, I hoped—it would be possible to show that, during a period roughly contemporaneous with the Reformation, the practice of the sacrament of penance in the traditional church had undergone a change which was important in itself and of general historical interest. The change, I thought, could roughly be described as a shift from the social to the personal. To be more precise, I thought it possible that, for the average layman, and notably for the average rural layman in the pre-reformation church, the emphasis of the sacrament lay in its providing part of a machinery for the regulation and resolution of offences and conflicts otherwise likely to disturb the peace of a community. The effect of the Counter-Reformation (or whatever one calls it) was, I suspected, to shift the emphasis away from the field of objective social relations and into a field of interiorized discipline for the individual. The hypothesis may be thought an arbitrary one: we can but see. I think it will be admitted that, supposing it turned out to be correct, we should have learnt something worth knowing about the difference between the medieval and the counter-reformation church, and something about the difference between pre- and post-reformation European society. If if did not turn out to be correct, we might nevertheless expect to pick up some useful knowledge about something which is scarcely a staple of current historical discourse, though it threatens to become so.

Looking through the more general accounts of the religious and other history of the sixteenth century, I did not find much light upon my problem. For Catholics as for Protestants, or most of them, the sacrament seemed to exist in a timeless and bloodless universe; if the Counter-Reformation made any progress with it, it can only have been in the sense of restoring to vigour what had become lax, removing dubious accretions, increasing the frequency of reception and perhaps the understanding of what was meant. Even so recent and so excellent a book as Jean Delumeau's *Le Catholicisme entre Luther et Voltaire* really gets one no farther than this; indeed the

quantitative 'religious sociology' which is his chief recommendation
for advance in the subject may here be a positive incentive for
remaining within a traditional frame of reference.[1] In any event, he
has no substantial comment to make about confession.

Had I then made my problem up? At this point I did two un-
fashionable things. I read a theological work, and I consulted Henry
Charles Lea's neglected masterpiece, the *History of Auricular Confession*.[2] When I had done that, I was sure that I had got a genuine
problem, though less sure that I had put it in the right place. To
begin with the theology. To one who had launched himself on the
subject with the hypothesis mentioned above in mind, it was a
remarkable experience to read Bernhard Poschmann's authoritative
account of the development of the theology of penance in the
Catholic church. Here you discover, if you did not know already,
that the original bearing of the sacrament was not individual but
collective: 'forgiveness . . . is not a matter which is concluded
simply between God and man; it comes through the mediation of a
church . . . which by his sin [the Christian] has dishonoured and
defiled'. Penance achieves reconciliation, not directly with God, but
with the church; the effect of the sacrament is to restore a condition
of peace (pax) between the sinner and the church; in return for the
acceptance by the penitent of his 'penance', the church extends its
forgiveness, restores to charity, and in charity prays to God that he
also may forgive. The restoration of peace is completed symbolically
when the priest lays his hand on the sinner who has fulfilled his
purgation. Adapted to different social forms, the social concept of
penance persisted through the centuries of the barbarian west until
scholastic theology interiorized the notions of sin and repentance.
Reconciliation to God, not to the community, became the object of
the sacrament; the change was institutionalized with the universal
imposition of private confession by the Lateran Council of 1215.[3]
As presented by Poschmann (and indeed by Lea), and considered
as a theological matter, the situation was perfectly clear: my
hypothesis would be correct, but would apply to the twelfth and
thirteenth centuries, not to the sixteenth.

---

[1] (Paris, *Nouvelle Clio*, 1971); see index. An exception to the generalization made
above is John Hale, *Renaissance Europe 1480–1520* (London, 1970), p. 27.

[2] *A History of Auricular Confession and Indulgences in the Latin Church* (3 vols., Philadelphia and London, 1896); cited hereafter as 'Lea'. In this paper I have neglected the subject of indulgences, dealt with in Lea's third volume. P. Michaud-
Quantin, *Sommes de casuistique et manuels de confession au Moyen Age (xii–xvi siècles)*
(*Analecta medievalia Namurcensia* no. 13, Louvain, 1962) is a helpful guide to the
authorities cited by Lea up to the 1520s.

[3] B. Poschmann, *Penance and the Anointing of the Sick* (London, 1964), pp. 7 ff,
34, 96–102, 158 ff, 208 and *passim*; Lea, i, pp. 50–54.

To believe that this is not the end of the question, we do not need to fall back entirely on a supposition about the difference between theology and life. We may consult Jedin's account of the debate on the sacrament which occurred at the Council of Trent in 1551.[4] For practically all the theologians present, it went without saying that the final result of the development described was an unquestionable and extra-historical *datum*. Most of them pushed the development somewhat farther by arguing that in the sacrament the priest exercised jurisdiction over the individual and his offences on the model of a secular criminal jurisdiction of Roman-law type. They seem to have had no idea that confession and penance might exist in a social dimension, and their view prevailed. There was however a dissenting voice, that of the German Johannes Gropper, who defended at some length the pre-scholastic view, arguing (from St Paul) that the reconciliation achieved was to Christ as well as to God in general, that Christ was to be understood as the members of Christ incorporated in the church as a community, and that this reconciliation was an essential part of the sacrament, since it was represented in the imposition of hands which the church had continually maintained in its practice. 'The absolution of the priest', he said, 'signifies . . . . the reconciliation of all the members of Christ, for the sinner in sinning offends . . . all the members of Christ, therefore by absolution . . . all the members are reconciled.' Gropper's demonstration was heard 'with great attention and applause', but had no effect on the outcome.[5] It is obviously important to know where Gropper had got his view from, and here I speak under correction. But, without wishing to underestimate what it may have owed to his own study of the sources or possibly to Protestant influence, I think it is fair to say that it represented tradition in two respects. It related to a subdued but fairly persistent element in the school-tradition which defended confession on the ground that, while mere contrition reconciled the sinner to God, only confession could reconcile him to the church: the position had been maintained by the well-known preacher John Geiler of Kaisersberg at the beginning of the sixteenth century.[6] It also showed that Gropper had given some attention to confessional practice as distinct from confessional theory.

---

[4] H. Jedin, *Geschichte des Konzils von Trient*, iii (Freiburg-im-Breisgau, etc., 1970), pp. 315–36.

[5] *Concilium Tridentinum*, vii, part 1, ed. A. Postina, S. Ehses, J. Birkner, T. Freudenberger (Freiburg, 1961), pp. 266–69; *cf.* the views of various opponents, pp. 275, 278, 279, and of Melchior Cano, p. 262, where the comparison with secular jurisdiction is made; *cf.* Lea, i, 281 ff. Gropper's text was II Corinthians, v, 18–20.

[6] Jo[hannes Geiler von] Keysersberg, *Navicula Poenitentiae* (Augsburg, 1511) fo. 23, col. 1; Lea, i, p. 214.

It seems possible that, both in theory and in practice, the tradition to which Gropper was appealing had persisted more vigorously in Germany than elsewhere.[7]

Bearing this theological background in mind I now propose to defend the view that the actual practice of pre-reformation confession did in fact continue to incorporate the social dimension which had been abandoned by the dominant scholastic tradition. I draw on two sources: on the manuals of advice to confessors which Lea used for his *History;* and—the choice is not perhaps so desperate as it may seem—on the view of the subject maintained by Luther.

Keith Thomas seems to me to have been fully entitled by the confessional manuals to discuss confession, as he does in *Religion and the Decline of Magic*, as part of a more general function of counselling and conflict-solving exercised by the clergy in rural society.[8] Medieval confession, we need to remember, was a face-to-face encounter between two people who would probably have known each other pretty well; we may also remember that it occurred, normally speaking, once a year, in the not-so-remote presence of a large number of neighbours, and more or less at the time (Maundy Thursday) set aside for the reconciliation to the community of public penitents in the pre-scholastic sense.[9] Given these circumstances, and a little *a priori* knowledge of rural society, we cannot be surprised at what we are told by the manuals, that the average person was much more likely to tell the priest about the sins of his neighbours than about his own.[10] It would be far-fetched to suppose that in doing this they were aware that they were carrying out the Gospel injunction to 'tell the church' if their brother had offended against them and refused to make amends;[11] but the fact is at least

[7] *Cf.* the 14th-century Augsburg ritual mentioned in *Lexikon für Theologie und Kirche*, ed. J. Höfer and K. Rahner, ii (Freiburg, 1958), col. 826 (Jungman).

[8] (London, 1971), pp. 154–59; *cf.* Hale, *Renaissance Europe*, p. 27. Zeldin, 'The Conflict of Moralities' (see below, n. 39), cites an Oxford D.Phil. thesis by A. L. Maraspini (1962) which suggests that this may still be true in [? southern] Italy.

[9] *Lexikon für Theologie und Kirche*, ii, coll. 823 ff. My idea of the practicalities of confession on the eve of the Reformation is derived from J. Toussaert, *Le sentiment religieux en Flandre à la fin du Moyen Age* (Paris, 1963), p. 106; *Decretorium Ecclesiae Gallicanae*, ed. L. Bochelli (Paris, 1609), pp. 210–12, 219 (councils of Laon 1404, Sens 1524, Paris 1557); Lea, i, p. 250 (council of Seville 1512).

[10] The point had struck various observers: *e.g.* B. L. Manning, *The People's Faith in the Time of Wyclif* (Cambridge, 1919), p. 33; Toussaert, *Le sentiment religieux en Flandre*, p. 119; Thomas, *Religion and the Decline of Magic*, p. 185; J. Bossy, 'The Counter-Reformation and the People of Catholic Ireland, 1596–1641', *Historical Studies*, viii, ed. T. D. Williams (Dublin, 1971), p. 167. Lea (i, p. 354) reports a model case from the manuals where a wife who brought up her husband's sins received two penances, one for herself and one for her husband.

[11] Matthew, xviii, 15–18.

not incompatible with a notion of confession as an annual settlement of social accounts. One thing we do know that people knew about confession was that the priest could not absolve a person from his sins if he proposed to remain in a state of social hostility with a neighbour: we know it because it was the most frequent reason why people refused to go to confession, and the only one which received a certain degree of official tolerance. But abandoning such hostilities was not purely a matter of the heart; the commentators were clear that a man was required to show forgiveness by performing the social acts of recognition and salutation which the relation of charity implied, to accept a proffer of hospitality if made.[12] If all this was to follow his confession, it was surely just as well for him to get all his grievances off his chest beforehand.

Had this not been an important aspect of the role of the priest in confession it would be hard to understand the concern shown in the manuals for the case where the hostility in question was between the penitent and the priest, or where a matter confessed would cause such hostility to arise. If, as John Myrc put the case, the penitent

> had done a synne
> By the priestes sibbe kin,
> Mother or sister or his lemmon,
> Or by his daughter, if he had one . . .

then he was advised to take his confession elsewhere, or omit the matter.[13] Only in this light, too, can we make sense of the inordinate amount of space given in the manuals to the question of restitution. This is the more remarkable in that, as every theologian was keen to point out, restitution had formally speaking no part in the sacramental process at all; though the word satisfaction was often used to cover both, it was held to be a completely different matter from sacramental satisfaction, simply a requisite preliminary *absque omni satisfactione pertinente ad reconciliationem peccatoris*. One may believe St Bonaventure when he remarked that people could not make head or tail of this: the more so since in the case of one

[12] Lea, ii, pp. 41 ff; Angelus de Clavasio [Angelo Carletti of Chivasso], *Summa Angelica* (n.p. or d. in the edn I have used, Brit. Mus. 847. m. 9; 1st edn 1486), fo. 111ᵛ; *Concilia novissima Galliae*, ed. L. Odespun (Paris, 1646), pp. 94 (council of Melun 1579; from Milan), 232 ff (council of Reims 1583: *Post confessionem absolutio nemini concedatur, qui non fuerit reconciliatus cum proximo, si quem oderat, saltem in voto*). Cf. J. Bossy, 'The Counter-Reformation and the People of Catholic Europe', *Past and Present*, 47 (1970), p. 56.

[13] Lea, i, pp. 285 ff, 349 ff, with enormous lists of authorities; also p. 454 for a melodramatic textbook case from sixteenth-century Spain where a murderer confessed accidentally to his victim's brother. John Myrc, *Instructions for Parish Priests*, ed. E. Peacock (E.E.T.S., 1868, revd. edn 1902), ll. 717 ff.

important offence (seduction) it was widely held that the proper restitution and the proper satisfaction were the same, *i.e.* marriage. Restitution was relevant to a wide variety of sins: not merely to theft or other ill-gotten gains, but to adultery, seduction, conjugal rights, abuse, slander and denial of common courtesy. It was certainly still a live issue on the eve of the Reformation, when Geiler of Kaisersberg preached on it vigorously and at length; he alleged a common proverb (on the lines of 'Thou shalt not be found out') to the effect that people felt shamed, not when they stole, but when having stolen they were obliged to make restitution. He also insisted that this should be made directly, and not by some convenient byway like giving to the poor.[14] In so far as restitution was an important feature of medieval confession, it must be clear that the social dimension of the sacrament remained established; even if it was less important in life than in the confessional literature, it would still be a solid witness to the lag between theology and practice for which I am arguing.

Seen in this context, Luther appears a radical or perhaps utopian traditionalist rather than a revolutionary. It is a striking fact that, despite his own well-known difficulties with the sacrament he spoke of it, at least in his middle years, with respect and indeed with affection: 'I would not wish it to cease; rather I rejoice that it exists in the church of Christ, for it is a singular medicine for afflicted consciences.' One has the impression that in this case Luther the connoisseur of rural life had come to the rescue of Luther the friar; as expressed in the *Babylonian Captivity* and other texts of the same period, his doctrine of confession was a single-mindedly social one. He made a clear distinction between sins which upset the community —'adultery, murder, fornication, theft, robbery, usury, slander, *etc.*'—and 'the secret sins of the heart', by which he seems chiefly to have meant interior sexual motions which had no overt consequences. The latter, he thought, might well be left between the individual and God, and were not a matter for sacramental or public confession; nevertheless, a man might be helped if they were

---

[14] Lea, i, pp. 439, 447; ii, pp. 43–58 (Bonaventure, p. 46; note the declining interest from seventeenth century, p. 53), 187 (marriage as penance; examples in M. Grosso and M.-F. Mellano, *La Controriforma nella arcidiocesi di Torino* (3 vols., Rome, 1957), iii, p. 274); Geiler, *Navicula Poenitentiae*, fos 43, col. 2–58, col. 2 (passage cited fo. 46, col. 3; quotation above, from Scotus, fo. 43, col. 4). There is a discussion of restitution in sexual offences in Martin de Azpilcueta [Navarrus], *Enchiridion sive manuale confessariorum et poenitentium* (Antwerp, 1581 edn; 1st edn Coimbra, 1553), pp. 263 ff. A case which would be worth a study in itself is that of restitution and the adulterine child: Lea, ii, pp. 50 ff; extended discussion in Hostiensis, *Summa Aurea* (Lyon, 1548 edn), fo. 285ᵛ; Geiler, *op. cit.*, fo. 51, coll. 3–4.

not left to fester inside him, and in that case he drew on the doctrine of the priesthood of believers (and ultimately, of course, on St James). The member of a community who was oppressed by secret sins might gain comfort and forgiveness by confession to any other member, 'a brother or a neighbour, at any time or in any place, in the house or in the fields'; the neighbour might or must grant him absolution, but would impose no penance, for 'the best satisfaction is to sin no more and do good to your neighbour, be he friend or enemy'. This doctrine left intact the traditional annual and private confession to the priest, but confined it to offences of a community-disturbing character, principally considered as arising out of hatred. In this sense confession survived the Reformation in Lutheran churches, though as time went on it clearly lost its social vitality; both in the private form which Luther had favoured himself, and in the collective form which tended to supplant it, it retained the symbol of social reconciliation, the imposition of the hand on the penitent. In his attitude to confession, as in his attitude to usury, Luther was a backward-looking figure, and I do not think it is perverse to interpret the practice of late medieval confession in the light of his attempt to reform it.[15]

For the historian of Catholicism, in any case, the winds of change were blowing in a different direction. To be more exact, they were blowing in two different directions at once. Of the two developments which may support a hypothesis of significant change occurring between the fifteenth and the seventeenth centuries, I propose to deal rather briefly with the first. There was a strong tendency to psychologize the sacrament: to reinforce the desocializing efforts of the earlier scholastics by suggesting that sin was essentially something which occurred in the mind. This tendency drew on a variety of different sources: on the *Devotio Moderna* with its development of the examination of conscience and of the practice of systematic meditation; on the Christian humanists whose inclination to treat sin as a purely psychological matter tempted them, it seems to me, to abandon the idea of sacramental penance altogether. Dr Fenlon's admirable exposition of what penance meant for Reginald Pole strikes me as a startlingly clear example

[15] For the *Babylonian Captivity*, I have used the translation in *Martin Luther: Selected Writings*, ed. J. Dillenberger (Garden City, N.Y., 1961), passage on confession at pp. 314–24; also *Luther's Works*, ed. J. Pelikan and H. T. Lehmann, vol. 35 (Philadelphia, 1960), p. 21; vol. 39 (1970), pp. 32–34; Lea, i, pp. 515–19; James, v, 16. Although Luther described the work of confessional writers like Prierias as 'bilgewater' he was not above competing with them on their own ground; compare his treatment of the case of the adulterine child in *Babylonian Captivity*, p. 337, with that of Hostiensis cited in the previous note. I should have thought this was a good instance of 'utopian traditionalism'.

of this.[16] Precisely for that reason the humanist influence was less likely to be fruitful for the future than the scholastic, and what seems to have mattered here was the success of the theologians of the Thomist revival, like Cajetan, in establishing the view that the primary element in sin was intention and elaborating the distinction between material and formal sin. Whether or not Lea was right to claim that this distinction brought to the sacrament a frame of mind 'wholly different from that which prevailed prior to the sixteenth century', it is clear that the psychological approach had made enormous progress by the end of the century, embodied as it was in the practice of the Jesuits and of others like François de Sales. Its effects may be clearly seen in the decline—which persisted in the teeth of the Council of Trent—of the satisfactory element in the sacrament; Cajetan, rather in the manner of a modern penal reformer, had affirmed that all penances were 'medicinal' or reformative, not 'satisfactory' or vindictive; the Jesuits seem to have been strongly inclined to abandon satisfaction altogether.[17]

It is ironical that the efforts of the psychological school were probably less successful in changing the confessional experience of the average soul in the direction they intended, than those of a man who was, on the face of it, utterly opposed to their point of view. The man was Charles Borromeo, whose corpus of instructions about confession, made during his twenty years as archbishop of Milan (1564–1584), was certainly the most important contribution to the practice of the subject made during the Counter-Reformation.[18] Superficially Borromeo might seem to have more in common with Gropper than with the dominant view expressed at Trent. His work

[16] H. O. Evennett, *The Spirit of the Counter-Reformation* (Cambridge, 1968), pp. 32 ff; Erasmus, *Enchiridion, militis Christiani*, in *The Essential Erasmus*, ed. J. P. Dolan (New York, 1974), *passim* esp. p. 90: 'The only person that can harm a Christian is himself.' Dermot Fenlon, *Heresy and Obedience in Tridentine Italy* (Cambridge, 1972), pp. 106 ff.

[17] B. Häring, *The Law of Christ* (Cork, 1961 edn) pp. 16 ff; Lea ii, pp. 375–86 (quotation at p. 375), 184 ff, 229 ff (satisfaction); for an example of Jesuit confessional practice which seems to contain no satisfactory element see *John Gerard: the Autobiography of an Elizabethan*, ed. P. Caraman (London, 1956 edn), *passim*. For François de Sales, see his *Advertissement aux Confesseurs*, in *Œuvres complètes*, vi, [ed. A. C. Peltier] (Paris, 1865), pp. 129–146; discussed in P. Broutin, *La réforme pastorale en France au XVIIe siècle* (2 vols., Tournai, 1956), i, pp. 90 ff.

[18] *Acta ecclesiae mediolanensis . . . Federici Card. Borromei . . . iussu . . . edita* (I have used the Milan, 1843–46 edn, 2 vols. with continuous pagination). Apart from various decrees of synods, *etc.* (pp. 16 ff, 98 ff, 229 ff, 312 ff, 447 ff), the chief texts are the instructions in the *Sacramentale ambrosianum*, pp. 579–95 (ritual pp. 584 ff; penitential canons pp. 586 ff), the section dealing with the confessional in the *Instructiones fabricae et supellectilis ecclesiasticae*, pp. 645–47, and the *Avvertenze* or *Monita ad confessarios*, pp. 868–904. A convenient recent edition of the *Instructiones abricae* is in *Trattati d'arte del Cinquecento*, ed. P. Barocchi, iii (Bari, 1962), pp. 1–113: confessional at pp. 63–68, and n. on p. 447 ff.

was in many respects an attempt at archaeological revival of the pre-scholastic penitential tradition; he tried to revive public penance, to make the confessional period conform more exactly to the ancient penitential season, to institute, by the systematic practice of delayed absolution, something akin to the ancient practice whereby satisfaction preceded rather than followed absolution. He added to his instructions a fearsome compilation of penitential canons from the Dark Ages. The form of ritual which he laid down included the *impositio manus* and a final injunction to the penitent to 'go in peace'. Nothing, it would seem, could more clearly exemplify a determination to regard sin as a social matter, to treat it as identical with exclusion from the Christian community and the sacrament as the *pax ecclesiae.*

And yet the impression *is* totally superficial. If by 'social' we mean what we have been meaning so far, I think Borromeo had a limited sense of the social dimension of sin. His historical reconstruction was vitiated in principle by the assumption—for which of course he cannot be blamed—that the reconciliation to be procured by the sacrament was a reconciliation to God and not to the community. Without their proper context the penitential canons were simply a list of vindictive punishments to be held over the penitent *in terrorem* in order to secure his acquiescence in a new disciplinary regime.[19] There is something totally incongruous about finding this appalling catalogue of Wagnerian iniquity cheek-by-jowl, in his instructions, with remarks about uniformity of dress, a bureaucratic proliferation of forms, receipts and files, and pedantic regulations about the dimensions of the confessional-box. Since the confessional was to be Borromeo's principal legacy to the population of Catholic Europe, it is important to notice that it showed up this incongruity in a very practical way. We have seen that a concern for the *impositio manus* was something like a litmus-paper test of whether or not one viewed the sacrament as possessing in its essence an element of social reconciliation; we have also seen that Borromeo firmly included it in his ritual. It does not take much reflection to realize that the introduction of the confessional made the act physically impossible to perform: on Borromeo's specifications you could not get a little finger through the grille which was to separate priest and penitent, never mind a hand.[20]

[19] As indeed he made clear himself: *Acta*, p. 886; Lea, ii, p. 179.

[20] Lea, i, pp. 54, 393 ff; *Lexikon für Theologie und Kirche*, ii, col. 826. The express stipulation about the little finger seems to have been first made by a decision of the Roman Congregation of Bishops and Regulars in 1645, but it is clearly implied by Borromeo's instruction that the holes in the grille were to be 'about the size of a pea'.

The point may seem a childish one (personally I do not think it is), but it does suggest that, when it came down to it, what mattered for Borromeo was not his penitential archaeology, but the new technology of the confessional. We can see fairly precisely his motives in introducing it. First he wished to create a scenario which would give a visible embodiment to the jurisdictional theory of the sacrament which had prevailed at Trent. It was to be a *sedes confessionalis*, where the priest sat in judgment *tamquam pro tribunali judex*.[21] Second he wished to ensure that no chance of sexual arousal or innuendo could arise from the practice of the sacrament. Ideally he seems to have wanted each parish church to possess two confessionals, one for women and one for men, so that men and women should not come to confession 'confusedly mixed up and squeezed together'; but in his legislation the confessional was only compulsory for women, and this remained the case when the *Rituale Romanum* generalized the invention in 1614.[22] In short he regarded face-to-face confession as dangerous on sexual grounds; whether it is a correct deduction to conclude that from now on confession was likely to be dealing more intensively with sexual matters is a question which I leave for the moment. Finally he clearly wanted to seclude both priest and penitent from the mass of people who were otherwise thought likely to press around them; if the confessional was to become an instrument for intimate self-examination, for instruction of the ignorant in the rudiments of Christian doctrine, and for encouraging the denunciation of neighbours to the Inquisition for heresy and similar matters, privacy of a kind was evidently called for.[23] Altogether Borromeo emerges as a confessional individualist *malgré lui*. His work embodied in the most concrete possible form the defeat of Gropper's Tridentine position; his invention provided a vehicle through which the departures of the psychological school could be made available to the average man. Between them they inaugurated a new and lasting regime.

I do not wish to suggest that with the appearance of the confessional the sacrament lost its social dimension overnight, or that Borromeo intended that it should. The role ascribed to the confessional in resolving social enmity in rural communities did not cease with the sixteenth century; Borromeo certainly thought it important, and so did the bishops in Italy and France who emulated him.[24]

[21] *Acta*, p. 230.

[22] *Ibid.*, pp. 645 (1573), 871 (1575), 229 (1579); *Rituale romanum* (Rome, 1952 edn), pp. 141 ff.

[23] *Acta*, pp. 581, 645, 872, 877.

[24] *Ibid.*, p. 581; *cf.* my 'The Counter-Reformation and the People of Catholic Europe' (above, n. 12), pp. 55–56.

One could argue that they saw the relation in a different way: that where the medieval church promoted penance as a means of removing social hostility, the counter-reformation church objected to social hostility because it prevented people going to confession. But even if that were untrue the case for seeing the introduction of the confessional as symbolic of some general shift of values would still seem very strong. Taking it as established, I propose to devote the rest of my paper to exploring two problems. What was the chronology and geography of this change? And to what extent did it involve any kind of Copernican revolution in the universe of what was felt to be sinful? The first question is certainly the easier one to answer.

Strictly speaking the confessional had not in fact been invented by Borromeo, and it was not imposed by any universal legislation: it advanced by a process of diffusion requiring initiative from bishops and local synods, a response from the parish clergy, and some degree of collaboration from the laity.[25] During the twenty-five years between the formulation of Borromeo's instructions and the end of the sixteenth century a series of visitations sought to impose the new model throughout most of northern Italy. The results are difficult to interpret, since where the subject is not mentioned it is impossible to know whether the situation was satisfactory or the visitor had not bothered. Thus in the diocese of Bergamo, visited by Borromeo himself in 1575 when the question must have been very fresh in his mind, no mention of the matter was made in two-thirds of the parishes, and the remainder were required to construct a confessional in due form.[26] It might be deduced that he was successful in establishing the new regime in about half the parishes of the diocese:

---

[25] Cf. W. M. Ploechl, *Geschichte des Kirchenrechts*, iv (Wien/München, 1966), pp. 148 ff, where Borromeo is described as the 'juristic initiator' of the confessional; Lea, i, pp. 394–94; *Dictionnaire de droit canonique*, ed. R. Naz, iv (Paris, 1949), col. 63. The first reference I have seen dates from 1551, council of Narbonne—*quae vulgo confessionalia vocantur: Concilia novissima Galliae*, p. 751.

[26] *Gli atti della visita apostolica di San Carlo Borromeo a Bergamo (1575)*, ed. A. G. Roncalli and P. Forno (2 vols. in 5 parts, Florence, 1938–57). Of the three parts of vol. ii, which deals with the rural parts of the diocese, the first makes scarcely any mention of confessionals at all; in the other two, which cover 141 parishes, there is no mention in 73 cases either in the *comperta* or the decrees, 2 are mentioned in the *comperta* as having a confessional wrongly constructed or in the wrong place, in 55 cases the subject is not mentioned in the *comperta* but the decrees require one to be constructed in due form, and 11 are mentioned in the *comperta* as having none. An idea of the situation in neighbouring dioceses may be got from Grosso and Mellano, *La controriforma nella arcifiocesi di Torino*, i, p. 172; ii, pp. 80, 272; iii, p. 200, *etc*, and M.-F. Mellano, *La controriforma nella diocesi di Mondovì* (Turin, 1955), pp. 139 ff, 165, 255, 299. It seems clear from *Torino*, ii, pp. 80, 272, that a non-visual confession was very difficult for the average peasant to manage.

differences in reception were probably due more to differences in the zeal and opinions of his deputy visitors than to social or geographical difficulties, but it does look as if the regime became firmly established in the towns, patchily in the country districts, and hardly at all in the mountains. This is perhaps as near as we can get to the position in the most favoured parts of northern Italy at the beginning of the seventeenth century: in the south and the islands, as in Spain, it does not look as if the confessional made much progress for a while to come.[27] In France, though one or two councils in the time of the Catholic League did legislate for the introduction of the Borromean regime in the south, it does not seem that much was done in practice until the seventeenth century, and the north was clearly slower in the matter than the south. In Normandy we are told that no actual confessional survives which predates the reign of Louis XIII and that there are few from before 1700; we can deduce from Vincent de Paul's account of his missions that it was not normal in rural France about 1640. It seems in fact fairly certain that the general introduction of confessionals did not occur before the onset of Borromeanism among the French clergy in the mid-century which led to the translation and publication of his instructions in 1657.[28] The situation looks much the same in the Netherlands: the first general legislation dates from 1607, though a well-known Louvain theologian could write on confession in the 1630s assuming that it did not exist. Germany appears to have accepted the innovation very late: here the confessional seems to have been a baroque introduction, perhaps connected with the reconstruction of churches after the Thirty Years' War and receiving a great deal of artistic elaboration during the eighteenth century.[29]

[27] In Rome and the Papal States nothing much seems to have happened until the days of Bernini and Borromini: *Enciclopedia cattolica*, iv, coll. 225–26 and *tavola* ix; R. Wittkower, *Art and Architecture in Italy, 1600–1750* (Baltimore, 1958), plate 69a—Borromini's confessionals at S. Carlo [Borromeo] alle Quattro Fontane. For the south I have nothing beyond a council of Cosenza, 1579 (Lea, i, p. 395) and the private information, which I have not checked personally, that a semi-enclosed confessional permitting the *impositio manus* is still in use in Sicily. Alessandro Sauli does not seem to have tried to introduce the confessional in Corsica: F. Casta, *Evêques et curés corses* . . . *1570–1620* (*Corse historique*, Ajaccio, 1965), pp. 134 ff; *cf.* p. 141 for evidence of the *impositio manus*. For Spain, see Lea, i, p. 396.

[28] *Dictionnaire de droit canonique*, iv, coll. 64 ff; *Concilia novissima Galliae*, p. 523 (Aix-en-Provence, 1585; Toulouse, 1590): it would appear from G. Baccrabère, 'La pratique religieuse dans le diocèse de Toulouse aux XVI–XVIIe siècles', *Annales du Midi*, lxxiv (1962), pp. 287 ff, that the decision of the latter council remained a dead letter; Broutin, *La réforme pastorale en France au XVIIe siècle*, i, pp. 104, 229, ff 276, ff; ii, pp. 374, 395; Delumeau, *Le catholicisme entre Luther et Voltaire*, pp. 279 ff.

[29] Toussaert, *Le sentiment religieux en Flandre*, pp. 104, 684, n. 1; Lea, i, p. 394 (Mechelen, 1607, with indications of resistance from clergy); compare G. Estius,

I am certainly assuming that this process of diffusion was in some way related to changes that were taking place in European society, and that its chronology and geography are of interest to the social historian. But it would be unwise to look for too immediate a relation, and in any case the subject is too large to be dealt with here. I remark only: that the diffusion of the confessional was a fairly slow process, which does at least help one to envisage it as an event in European social history; that among the social changes with which it might be correlated the reception of the Tridentine law of marriage has a claim to consideration; and that, given a certain degree of social development, it seems to have spread more rapidly in regions which had a tradition of Roman law than in those which did not.

I come to my final question: did the change which I hope to have established in confession also involve a Copernican revolution in sin? The argument, you may feel, would hardly be complete and perhaps not even convincing unless it had done. I approach the question by proposing another hypothesis: one which would be eminently compatible with my argument about the externalities of confession, and does not look too absurd. The hypothesis is that in the old confessional regime the primary material of the sacrament, as directed to the laity, was hatred and its consequences; in the new regime it was individual sexuality. Put in this form, the hypothesis does not require the implausible assumption that the medieval church was not concerned about sex: it would imply that in pre-reformation confession sexuality was mainly viewed as a prime creator of havoc in human relations, in post-reformation confession the object was sexuality as such. Crude as it may be, let us try and test it.

I think the evidence for the truth of the first leg of the hypothesis is extremely strong. Suppose we take, for convenience's sake, the conspectus of sin provided in Borromeo's penitential canons, which may I believe be taken as fairly representing the situation in the early middle ages. They occupy in the edition I have used about fourteen long columns, of which no less than five are devoted to the fifth commandment (murder), compared with two and a half on the seventh (here adultery, and including incest, fornication by priests, unnatural vice and masturbation). Sexual indulgence in thought is dealt with very briefly under the tenth commandment.[30] It may of

---

In quattuor libros sententiarum commentaria (4 vols., Paris, 1637–38), iv, p. 203, assuming an *impositio manus* visible to others; Ploechl, *Geschichte des Kirchenrechts*, iv, p. 149. Note the evidence in Lea, i, p. 396, that the confessional was generally regarded as an entirely optional device in 1630.

[30] *Acta ecclesiae mediolanensis*, pp. 588–93.

course be said that this comes from the pre-confessional epoch, and from an age when the penitential system formed a major part of the criminal law. All the same, I think we may take it as a starting point. When the concept of mortal or deadly sin emerged in the twelfth century with the growth of confession, it carried with it strong overtones of mortal or deadly feud.[31] Theologians were anxious to distinguish them, but did not find it very easy to do so: consider Thomas Aquinas's difficulties in defending as compatible the views (1) that the characteristic of a mortal sin was that it was contrary to charity, and (2) that every act of lechery was a mortal sin.[32] I am fairly convinced that the average person during the centuries which followed would have been more persuaded by the first branch of Thomas's argument than by the second (as indeed he seems to have been himself). Suppose we take, as such an average person, Geoffrey Chaucer, whose *Canterbury Tales*, we may remember, conclude with a sermon from the parson about confession, consisting chiefly of an exposition of the seven deadly sins.[33] The sequence in which Chaucer puts them is different from what a modern catechism would lead one to expect. After pride, we get the social sins, envy and anger, and finally the individual sins, accidie or sloth, avarice, gluttony and lechery. Envy—to borrow from the abstract conveniently provided by Neville Coghill—is sorrow at the prosperity of others and joy in their hurt; it is the worst of sins; its remedy is to love God, your neighbour and your enemy. Anger consists in a wicked will to vengeance; in its worst form, malice aforethought, it is the devil's furnace which stokes up hatred, manslaughter, treachery, lies, flattery, scorn, discord, menaces and curses. Among the solitary sins, two are described mainly in terms of their social effects: avarice because it leads to usury, and lechery because it is the greatest theft that there is, for it steals both body and soul. (I remark, *en passant*, that the assimilation of lechery to theft explains why the confessional manuals devote so much attention to restitution in connexion with it.) So for Chaucer, while we can see that since the days of the penitentials the idea of sin has become more internalized, since deadly sin is considered primarily not as a matter of acts but of dispositions of the mind; nevertheless the dispositions which most urgently require to be dealt with are those which disturb the reign of charity in the community: as Hostiensis had put it, referring specifically to the sins of peasants, 'homicides, perjuries, false witnesses, fornications and other principal

---

[31] *E.g.*, Lea, ii, pp. 43 ff; i, 417; ii, 233 ff for mortal sin.

[32] Expounded in Noonan, *Contraception* (below, n. 40), pp. 240 ff.

[33] *The Works of Geoffrey Chaucer*, ed. F. N. Robinson (London, 1957 edn), pp. 229–64; Coghill version, *The Canterbury Tales* (London, 1960 edn), pp. 505–06.

and common vices, injuries and damages committed by them on their neighbours'.[34] It is open to anyone to claim that my selection of witnesses is unbalanced, but personally I should be willing to defend it, and am prepared to regard the first leg of my hypothesis as sufficiently established.

To come to the second leg. I need to show that, between the age of Chaucer and the age of, say, Pascal, an economy of sin organized around the idea of hatred was converted into a different economy dominated by sexuality. If we look at the confessional manuals with the aid of Lea, we find a number of things which do suggest a transition of this kind going on. Consider what they say about some aspects of the relation between the priest and the penitent. Among the qualities in a priest which would relieve the parishioner of his duty of confessing to him one, as we have already seen, was that the two were in a state of social hostility, or would become so as a result of something said in confession; another, in the case of women, was that the priest was unchaste and that the penitent would expose herself to danger by going to confession. I think it is fair to say that in the traditional regime these two situations were considered about equally probable, and that during the period we are concerned with the second came to overshadow the first. Borromeo's confessional looks like some kind of a *terminus ad quem* of this development; from about 1560 solicitation in confession became a matter for the Inquisition.[35] Much the same might be deduced from the treatment of the reverse situation, where a priest was deprived of jurisdiction over the penitent because they were partners in the sin to be confessed. Originally this participation does not seem to have been envisaged especially as a sexual matter: it does not appear so, for example, in Borromeo's instructions, which seem to be traditional in this case. But generally the post-Tridentine commentators seem to treat the issue exclusively as a matter of absolution by the priest of a woman for sexual sin committed with himself.[36] I should be prepared to adduce other examples of this change of values, like the history of the term *delectatio morosa*;[37] but these may suffice to give some plausibility to the argument.

To establish it, however, we shall need to approach more directly the history of the treatment of one or two sins of a sexual nature, to

---

[34] *Summa Aurea*, fo. 277[r].   [35] Lea, i, pp. 285 ff, 349, 382 ff.

[36] *Ibid.*, pp. 382 ff; Ploechl, *Geschichte des Kirchenrechts*, iv, p. 146; *Acta ecclesiae mediolanensis*, p. 447.

[37] Lea, ii, pp. 262 ff. There is a classic exposition of the supra-sexual view in *T. de Vio Caietani . . . de peccatis summula* (Paris, 1530 edn; 1st edn Rome, 1526), fos 58–62. The German priest to whom belonged the copy of Azpilcueta's *Enchiridion* which I have used (above, n. 14) was evidently unfamiliar with the term, and translated it *langsamer list oder listigkeit*.

see if during this period an enhancement of their status in the hierarchy of sin occurred. Two of them have recently been the subject of some historical discussion: masturbation, which has received attention from Philippe Ariès in his study of the family and also from the demographers; and contraception, on which we have the admirable study of Dr Noonan. The first may be a disagreeable subject, but it is clearly a fairly crucial one in the context of our problem. Did it receive increasing attention during our period? For Jean-Louis Flandrin, who has written on the subject in *Annales*, there can be no doubt that it did. Having, he says, been more or less ignored in the early penitentials, it became, between the fifteenth and the eighteenth centuries, a matter of obsessive concern for confessional writers; the decisive innovator in the question was Jean Gerson, whose *De confessione mollitiei*, dating from the early years of the fifteenth century, launched a vogue. Ariès had also drawn attention to Gerson in this context.[38] If the case were as stated, I think we might regard the second leg of our hypothesis as proved, since *mollities* (as understood at the time) is a sexual activity which has no social consequences. It may be so; but I am afraid I am not sure that it is, or that the admittedly tempting case for associating the emergence of the confessional with the rise of masturbation can really be made out. Gerson at the beginning of the fifteenth century is a long way from Borromeo in the late sixteenth, and I see no clear evidence that there was any connexion between them; from what I have seen of the confessional manuals they do not take anything like the extreme view of the matter which Gerson took; most serious of all, there is much to suggest that during the sixteenth century confessors were being invited to go easy on the subject, partly because of the increasing confession of children, which one might have supposed to have intensified the degree of attention given to it.[39]

[38] 'Mariage tardif et vie sexuelle', *Annales*, 27ᵉ année (1972), pp. 135 ff— Flandrin suggests a connexion between this and an assumed rise in the age of marriage; Philippe Ariès, *Centuries of Childhood* (London, 1962 edn), pp. 106 ff; Jean Gerson, *Œuvres complètes*, ed. P. Glorieux, viii (Paris, 1971), pp. 71–74.

[39] Compare Gerson's rigorous inquisition with the comparatively mild remarks in *Summa Angelica*, fo. 258ʳ and Azpilcueta, *Enchiridion*, p. 257; Lea, i, p. 374. Noonan (see following note), p. 270, remarks that Gerson was 'hypersensitive' in sexual matters, and not typical; *cf. ibid.*, pp. 372 ff. Concern with the subject does seem to have become 'rampant' in the eighteenth century: Theodore Zeldin, 'The Conflict of Moralities: Confession, Sin and Pleasure in the 19th Century', in *Conflict in French Society*, ed. T. Zeldin (London, 1970), p. 50. Contrast the following story from a collection attributed to a country priest in Tuscany and published about 1515. A young peasant comes to confess at Easter, and after confessing a whole string of thefts, including that of a quantity of corn from the priest, pauses overcome with embarrassment. Encouraged to continue, he finally confesses that

The case of masturbation would seem to leave the second leg of my hypothesis in the air, neither established nor disproved. What I think does actually disprove it is the case of contraception. The essential text which governed the treatment of the subject in the Middle Ages was the canon *Si aliquis*. This said:

'If someone, to satisfy his lust or in deliberate hatred, does something to a man or a woman so that no children can be born of him or her, or gives them to drink, so that he cannot generate or she conceive, let it be held as homicide.'[40]

This text, with its confusion (to our mind) between practices engaged in by a couple for their own satisfaction and magical or other practices against their fertility engaged in by others, its air of indiscriminate *maleficium*, its parallel of lust and hatred, its identification of contraceptive practice with homicide, seems an eloquent illustration of what I have been claiming was the medieval idea of sin. If my hypothesis were true, we should have expected that during our period the subject might have lost its place among the contraventions of the fifth commandment, and found it among the contraventions of the seventh. There was indeed a tendency in this direction, but it did not get very far. Borromeo, the Tridentine *Catechism*, and most of all Pope Sixtus V, who issued a terrifying bull on the subject in 1588, maintained the traditional position that contraception was a matter of homicidal *maleficium*, not a matter of sexual irregularity. Admittedly, Sixtus V's bull was immediately repealed, but it was not until the middle of the eighteenth century that the modern doctrine of contraception was established. In the interval, as is clear from Noonan's discussion, confessional interest in the subject had declined.[41] What we learn from the history of the confessional treatment of contraception, it seems to me, is that the first leg of my hypothesis is correct, and the second leg is wrong. Whatever it was that governed the social universe of sin in the period

---

when he was 15 he used to go out in the meadows to masturbate, which gave him great pleasure. The priest told him to masturbate whenever he felt like it, but keep his hands off other people's property, and above all give him back his corn: '*Menati il tuo batisteo quando tu voi, e piu non rubare; lascia istare la roba d'altri, e sopra ogni cosa rendimi il mio grano*'. *Motti e facezie del piovano Arlotto*, ed. G. B. Folena (Milan/Naples, 1953 edn), pp. 34 ff. I hope the reader will be as grateful to Peter Burke as I am for this charming illustration, as for the information above n. 27.

[40] J. T. Noonan, *Contraception: a history of its treatment by Catholic theologians and canonists* (Cambridge, Mass., 1966), pp. 168 ff, 178.

[41] *Ibid.*, pp. 360–64, 349 f, 372 f, 379, 383. There is not much of interest for our period in H. Bergues and others, *La prévention des naissances dans la famille* (Paris, 1960), except (pp. 240–47) some evidence for the diocese of Liège which helps to show that the relative lack of interest among confessional writers is not necessarily explained by a lack of experience among the population.

during which the average Catholic was finding his way around the confessional, I do not think it can have been an obsession with individual sexuality.[42]

Alternative approaches might be suggested. Difficult as the concept may be for a social historian to manage, some credit must be given to the confessional as an instrument of Luther's *metanoia*, the experience of conversion.[43] More mundanely, there is a good deal about the new dispensation—a novel concern for the confession of children, the association of confession with catechism—to indicate that educational values lay close to its centre; or that it was designed to instil a new standard of obedience to the precepts of the church concerning religious observance.[44] But I end on a negative note, and this is perhaps appropriate. The confessional keeps its secrets, as it is entitled to do.

Queen's University, Belfast.

[42] It would appear from Zeldin's discussion (above, n. 39, *e.g.* p. 19), that this had become the case by the nineteenth century, at least in France; *cf.* Delumeau, *Le catholicisme entre Luther et Voltaire*, p. 321, and the classification of mortal sins by the nineteenth-century Jesuit Jean Gury in Lea, ii, p. 259.

[43] Thus Estius, *In quatuor libros senientiarum commentaria* (above, n. 29), iv, p. 183.

[44] Lea, i, pp. 155 ff, 400 ff; *Acta ecclesiae mediolanensis*, pp. 312, 645 ff, 869, 875 (education). On the precepts of the church note Gury in Lea, ii, p. 259.

OBSERVATIONS ON ENGLISH GOVERNMENT FROM THE TENTH TO THE TWELFTH CENTURY

By James Campbell, M.A., F.S.A., F.R.Hist.S.

READ 10 MAY 1974

PRUDENT historians, when they consider the ordered power of the late Anglo-Saxon state, are apt to indulge a professional instinct, to hedge their bets. Such phrases as 'specious uniformity' and 'rudimentary precocity' have found favour.[1] It has long seemed likely, and it has by now become certain, that such caution is superfluous.

Some of the most solid, and the earliest, evidence for a powerful and elaborate system of government in England has been provided by recent investigation of the forts of the 'Burghal Hidage'.[2] Nearly all thirty-three have been identified. It has been shown that some are very big, enclosing over eighty acres. Their earthworks were massive and sometimes revetted with timber. The lengths of the fortifications often correspond, sometimes closely, to those which may be deduced from the 'Burghal Hidage' by using its formula of a hundred and sixty hides to the furlong. So Alfred, or he and his son, not only built a vast system of fortifications, but also devised elaborate means of serving them, of which the 'Hidage' is the record. By the beginning of the tenth century West Saxon kings were capable of a feat of government on the largest scale.

The coinage from the end of Edgar's reign demonstrates how successfully the English could manage a system of great sophistication. Its main characteristics have been generally known since 1961.[3] An abundant silver coinage was kept under complete royal control. Every six or seven years (later every two or three) a new type was issued and previous types were then normally demonetized. The evidence of hoards is that such demonetizations, involving the frequent replacement of a coinage of, at the very least, ten million silver pennies, were very thorough, though less so in the Confessor's

---

[1] F. Barlow, *The Feudal Kingdom of England* (London, 1955), pp. 42, 46; V. H. Galbraith, *The Making of Domesday Book* (Oxford, 1961), pp. 46, 47.

[2] C. A. Ralegh Radford, 'The Later Pre-Conquest Boroughs and their Defences', *Medieval Archaeology*, xiv (1970), pp. 83–103, and the articles cited there.

[3] R. H. M. Dolley and D. M. Metcalf, 'The Reform of the English Coinage under Eadgar', *Anglo-Saxon Coins*, ed. R. H. M. Dolley (London, 1961), pp. 136–68.

reign. Not the least remarkable feature of the system was that a new type might be lighter, or heavier, than its predecessor, sometimes markedly so. Historians have been inclined to boggle at what numismatists show them to have existed here. Their difficulty is that of making sense of the evidence without attributing more sophistication than seems plausible. The evidence is nevertheless such as to render the implausible irresistible. The English kings were running the earliest known, and the best, example of the system of *renovatio monetae* which by 1200 had come into use in many states from Poland to Portugal.[4] A ruler could use a currency controlled in this way to bring in profits exceeding those of simpler systems. The currency became a means of taxation and subjects would sometimes, as in Aragon in 1236, grant heavy property taxes to be rid of *renovatio monetae*.[5]

For the best results it was desirable that there should be a close connexion between the monetary and fiscal systems. A passage (possibly interpolated) in *Dialogus de Scaccario* supports the supposition that in England the Crown insisted that all payments to itself should be in coin of the current issue.[6] Such a requirement would not only help to enforce the demonetization of old types; it could also provide the Crown with the means to play 'heads I win, tails you lose' by, for example, at some times requiring payment by weight and at others by tale. The variety of methods of payment, by tale, by weight and blanch, recorded in Domesday suggests the possibility of such a system. Its presence would accord with Miss Sally Harvey's suggestion that the payments in an *ora* of 20d., rather than of 16d., recorded from royal demesne in Domesday represented the means whereby the king averted loss when the weight of the penny was reduced from about 21·5 gr. to 17 gr. in *c.* 1062.[7] A converse explanation may account for the great increase in the weight of the penny, from 18 gr. to about 26 gr., in *c.* 1051. Various explanations have been offered for such increases. For example, the wish to 'avoid the creation of a bullion reserve of embarrassing magnitude'.[8] Or,

[4] H. Bertil A. Peterson, *Anglo-Saxon Currency. King Edgar's Reform to the Norman Conquest* (Lund, 1969). *Cf.* A. Suchodolski, '*Renovatio Monetae* in Poland in the Twelfth Century', *Wiadomści Numizmatyczne*, v (1961), pp. 57–75 of the supplement and C. S. S. Lyon, 'Variations in Currency in Late Anglo-Saxon England', *Mints, Dies and Currency*, ed. R. A. G. Carson (London, 1971), pp. 101–20.

[5] S. Bolin, 'Tax Money and Plough Money', *Scandinavian Economic History Review*, ii (1954), pp. 5–21, esp. p. 17.

[6] Ed. C. Johnson (London, 1950), p. 9; on the assumptions that *instantis monete* (last line) means 'of the current issue' and that the chronology is, as elsewhere in the *Dialogus* (*cf.* p. xx), unreliable.

[7] S. Harvey, 'Royal Revenue and Domesday Terminology', *Economic History Review*, 2nd ser., xx (1967), pp. 221–28.

[8] M. Dolley, *The Norman Conquest and the English Coinage* (London, 1966), p. 10.

in the case of the increase under discussion (granted a likely connexion with the suspension of the geld and the standing down of the
fleet) that Edward 'calculated that fewer coins would be needed
and decided that the opportunity should be taken to produce a
heavier coin which would give enhanced prestige'.[9] It seems more
likely that the heavier coin was a substitute for the tax, and intended
to increase the value to the Crown of payments by tale. The late
Old English coinage system was probably highly remunerative. If
it is true that Ethelred II did not introduce a hidage tax until
c. 1012, it may have been his new system of exploiting the currency
which did most to enable him to buy off the Danes.[10]

'The Anglo-Saxon financial system, which collected the Danegeld, was not run from a box under the bed.'[11] Indeed, it demonstrates the power of the state. A powerful instance of the fiscal
system at work has been provided by Dr Hart in an analysis of a
reassessment of Northamptonshire carried out between a date
probably not long after the Conquest and 1086.[12] The assessment
was not only reduced, but also reallocated between hundreds. This
reallocation was such as to restore a balance among the hundreds
which had existed at the time of the 'County Hidage', but had since
been upset by a reduction of the burden on some hundreds, but not
on others. The restoration of the earlier balance required the reduction of the hidages of different hundreds in different proportions:
in some in the ratio 2 : 1; in other 5 : 2; in other 9 : 3½; otherwise
in yet others. What must have been a central decision and plan was
executed in an elaborate and orderly way at the local level.

Few financial documents survive which are older than Domesday
Book. Of these the Northamptonshire Geld Roll is the most important. In addition Miss Harvey has shown that Domesday was
preceded by, and partly dependent on, hidage lists, some of them
arranged as it is, and some older than the Conquest. Such records
are known to have been kept in the Treasury with Domesday.[13]
Otherwise there is very little.[14] But it is likely, as Galbraith suggests,
that late Old English administrative documents were numerous, and
that nearly all have been lost, partly because they were commonly

---

[9] F. Barlow, *Edward the Confessor* (London, 1970), pp. 183–84.
[10] *Two of the Anglo-Saxon Chronicles Parallel*, ed. C. Plummer and J. Earle,
(Oxford, 1892), p. 173.
[11] V. H. Galbraith, *Studies in the Public Records* (London, 1948), p. 45.
[12] C. Hart, *The Hidation of Northamptonshire* (Leicester, 1970), esp. pp. 39–43.
It seems reasonable to take such a post-Conquest instance as indicative of English
practice, especially as the key document, the Northants Geld Roll, is in English.
[13] S. Harvey, 'Domesday Book and its Predecessors', *English Historical Review*,
lxxxvi (1971), pp. 753–73.
[14] But *cf.* pp. 50–51 below.

in English, as the Northamptonshire Geld Roll is.[15] Miss Robertson's collection of charters in Anglo-Saxon contains some twenty documents which are not charters, agreements, or records of lawsuits, but public and private administrative records of other kinds. Though few, they are very varied: a list of services for the repair of a bridge;[16] a memorandum on the recruitment of a ship's crew in Ethelred II's time;[17] estate lists and surveys;[18] lists of treasures;[19] stock inventories;[20] the Northamptonshire Geld Roll; the 'Burghal' and 'County' hidages. The chances for the preservation of such documents were poor. The best lay in their being copied into a cartulary, as the Northamptonshire Geld Roll was. But cartulary-making became widespread only in the twelfth century. Only one pre-Conquest cartulary survives and only two others of before 1100.[21] Many of the documents are of types which are not found in Latin in the Old English period. It is reasonable to deduce that those collected by Miss Robertson are indeed the survivors from a much larger number and that English was the ordinary language for much written business.[22]

The use of written English went with a considerable degree of lay literacy; no doubt as both cause and effect. Æthelweard's translation of the Chronicle was the first book written by an English nobleman and, for nearly four centuries, the last.[23] Two of Ælfric's theological treatises were written for thegns.[24] The relative abundance of inscriptions, not only on churches but also on, for example, brooches and rings, is suggestive.[25] A layman who learned to read in the Confessor's reign would be able to make out his father's will, the king's writs, the boundary clause of a charter, or a monastery's inventories. In Henry II's day mere literacy would have won him none of these advantages. If he wanted them he had to learn Latin. There is no doubt that some did so;[26] but it would be unwise to be

[15] *Studies in the Public Records*, pp. 37–40.

[16] *Anglo-Saxon Charters*, ed. A. J. Robertson (Cambridge, 1956), no. LII (possibly post-Conquest).   [17] *Ibid.*, no. LXXII.

[18] *Ibid.*, nos. LIV, LXXXIV, CIX, CX and App. I nos. IV and V, for which see pp. 50–51 below.

[19] *Ibid.*, nos. XXXIX, CIV and App. II nos. II–IX. *Cf.* p. 49 below.

[20] *Ibid.*, nos. XXXIX, CIV, App. II nos. III, IX and *cf.* J. Earle, *Hand-Book of Land Charters and other Saxonic Documents* (Oxford, 1888), pp. 275–77.

[21] G. R. C. Davis, *Medieval Cartularies of Great Britain* (London, 1958), pp. xi–xii.

[22] *Cf.* Professor Dorothy Whitelock's suggestion on the survival of letters in English, *English Historical Documents c. 500–1042* (London, 1955), p. 577.

[23] But see H. G. Richardson and G. O. Sayles, *The Governance of Mediaeval England* (Edinburgh, 1963), p. 273.

[24] Whitelock, *English Historical Documents*, p. 849.

[25] E. Okasha, *Hand-list of Anglo-Saxon Non-Runic Inscriptions* (Cambridge, 1971).

[26] Richardson and Sayles, *op. cit.*, pp. 265–84.

confident that they were more numerous than those who were literate in English a century or more earlier. If the late Anglo-Saxon state was run with sophistication and thoughtfulness this may very well be connected with the ability of many laymen to read.[27]

It would be tediously easy to multiply instances of the power of the late Old English kings. Nothing is more remarkable about them than the long series of innovations which they introduced and the power of experiment and of creation so displayed. The shires of the Midlands, the hundredal system, the burghal system, planned towns, Danegeld and the currency reveal a capacity for change and for order hardly matched until the nineteenth century. Those who find themselves unable to believe that this was so draw attention to, for example, inequalities in the taxation system and provincial differences in law and administration. But such inefficiencies and variations appear in fact to have been less marked than they were in most of the states of Europe in the eighteenth century.

Prima facie the Dark Age state most readily comparable with the English is that of the Carolingians. The best account of the relations between them remains that of Stubbs.[28] He pointed out the numerous and obvious similarities which suggest direct connexion. Carolingian counties and *centenae* with their courts bear a resemblance to those of England which extends to matters of detail. The earl like the count took a third of the profits of justice. Danegeld in England is preceded by similar taxes in Francia. Prescriptions which appear in ninth century Carolingian capitularies reappear in tenth century English laws.[29] He also drew attention to the dynastic and other relationships which would have enabled one area to influence the other. Nevertheless he warned that 'the parallels between Frank and English law must not be pressed without allowing for the similarity of circumstances which prompted them and the fundamental stock of common custom and principle which underlay them'. His conclusion was masterly: 'it is wiser and safer to allow the coincidences to speak for themselves, and to avoid a positive theory which the first independent investigator may find means of demolishing'.

For a generation after Stubbs the question was regarded as open. For example, Maitland took it for granted that Danegeld might have a Carolingian origin.[30] But in 1912 Helen Cam published her

---

[27] *Cf.* Galbraith, *Studies in the Public Records*, p. 57.

[28] W. Stubbs, *The Constitutional History of England*, i (Oxford, 1891), pp. 223–27.

[29] To the instances cited *ibid.*, p. 226, add those mentioned on pp. 45–47 below and by J. Yver, 'Les premières institutions du duché de Normandie', *Settimane di studio del centro italiano sull' alto medioevo*, xvi (Spoleto, 1969), p. 319. Some capitularies and some Anglo-Saxon 'codes' resemble one another fairly closely in general form.

[30] F. W. Maitland, *Domesday Book and Beyond* (Cambridge, 1897), p. 518.

M.A. thesis, addressed to the question Stubbs had raised. She concluded that in reply to the question: ' "Did the West Saxon kings borrow from the Carolingian emperors?", we can only reply that it is possible, but hardly probable.'[31] Her evidence hardly justified her conclusion, not least because she gave virtually no consideration to Stubbs's suggestions on, for example, Danegeld, general oaths and the relationship between English laws and Frankish capitularies. At the same time Liebermann's *Gesetze* were appearing and his inclination was to find early or common Germanic origins for institutions where he could, while he was only marginally concerned with some of the relevant evidence. The strange consequence has been that for sixty years the question of the relationship between English and Carolingian institutions has been only rarely and barely considered. In seeking the origins of English institutions scholars have preferred to look north and to later texts, rather than south and to earlier. For example, Dr Richardson and Professor Sayles suggest a Scandinavian origin for the earl's third penny, referring to the *Heimskringla*, even though the count's third share is a well-known Carolingian institution.[32]

Stenton wrote of the Danegeld that it was 'the first system of national taxation to appear in western Europe' and that 'as a piece of large scale financial organisation it has no parallel in the Dark Ages'.[33] In fact on several of the twelve or thirteen occasions when large payments were made to the Danes in Francia the money was raised by national taxation which, if it was more complex than Danegeld, nevertheless in some respects resembled it.[34] For example in 866 Charles the Bald levied 6d. on every *mansus ingenuilis*, 3d. on every *mansus servilis*, 1d. on every *accola* and on every two *hospitia*. He required all free Franks to pay the *heribannus* and merchants a tenth of their possessions.[35] (The levies on the *mansus* may have applied only to lands held as benefices or even only to monastic lands so held.[36]) It seems that the *mansus indomicatus* was generally exempt from such taxes, suggesting comparison with the exemption of manorial demesne in England.[37] The existence of such Carolingian taxation does not prove that English Danegeld has Frankish origins.

[31] H. M. Cam, *Local Government in Francia and England* (London, 1912), p. 156

[32] *The Governance of Mediaeval England*, p. 26, n. 1; F. L. Ganshof, *Frankish Institutions under Charlemagne* (Providence, R.I., 1968), p. 29.

[33] F. M. Stenton, *Anglo-Saxon England*, 3rd edn (Oxford, 1971), pp. 645, 648.

[34] E. Joranson, *The Danegeld in France* (Rock Island, 1923).

[35] *Ibid.*, pp. 72–73; *cf.* pp. 45–58, 62–92.

[36] F. Lot, 'Les tributs aux Normands et l'église de France au ixe siècle', *Bibliothèque de l'École des Chartes*, lxxxv (1924), pp. 58–78.

[37] Joranson, *op. cit.*, p. 191; R. Welldon Finn, *An Introduction to Domesday Book* (London, 1963), p. 254.

But it is at the very least in sufficiently strong contrast to Stenton's statements to suggest that even one of the most eminent of English historians could lose sight of what happened beyond the Channel.

Undoubted evidence for direct connexion is to be found in the coinage. It is generally agreed that the introduction of a penny coinage into England in the eighth century and the extension of royal authority over the coinage in the ninth and early tenth centuries reflect and partly depend on Carolingian policy.[38] For example when Athelstan introduced a penalty for false coining it was the unusual one of striking off the hand, which is required for the same offence in the capitularies.[39] The most remarkable feature of the later development of the English coinage, the successive demonetizations, also had Carolingian precedent. On several occasions between the time of Charlemagne and that of Charles the Bald an emperor gave orders for the demonetization of previous types in favour of a new one.[40] The edict of Pîtres, 864, gives detailed instructions on how such a demonetization was to be accomplished.[41] There is evidence that it was attended with some measure of success.[42]

There are other points of resemblance between the English and Carolingian systems where the evidence suggests something more than common origins and common needs. The earliest is an instance of English influence on the empire. When Charles the Bald introduced compulsory work on fortifications, which was well-known in England, but not in Gaul, he did so, he said, *iuxta antiquam et aliarum gentium consuetudinem*.[43] In the next century the case for English kings having Frankish precedent in mind when they established the hundredal system is strengthened by the word 'hundred' itself. Many of the features of the system appear new in England, but some of them had appeared earlier across the Channel.[44] No

[38] M. Dolley, *Anglo-Saxon Pennies* (London, 1964), pp. 14–15.

[39] Yver, 'Les premières institutions du duché de Normandie', *op. cit.*, p. 343, nn. 109, 110. Frankish moneyers were at work in the Danelaw in the late ninth and early tenth centuries, M. Dolley, *Viking Coins of the Danelaw and of Dublin* (London, 1965), pp. 17–20.

[40] K. Morrison and H. Grunthal, *Carolingian Coinage* (American Numismatic Society Notes and Monographs, no. 158, 1967), pp. 1–8.

[41] *Capitularia Regum Francorum*, ii, ed. A. Boretius and V. Krause (*Monumenta Germaniae Historica, Legum, Sectio II* (Hanover, 1890)), pp. 314–18.

[42] Morrison and Grunthal, *op. cit.*, p. 6.

[43] N. Brooks, 'The Development of Military Obligations in Ninth and Tenth Century England', *England before the Conquest*, ed. P. Clemoes and K. Hughes (Cambridge, 1971), p. 81.

[44] H. R. Loyn, 'The Hundred in the Tenth and Early Eleventh Centuries', *British Government and Administration*, ed. H. R. Loyn and H. Hearder (Cardiff, 1974), pp. 1–15, esp. 2–3; H. Dannebauer, 'Hundertschaft, Centena und Huntari', *Historisches Jahrbuch*, lxii–lxix (1942–49), pp. 155–219, esp. pp. 163-65.

instance is known before the tenth century of the word 'hundred' (or of any word, in English or Latin, meaning a numerical hundred) being used in England to denote a unit of government or of juris- diction.[45] The argument from silence carries weight here because we have so many early laws. It was on the Continent that such words were used to denote governmental divisions not dissimilar from later English hundreds.[46] Before the tenth century the English do not appear to have had either the institution or the name. The case for the institution, when it appears in the tenth century, having been developed under Continental influence is supported by the adoption of a corresponding name.

There is similarly a good *prima facie* case for direct connexion in regard to general oaths. The first possible reference to such an oath in England appears in Edward the Elder's Exeter code which refers to 'the oath and pledge which the whole nation has given' in a context which has to do with the prevention of theft.[47] Athelstan's fourth and fifth codes refer to an oath or oaths in a similar context 'given to the king and his councillors' and 'given at Grateley'.[48] In *c.* 943 Edmund's Colinton code gives the text of an oath by which 'Omnes', were to swear fidelity to the king, 'sicut homo debet esse fidelis domino suo'.[49] From Cnut comes the famous requirement that every man above twelve years 'take an oath that he will not be a thief nor a thief's accomplice'.[50] It is not clear how these references to oaths should be related together. But it is clear that they can be so related by considering them in comparison to what is known of Carolingian oaths. Charlemagne introduced or re- introduced the general oath in 789, taking elaborate precautions in 792 or 793 to ensure that every adult male above the age of twelve took it. In 802 a new text for the oath was introduced. All were to swear '. . . fidelis sum, sicut homo per drictum debet esse domino suo'. There was another general oath taking and the instructions to the *missi* make it clear that the oath was regarded as one not to engage in any unlawful activity.[41] There is no certain reference to a

[45] F. Liebermann, *Die Gesetze der Angelsachsen*, ii, pt. ii (Halle, 1912), p. 516.

[46] In important aspects and areas the *centena* may have been an innovation of Charlemagne's time: Loyn, *op. cit.*, pp. 2–3; Ganshof, *Frankish Institutions under Charlemagne* p. 32; B. Guérard *Le Polypytque de l'abbé Irminon* (Paris 1844), i, pp. 43–44.

[47] F. L. Attenborough, *The Laws of the Earliest English Kings* (reprint, New York, 1963), p. 121.

[48] *Ibid.*, pp. 149, 153.

[49] A. J. Robertson, *The Laws of the Kings of England from Edmund to Henry I* (Cambridge, 1925), p. 12.

[50] *Ibid.*, p. 185.

[51] F. L. Ganshof, *The Carolingians and the Frankish Monarchy* (London, 1971), pp. 112–17.

general oath in England before Edmund, while it had a much older history in Gaul. There is an important textual resemblance between the core of Charlemagne's oath and the core of Edmund's. The age limit mentioned by Charlemagne and Cnut is the same. Granted then that all the English references make sense if taken as referring to an oath of the Carolingian type, it would seem that in the absence of definite proof the onus should lie on those who maintain that we do not see here a Carolingian institution imported into England.

Such an importation would not be surprising. The dynastic and cultural relationships between England and the Carolingian world were close from at the latest the later ninth century. In the age of Alfred and Charles the Bald, Asser, Grimbald and Hincmar the nexus of relationships between the successful West Saxon and the struggling Carolingian realms was sufficient to ensure that many of the achievements of Alfred and his circle must be placed in a Carolingian context. Alfred's biography is exactly in the tradition of Carolingian royal biography.[52] The Chronicle recalls the Carolingian royal annals.[53] Professor Wallace-Hadrill has suggested that Alfred's producing a law code was a consequence of his resuming 'a practice that had been lost in England because he knew that, up to the time of Charles the Bald, the Carolingians had found a use for it'.[54] The suggestion is a very important one in the present context. At the time when the West Saxon dynasty was acquiring new scope for the exercise of power it came into a relationship with Frankish circles which were devoted to the memory and to the collection of the records of Carolingian glory.

In the tenth century dynastic relations with the sub-Carolingian world continued to be important; but Carolingian influence is most readily demonstrable in the thought and institutions of the English church, especially in the time of the monastic reformers and in the next generation. The writings of Wulfstan and Ælfric were deeply influenced by Carolingian thought.[55] A bishop writing a letter in the reign of Ethelred II could copy the larger part of it from one of Alcuin.[56] The monastic reformers looked to contemporary models of observance; but in establishing a series of monasteries which was

[52] D. A. Bullough, 'The Educational Tradition in England from Alfred to Ælfric', *Settimane . . .*, xix (Spoleto, 1971), p. 455, n. 2.
[53] J. M. Wallace Hadrill, 'The Franks and the English in the Ninth Century', *History*, new ser., xxxv (1950), pp. 212–14.
[54] *Idem, Early Germanic Kingship in England and on the Continent* (Oxford, 1971), p. 148.
[55] *E.g.* D. Bethurum, *The Homilies of Wulfstan* (Oxford, 1957), esp. p. 61; P. Clemoes, 'Ælfric', *Continuations and Beginnings*, ed. E. G. Stanley (London, 1966), pp. 182–83.
[56] F. E. Harmer, *Anglo-Saxon Writs* (Manchester, 1952), p. 22.

integral to the state and in drawing up such a document as the *Regularis Concordia* they looked much further back, to Louis the Pious and Benedict of Aniane.[57] Stubbs fairly commented: 'It would be very rash to observe that while the bishops who composed so large a part of the Witanagemot sought foreign models for their canons they did not also seek foreign models for their secular laws.'[58]

The seriousness of the difficulties, but also the importance of the possibilities, which are intrinsic to the attempt to consider Old English government in a Carolingian and sub-Carolingian context are most apparent in the case of Domesday Book. The Carolingians had written surveys made for a wide variety of purposes, often using the sworn inquest.[59] They had *mansus* lists. In 843 the empire was divided *per descriptas mansas*. A hundred and twenty commissioners toured to make the necessary *descriptio*, part of which probably survives.[60] The emperors had surveys made, in great detail, of particular estates. They pursued careful inquiries of other kinds. For example, in 864 Charles the Bald ordered a detailed inquiry into markets, past and present, the results of which were to be returned in writing, on *breves*, a term not unfamiliar to students of Domesday.[61] Carolingian taxation involved the listing and valuation of property.[62] There is very little about Domesday, considered as a piece of administration, which would have seemed unfamiliar to a Carolingian official of the period between Charlemagne and Charles the Bald. When the wide variety, the sometimes wide extent, and the techniques of Carolingian surveys are considered it is very difficult to avoid the conclusion that theirs is the tradition in which Domesday, somehow or other, must lie. The possibilities of connexion are numerous; the gap in the evidence is wide. No one knows when (no one indeed really knows if) surveys ceased to be used by the Continental rulers; no one knows when English rulers began to use them. If such techniques fell into desuetude in sub-Carolingian states

---

[57] D. Knowles, *The Monastic Order in England* (2nd edn, Cambridge, 1966), p. 42.

[58] *Constitutional History*, i, p. 224.

[59] W. Metz, *Das Karolingische Reichsgut* (Berlin, 1960), pp. 11–90; Ganshof, *The Carolingians and the Frankish Monarchy*, pp. 130–32.

[60] Ganshof, *op. cit.*, pp. 292–95.

[61] *Capitularia*, ii, *op. cit.*, pp. 317–18. For *breve* in its common Domesday meaning of schedule or return see Ganshof, *The Carolingians and the Frankish Monarchy*, p. 293 and E. Lesne, *Histoire de la propriété ecclésiastique en France*, iii (Lille, 1936), pp. 1–30, esp. 1–6. It was the term almost invariably used by Carolingian government in such contexts as: 'per omne regnum suum litteras misit, ut episcopi, abbates et abbatissae breves de honoribus suis quanta mansa quisque haberet . . . deferre curarent' ('Annals of St. Bertin', *s.a.* 869, ed. F. Grat, J. Vielliard and S. Clémencet (Paris, 1964), pp. 152-53

[62] Joranson, *The Danegeld in France*, p. 49.

some of them were preserved in the church. The tradition of the estate survey, the polyptych (or *descriptio*, another term familiar to students of Domesday Book) was continuous there from the ninth century to the twelfth.[63] Guérard, the founder of the study of such surveys, saw Domesday Book as one of them: 'De tous les documents qui peuvent être rangés dans la classe des polyptyques, le plus étendu et le plus remarquable'.[64] Something of what he meant can be seen in considering, for example, the compilation of the polyptych of the abbey of Prüm, in Lorraine, in 893, or somewhat before. Commissioners were sent to all the abbey's demesnes (which were scattered over some hundreds of square miles) to inquire into the number of manses of every description, into mills, and into other sources of income.[65] Perrin has shown, from variations in the text as it applies to different areas, that a number of different sets of commissioners were despatched and he discusses the way in which their original returns were put together and edited.[66] He goes on to emphasize the almost universal practice of writing out a polyptych in a book, rather than on the rolls normal for other kinds of record, and the status of such a survey as public record.[67] There is an echo of Domesday here, not too faint, and not inconceivably answering.

It may be then that the Carolingian techniques which are seen at their apogee in Domesday Book were transmitted to England by the church. True, there is no sign of a complete *descriptio* having been made for the lands of any pre-Conquest monastery. Such surveys were far from universal on the Continent. But Continental houses which did not have complete surveys could still make use of the techniques of written record which came from the world of the *Capitulare de Villis* and the *Brevium Exempla*. They could make inventories of stock and lists of treasure and survey their estates piecemeal, as occasion arose.[68] The handful of administrative documents from English monasteries, which have been argued to be the survivors from many more, are of just such kinds. Doubtless it is unremarkable that one list of men, oxen and flitches of bacon resembles another, even if one comes from Æthelwold's Ely and the

---

[63] Lesne, iii, *op. cit.*, pp. 1–30. The early meanings of *descriptio* commonly have to do with a record or survey made for purposes of taxation (Ducange, *Glossarium*, s.v.). In the Carolingian period it denotes a survey, *e.g.* of the kind which was made for the division of the empire in 843 (p. 48 above) or inventory *e.g.* such that 'by consulting it the king could discover not only what he possessed, but also what his possessions were worth' (Ganshof, *The Carolingians and the Frankish Monarchy*, pp. 293–94). For its use to denote an estate survey, see Lesne, *op. cit.*, iii, 11–20.

[64] *Polyptyque de l'abbé Irminon*, *op. cit.*, i, p. 25.

[65] C.-E. Perrin, *Recherches sur la seigneurie rurale en Lorraine* (n.p., 1935), pp. 3–93.

[66] *Ibid.*, pp. 47–64; *cf.* pp. 600–3.   [67] *Ibid.*, pp. 614, 607.

[68] Lesne, *op. cit.*, iii, pp. 19–20 76–77.

other from the *Brevium Exempla*.[69] But there are somewhat more specific resemblances between English and Continental documents. In particular there are Continental precedents for two English documents in which a list of treasures is followed by a list of sources of income.[70] In general the English documents do look as if they came from milieux whose techniques in the use of writing in estate management were in a Carolingian tradition.

Most of the documents in question come from monasteries, especially from Ely; and none is earlier than the end of the tenth century. English monastic reform is well-known to have owed much to Continental houses, especially Fleury, St Peter's, Ghent, and the reformed houses of Lorraine, notably Gorze and Verdun. From such houses could be learned, not only how monks should rightly live, but also, and no less important, how the property whereby monks lived should be looked after. Abbo of Fleury had much to do with the English reform. He well knew the value of a polyptych. In a letter to a fellow abbot he described the good use to which he had put *libri politici a temporibus Magni Caroli*, even though, *pene vetustate consumpti*.[71] The surviving documents from the Lorraine houses, especially Gorze and Verdun, show the careful use of writing in estate management. Better record keeping could indeed be directly associated with reform.[72] It is reasonable to suppose that English reformed houses were influenced by their foreign exemplars in this respect as in others. What such a potentate as Æthelwold learned in the church he could have applied in the state.

The use of the inquest is almost intrinsic to the Carolingian tradition of inquiry and survey. The possibility of the inquest's use in late Anglo-Saxon England is widely admitted, though there are differences of opinion on how formal it was and on whether it was used by the Crown.[73] There is a little evidence which has not been used by the main authorities. It has been acutely observed that the early part of what is called Ethelred's fourth code looks like a reply to an inquest on the customs of London.[74] In addition there are two surveys, one dating from between the Conquest and Domesday, the other of about the time of Domesday, recording dues owed to, respectively, the bishop of Winchester at Taunton and to the

---

[69] Robertson, *Anglo-Saxon Charters*, no. XXXIX; *Capitularia*, i, pp. 250–52.

[70] Robertson, *op. cit.*, nos. XXXIX and CIV (pp. 194–97); *Capitularia*, i, *loc. cit.*; Lesne, *op. cit.*, iii, p. 156.

[71] *Patrologia Latina*, ed. Migne, cxxxix, col. 442.

[72] Perrin, *Recherches sur la seigneurie rurale en Lorraine*, pp. 101–239, 599.

[73] R. V. Turner, 'The origin of the medieval English jury', *Journal of British Studies*, vii (1967–68), no. 2, pp. 1–10.

[74] H. G. Richardson and G. O. Sayles, *Law and Legislation from Æthelberht to Magna Carta* (Edinburgh, 1966), p. 28.

church at Lambourne.[75] Both are in English, and witnessed. A witnessed survey of dues comes close to a record of a sworn inquest, especially when, as in the Taunton document, they are dues owed in the past. It relates to the state of affairs on the day of the Confessor's death, so recalling Domesday. The other claims royal participation in some way. These documents strengthen, though they do not clinch, the case for the pre-Conquest inquest and for its use by the Crown. It is curious, but characteristic, that while it has long been admitted that the English inquest may have had a Carolingian ancestor, it has nearly always been assumed that the descent could only be via the Normans.

It is sobering to consider what account historians would have given of the history of English administration had Domesday and the early records of the Exchequer been lost. Left to squeeze what they could from charters and annals they would gravely have underrated the English state. One may wonder how far other European states have been underrated by their historians, lacking financial records older than the thirteenth century. That administration on the Continent in the tenth and eleventh centuries may have been more sophisticated than is commonly assumed multiplies possible explanations for the resemblances between Carolingian and English government. While it is very likely that some important developments in England reflect the influence of the ninth-century empire, its memory, or its records, others may derive from France, Germany or Normandy. Nevertheless, if it is granted that when the Domesday survey was made and the *breves* incorporated in the great *descriptio*, this was much more likely to have been the fruit of a strong administrative tradition which had been continuously maintained from Carolingian times than of the adoption of *ad hoc* procedures, and if it is asked where that tradition had found a home in the century preceding 1086, the answer must be: just possibly Normandy,[76] but much more probably England.

The framework of the Old English state lasted long. Some of it still endures. Nevertheless it came under heavy strain in the twelfth century, which was not a period of universal progress in English administration. It is possible that the Anglo-Saxon fiscal system was never afterwards so efficient, or oppressive, as it had been under Ethelred and Cnut;[77] it is likely that Stephen's reign did much to ruin it; but it was Henry II who actually dismantled it. Henry I

[75] Robertson, *Anglo-Saxon Charters*, App. I, nos. IV, V.

[76] Yver, 'Les premières institutions du duché normand', p. 339 for recent work on the early Norman fiscal system.

[77] Maitland, *Domesday Book and Beyond* (1960 reprint), pp. 25–26, 514; Dolley and Metcalf, 'The Reform of the English Coinage under Eadgar', p. 157.

had continued the Danegeld. It is not known whether Stephen levied it. Henry II did so for the last time in 1162. Although the old assessment continued to be used occasionally for shire *dona* and hidage or carucage taxes were revived between 1194 and 1220, the balance of the fiscal system shifted towards scutage, the exploitation of feudal incidents and the sale of royal rights.[78] Regular changes of coin type continued until 1158. '1158 and not 1066 is the year for the numismatist to have always in mind'.[79] In that year Henry completely abandoned the system of *renovatio monetae*. The coinage of ugly and ill-struck pennies of the 'Tealby' type which was then introduced was maintained until 1180. By the end of the century the English coinage had gone over to the sub-Carolingian simplicity of the *type immobilisé*.

It is possible to regard both these changes as reforms. Yet though Danegeld was, as we are often assured, riddled with anomalies (which Henry increased), it was the largest item in the king's not very large revenue; and the Angevin fiscal system, as we follow it along the road to Runnymede, is not without anomalies of its own. It is highly probable that Henry lost money by the currency revolution of 1158.[80] It may be that both abandonments were concessions. Certainly, in both instances, something which was, or once had been, very elaborate and orderly was replaced by something simpler to administer.

A marked change, certainly in the frame of mind in which England was governed, arguably in the power and coherence with which it was governed, may be seen in the treatment of administrative areas and boundaries. Tenth-century government created new units and suppressed old. The shires it made lay orderly on the map until 1 April 1974. On that map were elements of disorder: the foolish little shire of Rutland and the oddly disposed counties of the north west. These were not Saxon, but Angevin muddles. Although Rutland had a distinct status in the Anglo-Saxon period, its rise to the status of a shire and the dignity of a sheriff was the product of a confused process in the twelfth century.[81] Similarly in the north west. Until John's reign Westmorland was treated in an anomalous way, having a sheriff only when one of the two lordships which made it up was in the king's hand.[82] The odd northern boundary

---

[78] Painter, *Studies in the History of the Medieval English Feudal Barony* (Baltimore, 1943), pp. 74–79; J. C. Holt, *Magna Carta* (Cambridge, 1965), pp. 19–42.

[79] Dolley, *The Norman Conquest and the English Coinage*, pp. 35–36.

[80] D. F. Allen, *A Catalogue of Coins in the British Museum. The Cross-and-Crosslets* (*'Tealby'*) *Type of Henry II* (London, 1951), p. lxxxviii.

[81] F. M. Stenton in *Victoria County History of Rutland*, i (London, 1908), pp. 134–36; J. M. Ramsay, *ibid.*, pp. 165–71.

[82] J. C. Holt, *The Northerners* (Oxford, 1961), p. 199.

of Lancashire is that between the fiefs of Roger of Poitou and Ivo Taillebois in 1094; among other eccentricities it bisects a parish. The early history of Lancashire is anomalous in other ways. For a time it was a kind of private shire, Roger of Poitou having his own sheriff. The Angevin Exchequer treated it as a unit of lordship rather than of administrative geography, in that the other lands of Roger were always included with it for Exchequer purposes.[83] These were shires which Old English government had not reached. What appears in them is not its system, organized in a way which seems rational to the modern eye, but a different one, whose instinct was to organize *ad hoc*, and largely by reference to who owned what.

The same contrasts can be seen, on a wider scale, between the way in which the English kings ordered their acquisitions in the tenth century and that in which the Capetians ordered theirs from the twelfth. In the one there is a reduction to uniformity; in the other the superimposition of royal government on whatever already existed, with as a consequence the France of the *ancien régime*, in some ways formidably united, in others with anomalies numberless and, for example, far more provincial distinctions in law than anyone has found in eleventh-century England. That the essential difference between the two states lies in the time of their unification can be seen in considering that astonishing survival of *ancien régime* attitudes, the independent status allowed the Channel Islands and the Isle of Man, or the centuries for which Berwick-on-Tweed was left with a totally anomalous status, or the long delay in shiring most of Wales. Lands which were added to England after 1200 were treated in the spirit with which the Capetians treated their acquisitions.

The church presents a similar contrast between what happened before and after the twelfth century. Edward the Elder and Athelstan could create new dioceses on what appears a rational plan. If what they did was sometimes undone by amalgamations in the following century one can in either case see that innovation was possible and that administrative units were not regarded as immutable.[84] In the late Anglo Saxon and Norman periods new parishes were created, at least in the east, almost at will, and as necessity or greed required.[85] In the twelfth century new bishoprics ceased to be created; Ely (1108) and Carlisle (1133) were the last. It became very much harder to make new parishes.[86] In consequence

[83] J. Tait, in *Victoria County History of Lancashire*, ii (London, 1908), pp. 181–82, 187–88.
[84] Stenton, *Anglo-Saxon England*, 3rd edn, pp. 438–40; F. Barlow, *The English Church 1000–1066* (London, 1963), pp. 162–65.   [85] *Ibid.*, pp. 183–208.
[86] *E.g.*, J. H. Round, *Family Origins and Other Studies* (London, 1930), pp. 272–74.

the disproportions between English sees remained unquestioned through the middle ages; while the distribution of parishes in the nineteenth century remained what it had been in the twelfth (a phenomenon which had an effect on the geography of the Liberal vote).[87]

A serious effort to explain why medieval states were in important ways less powerful, less capable of *au fond* organization and re-organization, than those of a Carolingian type would extend this paper too far. It may be that much in the regularity of the earlier period was very old indeed. Orderliness in the disposition of men and land is not necessarily the fruit of progress. Something of the answer may perhaps be glimpsed in the reasons for the cessation of the creation of new parishes. This was the result of the development of canon law and of papal jurisdiction, which secured innumerable vested interests and so half froze the church. The number of vested interests, and of individuals, which kings had to respect may similarly have increased. It is worth noticing that the Anglo-Normans seem to have been the last rulers in England to have used forced and unpaid labour to build great earthworks and the last to employ harrying as an instrument of government.

For whatever reasons the attitudes and powers of government and its approach to institutions and to boundaries changed. The changes which can be traced in twelfth-century England are not simply to be explained as a transformation of the archaic, if some-times oddly regular, into the more developed or modern. For the late Anglo-Saxon system of government had not been specious in its uniformity or rudimentary in its precocity. It was uniform and sophisticated and reflected not only power, but intelligence. It was in important ways the continuation and the heir of the Carolingian state and our knowledge of it may provide our nearest approach to apprehending what the Carolingian state was like. If, ultimately, England avoided the fate of the rest of *ancien régime* Europe it was largely thanks to a framework established by a regime yet more ancient.[88]

Worcester College, Oxford.

[87] H. Pelling, *The Social Geography of British Elections 1885–1900* (London, 1967), pp. 108, 206, 289.

[88] I am indebted to Miss P. A. Adams for her help with this paper and to Dr D. M. Metcalf, who advised me on the Anglo-Saxon coinage but is not responsible for any errors.

PLACE AND PROFIT: AN EXAMINATION OF THE ORDNANCE OFFICE, 1660-1714 THE ALEXANDER PRIZE ESSAY

By H. C. Tomlinson, B.A.

READ 7 JUNE 1974

AS far as Professor Trevor-Roper was concerned public office in the seventeenth century was commensurate with wealth, and the gaining of office was one of the causes of such rises of the gentry that occurred before the civil war.[1] This view has been substantially modified by a number of historians who have delved more deeply into the mire of departmental records, and have concluded that the rewards of officialdom were usually modest, especially under Elizabeth I and Charles I, and that the more spectacular beneficiaries were small in number.[2] Very little work on the profits of office in the later Stuart period, however, has been atttempted. Excellent departmental studies on the post-Restoration Treasury, for instance, exist,[3] but although they detail the official salaries of treasury personnel they do not indicate all the remunerations that they might expect from their daily toil. One of the main reasons for this neglect is the lack of evidence on which to base any far-reaching conclusions on the unofficial spoils of office. Myriads of departmental records are extant but they do not throw much light on illicit profiteering. It would be a very careless official who admitted all his gains in his accounts or departmental correspondence. Such evidence as does exist in official documents is necessarily scanty and has to be pieced together with scraps of information from private sources. Even then

---

[1] H. R. Trevor-Roper, *The Gentry, 1540–1640* (Economic History Review, Supplement 1, 1953); *idem*, 'The General Crisis of the Seventeenth Century', *Past and Present*, xvi, (1959), pp. 31–64.

[2] See, *e.g.*, L. Stone, 'Office under Queen Elizabeth: The Case of Lord Hunsdon and the Lord Chamberlainship in 1585', *Historical Journal*, x (1967), pp. 279–85; *idem*, *The Crisis of the Aristocracy, 1558–1641* (Oxford, 1965); G. E. Aylmer, 'Office Holding as a factor in English History, 1625–42', *History*, xliv (1959), pp. 228–40; *idem*, *The King's Servants: The Civil Service of Charles I, 1625–42* (London, 1961); *idem*, *The State's Servants: The Civil Service of the English Republic, 1649–60* (London, 1973).

[3] S. B. Baxter, *The Development of the Treasury* (London, 1957); H. G. Roseveare, *The Treasury* (London, 1969); J. C. Sainty, *Treasury Officials, 1660–1870* (London, 1972); H. G. Roseveare, *The Treasury, 1660–1870: the Foundations of Control* (London, 1973).

some of the remaining evidence has to be treated with circum-
spection for, as Professor Hurstfield has pointed out, allegations of
corruption are not necessarily good evidence and have to be heavily
substantiated.[4] Ultimately, then, the extent of corruption in government is unmeasured and immeasurable if only because the clever
official did not get caught and left very little account of his proceedings. In this paper, however, an attempt will be made to
elucidate the unofficial as well as the recognized payments of
ordnance officials in a department, which at least one historian has
castigated as having enjoyed 'an unbroken reputation for pro-
crastination and corruption' throughout its existence.[5]

An ordnance officer in this period was well endowed with official
allowances. Patent fees, quarter salaries, additional allowances for
extraordinary services, and fringe benefits such as travelling and
diet allowances, allowances for dependents, tax exemption and a
free house were the official rewards, paid out of the exchequer or
ordnance treasury, which were available to ordnance personnel.
An officer could also hope to gain other equally profitable recom-
penses: the spoils from selling his office and the gains from subsidiary
fees. These were the unofficial rewards of office holding as the fees
were paid privately to an official by an interested party.

The ordnance patent fees, paid out of the receipt of the exchequer
to those officers who received their office by virtue of the king's
patent, varied little from the fees paid earlier in the seventeenth
century[6] and remained unchanged throughout the period. The
master of the ordnance received £175 18s. 4d. *p.a.* plus the wages
for four servants, the lieutenant £63 13s. 4d. *p.a.*, the storekeeper
£54 15s. od. *p.a.*, the surveyor, clerk of the ordnance and master
gunner £36 10s. od. *p.a.* and the clerk of deliveries £18 5s. od. *p.a.*
from these sources.[7] These payments were the ancient methods of
reward to government officials and were supplemented by other
fees exacted from private individuals.

One of the most lucrative fees was poundage, a levy of 6d. in the £
on payments made by the lieutenant when he acted as treasurer
from 1660–70. A private account shows that William Legge received £8,011 13s. 6d. poundage money between the Restoration
and December 1665.[8] In a letter written to Arlington in January
1667/8, however, Legge himself observed £558,118 2s. 2½d. had

---

[4] J. Hurstfield, *Freedom, Corruption and Government in Elizabethan England* (London,
1973), pp, 173 ff.

[5] J. Ehrman, *The Navy in the War of William III* (Cambridge, 1953), p. 176.

[6] Compare a list of 1663 (P.R.O., W.O. 49/112) with one of 1619 (B.L. Add
MS. 36,777, fols 14ᵛ–16ʳ).

[7] For a full list of exchequer payments *c.* 1670 see Staffs. County Record Office,
D.1778/v, 71.   [8] *Ibid.*

been received on all assignments between midsummer 1660 and the 31 December 1666, the poundage on this sum due being £13,219 10s. 6d. or £2,033 15s. 5½d. *p.a.*[9] A poundage fee of 3½d. in the £, which was worth £1,000 *p.a.*, was also levied by the clerk of the ordnance until 1664.[10] There were certain other commission fees which particular officers exacted. The clerk of the ordnance was allowed £2 for the entry of a principal officer on the quarter books, £1 for an under minister and 10s. for a gunner.[11] The allowances to the master's clerk were similarly graded. £2 was to be given as fee for a labourer's place, £1 for a gunner's commission and 10s. for any other warrant.[12] The master gunner was awarded similar fees— 10s. for the examination trial and certificate of a gunner, 5s. for taking his oath and 2s. 6d. for his entry onto the muster roll.[13] These allowances must have been a sizeable perquisite, considering that there were seven principal officers (including the master and the treasurer) who constituted the ordnance board, numerous miscellaneous under-ministers, twenty to sixty labourers, and sixty to a hundred gunners on the permanent ordnance establishment.[14] In addition extraordinary personnel were given commissions on the establishment of artillery trains,[15] and all commissions were renewed at the coming in of a new master general or at the beginning of a new reign. It is probable, however, that commission fees were not appropriated solely by the clerk of the ordnance, the master's chief clerk, or the master gunner, but were partly distributed by them to the personnel who worked under them. The storekeeper had no right to commission fees, but he could exact fees from traders for using the king's gunwharf[16] and he was allowed to take fees for showing stores to the public. At the Restoration the fee for seeing the Tower and the Armouries was 33s.[17] The value of what was probably the most lucrative fee of all, however, is unascertainable. This was the money exacted for the disposal of places. The master of the ordnance had the most extensive powers of patronage in the department and each principal officer was free to choose his own

[9] P.R.O., S.P. 29/189, no. 33, Legge to Arlington, 23 Jan. 1666/7.

[10] P.R.O., S.P. 29/215, no. 37, memorial, 27 Aug. 1667.

[11] B.L., King's MS. 70, f. 13, instructions, 25 July 1683.

[12] P.R.O., S.P. 29/112, f. 166ʳ, order, 13 Feb. 1664/5.

[13] B.L., King's MS. 70, f. 34ᵛ, instructions, 25 July 1683.

[14] For an indication of the size of the ordnance establishment see P.R.O., W.O. 54/20–72, ordnance quarter books, Sept. 1660–Dec. 1714.

[15] In Sept. 1716, for instance, when a new artillery train was established, £61 10s. was paid to the clerk of the ordnance and £42 5s. to the master's chief clerk; P.R.O., W.O. 47/29, p. 226.

[16] See below p. 59.

[17] C. J. Ffoulkes, *Inventory and Survey of the Armouries of the Tower of London* (London, 1916), i, p. 35.

clerks. In addition Storekeeper Richard Marsh in the 1660s had rights of appointment to posts of junior storekeeper at the Tower, the Minories, Woolwich and Chatham.[18]

Such a system of private fee payment was obviously highly unsatisfactory as it meant that the public welfare was being sacrificed for private interest. Poundage gave the lieutenant a vested interest in keeping office expenditure at a high level; commission fees possibly resulted in more officers being engaged than was desirable; the showing of ordnance stores affected security; and the patronage network did not necessarily ensure the appointment of the ablest officials. There is evidence, however, that in this period attempts were made to reform the old administrative system by abolishing some private fees and making regular payments in lieu of them.

The origin of such reforms may be traced back to the Cromwellian period when the establishment was reduced and increased salaries were paid to some of the principal ordnance officers.[19] At the Restoration the old ordnance board was reconstituted with its pre-civil war fees and salaries.[20] A radical reformation of the fee system, however, was undertaken by the ordnance commissioners who held office from October 1664 to June 1670.[21] The previous master, Sir William Compton, had enjoyed 'the liberty of disposing of all places under his command to his advantage', as well as his patent fee and a sizeable pension, but on the appointment of the master-commissioners a fixed salary of £500 each *p.a.* was awarded them in lieu of 'all advantages of perquisites whatsoever', at the commissioners' own request to the king.[22] At the appointment of the master commissioners the poundage fee of the clerk of the ordnance was also abolished.[23] Of far greater importance to the future constitution of the Office, however, was the order issued on the 13 February 1664/5 which abolished the lieutenant's poundage fee after the death of the then incumbent, William Legge, when the

[18] Marsh also claimed the rights of patronage at other places but this was quashed; P.R.O., W.O. 55/330, pp. 333–34.

[19] W. Reid, 'Commonwealth Supply Departments within the Tower and the Committee of London Merchants', *The Guildhall Miscellany*, ii (Sept. 1966), pp. 319–52.

[20] For the establishment of the office in 1660 see P.R.O., W.O. 54/20, quarter book for Sept. 1660.

[21] These were Lord John Berkeley, Sir John Duncombe and Sir Thomas Chicheley. For their patent of appointment see P.R.O., C/66, 3061. They were succeeded on 4 June 1670. Sir Thomas Chicheley was appointed sole master-general; C/66, 3117.

[22] P.R.O., S.P. 29/215, no. 37, report, 27 Aug. 1667.

[23] *Ibid.*

office of paymaster was to be executed separately by a treasurer who was to receive a salary of £400 *p.a.* in the place of all fees and gratuities. The succeeding lieutenant was to be compensated with a salary of £800 *p.a.*[24] There was a further limitation of the poundage fee on saltpetre payments before it was abolished on the death of William Legge in 1670, although it cost the crown £1,000 plus 10s. in every £100 on all saltpetre payments.[25]

After the disbanding of the 1664–70 commission the policy of abolishing private fees in exchange for monetary compensations was continued. The keeper of the rich weapons and the deputy-keeper of the armoury were allowed £70 *p.a.* each and the principal storekeeper and keeper of the small guns £50 *p.a.* each, after various prohibitions were made against the showing of stores,[26] although one observer commented that the keeper of the rich weapons continued to show the stores and to receive the fee.[27] The principal storekeeper was also compensated for various other lost fees or rights. On 30 December 1670 Richard Marsh was allowed £30 *p.a.* for rent lost when the old Woolwich gunwharf was sold, and a further £100 *p.a.* was paid to his son, as storekeeper, in consideration of the loss of his patronage rights at Woolwich and Chatham.[28]

These were the only private fees to have been abolished and no attempt was made to do away with commission fees. The extent of these fee reforms, however, should not be minimized. Fee payments were the traditional way of rewarding government officials, who had a vested interest in continuing such a system, for allowances paid in compensation were unlikely to match the profits of the private rewards. Fees, therefore, could only be abolished piece by piece after the death of an officer who had enjoyed the fruits of the system. The Treasury's shortage of money was also a principal stumbling block in the way of an abolition of all fees. The argument Legge used in defence of the poundage he claimed on saltpetre payments, that the king should not be charged because the petremen had always been willing to pay the money,[29] was a telling one if a Lord Treasurer was pressed for cash. It also illustrates the difficulties

---

[24] P.R.O., S.P. 29/112, ff. 166–68.

[25] P.R.O., S.P. 29/189, no. 34, Legge to Arlington, 22 Jan. 1666/7; W.O. 51/8, f. 30ᵛ, payment to Legge, 6 Apr. 1667; *Cal. S.P. Dom., 1666–67,* p. 556, warrant 11 Mar. 1667 (n.s.).

[26] P.R.O., W.O. 48/13, p. 161, payment to Batchler, grounded on warrant 2 Dec. 1670; W.O. 54/32, quarter payment note of compensatory payment from 24 Mar. 1673/4; W.O. 48/27, 22 Feb. 1688/9, payment to Franklyn. W.O. 47/18, p. 305, 15 Feb. 1695/6; Staffs. C.R.O., D. 1778/I i, 780.

[27] Staffs. C.R.O., D. 1778/v, 41; unsigned memo.

[28] P.R.O., W.O. 54/28, 29; W.O. 48/12, p. 106, payment to George Marsh, 26 July 1673.

[29] P.R.O., S.P. 29/189, no 34, Legge to Arlington, 23 Jan. 1666/7.

of a reform being instituted by the establishment of a salaried structure of government allowances, when the alternative was the continuation of private fees, which in the short term saved the crown an enormous amount of expense.

Nevertheless, salaries were established as a complementary process to the abolition of private fees. Over the whole period the salaries of the principal officers increased substantially. Compton received a yearly salary of £150,[30] but the next sole master, Sir Thomas Chicheley, was granted £1,500 p.a., which became the basic yearly salary for his successors.[31] The increase, as has been shown, occurred in the interim administration of the master commissioners from 1664-70. Their first salary of £500 p.a. each was increased to £1,000 p.a. in December 1666, but was reduced to £600 in March 1667/8, the same salary as the 1679-82 commissioners. The lieutenant's salary was £384 p.a. in 1660, which was raised to £800 p.a. after Legge's death in 1670. The surveyor was paid £194 p.a. in 1660, £250 p.a. in December 1674, and £400 p.a. from December quarter 1683, whilst the salaries of the clerk of the ordnance and the storekeeper were raised from £215 4s. p.a. to £400 p.a. and from £216 12s. p.a. to £400 p.a., respectively, in the same quarter. The clerk of deliveries received £155 16s. in 1660, £200 p.a. from the June quarter of 1682, and £300 p.a. from the December quarter of 1683. The salary of the treasurer was fixed and remained at £400 p.a. in 1670. Certain additional allowances were paid to the principal officers which did not appear on the quarter books. A grant of £300 p.a. was paid to successive lieutenants after the sale of land and property in the minories in 1673 over which the lieutenant had proprietory rights,[32] and the surveyors were also awarded £300 p.a. above their salaries for acting as deputy to the lieutenant.[33] Sherburne, as clerk of the ordnance, was given £100 p.a. for keeping a check ledger on the storekeeper, which payment

[30] By warrant of 29 Apr. 1662; P.R.O., 30 37/14. Compton was master from 1660 to his death in 1663.

[31] This and other salaries have been calculated from the ordnance quarter books; P.R.O., W.O. 54/20-72, Sept. 1660-Dec. 1714.

[32] Cal. S.P. Dom., 1673-75, pp. 54 (warrant to Chicheley, 11 Dec. 1673), 66-67 (petition of Knollys and report by lord keeper); Cal. S.P. Dom., 1687-88, no. 401, p. 81, 9 Oct. 1687; Cal. S.P. Dom. 1689-90, p. 97, 10 May 1689; P.R.O., MS. Cal. S.P. Dom., Anne, p. 901, 20 Nov. 1712, grants of £300 p.a. to Tichburne, Goodricke and Hill.

[33] Cal. S.P. Dom., 1687-88, no. 377, p. 76, allowance to Shere, 26 Sept. 1687; P.R.O., W.O., 48/29, 13 Aug. 1690, payment to Charlton; W.O. 46/6, pp. 105-6 (petition of Bridges and letter to Marlborough re the lack of payment of this award. Back payment was eventually made to him totalling £1,500); W.O. 48/48, list 30 June 1710, 1st payment, 4 Apr. 1710.

was continued to his successors,[34] and Mordaunt, as treasurer, enjoyed a present of £300 *p.a.*, part of which he probably shared with his deputy.[35] The principal officers also claimed the master's salary when that office was vacant, although their right to this money was not always uncontested.[36]

The quarter salaries paid to the under ministers did not rise as dramatically as those of the principal officers, although the master's chief clerk's salary was increased from £40 to £200. In March 1664/5 the salaries of the ordnance's first clerk were increased from £60 to £75 *p.a.*, that of the minuting clerk from £50 to £65, and those of the other first clerks from £40 to £60.[37] The quarter books do not show an increase for the chief clerks' salaries after that date but they were in fact augmented. In 1696 it was proposed by the board that the salaries of all the clerks in ordinary should be substantially increased, as in the navy offices, because of the vast increase of business since the Restoration.[38] Nothing was done about the proposal until 1704/5 when £40 *p.a.* was added to the salaries of the first seven clerks, augmenting the salary of the first clerk to the Clerk of the ordnance to £115 *p.a.*, that of the minuting clerk to £105 and those of the other five first clerks to £100 each *p.a.*[39] For the other clerks in ordinary, however, there was no such recompense and no attempt was made to implement the 1696 petition *in toto*. Over the whole period the salaries of the under clerks, which varied from £60 to £40 *p.a.*, were not improved, apart from the increase for the second clerks in 1664/5.

The storekeepers' quarter salaries varied between the £20 *p.a.* paid to the man at Chepstow, to £120 *p.a.* for the storekeeper at Portsmouth and Chatham. The salaries which showed the most marked increase in this period were awarded to those officials at the larger ports and garrisons. The storekeeper's salary at Chatham was

[34] *Cal. S.P. Dom., 1665–66*, p. 261, warrant 21 Feb. 1666 (n.s.); P.R.O., S.P. 32/5, no. 75, warrant Apr. 1694; *Cal. S.P. Dom., 1696*, p. 162, warrant, 2 May 1696.

[35] Churchill Coll. Cambridge, Erle MS., 2/13; Craggs to Erle, 7 July 1705. Trumbull was prepared to allow his deputy one-third of his salary; B.L., Add. MS. 52,279 (his diary, 30 Oct. 1685).

[36] In 1698 the officers were paid £4,125 for acting as master general for 2¾ years, 1690–93 (P.R.O., W.O. 48/37, p. 284, 26 Nov. 1698), despite the ruling at the Treasury some months previously that such interim salaries should be saved; *Cal. Treas. Books, 1697–98*, p. 95, 25 May 1698. The auditors of the imprests queried the payment but it was finally allowed; *Cal. Treas. Books, 1702*, p. 97, 8 Dec. 1702; *Cal. Treas. Books, 1703*, pp. 75–6 (18 Aug. 1703), 401 (10 Sept. 1703); P.R.O., T 1/162, no. 31(a), warrant 10 Sept. 1703.

[37] P.R.O., S.P. 29/112, ff. 166–68, order 13 Feb. 1664/5.

[38] P.R.O., W.O. 46/4, p. 8, board to Romney, 28 Apr. 1696.

[39] P.R.O., W.O. 55/488, p. 57, 22 Mar. 1704/5.

increased from £40 to £120 *p.a.*, and storekeepers at Portsmouth and Tilbury gained increases of £60 to £120 and £20 to £100. Numerous miscellaneous officials—armourers, clerks of the check, gentlemen of the ordnance, messengers, overseers, proofmasters, purveyors, surgeons, waggon masters and yeomen of tents and toils —also received quarter salaries, which ranged from £100 *p.a.* to the waggon master to £20 *p.a.* to the yeomen.

Labourers, fireworkers, engineers and gunners remain to be considered. Labourers were paid £21 1s. 8d. *p.a.* in 1660, which payment was increased by £5 *p.a.* in August 1673 for twenty of the old established labourers. The fireworkers' salaries were finally fixed at £250 *p.a.* for the comptroller, £150 *p.a.* for the chief firemaster and £80 *p.a.* to his mates, and £40 *p.a.* for the ordinary fireworkers, although there were considerable variations in these payments in the early years after the Restoration. There were also considerable fluctuations in the quarter payments made to engineers, before they settled at £300 *p.a.* for the chief engineer, £250 *p.a.* for the second, £150 *p.a.* for the third, and £100 *p.a.* for the ordinary engineers. The salary of the master gunner increased from £171 to £190 *p.a.*, his mates' salaries were established at £45 10s. *p.a.*, and the exchequer fees of 6d., 8d. or 12d. per day to the ordinary gunners, which had been transferred to the ordinary of the office in 1660/1,[40] were regularized at 12d. per day for all gunners in the early 1680s.[41]

It is difficult to determine whether the increase of salaries for ordnance officials compensated for their loss of fees: in the case of the lieutenant, the new allowance did not match the annual poundage that Legge claimed to have levied. Nevertheless, in a period of general price stability,[42] ordnance salaries were sufficiently high to enable the office-holders to enjoy a comfortable standard of living. Nor were such salaries exceptional among government servants. By the end of the period printed lists show that in many departments high salaries had been instituted for officials. To take just random examples from among the top tier of officials, by 1708 the commissioners of customs were receiving £1,000 *p.a.* each, the commissioners

---

[40] P.R.O., W.O. 55/386, p. 151, preamble to warrant, 13 May 1661.

[41] Ordnance officers were exempt from taxes on these salaries, although an Act passed after the Revolution only exempted those military officers in muster by the muster-master general of the army. For a discussion of this question see P.R.O., T. 1/27, no. 30 (petition); T. 1/29, ff. 147, 163; W.O. 46/3, pp. 11, 12, 13, 31–2, 70. In subsequent years exemptions were allowed; W.O. 46/5, p. 128; W.O. 47/23, p. 332; W.O. 47/25, pp. 100, 485–86; W.O. 47/28, pp. 17, 94.

[42] Prices were, of course, subject to seasonal variations, but in the late seventeenth century both agricultural and industrial prices appear to have fluctuated around a fairly level trend. See R. B. Outhwaite, *Inflation in Tudor and Early Stuart England* (London, 1969), pp. 10–11, table and fig. 1.

for the salt duty £500 *p.a.* each and those for wine licences £200 *p.a.* each, the treasurer of the navy £2,000 *p.a.* and the members of the navy board £500 *p.a.* each and the commissioners for victualling and transports £400 *p.a.* each. Clerks in such offices could expect at least £40 *p.a.* and lowly figures such as watchmen and labourers £20 *p.a.*[43] These salaries compare favourably with those of other members of the community. By the eighteenth century it has been estimated that the average annual income for the largest landowners were no more than £5,000 for a peer, £1,200 for a baronet and £400 for a member of the gentry.[44] At the other end of the scale, Gregory King guessed that in the 1690s the yearly income for the family of a labourer or outservant would be about £15, whilst a cottager's family might have to subsist on £6 *p.a.* King also estimated that the average family income of a merchant would be no more than £400, a lawyer £140 and a clergyman £60 *p.a.*[45] It would thus appear from their salaries alone that government officials were generally well paid, and the highest officials were among the wealthiest men in the country.

But government officials did not have to live solely on their salaries. For the ordnance officers there was the hope of additional allowances for extraordinary services. A special rate of pay was established for those officers involved in stock-taking. It was normally the practice to grant £50 each to the principal officers, £20 each for the clerks and the messenger, and £10 each to the extraordinary clerks.[46] Extra payments were also made to ordnance officers for numerous other services. Rewards were made to the surveyor, Jonas Moore senior, of £200 and £150 for attending the building of Sheerness Fort in 1668, and for 'taking a due and perfect description of the coast from Folkestone . . . to Southwell Bay'.[47] Engineer Beckman received allowances of £37 12s. for 'his invention of a defence against small shot' in 1673, and £100 in consideration of his

[43] For these lists see John Chamberlayne, *Magnae Britanniae or the Present State of Great Britain* (22nd edn, London, 1708), part ii, book iii.

[44] G. E. Mingay, *English Landed Society in the Eighteenth Century* (London, 1963), pp. 20–23.

[45] Although King's figures seem too low. See Gregory King, *Two Tracts . . .*, ed. George E. Barnett (Baltimore, 1936), p. 31.

[46] Staffs. C.R.O., D. 1778/v, 27, report 28 Oct. 1684; D. 1778/v, 71, report 30 Apr. 1688; P.R.O., W.O. 48/40, list 30 June 1702; W.O. 48/50, list 31 Mar. 1712 (3rd and 4th payments); W.O. 49/226, copies of bills for the 1710, 1713 remains. No allowances appear to have been paid for those involved in the 1679 and 1686 remains, although a retrospective payment of £25 to the principal officers and £10 to the clerks was later made for the 1679 remain. In 1683 only the clerks were paid.

[47] P.R.O., 30 37/17, warrant 20 October 1668; W.O. 51/11, f. 48ʳ, 12 Feb. 1669/70.

good service at Tangier in 1680.[48] Gratuities would be paid to principal officers and their clerks for their care in supplying stores for expeditions.[49] Clerks were especially likely to receive supplementary benefits. Francis Povey was allowed £40 for transcribing accounts from March 1675 to March 1676,[50] Abell Barton was paid £30 compensation for recovering stores when commissary to the 1685 artillery train,[51] and Thomas Townesend was awarded £100 for services performed, by which he 'was constrained to write many extraordinary hours in the night times'.[52] The other ordnance officers were not excluded from such payments. Storekeepers at the out ports might be given £30 and labourers £3 or more for extraordinary services,[53] and gunners gained allowances for attending at Whitehall or for firing guns on triumph days.[54]

Small *ad hoc* allowances were also made to the widows and dependents of those who had died or had been disabled in the king's service. The amounts awarded varied from a few pounds to more substantial payments.[55] Sometimes such bounty payments were renewed annually, becoming in effect pensions, the size of pension awarded usually depending on the importance of the deceased officer. Elizabeth Hill received £8 *p.a.* as recompense for the services of her late husband who was a purveyor; the widow of John Browne, firemaster, who lost his life by breaking a shell, was given £20 *p.a.*; whilst £100 *p.a.* was awarded to the widow of Colonel George Browne, who died commanding an artillery train.[56] It was less usual for a pension to be given to an officer who had been removed from office, although it was reported that Sir John

[48] P.R.O., W.O. 51/15, f. 90ᵛ; W.O. 48/19, p. 297.
[49] P.R.O., W.O. 48/6, pp. 93, 228 (£20 to clerk of ordnance, £15 to other principal officers, and £20 and £10 to clerks); W.O. 55/332, p. 96, warrant 9 Jan. 1666/7; W.O. 48/52, list 31 Dec. 1713, 2nd payment, £20 each to clerks in ordinary and £10 each to extraordinary clerks for war services.
[50] P.R.O., W.O. 48/14, p. 48.   [51] P.R.O., W.O. 48/25, p. 197.
[52] P.R.O., W.O. 55/336, ff. 1–2.
[53] *E.g.*, P.R.O., W.O. 46/1, f. 261ʳ, £30 to storekeeper Watkinson at Hull, 11 Jan. 1682/3; W.O. 51/4, f. 62ʳ, warrant 30 Sept. 1664, for £60 to 20 labourers.
[54] P.R.O. 30 37/14 (warrant 3 June 1662, 21s. per week between four gunners for service at Whitehall); W.O. 48/14, p. 34 (payment to Loop 2s. 6d. per day for same); W.O. 44/714 (petition of feed gunners re 20s. formerly paid on every firing day).
[55] *E.g.*, *Cal. S.P. Dom. 1670*, p. 140 (warrant 30 Mar. 1670); P.R.O., W.O. 48/9, p. 535, payment of £600 to widow of George Clarke for his service 'during the late rebellion and usurpation'. This was an exceptionally high sum. See P.R.O., W.O. 47/19a, pp. 383, 426 (two payments of £10 to widow of firemaster); P.R.O., W.O. 47/5, p. 220 (£50 to widow of man killed in moving a great gun).
[56] *Cal. S.P. Dom.*, *1685*, no. 1603, p. 325, Sunderland to Dartmouth, 8 Sept. 1685; *Cal. S.P. Dom.*, *1680–81*, p. 101, warrant 10 Dec. 1680; *Cal. S.P. Dom.*, *1703–04*, p. 470, 5 July 1703.

Chicheley received a £1,000 pension after the break up of the second commission in the 1680s, and Sir William Trumbull was allowed £200 *p.a.* for a short time after his dismissal as clerk of the deliveries.[57]

All officers received diet and travelling allowances, the amount awarded to each officer depending on the rank that officer held, the master receiving £4, the lieutenant £3, the surveyor £2 and the clerk of the ordnance and storekeeper £1 10s. per day.[58] Payments to the clerks and other civil officers for travelling charges were either at a rate of 6s. 8d. or 10s. a day.[59] The engineers fared somewhat better, the chief engineer receiving £1, the second engineer 13s. 4d. and the other engineers anything from 5s. to 20s. a day.[60] Such payments for travelling expenses could add up to hundreds of pounds. Sir Thomas Chicheley and Dartmouth frequently received over £100,[61] and bills were made out for the Duke of Marlborough to receive two payments of £1,120 and £896 for his travelling charges in 1705 and 1706.[62] Disbursements to officers other than the master generals were not as large and were more likely to add up to tens rather than hundreds of pounds, although occasionally extraordinarily large sums were awarded.[63] It is impossible to determine the extent of profit made on such travelling allowances, but there are instances of claims being disallowed[64] which suggests that some officers were abusing the system and making excessive gains.

[57] *Hist. MSS Comm., Ormonde*, n.s. vi, p. 244, Longford to Ormond, 3 Dec. 1681; *Cal. S.P. Dom., 1686–87*, no. 1751, p. 422, warrant, 9 May. For the circumstances surrounding Trumbull's dismissal, see his diary, B.L., Add. MS. 52,279.

[58] P.R.O., W.O. 51/26, f. 58ʳ, payment to Legge, 7 Oct. 1682; W.O. 48/42, list, 30 June 1704, payments to Granville and Bridges; W.O. 48/26, 29 May 1688, payment to Shere; W.O. 48/10, pp. 135 (payment to Sherburne), 174 (payment to Marsh). I have no record of travelling payments to the clerk of deliveries or the treasurer.

[59] P.R.O. 30 37/14, warrant 9 Jan. 1662/3 for 6s. 8d. to Fleetwood; W.O. 51/7, f. 132ʳ, 3 Nov. 1666 (payment to Cheltenham at 10s. per day for the first four days and then 6s. 8d.); W.O. 48/17, p. 50, 14 June 1679 (payment to Hubbald at 10s. per day); W.O. 48/18, p. 406, 29 June 1680 (payment to waggon master at 10s. per day).

[60] *Cal. S.P. Dom., 1685*, no. 2101, p. 420, warrant 23 Dec.; *Cal. S.P. Dom., 1696*, p. 33, Feb. 1696 (n.s.), warrant; P.R.O., W.O. 48/33, p. 449, 12 Dec. 1694, payment to Romer; W.O. 48/48, list 31 Dec. 1709, 12th payment to Moore.

[61] P.R.O., W.O. 48/10, p. 132; W.O. 48/12, pp. 163–64 (payments to Chicheley of £112 and £120); W.O. 48/24, 26 Jan. 1685/6; W.O. 48/26, 28 Jan. 1687/8 (payments to Dartmouth of £252 and £140).

[62] P.R.O., W.O. 47/23, p. 93; W.O. 47/24, p. 183.

[63] P.R.O., W.O. 47/25, pp. 74, 168, 329 (£543 and £696 to Erle (lieutenant), £350 to engineer Lilly).

[64] P.R.O., W.O. 47/29, p. 86, 17 Apr. 1716; W.O. 47/31, p. 74, 21 Mar. 1717/18.

Free accommodation or rent in lieu of a house was a further perquisite available for a number of officers. The houses given to the principal officers were quite substantial. A plan of the Tower made in the 1680s shows that the dwellings of the surveyor, the clerk of the ordnance and the storekeeper occupied large sites to the north-east of the White Tower.[65] Personnel at the major outports also enjoyed the convenience of comfortable houses at the expense of the Ordnance Office.[66] Not every officer, however, was provided with a home, as is evidenced by petitions for accommodation from ordnance clerks when official residences within the Tower became vacant.[67] This shortage of Tower houses was aggravated by the practice of sub-letting official lodgings.[68] If an officer was not provided with a house he was sometimes compensated by the payment of rent which could be as high as £40 p.a.[69]

A structured system of salaries with additional allowances and grants in kind, then, became firmly established within the Ordnance Office in this period. It was realized that such a system was the only solution to corrupt practices. James II once noted that a good salary could make officials 'value their employments and not subject them to a necessity of base compliances with others to the king's prejudice',[70] and his words were echoed by ordnance personnel throughout the period. In 1661, for instance, the principal officers petitioned that they might have a 'competency of subsistence and be debarred from embezzling any of the provisions under their charge',[71] and in August 1667 the master general commissioners defended the increases they had made to the salaries of various ordnance officials by arguing that this was the only possible remedy to prevent corruption.[72] How successful were such rewards in preventing ill-gotten gains?

[65] Tower, Armouries library, plan c. 1685.

[66] See B.L., King's MS. 45, f. 45, house on Plymouth gunwharf, 1715; King's Top. Coll., xi, t, u, w, elevations and plans of houses for labourers, storekeeper and clerk on Portsmouth gunwharf, 1717.

[67] See P.R.O., W.O. 44/714, petitions of Hooper (endorsed 23 Feb. 1685/6) and Katherine Reade, endorsed 24 Oct. 1689.

[68] P.R.O., P.C. 6/18, p. 198, 10 May 1683, order that such practices should cease; W.O. 47/32, p. 157, 16 Apr. 1719, no house should be let without leave.

[69] The clerk of deliveries was allowed £20 in lieu of a house, which rent was later doubled; P.R.O., W.O. 48/11, p. 123, payment to Fortrey; W.O. 48/47, list 28 June 1709, 4th payment to Craggs. Moore senior, as assistant surveyor, received £20 p.a., Povey, the storekeeper at Portsmouth, £10 p.a., and the eleven labourers at Portsmouth and Chatham £4 p.a. each; W.O. 51/8, f. 116; W.O. 48/9, p. 398; W.O. 48/46, list 14 Aug. 1707, 14th payment.

[70] Quoted in J. R. Western, Monarchy and Revolution: the English State in the 1680s (London, 1972), p. 88.

[71] P.R.O., P.C. 2/55, 4 Mar. 1660/1; W.O. 55/330, pp. 304-6, 7 June 1661.

[72] '[It is] impossible . . . by any rigour whatsoever to keep officers either in

The buying and selling of most public offices was made illegal by a law of 1551/2, which remained unchanged for more than two and a half centuries.[73] In the seventeenth century, however, office was looked upon as part of a man's freehold to be bartered on the open market, and there is evidence that trade in offices continued within the ordnance among all ranks of officials, especially in the 1660s and 1670s, despite several proclamations against the practice.[74] Sir George Savile observed that Sir Thomas Chicheley had bought a place in the ordnance and it was later confirmed that he had agreed to sell the mastership of the ordnance in Ireland to the Earl of Longford.[75] Legge's clerk informed him that the then surveyor, 'perceiving . . . something of a design against him', had asked one of the commissioners to persuade Jonas Moore to give him money for his place, provided the other officers did not 'envy such his happiness'.[76] Edward Conyers was charged with giving 'a very considerable sum of money' for his storekeeper's place, and then setting up a trade in offices by selling his clerks' places.[77] Daniel Benson, bricklayer to the office, assumed the authority of selling the plasterer's place.[78] The general of the Scottish artillery petitioned the king in January 1666/7 to name the sum he was to be allowed in lieu of the office of master gunner.[79] A gunner's warrant confirmed that the places of gunners and matrosses were bought and sold to the highest bidder.[80] There is little evidence, however, on the actual amounts received and paid for office and these are the only instances that have been uncovered of the sums involved: Lord Conway was willing to pay £1,000 to the wife of the dying Sir Robert Byron for the mastership of the ordnance in Ireland; William Legge was offered £10,000 for his lieutenantship; it was reported that a principal officer had received £100 or more from selling a clerk's place; a labourer affirmed he had paid over £60 and another labourer £70 for their positions; and a garrison gunner claimed he

---

peace or war from irregular gain in their places . . . unless their lives be rendered easy and comfortable to them by constant pay of good salaries'; P.R.O., S.P. 29/215, f. 69ʳ, 27 Aug. 1667.

[73] K. W. Swart, *Sale of Offices in the Seventeenth Century* (London, 1949), pp. 45 ff.

[74] B.L., King's MS. 70, ff. 6ᵛ–7ʳ, 1683 instructions to master-general; P.R.O., W.O. 46/2, p. 22, order 6 May 1684 re Watkinson's place at Hull; W.O. 47/31, p. 252, 4 Sept. 1718; W.O. 47/32, p. 318, 4 Aug. 1719.

[75] H. C. Foxcroft, *The Life and Letters of Sir George Savile* (London, 1898), i, p. 29; *Cal. S.P. Dom.*, *1679–80*, pp. 268 (Gwyn to Conway, 25 Nov. 1679), 372 (Rawdon to Conway, 14 Jan. 1680 (n.s.)).

[76] Staffs. C.R.O., D. 1778/I i., 155, Wharton to Legge, 21 July 1665.

[77] Staffs. C.R.O., D. 1778/I i., 780.

[78] P.R.O., W.O. 55/388, f. 51ʳ, 22 Mar. 1663/4.

[79] *Cal. S.P. Dom.*, *1666–67*, p. 459, 18 Jan. 1667 (n.s.).

[80] P.R.O., S.P. 29/443, no. 3.

had given £63 for his office.[81] If these claims were accurate and representative of the values of other ordnance positions a poorer ordnance place was worth about three times, and a more lucrative office more than three times, its own annual value.

There were many unofficial rewards which could be gained by an ordnance officer. Unwarranted fees were sometimes claimed. Matthew Bayly, the Master's secretary, 1660–63, caused one gunner to pay £21 and the others £5 for their warrants,[82] and in the 1690s gunners commissioned for a train of artillery claimed that they were ordered to pay £3 4s. each for their warrants and copies of their oaths,[83] which was far in excess of the official rate. It seems that under the Duke of Schomberg, master 1689–90, several clerks were enriching themselves by collecting fees from fraudulent warrants, for he warned the board that Cardonnel, his chief clerk, had 'much magnified his services' in several postscripts to Schomberg's own letters and had issued unauthorized warrants for storekeeper's places.[84] A little prior to this a number of clerks had been caught forging Schomberg's signature.[85] Other clerks profited by taking presents to ensure that payments were made and by collecting poundage money. These payments were quite unofficial and records of them do not appear in ordnance registers, but a series of private letters from minor officials to Edward Hubbald, a senior clerk in the ordnance treasury, does exist among the mass of official ordnance *impedimenta*, which show that profits of this kind were made.[86] Hubbald was allowed 6d. in the £ for all payments he made on behalf of John Duxbury, storekeeper at Hull, and Duxbury also gave him several gifts for his services.[87] Even the under clerks received the benefits of such largesse.[88] A number of letters in the series show that payments were made to clerks to forward the pay-

[81] P.R.O., S.P. 63/333, no. 127, Essex to Arlington, 19 Apr. 1673; S.P. 29/189, no. 34, Legge to Arlington, 23 Jan. 1666/7; Staffs. C.R.O., D. 1778/v, 24, report of Duxbury; W.O. 47/19a, p. 130, 3 Nov. 1668; W.O. 44/714, petition of Lowe; W.O. 55/1782, Trollapp to board, 9 Dec. 1684.

[82] P.R.O., W.O. 55/388, f. 32ʳ, petition of thirty-seven gunners, 3 Feb. 1663/4.

[83] P.R.O., T. 1/23, no. 3, ff. 13–18, Guy to board, 1 June, board's report, 1 July 1693.

[84] P.R.O., W.O. 55/337, ff. 102ᵛ–03ʳ, Schomberg to board, 7 Feb. 1689/90. See W.O. 44/715, petition of John Grahme re a commission to De Cardonnel, 'who inserted his own name' for the place of gentleman of the ordnance.

[85] P.R.O., W.O. 55/336, f. 173ᵛ, Holford to Goodricke, 11 Aug. 1689.

[86] P.R.O., W.O. 55/1796.

[87] *E.g.* a twelve gallon cask of ale and a promise of 'a keg of ale and a furkin of good butter'; *ibid.*, Duxbury to Hubbald, 7 Aug., 7 Sept. 1687.

[88] In March 1685/6, for instance, Duxbury authorized Hubbald to pay a 5s. piece and 2s. 6d. to two clerks, Whiteing and Scattergood; *ibid.*, same to same, 3 Mar. 1685/6.

ment of salaries and bills or for other services. Richard Wharton, an ordnance engineer, asked Hubbald to accept 10s. 'to buy a pair of gloves' as his quarter salary had come so 'opportunely',[89] and in December 1687 Henry Hooke, storekeeper at Plymouth, promised 'two guineas besides a thousand thanks' if Hubbald would draw up a petition for him for back payments for Tangier freight charges.[90] There is other evidence of ordnance officials receiving presents from merchants and artificers. Hubbald himself claimed that Sir Jonas Moore junior, surveyor 1679–82, had demanded and received two cases of pistols from some gunmakers 'for the great kindnesses he had done them',[91] and Lord Dartmouth, master 1681/2–89, ordered that clerks were to be suspended and then dismissed, if they continued 'to take frequent treats and entertainments' at taverns from ordnance tradesmen.[92] Any artificers who attempted to 'seduce' clerks were also to be discharged.[93]

Tradesmen may well have made such payments to ordnance officials in order to gain contracts, as William Warren, the timber merchant, did to Pepys when he was at the Navy Board.[94] Pepys, however, was not the only official to profiteer through the manipulation of contracts. William Legge, lieutenant 1660–70, was accused by Pepys himself for charging excessive prices for Tangier stores in order that he and other ordnance officials might have a share in the profits. Pepys made comparisons between the previous month's prices paid for such stores, which had been contracted for Tangier by the ordnance office, and the then naval price, and concluded:

> From whence we see how the king is served: bad at best and very bad in other places compared with the present prices we buy in the navy.[95]

Pepys's list of prices and Legge's suspicious actions at the Tangier committee—his heated words with the navy officers and his concealment of the estimate after he left the meeting—perhaps suggest that the ordnance officers were guilty of corruption in this particular case, although too much reliance must not be placed on Pepys's words for he had a vested interest in contesting the contract. The

---

[89] *Ibid.*, Wharton to Hubbald, 30 Sept. 1687.

[90] *Ibid.*, Hooke to Hubbald, 2 Dec. 1687.

[91] Staffs. C.R.O., D. 1778/I i, 780, testimony of Hubbald, 14 Dec. 1680.

[92] P.R.O., W.O. 55/334, f. 16ᵛ, 8 Oct. 1685.

[93] *Ibid.*

[94] See R. G. Albion, *Forests and Sea Power: the timber problems of the Royal Navy, 1682–1862* (Cambridge, Mass., 1926), pp. 50–51.

[95] Taken from a transcript of Pepys's Navy White Book by Professor Matthews in the possession of the librarian of the Pepys Library at Magdalene College, Cambridge, pp. 61 ff., 24 Sept. 1664.

most significant comment on the whole affair occurs in Pepys's diary entry for the same day:

> To the Tangier committee and there I opposed Colonel Legge's estimate of supplies of provisions to be sent to Tangier till all were ashamed of it. . . . Mr. Coventry seconded me and between us we shall save the king some money . . . and yet purpose getting money to myself by it.[96]

It is highly likely that both the ordnance officers and Pepys were guilty of overcharging on the Tangier contracts and pocketing the remains.

Ordnance officials made profits by trading in and by embezzling ordnance stores. Members of artillery trains could profit from broken ordnance. William Hubbald, paymaster of an artillery train, reckoned that he could make about a 30 *per cent* gain by buying up the 'clearings' of a disbanded train and reselling them,[97] which practice was strictly forbidden.[98] Alexander Eustace, a clerk in the office, similarly profited from private trading.[99] Others were caught abusing their privileges as ordnance officers. Samuel Palmer, a labourer at Portsmouth, received money for allowing stores other than ordnance stores to be deposited in the official storehouses and James Rolfe, another labourer there, acted as agent to private transporters of stores.[100] Both men were also accused of embezzling stores.[101] There are further instances of petty pilfering by ordnance personnel,[102] but the evidence suggests that acts of embezzlement were more likely to be committed by the establishment of garrisons and private persons than by ordnance officers.[103]

Evidence also exists that petty thievery of money occurred as well

---

[96] Pepys Diary, ed. H. B. Wheatley (London, 1904–05), iv, p. 234, 24 Sept. 1664.

[97] Staffs. C.R.O., D. 1778/v, 71.

[98] B.L., King's MS. 70, f. 42ʳ, 1683 instructions.

[99] He was suspended from office for a time for allowing private goods worth £115 to be put on board an ordnance ship, and he claimed in his defence that there were many instances of officials not being penalized for similar offences. Blenheim Palace MS., B I 23; P.R.O., W.O. 46/4, p. 54, Pendlebury to board, 4 Aug. 1699.

[100] P.R.O., W.O. 55/1802.   [101] *Ibid.*

[102] *The Bulstrode Papers, i, 1667–75* (1897), p. 64, 26 Sept. 1668 (Thomas Robson, a Chatham storekeeper, selling ordnance in Flanders for 2,000 livres); P.R.O., W.O. 47/31, p. 127, 2 May 1718 (storekeeper at Edinburgh Castle changing good arms for bad).

[103] See, *e.g.*, P.R.O., W.O. 46/1, ff. 212ʳ, 250, 253ʳ, 255ʳ, 268–69 (embezzlement of stores at Hull); *Cal. Treas. Books, 1681–85*, p. 375 (same); W.O. 46/4, pp. 66 ff (embezzlements at Dover Castle); W.O. 49/112, report on gunners taking powder from cartridges; W.O. 55/1802, embezzlement book 1701–17; W.O. 47/7, pp. 113, 114, 122; W.O. 47/19a, pp. 8, 10, 27, 39, 157, 177, 245, 323, miscellaneous embezzlements.

as peculation of stores, among minor office holders.[104] Those more important officials directly responsible for ordnance finances, however, had far greater opportunities to misappropriate government money. Ordnance treasurers were notoriously slow in handing over the balance of their accounts to the succeeding treasurer, and their accounts were not declared for many years, so that use could have been made by succeeding treasurers of money remaining surplus on the account until it was balanced. This occurred in the late sixteenth century before interest was charged on such 'loans' in 1608.[105] This is no hard evidence for this period that such misuse of arrearages occurred, but the accounting system of the day undoubtedly facilitated misuse of government money. This danger was indeed pointed out by the board to Romney, master 1693–1702, when they demanded that Mordaunt should give a sufficient security for the office of treasurer in 1699.[106]

One ordnance treasurer, Sir George Wharton, was in fact accused by Edward Conyers, the storekeeper, of corrupt practices. Evidence was brought forward which suggested that several debentures had been bought from contractors at a discount, and that Wharton had received gifts after he had lent money to ordnance creditors, and had accepted up to twenty guineas to ensure that creditors were repaid.[107] Wharton himself, however, vigorously denied the charges and accused Conyers of altering sworn statements.[108] Further evidence also suggests that Conyers attempted to discredit Wharton by suborning witnesses.[109] Some of Conyers charges, however, probably had a foundation of truth. Wharton himself did not deny that he had voluntarily lent his own money and had received gratuities on the money lent.[110] He also admitted that his chief clerk Edward Hubbald, had disposed of a number of debentures, though with the consent of the owners.[111] Conyers, himself, however, could not claim to be innocent of all malpractices.

---

[104] *E.g.* P.R.O., W.O. 47/29, pp. 95 (27 Apr. 1716), 232 (18 Sept. 1716), 271 (15 Nov. 1716, desertions with ordnance cash); W.O. 47/29, p. 169, 12 July 1716; W.O. 47/30, p. 39, 20 Feb. 1716, misappropriation of wages.

[105] R. Ashley, 'The Organisation and Administration of the Tudor Office of Ordnance' (Oxford Univ., B.Litt. thesis, 1973), p. 125.

[106] . . . 'a treasurer's own bond would not answer the many accidents which may happen, as in case a treasurer dies his under officers may convert the cash to his own use . . . and the circumstances of a treasurer at his death may be such . . . that his heir may not think it in his interest to make up either his accounts or his cash'. P.R.O., W.O. 46/4, pp. 49/50, board to Romney, 6 July 1699.

[107] P.R.O., W.O. 49/111, testimonies of Freeman, Marshall, Walker, Herringe, Tough.

[108] Staffs. C.R.O., D. 1778/I i, 780, 'The Answer of Sir George Wharton. . . .

[109] *Ibid.*, 'Sundry Informations . . . touching . . . Conyers.'

[110] 'The Answer of Sir George Wharton . . .'. *Ibid.*   [111] *Ibid.*

As a clerk to the storekeeper, he was dismissed by the ordnance commissioners for receiving money from artificers for bills which he had purposefully delayed, for claiming money for false bills, and for appropriating several stores without their having been first viewed by the board.[112] Conyers was later reinstated and eventually succeeded as storekeeper, but he continued to undertake sharp practices.[113]

Is it possible from this fragmentary evidence to estimate the overall extent of venality within the Ordnance Office? Buying and selling of offices undoubtedly occurred, unofficial fees were claimed, stores were purloined and money misappropriated. The weight of this evidence, however, is insufficient for a valid indictment of extensive corruption to be made against the Ordnance Office. Only a small percentage of officials seem to have been involved in gross corruption, and the majority of these officials held office in the years immediately after the Restoration. It is indeed significant that the commissioners of accounts in the early eighteenth century did not make any charge against the Ordnance Office, although substantial charges of venality were made against the victuallers and sick and wounded commissioners.[114]

Many ordnance officials in this period then profited from the best of both worlds: the tradition of private fee payments, handed down from medieval bureaucracy, and a newer salaried system, struggling for recognition against the old. The richest officials were those who commanded a large salary and could still exact substantial private rewards: the master who had extensive powers of patronage; the master's secretary, the clerk of the ordnance, and the master gunner, who could still officially exact commission fees; the storekeeper, who could show his stores and had small reservoirs of patronage

---

[112] P.R.O., W.O. 47/8, 15 Feb. 1665/6; W.O. 47/19a, p. 251, 1 Apr. 1669; 'Sundry Informations . . . touching . . . Conyers.' *loc. cit.*

[113] *Ibid.*, D. 1778/v, 24, report of Duxbury, May 1679. He apparently accepted payments of over £70 from ordnance creditors. He also acted as middleman in a bargain between a powdermaker and a French merchant for the sale of 1,000 barrels of the king's gunpowder, and he resold decayed gunpowder to powdermakers, for which transaction he received £370 18s. 6d.

[114] *William Cobbett's Parliamentary History* (London, 1806–20), vi, pp. 1001–03 (15 Feb. 1710/11), 1026–31 (4 June 1711); *Richard Chandler's History . . . of The House of Commons* (London, 1742–4), iv, pp. 363–66; v, pp. 7–8. Two ordnance officials, William Churchill, a deputy treasurer, and his brother-in-law, John Pearce, a treasury clerk 1701–13, were involved in abuses in the contracts for transporting prisoners. *Ibid.* James Craggs, ordnance clerk of deliveries 1703–11, 1714–15, was also indicted by the commissioners of accounts for paying huge bribes in order to gain army clothing contracts. *Ibid.*, pp. 79 ff (report 13 Apr. 1714). There is no evidence, however, of these officials having indulged in these practices within the Ordnance Office.

in the early years after the Restoration; and the lieutenant before 1670 and the treasurer after that date, who could manipulate their control of ordnance finances. The most lucrative of these offices probably had an annual value of thousands rather than hundreds of pounds. Some other officials might also be fortunate enough to hold more than one office at the same time. Richard and George Marsh and Edward Conyers, for instance, were storekeepers (£216 12s. *p.a.*) and also keepers of the rich weapons (£20 *p.a.*) and Philip Musgrave, Pulteney, Craggs and Ousley held the clerk-ship of deliveries (£300 *p.a.*) with the office of the master's chief clerk (£200 *p.a.*).[115] Those who probably did best out of the ordnance office, however, were not strictly ordnance officials but ordnance contractors. John Fuller, the gunfounder, for instance, showed a 40 *per cent* profit margin on the sales in 1746,[116] and one of the lead-ing gunpowder makers of the period claimed he could make £300 from the working of 1,200 barrels of gunpowder.[117] If these figures are representative, the total profits gained by the largest ordnance gunfounders and gunpowder makers of the period must have been extremely high.[118] Ordnance officials were excluded from such gains, as the supplying of all ordnance stores were contracted out to tradesmen who were not in a position to influence their price.

Against these sort of profits, however, must be set the expenses of office and the irregular payment of allowances, fees and quarter salaries. The very number of petitions from disillusioned office holders suggest that office was not necessarily commensurate with wealth. Early in the period ordnance officers petitioned that be-cause their wages were three and three quarter years in arrears, they had been forced to take out money at interest for their main-tenance, which they considered would in time 'consume and eat out their estates'.[119] The principal officers gained a rise shortly after this supplication, but for some of the clerks in ordinary there was no

[115] See P.R.O., W.O. 54/20–72, ordnance quarter books. The offices of feed gunner (until the reorganization of the 1680s) and of gentleman of the ordnance were also held in conjunction with clerkships.

[116] E. Straker, *Wealden Iron* (London, 1931), p. 200. These were his profits for that year: £2,179 16s. from sales totalling £5,966.

[117] P.R.O., T 1/58, f. 298, petition of Sir Polycarpus Wharton.

[118] From July 1664 to May 1678 the Browne family of gunfounders supplied something like 3,871 tons of iron guns worth about £136,693; P.R.O., W.O. 51/4–20, *passim*, ordnance bill books. Wharton's profits on the 32,852 barrels of gunpowder he supplied between Dec. 1687 and Apr. 1695 (*V.C.H.*, *Surrey*, ii, p. 326) must have been well over £8,000.

[119] P.R.O., W.O. 49/112, n.d. (? early 1660s). They also indicated that their allowances were no greater than those paid in the time of Henry VIII, 'when a shilling would go further than ten now'.

such recompense.[120] Other ordnance officers found their salaries an insufficient reward to compensate for the strains and expenses of office. Storekeeper Watkinson at Hull considered that it was impossible for him to subsist on his salary, and he left office a sick and embittered man, with several hundred pounds still owing him from the ordnance.[121] His successor in office, John Duxbury, confirmed that, because of the high cost of provisions at Hull, the salary of that particular garrison was barely sufficient for a man with a large family.[122] The career of Edward Sherburne perhaps affords the best example of the difficulties that might confront a conscientious office holder. He was constituted clerk of the ordnance for life under Charles I, but he was deprived of his place in 1642. At the Restoration he was restored to office, and he continued as clerk of the ordnance until 1688, when he was again deprived of his place for being a Roman Catholic. Sherburne was a loyal and efficient administrator but it is clear that office did not bring him great wealth. Towards the end of his life he was reduced 'to the lowest of extremities and a deplorable poverty', depending for his livelihood on charitable handouts from the Treasury. [123]

The profits made from a place in the ordnance office in the late seventeenth century, then, finally depended on the extent to which ordnance officials were prepared to exploit their office for personal gain. There were some rotten apples in the organization, like Edward Conyers, who were quite prepared to do this regardless of the public cost, but there were other ordnance officials who were diligent and benevolent administrators.[124] These officials were not immune from making use of their office for private gain, but this did not necessarily mean that the public interest was being sacrificed for private advantage. Many officers must, like Pepys, have felt that 'the expectation of profit will have its force and make a man

[120] See petitions of clerks; P.R.O., W.O. 46/6, pp. 2–3, Mar. 1703/4. In 1741 it was still reported that the salary of some of the under clerks had not altered since the Restoration, 'notwithstanding the almost inconceivable increase of business and the vast increase in the price of necessaries'; W.O. 55/1796.

[121] P.R.O., W.O. 46/2, pp. 208–10 (Watkinson to Dartmouth, 20 Apr. 1684), 217 (same to board, 13 May 1684), 301 (same to same, 13 Dec. 1684).

[122] P.R.O., W.O. 55/1796, Duxbury to Hubbald, 31 Mar. 1686.

[123] C. Davies Sherborn, A History of the Family of Sherborne (privately printed, 1901), pp. 83 ff. B.L., Sloane MS. 836, ff. 85–86 (draft petition); Sloane MS. 1048 (petition); Sloane MS. 4067, f. 148 (petition); P.R.O., T. 1/80, p. 108 (petition).

[124] I am thinking of men like George Legge, Lord Dartmouth, master 1681–89; Sir Henry Goodricke, lieutenant 1689–1702; Sir Jonas Moore, senior, surveyor 1669–79; and Sir Edward Sherburne, clerk of the ordnance 1641–42, 1660–88. See D.N.B.

the more earnest'.[125] What is important is not to condemn such practices in the light of later standards of bureaucracy, as some whig historians have done.[126] Methods which do not conform with the standards of modern administration were, of course, prevalent in late seventeenth-century government. Within the Ordnance, officers sold places and extracted fees, but this was not unusual at this period[127] and such practices must simply be looked upon as part of a process a developing country goes through before it reaches maturity.[128] If the ordnance officers of our period, then, are accepted on their own terms they cannot be shown to be especially corrupt. Indeed, an historian looking for evidence of corruption with which to damn the Ordnance Office and its officers is much more likely to find it in the late sixteenth and early seventeenth centuries than in the later seventeenth and early eighteenth.[129] If, however, this historian in his wisdom carried his designs too far, I would simply remind him of the recent scandal over naval victualling and suggest that until government is in the hands of automatons it will be subject to the whims and vagaries of human behaviour.

Bedford College, London, and Reading University.

[125] Quoted in Albion, *Forests and Seapower*, p. 52, from Pepys' Diary, 19 Dec. 1663.

[126] See *e.g.* D. B. Eaton, *Civil Service in Great Britain* (New York, 1880), pp. 61, 69–70.

[127] See Swart, *Sale of Offices*, p. 55; Western, *Monarchy and Revolution*, pp. 116–17.

[128] In some respects corruption today in the emergent African nations seems to be at a similar stage as it was in early modern England. See S. Andreski, *The African Predicament* (London, 1968), chap. 7 ('Kleptocracy or Corruption as a System of Government'). I am very grateful to Miss Lesley Allen for this reference.

[129] See Ashley, 'The Organisation and Administration of the Tudor Office of Ordnance', pp. 130 ff; Menna Prestwich, *Cranfield: Politics and Profits under the Early Stuarts* (Oxford, 1966), pp. 218, 221, 392 ff.

ENGLAND, SCOTLAND AND EUROPE: THE PROBLEM OF THE FRONTIER

By Professor D. Hay, M.A., D.Litt., F.B.A., F.R.Hist. S.

READ AT THE SOCIETY'S CONFERENCE
19 SEPTEMBER 1974

IN what follows I propose to discuss certain questions concerning frontiers as they affect historians. Most of my time will be devoted to the Anglo-Scottish frontier, for the reason that it displays phenomena much more easily identified and documented than those associated with the frontiers of Europe. Some of the lessons one may draw from Anglo-Scottish frontier history are, moreover, of relevance elsewhere within the Continent, not only between countries but in some instances inside countries.

Our present concern with sharp lines on maps conditions us in all sorts of ways which may interrupt a clear view of political and cultural contacts in earlier times. For a century and a half statesmen have been trying to solve international conflicts of all kinds—political, economic, religious and sentimental—by adjusting boundaries between areas of sovereignty. Never has such activity been more intense than in the last ten years. Indeed at the very moment when I write, in Asia, in the Middle East and on our own doorstep in Ireland frontiers and the hopes and fears attached to them obtrude themselves daily and tragically on public attention. In our present troubles divisions are due to ethnic, religious and ideological conflict. But it is reasonable to suppose that awareness of such antitheses is never far from the surface anywhere. It is a curious commentary on the Enlightenment that it has proved so feeble a constituent in later attitudes among intellectuals, let alone in the public at large, even in regions of high literacy. As the nineteenth century progressed it became more and more difficult to become a member of the 'Heavenly City of the Eighteenth Century Philosophers', to use the title of Carl Becker's famous book.[1] What intelligent man today could describe himself as a 'citizen of the world'? We can, of course, console ourselves to some extent by our modern acceptance of the reasonableness of unreason and by pretending that one can scientifically study the dark irrational forces within each of us.

[1] New Haven, 1932.

I venture to mention these imponderables at the outset because we should remember that behind most political tensions lie assumptions which (for want of a better word) might be called moral. These are to be found whenever a man enters an unfamiliar environment—when the poor man crosses the threshold of a rich man, even more perhaps when the rich man crosses the threshold of the poor. At a higher point of social organization come the distinctions between larger groups. The earliest of these was surely the town-country dichotomy and I cannot do better than quote a few lines by Carlo Cipolla:

> The city represented for people in Europe during the eleventh, twelfth and thirteenth centuries what America was for nineteenth-century Europeans. The city was 'the frontier': a dynamic and new world in which men had the power to break the shackles of the past, where people saw or thought they saw new opportunities for economic and social success, where the old institutions and old prejudices no longer counted, where institutions and fortunes were all to be made or moulded as a reward for initiative, boldness and risk.[2]

One is reminded here, of course, of Marc Bloch's famous description of the chasm which separated the bourgeoisie from the feudal society around them, symbolized by the sworn commune between equals.[3] One is also reminded of the equally celebrated discussion by Braudel of the mountain and the plain in Mediterranean history.[4] For my purposes, in fact, Braudel's *montagnards* and agriculturists are more to the point than the townsmen of Bloch or Cipolla. Cipolla's city 'frontier' is obviously an application of Frederick J. Turner's interpretation of the American experience, where the frontier was on the move for generations and the type of society associated with it conditioned the whole development of United States history. Such a view does not have much if any relevance in the continent of Europe, where the concept of the frontier was very different. Nor is it applicable in the context of England and Scotland.

The Anglo-Scottish frontier was long in establishing itself. For centuries after the departure of the Romans the island they had called Britain was divided and subdivided into clans and petty kingdoms. After the English invasions some of these divisions were

---

[2] Carlo M. Cipolla, *Storia economica dell' Europa pre-industriale* (Bologna, 1974), p. 200.

[3] *Feudal Society*, trans. L. A. Manyon (London, 1961), p. 355.

[4] F. Braudel, *La Mediterranée et le monde mediterranéen à l'époque de Philippe II* (Paris, 1949), esp. part 1, chap. 1.

modified but the future boundary between the two kingdoms was overlaid by Celtic peoples in Cumbria (later Cumberland and Westmorland with S. W. Scotland) and English tribes in the North East—a Northumbria which stretched from the Firth of Forth to the Humber. Subsequently the Scots were compelled to recognize a single king. By the time of the Norman conquest the Scots not only exercised some control over Cumbria but had conquered that part of Northumbria which lay north of the Tweed. When William Rufus made good his recognition in Cumberland and Westmorland something like the later frontier had emerged. It was not until the Treaty of York in 1237 that these *ad hoc* arrangements were in some sense recognized, although the armed incursions of one country with the other were, of course, to continue for centuries. The Treaty of York was, it has been said, 'an incident' in the process of Scottish unification, part of the 'southern phase of the process'.[5] It should be stressed that 1237 was not in any way a deliberate delimitation of territories. It is simply the case that, in subsequent wars between England and Scotland, the border then accepted was not subsequently greatly modified, save by the incorporation in England of Berwick and its 'bounds', permanently after 1482. The chronology of the establishment of a firm ecclesiastical frontier between the two countries was somewhat different, but the archbishop of York's claims to metropolitan jurisdiction in Scotland were not seriously pressed after the thirteenth century.

I have set out in brief these developments because, and this is surprising, there is very little discussion of the frontier in ordinary surveys of Scottish or English history.[6] Books there are which do discuss the frontier, but they do not seem to have attracted much attention, since major conflicts between the two countries were affected only marginally by the ambiguities of the Tweed-Solway line.[7] In the long tally of wars and treaties, of dynastic claims and dynastic marriages, the details of demarcation are certainly not negligible (witness the Debateable Land); but they are subsidiary to wider international issues, and notably the relationships of each country with France. However, the prolonged hostilities meant that the frontier had to be guarded and Wardens of the Marches were appointed on each side and to them was committed not only the defence of the respective kingdoms, but also the much more

[5] F. M. Powicke, *The Thirteenth Century*, 2nd edn. (Oxford, 1962), p. 574.

[6] Powicke, *op. cit.*, is exceptional; now see Geoffrey Barrow, 'The Anglo-Scottish Border', *Northern History*, i (1966), pp. 21–42.

[7] James Logan Mack, *The Border Line* (Edinburgh, 1924), is a careful account of earlier descriptions and maps, together with an on-the-ground perambulation. The standard narrative remains George Ridpath, *The Border History of England and Scotland* (Berwick, 1776; revd. edn., Berwick, 1848).

difficult task of managing the Borders in time of official peace. They have been well studied,[8] and, if the establishment of a fixed boundary has been somewhat taken for granted, this has not been the case with the Marches as two areas to be administered. One in England, the other in Scotland. For the Border was not merely a line, notionally following rivers and burns and leaping to standing stones and ditches or dykes. It was a tract of territory separated in some senses from the countries on either side of it. It was thus a frontier of a peculiar kind.

This was evident to any sharp observer. Here is Polydore Vergil writing in the early sixteenth century. Having given some information regarding the dimensions of Scotland (grotesquely distorted because seen in the shape of a contemporary map) he goes on: 'Beside the Tweed, which rises from the hills not far from Roxburgh, a region lies to the South which they call the March, that is the frontier of the kingdoms of the English and the Scots. The Tweed separates this from Northumberland, the last region of England, which faces on to the German ocean and whose main town is Berwick'. He then turns to the *Scotiae limes* in Cumbria and the Solway. 'Between these two regions Mount Cheviot rises in the heart of the land'.[9] For Vergil—this is the point I am making—the Anglo-Scottish *limes* is the centre of a *regio*.

It is not entirely true, of course. The bounds of Berwick were clear enough, and the great medieval and early modern fortifications a permanent reminder that near the town the Tweed began the frontier. But it was then readily fordable even near Berwick and soon ceased to be more than an occasion for irritating riparian quarrels over fishing rights; these were the limits of the East March. In the West the great tidal estuary of the Solway was also fordable at several points and so were the rivers north and west of Carlisle; the West March in Scotland comprised modern Dumfriesshire and Kirkcudbrightshire and in England the counties of Cumberland and Westmorland. As for the central section, the Middle March in each country, the great rolling masses of the Cheviot Hills were traversed by many well-worn cattle roads. On this large extent of moorland agriculture was only possible in the lower valleys and, in the east, in the level Merse. The agricultural areas were more extensive nearer to the line of the frontier on the Scottish than on the English side. In the moorland proper there was only grazing

---

[8] R. R. Reid, 'Office of Warden of the Marches', *Eng. Hist. Rev.*, xxxii (1917), pp. 479–96; D. L. W. Tough, *The Last Years of a Frontier* (Oxford, 1928); Thomas I. Rae, *The Administration of the Scottish Frontier 1513–1603* (Edinburgh, 1966).

[9] *Anglica historia*, ed. Thysius (Leyden, 1651), p. 12; *cf.* the anonymous English version, ed. H. Ellis (Camden Soc., 1846), p. 6.

and sheep and cattle were allowed, by consent, to pasture in-differently on either side. To the activities of the shepherd, rein-forced where conditions permitted by some crops, the land afforded one other economic activity: banditry or, in the local expression, reiving. Reiving was hunting for booty or 'prey', a word which fairly catches the grim overtones of *praeda*. Throughout its history down to and even after the Union of the Crowns, 'prey' was sought by borderers from both sides of the boundary. It was, perhaps, commoner for Scots to raid English and English to raid Scots, but the English and Scots also preyed on their own countrymen. Prey meant, especially before the sixteenth century, absolutely anything: men for the ransoms they would fetch, or pay to avoid destruction (let us remember the Border origin of the expression 'blackmail'), money and articles of value but above all moveable wealth on the hoof—sheep, cattle, horses.[10] These last commodities had one enormous attraction: they were self-propelling. A few men and a few dogs on a drove road with a days' start took a great deal of catching before the beasts were safely away.

All of this led to vendettas and rapine, to burnt farmsteads and castles and even churches. Policing the area was virtually impossible and however carefully international agreements were reached for Wardens to apply the 'Law of the March', its official application was always retrospective. Border law was, in its essentials and in so far as it was effective, a law of self-help. It was a primitive law, matching the primitive conditions of the area. It deserves study, and so do the social habits—not so different, it seems—in the south of Scotland and the north of England. Dr Rae has recently reminded us how clans or 'surnames', under one or more leaders, emerged in the later Middle Ages to exist beside the old 'feudal' tenurial dependents of the greater families, or even to develop at the expense of the older nobles[11]. It was a world in which gangs and gang warfare could flower and even seem patriotic. This structure of society was paralleled south of the border and in both countries great magnates found the office of Warden a useful adjunct to tenurial resources and family loyalties. The Douglasses and the Percies and Nevilles are not just story-book figures. They stain the pages of history as well as glorify those of romance.

It is not my purpose to display how nasty, brutish and short life was in and near the wide swathe of the Marches between England

[10] Hay, 'Booty in Border warfare', *Trans. Dumfriesshire and Galloway Nat. Hist. and Antiquarian Society*, xxxi (1954 for 1952–53), pp. 148–66.

[11] Rae, *Administration of the Scottish Frontier*, pp. 5–7; for the English side *cf.* J. A. Tuck, 'Northumbrian society in the fourteenth century', *Northern History*, vi (1971), pp. 22–39, esp. pp. 27–28 and refs.

and Scotland[12] but to add one or two complications to the picture I have sketched and then to put before you some observations regarding the confrontations of the two countries separated as they were by a human undergrowth (if this word may be applied to an area which observers agreed was singularly treeless) of gentry and shepherds, lords and men accepting mutual violence not as an exceptional occurrence but as a way of life.

First of all, the complication of the Debateable Land, or rather Lands. These tracts lay between the English West March and the confines of the Middle and West Marches of Scotland and (two smaller areas) between the two Middle Marches. They were for long a monument to the intractable character of the natives, for while it was agreed that one might by day graze them, no one might live there. Any habitation erected by Scots could be destroyed legally by English; and *vice versa*. These absurdities were partially removed in 1552, when the main disputed area was successfully partitioned. Second, even without violence, it was manifestly absurd to operate in any meaningful way a frontier crossing wild hills which gave a livelihood to men only by being grazed by beasts. The very pattern of transhumance, which was followed in parts of the Borders, stressed this. The high shielings at heads of valleys were found everywhere and survive widely, if only in little ruins, as evidence of this activity which persisted, of course, well beyond 1603 or 1707.[13] The present shared grazing of all our northern moorland shows that even today, with our acuter sense of property and territorial rights, the highlands of Cumberland or North Northumberland are indivisible. This is clearly seen in countless ways in the years before the Union. At one stage the English complained that 10,000 Scottish sheep daily grazed in England. And we have a safe-conduct issued in 1389 for 1,600 sheep belonging to the countess of March and Lady Hering to graze daily within five leagues of Cockburnspath for three years or the duration of the truce.[14]

A third consideration. It was the case, it seems, that many of the indwellers in the north of England were in fact Scots. This would be proved alone by the distrust of Scottish servants and the punishment of men of substance for having Scottish dependents. Lord

[12] A fine brief picture of this in Edward Miller, *War in the North* (St John's College Cambridge lecture 1959–60 . . . at the University of Hull. Hull, 1960). An older but equally unromantic picture in G. M. Trevelyan's essay, 'The Middle Marches', best read in the reprint published at Newcastle in 1934 for the Northumberland and Newcastle Society.

[13] H. G. Ramm, R. W. McDowall, Eric Mercer, *Sheilings and Bastles* (H.M.S.O., 1970).

[14] Hay, 'Booty' p. 165 and refs.

Hunsdon estimated that '2500 Scots, few of them denizens, lived in the East March in 1569; later on English estimates put the number of Scots within ten miles of the frontier as one in three'.[15] There was also a fair amount of intermarriage,[16] so it was not only banditry and the hostility of the rugged reivers to pressure from either Edinburgh or London which gave the region its coherence. It was the economic pressure of a pastoral economy, which made the borderers suspicious and alien to their more civilized neighbours and drove them in on themselves and out against everyone else.[17] This coherence may, perhaps, be reflected in the language used. To a southern Englishman the English borderers even in the sixteenth century sounded Scottish.[18] And in the modern and highly technical linguistic studies which have been made of this area there are some traces of a spill southward, especially in the East March, of words associated in recent times with the south of Scotland rather than the north of England.[19] But this evidence from today or even yesterday tells us little for sure about the sixteenth or seventeenth centuries let alone earlier times. We can however say with confidence that there was no linguistic frontier such as that which separated Romance and Teutonic areas in continental Europe. Here we have at any rate a further reason for some unity within the region. Shepherds and lords could communicate across the frontier which separated and united them in their ambiguous relationship. The pastoral economy itself meant that for months at a time men whose permanent dwellings were perhaps twenty miles apart came together on one sheiling ground during the summer months.[20] It was much more difficult for a burgess of Edinburgh and a Londoner to communicate by word of mouth.

Nor was living in the Border region without its compensations. In a cruel age it offered shelter to men on the run. Some were doubtless malefactors who sought the sanctuary of the hills in order not only to avoid harsh justice but to make a living by the wicked ways they knew—thieving, murdering, counterfeiting the coins of either realm. But the misty moors and their remote farms and castles offered sanctuary to religious refugees: I am thinking of catholics, presbyterians and even Anglicans, trying to exercise

---

[15] Tough, *Last Years of a Frontier*, p. 179.
[16] Rae, *Administration of the Scottish Frontier*, pp. 10–11.
[17] *Cf.* Braudel, *La Mediterranée*, pp. 650–52.
[18] Tough, *Last Years of a Frontier*, pp. 34–35.
[19] See Beat Glauser, *The Scottish-English Linguistic Border. Lexical Aspects* (Bern, 1974); Hans-Hennig Speitel, 'An areal typology of isoglosses: isoglosses near the Scottish-English Border', *Zeitschrift für Dialektologie und Linguistik*, xxxvi (1969), pp. 49–66. I have to thank Dr Speitel for allowing me to consult him.
[20] P. W. Dixon in *Archaeologia Aeliana*, 4th ser., 1 (1952), p. 251.

liberty of conscience. This was all the easier since changes in religious policy arrived at by central governments left many leading families in the Border region for long unaffected.[21]

Another curious compensation for occasional war and endemic freebooting was the money it brought to a poor region.[22] The provision for wardens and supporting troops in each of the three Marches produced fair sums of money even on the Scottish side, where stipends were small and the notion of a paid soldiery was not yet established by the sixteenth century. On the English side large retainers were paid and some garrisons (such as that at Berwick) were substantial. It is of course true that the cash did not always arrive: the famous episode of the dishonoured tallies in Henry IV's reign was among the factors which led the Percies to revolt.[23] But overall a very considerable amount must have been spent locally on troops and by the troops on victuals and other goods. Here again was a bond between Borderers. The garrison at Berwick was largely fed by the provender purchased in the Merse.[24] Building of fortifications obviously gave employment, especially at seasons when normal reiving was difficult, as in long summer days. Such building was by no means restricted to castles for the rich or for agents of the government such as the Wardens. One of the characteristic features of the whole Border area, from Firth to Tyne, was the construction of fortified farms or 'bastles' 'fortalices', towers and churches—places where men and cattle might seek safety against raiders and their swords and torches. These buildings were by the sixteenth century, it seems, frequently erected by tenant farmers. Rents were low in the Borders, especially on Crown land which gradually controlled 'the whole of the upland border by the later sixteenth century'[25]

Finally it would be absurd to omit among the more creative side of Border life the emergence of a ballad literature which bears comparison with any such elsewhere.[26] The heroic element in the life of the Marches was paid for, we may think, at a terrible price in brutality and boorishness. But it was based on concepts of undying and unquestioning loyalty, reflected in ballad after ballad. The propriety of singing the praises of *Outlaw Murray* or *Johnny Armstrong* may be questioned: they were sung at the time, and

[21] 'The religion of the Borderers' in Tough, *Last Years of a Frontier*, pp. 61–75.

[22] Hay, 'Booty', p. 13. Was the general decline in the later medieval economy intensified or retarded in the Borders by war and reiving? I understand from Dr. Tuck that there is debate on the question.

[23] J. M. W. Bean, 'Henry IV and the Percies', *History*, xliv (1959), pp. 212–27.

[24] Tough, pp. 45–46.

[25] Dixon, *loc. cit.*, pp. 254–55, an extended assessment and supplement to *Shielings and Bastles*, above, p. 82, n. 13.

[26] An excellent recent book is by James Reed, *The Border Ballads* (London, 1973).

Bishop John Leslie, writing about 1570, describes this musical
activity as spontaneous and moving.[27] Moving it still is, but also
extraordinarily revealing of all aspects of border life—resistance to
central authority, lust for prey, kinship ties and so on. The Scottish
ballads are truer, less sophisticated than the English ones, perhaps
because the ethos of the frontier area lingered longer in southern
Scotland.

If the borderers may sometimes seem enviable, that was hardly
how they struck contemporaries, especially by the sixteenth century.
The gentry of southern England who visited the North as soldiers,
merchants or missionaries were appalled at the bestial lives of the
upper valleys and the hills. Feuds and violence made any regular
life a mockery, and not least the regular life of the Church.[28] As a
boy born in Cumberland the situation must have been well-known
to Bernard Gilpin; later, a saintly don and archdeacon of Durham,
he took his duties seriously, pastoralism of a different sort. He found
churches desolate, parsons ignorant, the people divided by hate.
The Prayer Book calls to Communion those who are 'in love and
charity with their neighbours', an echo of the Pax which had
latterly become a favourite part of the old Mass. It was difficult in
small neighbourhoods for feuding families to love neighbours they
were at odds with. They either lost face, or provoked a fracas, or
they stayed away from church.[29] They usually stayed away.

The perpetual disturbances on the Border were intensified by
weak or divided government in England and Scotland. On balance
the Scottish government was less capable of managing its border
region and the traditional families maintained their independence
with considerable success. On the English side central government
was stronger and, as Mr James has demonstrated, 'the values of
lineage, good lordship and fidelity' on the English March were
perceptibly dissolving in the later sixteenth century.[30] There were
regular attempts at government level to iron out differences[31] and
the Border itself was the subject of serious negotiation. I have
mentioned the division of the main debateable area in 1552; for the
rest it is clear that in 1552, and perhaps earlier, the watershed was
regarded as determining the boundary in the wastes of the Cheviot

[27] Tough, *Last Years of a Frontier*, p. 36; again *cf.* Braudel, *La Mediterranée*, p. 651.
[28] Tough, *op. cit.*, p. 64.
[29] *Northumberland County History*, xv (Newcastle upon Tyne, 1940), p. 312
(Gilpin at Rothbury). *Cf.* John Bossy, 'The Reformation and the people of Catholic
Europe', *Past and Present*, 47 (1970), p. 55.
[30] M. E. James, 'The first earl of Cumberland and the decline of northern
feudalism', *Northern History*, i (1966), pp. 43–69; *id.*, 'The concept of order and the
Northern Rising of 1569', *Past & Present*, 60 (1973), pp. 49–63.
[31] Tough, *Last Years of a Frontier*, pp. 175–77, 187–278.

hills in the Middle March.[32] This was certainly the case in the abortive memorandum submitted to Elizabeth in 1580. The phrase is clumsy but its meaning is inescapable: 'the height whereof (in the forest of Cheviot) as the water falleth, is the march of England and Scotland'.[33] But the long tale of war and rapine was in theory brought to an end by the accession to the English throne of King James VI of Scotland. The repeated attempts at a dynastic solution had finally paid off.

The learned monarch attempted at once to ordain a union of the two realms under the title 'Great Britain'. Professor Bindoff has shown how futile such a gesture proved at the time and for long after.[34] This was despite the precedents for such a usage which, as I have explained elsewhere, were indeed plentiful through the later Middle Ages and which became even more intense under the influence of humanist secretaries, ambassadors and men of letters.[35] James VI and I even had designs prepared for a flag which combined the crosses of St Andrew and St George; and a proclamation set out the manner in which British ships were to show the flag.[36] But all of this was part of a programme which was far from being effective. James as king of Scotland had made fruitless and some-times bloody efforts to enforce his authority in southern Scotland. 'Of the nine judicial raids which took place, James VI attended seven in person . . .'.[37] After 1603 the problem changed. As Dr Rae says, 'the international aspects of the problem had been eliminated, and a problem of frontier control involving two states became a domestic problem of administering the unruly Middle shires of King James's "united kingdoms"'.[38] It was far from easy to ad-minister these unruly shires, and the desire to make money out of the customs levied on border traffic was a strong incentive to

[32] Bowes' survey of 1550 is reprinted in Mack, *The Border Line*, pp. 32–40.

[33] *Calendar of Letters and Papers relating . . . to the Borders . . .* , ed. J. Bain, 2 vols. (Edinburgh, 1894–96), i, p. 31. *O.E.D.* gives the first use of 'water-shed' as 1803.

[34] S. T. Bindoff, 'The Stuarts and their style', *Eng. Hist. Rev.*, lx(1945), pp. 192–216.

[35] 'Great Britain in the Middle Ages', *Proc. Soc. Antiquaries of Scotland*, lxxxix (1955–56); I published a revised version of this as an appendix to the second edn. of my *Europe—the Emergence of an Idea* (Edinburgh, 1968). Much additional material could be adduced.

[36] National Library of Scotland MS. 2517 (a miscellany of heraldic papers), fos. 67–68, consist of a folded sheet of designs for a union 'jack'. Four of these are designs in colour; a further monochrome sketch displays a fifth way of combining the two national crosses. The earl of Nottingham (Charles Howard) signs, indi-cating his preference for a design where the colours will not run, presumably in his capacity as Admiral. None of these was the pappern adopted in 1606, on which see Sir W. L. Clowes, *The Royal Navy. A History*, ii (London, 1898), p. 25 and n.

[37] Rae, *Administration of the Scottish Frontier*, p. 212 and pp. 206–22, *passim*.

[38] *Ibid.*, p. 233.

maintain economic separation.[39] There was also regular pressure
from over-mighty subjects on both sides which led, *inter alia*, to the
attempt virtually to eliminate the Grahams (Graemes) of Eskdale
early in James I's reign, the subject of the *saeva indignatio* of a
descendant of the surname writing only fifty years ago.[40] Other
similar barbarities were only slowly abandoned and when the mid-
seventeenth century revived in effect a state of war between the two
countries principles could again shelter factions. But unhappily the
history of the Borders after 1603 remains to be written. All one can
be sure of is that the sheep and cattle went on grazing; that more
agriculture came to be practised; that more Scottish farmers drifted
southward into Northumberland and the Lake counties, bringing
with them industrious ways and the reformed religion,[41] a process
which was still going on in the eighteenth and nineteenth centuries.
This process of eroding ancient ways had at any rate reached the
point when in 1707 the bad habits, or the old habits, were no
impediment to the legislative Union which in the end brought the
Britain of James VI and I to something like a reality.

The Borders were a region and remain a region: the sheep have
seen to that, and until a century ago not just the border sheep but
the cattle from further north which followed drove roads over the
Cheviots to feed the hungry industrial towns of England, until the
railways completely took over the job.[42] Berwick was and is a
shopping centre for Berwickshire as well as north Northumberland;
the Scottish border towns have long had markets which attract
southern farmers just as more recently the licensing laws brought
droves of thirsty Scots into England on a Sunday. Much of this, as
can readily be imagined, is reflected in the current speech of the
area.[43] I do not wish to evoke the modern Border as to some extent
still a self-contained social entity, although as I have remarked its
history in such a context deserves to be written, especially for the
period after 1603. My point is that we have not merely a region
with a surviving life of its own (based to some degree on its history);
there are, after all, many such territorial groupings in Britain—
especially those where linguistic differences invoke old ethnic
patterns, as on the edges of the Highlands and Islands of Scotland,
Wales, and perhaps even the South West of England, where we

[39] A. R. B. Haldane, *The Drove Roads of Scotland* (Edinburgh, 1952), pp. 16–19.
The drovers of course did not find it hard to avoid such taxes.

[40] John Graham, *The Condition of the Border at the Union: Destruction of the Graham
Clan*, 2nd edn., (London, 1907).

[41] Trevelyan, *The Middle Marches*, p. 29; I wish I could agree that 'vulgarity
has not invaded from the cities', for it has since 1950.

[42] Haldane, *The Drove Roads of Scotland*, pp. 168–86.

[43] *Cf.* above p. 83, n. 19.

are meeting this evening. In all such regions, and indeed throughout the land, moss-trooping and reiving, piracy, highway robbery, blackmail, murder and rapine were endemic in the Middle Ages and the early modern period[44]. But none of such regions constitutes historical let alone present-day frontiers. The Welsh Marcher counties were not in any sense a frontier zone surviving the thirteenth century, although up till then it is true that the great Marcher lords claimed a right of private war in terms not dissimilar to those liberties arrogated to themselves by border magnates. Outlaw Murray in the ballad that bears his name made his position clear to an officious king:

> 'These lands are mine', the Outlaw said,
> 'I ken nae king in Christentie;
> Frae Soudron I this Foreste wan,
> When the King nor his Knightis were not to see'.

Just as Murray had 'won' his lands from the southerner, so Gloucester and Hereford in 1920 based their privileges on right of conquest of Welsh lands. Edward I effectively killed that,[45] even if the valley sheep, being fatter, still attracted the hillsmen.

In the United Kingdom of England and Scotland the Border region remained distinct from the others because it continued to mark an administrative division, as in certain respects it still does, while existing within a larger political entity. Here again I do not wish to imply that the Anglo-Scottish border has no parallels in other parts of Europe. What were the county (later duchy) of Piedmont and the kingdom of Navarre but marcher lordships, straggling across mountains? The count of Armagnac held his fief 'of the eagle', as many a border lord could have claimed to hold his of the buzzard or the falcon. There were debateable lands inside France and everywhere there were liberties where asylum could be found, and sub-frontiers where jurisdictions changed and the original writ had to be replaced by some new authorisation if a criminal was to be punished.[46] Banditry was worst, as Braudel says, where governments were weakest, in mountainous areas and in frontier zones; and he instances the Dalmatian uplands between Venice and Turkey, the Hungarian frontier, Catalonia and the Pyrenees, Messina, Benevento, the boundary of the Papal States and Tuscany,

---

[44] Cf. B. W. Beckingsale, 'The characteristics of the Tudor North', *Northern History*, iv (1969), pp. 67–83.

[45] Powicke, *The Thirteenth Century*, pp. 329–30; Hay, 'The divisions of the spoils of war in fourteenth-century England', *Trans. Royal Hist. Soc.*, 5th ser., 4 (1954), 108–9 and refs.

[46] Hay, 'Geographical abstractions and the historian', [*Irish*] *Historical Studies*, ii (London, 1959), p. 12 and refs.

and those between Milan and Venice, Venice and Austria.[47] One could make a longer list if one left the Mediterranean countries.

Borders represent divisions. But the tension of division forges bonds at the same time. The inter-feuding and intermarriage already mentioned as a unifying feature of Border life existed from the Normans onwards as between England and Scotland. Apart from Celtic areas in Wales and the Highlands, the two countries shared common linguistic backgrounds (Latin, Teutonic and French), a common religious tradition (Catholic and then, in broad terms, reformed), and a common literature. Differences remained after 1707, even after the spate of nineteenth-century Westminster legislation; education, law, the official relationship of Church to State. These however were not enough to nullify the basis of Union, which in the end offered opportunities especially to Scots, comparable in some sense to those in the Empire they helped so vigorously to create. In such circumstances the Border ceased by the eighteenth century to have any disruptive effect. On the contrary, it became an area of romance which the sophisticated of both countries could enjoy. Walter Scott published the *Minstrelsy of the Scottish Border* in 1802–3; James Hogg, the Ettrick Shepherd, was already producing verses and gathering material for his stories.[48]

You may have noticed that in the ballad I quoted the bard refers to 'Christentie' or Christendom as the widest area he and his listeners could know. Christendom (perhaps this was its main weakness) can have no conceivable frontiers: this would be a contradiction in terms. But Christendom bequeathed to Europe a large part of its ideological content, and I conclude with a few, I fear fairly obvious, reflections on the frontier of Europe, that area whose history has been as full of wars as has that of our own island. My first and most banal observation is that Europe has only one certain frontier—the seas which bound it to west and south. To the east it has only artificial limits, marks on a map which, as I have pointed out elsewhere, are now made entirely by Soviet administrators and geographers.[49]

---

[47] I paraphrase Braudel, *La Mediterranée*, p. 651; but the whole section, pp. 643–59, on poverty and banditry and the role of the noble malefactor, is relevant to Border conditions. *Cf.* also Braudel's comparison, p. 534, between well-governed Castile and anarchic Aragon, with its semi-independent lords, which can be applied more or less to the Anglo-Scottish scene.

[48] *E.g. The Brownie of Bodsbeck* (1817). *The Confessions of a Justified sinner* is by no means typical of James Hogg's work, as Professor William Beattie rightly points out in his introduction to the Penguin *Border Ballads* (Harmondsworth, 1952), p. 25. For the change in fashion which made popular ballads so appealing see Reed, *The Border Ballads*, pp. 1–8.

[49] For this paragraph and for what follows see my *Europe—The Emergence of an*

I confess that whenever I consider Europe as a political or cultural abstraction I realize that I am at the mercy of public pressures which I find it hard to resist, or if I resist I suspect that I over-react to them, to use current cant. When I began collecting material for the book I wrote on the idea of Europe it was 1950 and I was drenched in pro-European sentiment. This sentimental affection distorted my approach, or so I felt when I came to prepare a new edition in the mid-sixties. Now, when the selfishness and stupidity of the countries constituting the Community have all but destroyed its credibility, my heart again is stirred as I remember the inheritance by Europeans of Greece and Rome, of Christianity and Judaism, of an ideal of tolerance and material comfort which distinguishes the Continent from its neighbours in Asia and Africa. Apologies are due for such a series of personal revelations, although I daresay some of you may find echoes of current preoccupations affecting your work, especially if it lies in the very modern field.

Especially, but not entirely. In the last resort I suspect every topic in which we interest ourselves has its origins in some external suggestion and usually reflects contemporary interests. In any event it is the historian's job to destroy legends and if he is aware that he does this by creating new ones (they are called 'models' nowadays) than that is no bad thing. To understand how Britain as an abstraction survived from antiquity to become politically useful in the seventeenth century is to realize the power of a word. And when *Europe*, after centuries as a geographers' term, assumes a new role in the years after the Second World War we witness a similar phenomenon. Even 'Western Europe' can seem to have a role of its own, as it did to Yves Renouard in 1958—I suppose as a consequence of his being moved by the negotiations leading to the Treaty of Rome.[50]

What I suspect we will all do well to heed is the vulnerability of such abstractions. Europe, with or without frontiers, comprising only western Europe (and how western is western?), contains only so much meaning as its inhabitants and the outside world put into it, which at the moment is very little. And I venture to suggest that we should treat the concept Britain with similar reserve. Nothing is permanent in the no-man's-land where political relationships reflect patriotic sentiment. We were brought up—it is implicit in

---

idea (cited above, n. 35). In that edition there is a new preface and a new conclusion. 'Christentie'=Christendom, *ibid.*, pp. 22–23 and refs; this is a Middle English usage, not specifically southern Scottish or Border.

[50] Treaty of Rome, 1957; Yves Renouard, '1212–1216. Comment les traits durables de L'Europe se sont définis au début du XIIIe siècle', *Annales de l'Université de Paris*, xxviii (1958), pp. 5–21.

Renouard's 1958 article—on the assumption that there were great verities—France, Spain, Britain—which were the product of thirteenth-century settlements, bloody at the time but in the end sealed by the inexorable physical facts of the Pyrenees and the Alps and the English Channel. We were brought up to believe that after Ferdinand and Isabella, or at any rate after Charles V, Spain was 'unified' just as England and Scotland were after 1603 and 1707. Can any one of us be so sure today that even France, where the very word patriotism was born,[51] may not embark on processes of devolution which may go far, as may those, more obviously, in Spain and perhaps in the United Kingdom? If such developments do occur it will bring the old 'nation states' of Europe into line with the fractionalized systems that have returned to Germany and from which Italy has never departed.

My remarks about the frontier lead me to a hopeful generalization: frontiers are man-made and therefore admirable subjects for an historical approach. The absurd concern with natural features, above all the terrible effects of using watersheds to carve up peoples, display an approach to political predicaments which has done terrible damage, at any rate within the European area. Let us remind our students and our readers that the future is what we make it, just as were all the futures which lay in front of our forefathers. Nothing is inevitable, not even patriotism, not even a frontier.[52]

University of Edinburgh.

[51] For some relevant considerations see Jean Lestocquoy, *Histoire du patriotisme* (Paris, 1968).

[52] This lecture was delivered before I had the advantage of reading Mr A. C. Goodman's paper, 'Reformation and society in the Scottish Marches', delivered to the Second International Colloquium in Ecclesiastical History organized by the British Sub-Commission for the Comparative Study of Ecclesiastical History, Oxford, September 1974. I understand that this will be published. I have also now seen a useful summary by Dr D. P. Kirby, 'The evolution of the frontier, Part II, 1018–1237', contributed to the forthcoming *An Historical Atlas of Scotland*, edited by Peter McNeill and Ranald Nicholson.

SKILLS AND THE DIFFUSION OF INNOVATIONS FROM BRITAIN IN THE EIGHTEENTH CENTURY

By Professor Peter Mathias, M.A., F.R.Hist. S.

READ AT THE SOCIETY'S CONFERENCE
19 SEPTEMBER 1974

I

THIS paper stems from an initial interest in the relationships between science and technology in the eighteenth century.[1] Hence its concern lies principally with the nature of technical innovation and the sources of technical change during the Industrial Revolution. Exploring the ways in which new technology is diffused can shed light on the nature of technical change itself, which is a complex amalgam of influences governing invention, innovation (the bringing of inventions into productive use) and the diffusion of new techniques. Taking as a topic the diffusion of technology, particularly in machine-making and engineering, between Britain and Europe in the late eighteenth century is thus not meant to be a peg on which to hang wide-ranging animadversions on the differing economic fortunes and pace of advance of Britain and Europe, or a discussion of why industrialization came first and fastest to Britain and lagged elsewhere: it is a much narrower enquiry into seeing what light the processes and difficulties of diffusing new technology cast upon technical change itself at this time.

Such a limiting proviso is important because any enquiry into the general reasons for the failure of new technology on a wide front to get indigenized in a country other than that of its birth does lead into the widest realms of explanation, invoking the whole range of possible reasons for lags in rates of economic growth and industrialization in different countries, the net result of which collectively leads to a failure to adopt modern technology, at once the symbol, the measure and the means of modernization. Secondly, there is in-built bias in setting up an enquiry to look at the diffusion

---

[1] P. Mathias, 'Who Unbound Prometheus?', in *Science and Society, 1600–1900*, ed. P. Mathias (Cambridge, 1972); reprinted in *Science, Technology and Economic Growth in the Eighteenth Century*, ed. A. E. Musson (London, 1972); 'Technological Change on the Grand Scale', *History of Science*, x (1971).

of such technology from Britain to Europe which isolates a principally one-way flow in what was, in fact, a very turbulent stream of
change moving in different directions. The view from Russia in
1815, for example, shows French and German entrepreneurs more
prominent than British in many fields (save in machine-making and
cotton textiles) with Dutch and French skilled artisans present in
large numbers.[2] Estonia was largely a technological and business
dependency of German groups. Germans were most prominent in
the Russian Academy and as technical advisers to the government
(with notable exceptions like Sir Samuel Bentham and General
Wilson).

A similar picture is drawn in the Spanish royal manufactories
during the eighteenth century: French artisans and entrepreneurs
(with some Italians) dominated the transfers of technology in the
silk industry, as they did throughout Europe (not just as a consequence of Huguenot persecution); Germans and French in linen;
English and Irish in fine woollens and cotton; the Dutch in some
other cloths.[3] The Guadalaxara woollen mill, for example was
principally worked by English, Irish, French and Dutch artisans
(sought in integrated groups with complementary skills), but
others came from Poland, Prussia, Switzerland and Italy. France
was a principal source of new inventions and technology in Europe
during the century, leading a counterpoint between French inventions and English development in the basic development of branches
of the chemical industry, in paper-making and in the glass industry,
amongst others.[4] During the Revolutionary and Napoleonic Wars

[2] J. T. Fuhrmann, The Origins of Capitalism in Russia (Chicago, 1972); W. L.
Blackwell, The Beginnings of Russian Industrialisation, 1800–1860 (Princeton, 1968),
pp. 18, 29, 47, 62–64, 79, 90, 114, 230–33, ch. x.; P. I. Lyaschenko, History of the
National Economy of Russia (New York, 1949), pp. 327–29; J. P. McKay, Pioneers for
Profit (Chicago, 1970).

[3] J. Vicens Vives, An Economic History of Spain (Princeton, 1968), pp. 525–30,
538; J. C. la Force, 'Royal Textile Factories in Spain, 1700–1800', Journ. of Econ.
Hist. xxiv (1964); id., 'Technological Diffusion in the Eighteenth Century: the
Spanish Textile Industry', Technology and Culture, v (1964), pp. 322–43; id., The
Development of the Spanish Textile Industry, 1750–1800 (Berkeley, 1965).

[4] See, amongst many other sources, W. Cunningham, Alien Immigrants to England
(London, 1897), ch. vi; T. C. Barker, Pilkington Brothers and the Glass Industry
(London, 1960), esp. chs. 2, 5; D. C. Coleman, The British Paper Industry (Oxford
1958), chs. ii, iii, vii; P. Thornton and N. Rothstein, 'The Importance of the
Huguenots in the London Silk Industry', Procs. of the Huguenot Society, xx (1958);
W. C. Scoville, The Persecution of Huguenots and French Economic Development
1680–1720 (Berkeley, 1960), esp. ch. 10; 'The Huguenots and the Diffusion of
Technology', Jour. of Political Economy, lx (1952); 'Minority Migrations and the
Diffusion of Technology', Journ. of Economic History, xi (1951); S. T. McCloy,
French Inventions in the Eighteenth Century (Lexington, Ky., 1952); A. E. Musson and
E. Robinson, Science and Technology in the Industrial Revolution (Manchester, 1969).

French scientific administrators and civil engineers vigorously set about surveying for minerals and promoting mining techniques throughout the territories they controlled or influenced, in a European-wide endeavour to develop materials, skills and productive capacity for the armament industries.[5] Professor Rondo Cameron's study, *France and the Economic Development of Europe, 1815–1914*, which isolates a different flow, shows the extent of French technological influence, tightly packaged with French capital and business initiative. The closer technology depended upon formal scientific training at the end of the eighteenth century, the greater the influence of France as the mentor of Europe.

But with the basic mechanization of the textile industry after 1770, the growth of deep mines and large-scale metal fabrication, and the associated growth of engineering, it was principally British engineers and artisans who sponsored diffusion of these new techniques abroad. This was particularly true of machine-making and mechanical engineering generally (although not of civil engineering) —technologies that were to have the widest influence in the spread of mechanization and the engineering industries during the nineteenth century.[6] British technology also spread indirectly; when direct exports of machinery were prohibited (if never prevented), Russian textile factories drew on French and Belgian machines, much dependent on British expertise. In the 1840s, after repeal of the laws, a much more direct invasion of British textile technology took place.[7] As will be apparent, individual examples of best-practice technology—particularly dramatic new machines like the steam engine, installed in state-promoted or state-favoured plants— were transferred relatively rapidly in continental Europe, but they failed so often to become adopted more generally so that a much larger gap existed between best practice and the representative level of diffused techniques in such industries than was the case in Britain.

There was also a significant gap between the record of invention

[5] F. B. Artz, *The Development of Technical Education in France, 1500–1850* (Cambridge, Mass., 1966); R. E. Cameron, *France and the Economic Development of Europe, 1800–1914* (Princeton, 1961), chs iii, xii; D. Landes, *The Unbound Prometheus* (Cambridge, 1969).

[6] There is a large bibliography on this general theme. See surveys in Landes, *The Unbound Prometheus*; W. O. Henderson, *Britain and Industrial Europe, 1750–1870* (3rd edn., Leicester, 1972); C. Ballot, *L'introduction du machinisme dans l'industrie française* (Paris, 1923); *L'Acquisition des Techniques par les pays non-initiateurs* (Colloques internationaux du CNRS No. 538, Pont à Mousson, 1970) (particularly contributions by Dr. M. Teich and J. Lukasiewicz). The best recent analytical study is to be found in A. Milward and S. B. Saul, *The Economic Development of Continental Europe, 1780–1870* (London, 1973), esp. ch. 3, and pp. 270–87.

[7] Blackwell, *The Beginnings of Russian Industrialisation*, pp. 47, 114.

and development in many fields. The English had long been known as the perfecters of other people's ideas; but this continued in many fields. A Swiss calico printer remarked in 1766 of the English: 'they cannot boast of many inventions, but only of having perfected the inventions of others; whence comes the proverb that for a thing to be perfect it must be invented in France and worked out in England.'[8] All this is significant evidence that the general economic and commercial context was not so favourable in these countries.[9] In such an economic climate single swallows do not make a summer.

Doubtless a principal explanation for such lack of momentum in adopting new technology was the absence of the requisite extent of demand. A cumulative extension of demand for the products of these industries in continental countries would have put the necessary strain upon the inputs of conventional resources, threatened the traditional balance between techniques, materials and skills, forced up prices of the scarce factors and created the requisite incentives for adopting new technology. Britain was fortunate in her shortages in this period. These seem to have underpinned the diffusion of innovations such as coke-smelting in England and explained their timing in a commercial context.[10] Pointing to insufficient demand as one general explanation, of course, is to identify not a single relationship but a large bundle of economic and social, institutional, legal, political and motivational factors which underlie a highly abstract and conceptualized entity such as 'the level of effective demand'. An equivalent bundle of relationships lies at the back of the 'single' entity called a 'market economy'.

Of course the resource position with factor costs for cheap coal and iron was more favourable in the U.K. and in certain ways the commercial context less favourable in France and other continental states further east. The state willed certain of the ends of industrialization, such as the acquisition of new skills, but opposed (consciously or through the effect of other policies and positions supported by government) many of the general means to attain those ends and other preconditions of the process, such as general mobility of labour, growth of commercial institutions and the like.

There is also the question of economic or commercial rationality

[8] A. P. Wadsworth and J. de L. Mann, *The English Cotton Trade and Industrial Lancashire, 1600–1780* (Manchester, 1931), p. 413.

[9] For a theoretical exposition of some of these themes in a modern context see W. E. G. Salter, *Productivity and Technical Change* (2nd edn., Cambridge, 1969).

[10] C. K. Hyde, 'The Adoption of Coke Smelting by the British Iron Industry, 1709–1790', *Explorations in Economic History*, x (1973).

about the adoption, or absence of adoption, of such innovations.[11] If the relative prices of labour (in different grades, skill for skill), capital and materials were very different from what they were in the region where these devices were developed and adopted, then strict economic rationality of maximizing returns from a 'minimum cost' mix of inputs might have dictated that they be not adopted. There can be a sharp contrast (as we are still forcibly reminded from time to time) between the most technically advanced methods and the most commercially effective and most economic arrangements. There would have been, in the areas of these economies subject to market pressures and where changing price levels acted meaningfully as signals for action, a lower incentive to move along a production function substituting expensive capital equipment for labour, or adopting devices making large demands on scarce resources (whether skills or materials); and, doubtless, less commercial incentive also for wider reasons to move to new combinations of factors through technical progress and new innovation. Technical and economic criteria merge in such an analysis. The costs of getting the exactly suitable fuel, or the precise grade of labour required to maintain and operate new machines, for example, could prove too high, although expressed in terms of local shortages of suitable resources or suitable skills. These problems of relative shortages and differential factor prices are not to be conceived as offering an infinity of choices smoothly phased over a spectrum from highly capitalistic to highly labour-intensive techniques. Shortages of particular kinds of skills and particular sorts of material can be, in practical terms, absolute: differentiation in price would not reflect the degree of shortage, save that no supply would be forthcoming in the short-term at any price. In much technology the choice is set by such barriers. And for many techniques, particularly those involving new products, there is, in practice, not much choice; in others new techniques are so superior on all counts, in saving labour and capital and in the quality of product relative to price, that they offer no graduated choice according to differential prices of inputs.[12]

Technical problems of diffusing skills and technology still apply,

---

[11] For the best survey of recent theory and applications see *The Economics of Technical Change*, ed. N. Rosenberg (Harmondsworth, 1971), with bibliography. Major individual studies are: E. Mansfield, *The Economics of Technical Change* (New York, 1968); Salter, *Productivity and Technical Change*; J. Schmookler, *Invention and Economic Growth* (Cambridge, Mass., 1966); E. M. Rogers, *The Diffusion of Innovations* (New York, 1962); *The Rate and Direction of Inventive Activity*, ed. R. R. Nelson (N.B.E.R., Princeton, 1962).

[12] S. B. Saul, 'The Nature and Diffusion of Technology', in *Economic Development in the Long Run* ed. A. J. Youngson. (London), 1972, ch. 3.

particularly in situations where economic incentives are not of major relevance, or in the enclaves of technology where the imperatives for diffusion do not depend directly upon criteria of profitability —as in militarily useful technology, or other technology sought by the public sector, not subject to cost-effective decision making. Mechanisms for the diffusion of skills and the ways in which the production of skills have been institutionalised at the very least also affect the length of the time-lags involved in the diffusion process; and here, as in so many other fields, there is no clear-cut division between the short and the longer run. Economic history, like any other sort of history, is essentially concerned with time lags. Technical problems and skills have so often been assumed as a dependent variable in theoretical formulations about processes of economic development, but theoretically any other single constraint can be wished away from the analysis as a 'dependent' variable on the argument that if demand, or capital, or resources are there then the skills will surely follow. Questions of technical change and the diffusion of new techniques were (and are) much more complex than the application of neo-classical models and the logic of relative factor prices might suggest.[13] In the continental economies the reception-points for new technology and development were often outside the market-sector, as they are in much of the world in our own day, either formally within the state sector, where prices do not have a direct significance in market terms, or sheltered from market forces in the private sector.[14] It is for this reason, amongst others, that the *technical* problems of the diffusion of new technology can be considered meaningfully outside strictly commercial criteria of relative prices, costs and profits, determined in a competitive market with freely moving prices.

Continental governments made systematic efforts to promote technical change, new industrial skills and modernized technology into their countries.[15] Encouragement came partly from tariff walls or physical restrictions on competing imports, behind which monopolies could flourish undisturbed. There were royal monopolies,

---

[13] See below pp. 109–11.

[14] As Arthur Young commented wryly on the lack of progress in completing the Canal du Charolais: '. . . it is a truly useful undertaking and therefore left undone; had it been for boring cannon, or coppering men of war, it would have been finished long ago.' *Travels in France during the Years 1787, 1788 and 1789 by Arthur Young*, ed. C. Maxwell (Cambridge, 1950), p. 199.

[15] See, for example: S. T. McCloy, *Government Assistance in Eighteenth Century France* (Durham, N.C., 1946); W. O. Henderson, *The State and the Industrial Revolution in Prussia, 1740–1870* (Liverpool, 1958); W. Fischer, 'Government Activity and Industrialisation in Germany (1815–70)' in *The Economics of Take-off into Sustained Growth*, ed. W. W. Rostow (1963); W. Fischer, *Der Staat und die Anfänge der Industrialisierung in Baden, 1800–1850*, i (Berlin, 1962).

directly promoted state arsenals, shipyards, gun-foundries, manu-factories, some with research laboratories and scientists in atten-dance. Most continental governments had established departments of state which were virtually ministries of industrial progress deploying a whole range of economic policy weaponry: public subsidies and direct financing of investment; purchasing by the public sector focussed upon the publicly favoured plants or the state monopoly at lavish prices; public finance to attract entre-preneurs and workmen possessing new and scarce skills from other lands with fancy offers of reward in monopolies, guaranteed profits, high wages and other benefits in kind; ambassadors mobilized as recruiting agents. Jean Rulière, the French entrepreneur in Spain, had the foresight to negotiate with the King in advance: noble status, a very large salary, free house and living expenses, all travel costs for his family, an assured pension and a fixed percentage of the profits of the mill. The latter provision alone proved superfluous. Such state promotional agencies and inspectorates employed some of the most distinguished scientists and publicists of the new tech-nology on their payrolls—as Réamur, Gabriel Jars, Chaptal and Faujas de St Fond in France. Academies of Science had obligations to apply scientific knowledge to the advance of technique. There was nothing in England like the *Seehandlung* of Prussia, the Corps des Ponts et Chaussées (from which came the Ecole Polytechnique in 1795), the Ecole des Mines, the Conservatoire des Arts et Métiers, or the royal factories in the public sector of France. Institutionally, by public endeavour and by aspiration, all was orchestrated to the grand design of promoting new industrial techniques in these lands; more particularly because governments were conscious that ranges of new techniques were being developed more progressively elsewhere and that normal commercial processes did *not* produce sufficient incentives for their diffusion.

Such policies of direct and indirect state promotion for the attraction of new technologies had certain counter-productive effects, quite apart from the more general inhibitions to economic development associated with *ancien régime* political and social systems. Skills and capital were lavished upon luxury industries, such as fine cloths, silks, tapestries, porcelain, clocks, mirrors and plate glass and the like; or upon specialised military purposes. 'Spin-offs' could come from both; but cost-effectiveness featured in neither group. New technologies associated with immigrant skills and state promotion tended to become locked away from the rest of the economy in special enclaves of high cost. Inefficient administration, functional efficiency sacrificed to the dictates of patronage, great wastage of resources, characterized most of these operations.

Sometimes (as in Spain) they were deliberately sited in backward regions, unsuited for commercial success. High import tariffs on raw materials and capital goods, to encourage local production and investment in these branches of enterprise, forced high costs and uncertain supply upon private entrepreneurs using these products as inputs for their own enterprises, and prejudiced their own commercial efficiency. There is, however, a partial defence in that such establishments should not be judged as commercially efficient businesses but as training grounds for the diffusion of new skills: foreign artisans as part of their contracts accepted the obligation of teaching a regular number of local people their skills.

II

Institutions and processes for diffusing formal knowledge and scientific ideas in western Europe and North America in the seventeenth and eighteenth centuries were remarkably effective. In Nassau Senior's phrase, transfers of 'mental capital' were most easily effected.[16] Communications amongst the geographically dispersed elite of interested, largely leisured, groups were very active; by visits, publications of proceedings and transactions, astonishingly assiduous correspondence amongst members of academies and their secretaries through the *linguae francae* of French, English and Latin, supported by a lively European trade in important scientific books. The correspondence of Henry Oldenburg, first Secretary of the Royal Society, exemplifies this.[17] Sometimes small local societies in England had, like the Royal Society, 'corresponding members' and secretaries to maintain links with others— precisely to ensure the international diffusion of ideas. Encyclopaedias, periodicals such as the *Monthly Magazine* and *Gentleman's Magazine* in England, translated simplified versions of ideas and experiments from the professional literature of the Academies, like the *Philosophical Transactions*, in a transmission belt to a wider educated if unprofessional public. The republic of science was truly international at this time; possibly more so even than today, if only because of the much lesser degree of specialization in scientific subjects, institutions, and literature in the eighteenth century, with the much smaller number of persons engaged. The paradox concerning obstacles to the rapid transfer of new technology is therefore heightened, if formal scientific knowledge is considered the

[16] N. Senior, *An Outline of the Science of Political Economy* (London, 1836), pp. 193–4. I owe this reference to Miss M. Berg.
[17] *The Correspondence of Henry Oldenburg*, ed. A. R. Hall and M. B. Hall (Madison, Wisc., 1965–73).

crucial carrier of the innovations, as a necessary and sufficient condition.

Equally, at a more empirical level, the operative means of diffusing formal knowledge of the new technology were becoming extant in 'blue-prints' (in the form of detailed engravings) and models of machines, with detailed printed specifications and plans in patents. By the beginning of the nineteenth century leading British engineers commonly registered patents in France as well as England (to prevent pirating of the specifications available for inspection in London, in the absence of any international code of protection), thus describing their projects exactly and in detail for overseas consumption. British patents were available for an international audience, if interested. Of course it was more difficult to provide formal knowledge about new processes than new devices. These patents became more important as sources of exact formal knowledge about technology during the second half of the eighteenth century. In the mid-century many patent specifications were equivocal, relating to quite unpractical devices or drawn in terms which were difficult, if impossible to understand. The motivations for taking out such unoperational patents lay in the wish to stake out claims over an indeterminate field which might frighten rivals away, or even to snare unfortunate competitors into the coils of legal actions based upon the uncertain formulations. But, as patent law changed and 'case-law' in patents developed, the 'professional-ization' of patent registrations in the hands of specialized attorneys meant that descriptions had become much more specific by the end of the century, and needed to be if they were to stand a chance of being upheld in the courts.[18] A patent system invites more detailed discussion about its effects on the diffusion of techniques; but the relevant point here is to note that the existence of patent registrations added one more mechanism to the means of diffusing formal knowledge about new techniques.

Very extensive visiting by foreigners (scientifically literate and technologically aware visitors) took place to British workshops, mines and industrial plants, even if they were not allowed to see certain secret processes in places such as the Carron iron foundry.[19] Many such visits were officially sponsored. Technical encyclopaedias

[18] A critical investigation into the economic and financial implications of the patent system in the eighteenth century is still awaited. See K. Boehm, *The British Patent System*, i (Cambridge, 1967), ch. 2; E. Roll, *An Early Experiment in Industrial Organisation* (London, 1930), App. vi; E. Robinson, 'James Watt and the Law of Patents', *Technology and Culture*, xiii (1972).

[19] For example: G. Jars, *Voyages Métallurgiques* (3 vols., Paris, 1781; F. de St Fond, *Voyages en Angleterre . . .* (Paris, 1797); W. O. Henderson, *J. C. Fischer and his Diary of Industrial England, 1814–51* (1966); J. Chevalier, 'La Mission de

and dictionaries giving details, engravings and descriptions of machines had an international sale. Much purchasing of individual machines went on, again often officially conducted. Formal knowledge of technology was thus transferable, as formal knowledge of science, but the operational problems of diffusing the effective operation of innovations did not, it seems, lie principally at this level—that is, within the range of formally acquirable knowledge and ideas at all.

It is remarkable how quickly formal knowledge of 'dramatic' instances of new technology, in particular steam engines, was diffused, and how quickly individual examples of 'best-practice' technology in 'show piece' innovations were exported. The blockage lay in the effective spread of technical change more widely— diffused average technology rather than single instances of best-practice technology in 'dramatic' well-publicized machines. To take Newcomen engines as an example. The first commercially operating Newcomen engine was erected at Dudley Castle, in Worcester, in 1712. There were reports of a Newcomen engine at Konisberg in Hungary in 1721-2; at Passy, on the outskirts of Paris in 1726. The first were installed to pump out mines, the Passy engine for supplying Paris with water. By 1729 individual engines were in use in Belgium, France, Hungary, Austria and Sweden. In 1732, two engines were reputedly made in Hungary by Fischer Van Erlach (superintendent of the Royal Mines). An accurate engraving of a Newcomen engine dates from 1717; there were accurate designs published in a quite obscure German journal in 1727, and also in France in 1735. The first known international licensing agreement, with English down the right-hand side of the page and a German translation down the left-hand side, giving a local power of attorney in Hungary by Isaac Potter, the English erector of the engine, dates from 1730.[20] All these engines were erected and adjusted by English mechanics sent out from the workshops where they were made; and they had a very brief working life, most of them working only spasmodically during that formal existence.

Within the fields of large-scale iron working, machine construction, steam-engine manufacture, later machine tools and associated

Gabriel Jars dans les Mines et les usines Britanniques en 1764', *Trans. of Newcomen Soc.*, xxvi (1947–49); M. W. Flinn, 'The travel diaries of Swedish engineers of the eighteenth century as sources of technological history', *ibid.*, xxxi (1957–59); W. O. Henderson, *Industrial Britain under the Regency* (London, 1968).

[20] I am grateful to Dr M. Teich for this information. See M. Teich, 'Diffusion of Steam, Water and Air Power to and from Slovakia during the Eighteenth Century and the Problem of the Industrial Revolution', in *L'Acquisition des Techniques par les pays non-initiateurs* (note 6 above).

skills the story for the rest of the century was much the same: almost all such initial transfers involved English fitters and mechanics, if not English entrepreneurs. The sources already cited contain a very long list of instances which space does not allow to be elaborated here.[21] The implications of this veritably commonplace and universally acknowledged fact—that transfers of new technology initially always involved the movement of the artisans, in whom these skills were embodied, and capable entrepreneurs (also having such skills in addition to business capabilities)—have not fully been drawn in general discussions about the sources of technical change in the Industrial Revolution. The rest of this article seeks to investigate certain aspects of the matter. From the processes and difficulties involved we can learn much about the advance in techniques during these first phases of industrialization. From the struggles to indigenize this technology elsewhere we can gain insights into the context which favoured the development of these skills and techniques in Britain.[22] It is not to say, of course, that the skills discussed in this paper were the sole requirements for invention and innovation. But invention and successful innovation in new technology had to be translated into action through such skills, which remain a conditioning factor in their success or failure.

III

The critical technical blockage to attempted diffusion is probably not to be explained in terms of effective legal prohibitions at the British end. By the end of the eighteenth century, a battery of statutes had consolidated against the export of certain pieces of technology (particularly textile machinery) and the emigration of certain skilled artisans. Some such prohibitions had a paradoxical effect, as so often. For example, when the export of rolled copper was prohibited in 1779, to deny England's continental enemies the only main source of sheathing for naval vessels, this at once stimu-

[21] Casual observations are scattered through many travellers' diaries, Arthur Young offering a particularly interesting contemporary account of such immigrant enterprise in France in 1787–89. For example: (at Nantes) '. . . to view the establishment of Mr Wilkinson, for boring cannon . . . Until that well-known English manufacturer arrived, the French knew nothing of the art of casting cannon solid, and then boring them.'; (at Louviers) 'View the cotton mill here, which is the most considerable to be found in France . . . It is conducted by 4 Englishmen from some of Mr Arkwright's mills. Near this town also is a great fabric of copper plates, for bottoming the King's ships, the whole an English colony.' *Travels in France*, pp. 117, 310; and 119.

[22] For a brief discussion see P. Mathias, *The First Industrial Nation* (London, 1969), pp. 134–44.

lated the export of rolling equipment, and exposed the problems of technological interrelatedness in such specialized heavy engineering equipment that was experienced with the Newcomen engines.[23] Prohibitions on the export of capital equipment stimulated greater efforts to entice entrepreneurs and artisans abroad to establish local plants. There are, however, many reasons for doubting the effectiveness of these prohibitions.[24] In the Parliamentary enquiries considering their abolition in 1824 and 1841–3 much was made, sometimes tendentiously, of their weaknesses. Artisans, in fact, emigrated very frequently, even in war-time to enemy countries. Prohibited machines could be sent abroad as component parts without much difficulty. Prohibitions did not apply to plans or models, or to general ranges of castings which might be used eventually to make up into machinery. Smuggling was said to be easy because of the lack of expertise amongst customs inspectors. More particularly, some new inventions of the late eighteenth century, unmentioned in the general schedules of mainly textile machines, were not covered by the statutes, amongst the more important of which were the steam engine itself and various machine tools, such as pre-set lathes, etc.

The contract for the sale of Boulton and Watt's famous first engine to France was made on 12 February 1779 at the height of the American War of Independence.[25] Boulton and Watt had been granted a fifteen-year monopoly by the Council of State in France for making and selling their improved engines in the kingdom, and they pronounced in the contract that they were 'desirous of establishing the use of their fire engines in France'. The contract involved, as was usual, not only the sale of the machine, but transfers of 'plans, sections and drawings', supplies of necessary collateral equipment, such as piping, and, in practice, fitters to assemble, adjust and maintain the engine. Significantly the brothers Perier also wanted English files and what we should now call 'special steels'— hardened steel for metal-cutting, *'principalement de celui qui réussit le mieux pour tourner les métaux'*—all these being related aspects of the new technology of large-scale, precision metal-working where the technological gap between the two countries was at its widest. No insuperable difficulty seems to have been experienced in getting the engines to France, either in obtaining the requisite documents for

[23] W. H. B. Court, *The Rise of the Midland Industries, 1600–1838* (Oxford, 1938), pp. 241–43; J. R. Harris, 'Copper and Shipping in the Eighteenth Century', *Econ. Hist. Rev.*, xix (1966).

[24] T. S. Ashton, *Iron and Steel in the Industrial Revolution* (2nd edn., Manchester 1951), pp. 200–5; A. E. Musson, 'The Manchester School and the Exportation of Machinery', *Business History*, xv (1972).

[25] J. Payen, *Capital et machine à vapeur au XVIIIe siècle* (Paris, 1964).

export and import or in making arrangements for the ship. There were bureaucratic delays, tedious technical problems about insurancing, even the suggestion that they might need to organize a neutral vessel from Ostend; but in the end transporting the machines to France during the war was much speedier than getting the remittance from Paris in peace-time, five years later, with the Perier firm dependent upon official subsidies.

The whole tenor of Boulton and Watt's relations with overseas operations emphasizes the equivocal character of the legal restrictions officially governing the exports of new technology.[26] In some ways the firm sought to use the existing laws to enforce restraint in their own interests; they tried to bring what action they could against foreign entrepreneurs whom they thought might be taking pirated cylinders of other parts from John Wilkinson and others; they energetically pursued their erstwhile fitters who went abroad to a lucrative official monopoly on their patented inventions (or even just as commercial rivals). They were hypersensitive to reports of foreigners visiting Birmingham to inspect industrial establishments or to seduce artisans into emigrating. They sought to prevent such skills being exported, but only where this was against their own direct business interests, conceived in the interests of their firm, rather than industry as a whole or the national interest. More generally, as the manufacturers of capital goods, they eagerly sought export orders for themselves and were willing to adopt all necessary means to establish such an export of the new technology—entertaining potential customers at their works, taking monopolies overseas, giving long credits, lowering their terms for initial orders in the interests of the long-term advantages which the demonstration of the new devices in foreign countries might yield, sending over fitters to assemble and look after the machines and train their operators. They stood ready to supply the whole package of supporting skills and technology as required. Where Boulton and Watt led, William Wilkinson, Aaron Manby, John Cockerill and his son, and a steady trickle of other British engineers followed.

Thus, already by the end of the eighteenth century, a commercial interest had become established in the British economy developing an impetus of its own for the diffusing overseas of the crucial new technology—a 'push effect' supplementing the many officially sponsored 'pull effects' for importing such desirable new skills in other lands. When the engineering industry and the machine-

---

[26] E. Robinson, 'The International Exchange of Men and Machines 1750–1800', *Business History*, i (1958), reprinted Musson and Robinson, *Science and Technology in the Industrial Revolution*, ch. vi.

makers, the capital goods suppliers, emerge as independent firms, identifying a specific commercial interest in selling capital goods to other manufacturers, and claim export markets for themselves a new impetus is added to the process of diffusing technology; and a force begins to operate against the older tradition of official restraints against letting foreigners acquire such secrets on the grounds that products made by them would undercut exports of manuactured final-products.

IV

Where were the critical *technical* blockages holding back the spread of the new innovations, when so much effort was focussed upon their diffusion? It seems to have been at the level of what can be called 'artisan technology' where 'learning by doing' was all important, but not artisan technology in such traditional skills as handicraft textiles, carpentry, mill-wright and blacksmith skills, which were widespread across Europe, but in a narrow range of more specialized expertise which ruled the passage into the new world of iron machinery, mineral fuel technology, power technology. It lay in engineering rather than in science. In particular, precision metal-working on the scale necessary for large machines and the metal fabricating required for this was crucial; and this involved very hard steels, for files, etc., eventually machine tools, cutting edges for shaping metals, the means of establishing plane surfaces, exact joints for pipes, valves, cylinders, pistons and bearings at the precision end of the scale and cheap mass-produced iron for constructional uses, castings, etc. at the 'bulk' end of the scale. Skills for exact fashioning of small metal objects were traditional and wide-spread in Germany, France and elsewhere. Exact working of large objects in iron proved a main blockage—cylinders, crankshafts, and piping, for large-scale power technology and iron machinery. The problems of scale changed the *nature* of the operations and not just their *degree* of difficulty, quickly invoking special tools for boring, planing, turning and cutting; special materials in hard steels, with special skills, in an interrelated group. A later example showed this interrelatedness at the frontier of technology when James Nasmyth developed the steam-hammer as a precondition for forging the crankshaft of the paddle-drive for the *Great Britain*, a steamship of unprecedented size.[27] These formed a crucial, if narrow, zone on the frontiers of advance of the new technology, as clearly a precondition for progress in the late eighteenth century as new

[27] *James Nasmyth Engineer: an Autobiography*, ed. S. Smiles (London, 1883), ch. xiii.

metals or carbon fibres are for aeronautics in our own day; or solid-state physics for electronics. The blockage may be on a narrow front, but failure to overcome it can hold up innovations and development in a widening arc of activity behind it. Hewing coal was done by pick and shovel, in traditional medieval technology, but the extension of output, as mines got deeper in the main English coalfield, depended increasingly on steam pumps. This was not just a matter of factor prices—that coal was cheaper in England than elsewhere in eighteenth-century Europe—but a matter of developing skills integral with resources. The period of strategic advance, as Professor J. R. Harris and others have argued, may well have been 1660–1720, when all metals except iron swung onto mineral fuel and such industries as glass and pottery were set within the new matrix of a coal-fuel technology.

Scientific or formal knowledge at a certain abstract level, was not, it seems, the crucial mode of knowledge for these skills and their transference. Artisan technology and skills, even simple traditional skills, were not very amenable to literary descriptions or to instruction books (as anyone can discover by trying to build a stone wall or make a water-tight barrel). 'Knack', 'know-how'—all that is summed up in the modern phrase 'learning by doing'—lie behind this. Professor Harris stresses this point with 'coal fuel technology'.[28] Very subtle adjustments have to be made according to individual variations in the quality of materials, which governs all processes and the making of all objects. Different grades of raw materials and fuels demanded slightly different management or mixtures of fluxes in furnaces.[29] Even methods of stoking had to be different, as well as the design of the furnaces and chimney. Coal and iron are very far from being homogenous commodities. Before precision machine tools everything was 'one-off', save in crude castings and for some very specialized manufacturing processes such as watch components, where mini-machine tools such as pre-set lathes, screw-cutting lathes, fusee lathes, were already giving greater precision by the mid-eighteenth century. Thus all rested upon the individual skills of the artisan, given the better materials and therefore tools available. It is difficult to realize how scarce these specialized skills were in the late eighteenth century; how few the centres where precision metalwork in iron on a large scale could be

[28] Professor J. R. Harris is extending his enquiries into this field, the first results being reported in his inaugural lecture, *Industry and Technology in the Eighteenth-Century: Britain and France* (Birmingham, 1971).

[29] Some of these intricacies can be inferred from the diary of an informed visitor: *The Hatchett Diary: a Tour through . . . England and Scotland in 1796 visiting their Mines and Manufactories*, ed. A. Raistrick (Truro, 1967), pp. 35–36, 50–51, 58–59, 74–76.

conducted and could be learned; how limited the institutional means of acquiring such skills. The equivalent scarcities today would lie in coping with such problems as designing the operating parts of a nuclear power station or a linear accelerator or putting out a large fire at an oil well. This was a world without mechanics institutes or technical schools, without large apprenticeship schools in such businesses as railway workshops or large engineering works producing their own supply of skilled fitters. In the late eighteenth century the centres were few and small: Boulton and Watt above all, Maudslay's workshop in London, Woolwich arsenal, a few others. The only way of getting training therefore was to work in these very few specialized workshops for some years if they would take you on.

The profile or pyramid of skills in this eighteenth-century context had very steeply sloping sides, with a sharply pointed apex. Below the very few centres of top skills, the next echelons were much inferior. This is often a characteristic of an underdeveloped country —an acute shortage of special skills in its modernized sector— whereas the pyramid of skills in an advanced economy has sides with a very shallow slope and a wide plateau at its top. For every top man, or ten men, there are ten almost as good, for each of them a hundred almost as good. Where skills are scarce, dependence on the single person, or the small group, can be extreme. Pinch off a few at the top and the whole technology embodied in their skills could be at risk. Loss of the skilled artisans was crucial to a firm or a process, as Boulton and Watt knew well when seeking to prevent their own fitters from emigrating. Conversely the only way to transfer new technology was to attract the skilled artisans overseas. Virtually all recorded instances of transfer of new equipment, the invariable mechanism of diffusion, involved the emigration of skilled artisans and fitters. It was not just a question of erecting and adjusting the machine but staying to operate, maintain and repair it. The position in France, Petersburg, Sweden, Prussia, Bohemia, Hungary, Spain, in these new skills exemplifies this sort of dependence—for machine-building, power technology, producing things like calendering machines, roller-printing machines, copper sheathing rollers and sheathing nails for ships.

Where technology was so specifically embodied in the persons of the skilled artisans many of the problems of diffusing skills centred upon the difficulties of their settlement in alien lands. Of necessity they formed very high-cost, privileged groups as a condition of their emigration. Not infrequently they were feckless people, leaving their own countries for dubious motives and succumbing to the delights of drink and other distractions in their new-found prosperity. Social acclimatisation proved difficult outside major commercial centres because, as privileged aliens, they attracted local hostility, the enmity of guilds and the like. The process of settling foreign artisans generally proved much more difficult than attracting them in the first instance.[30]

V

Analogies with twentieth-century experience are legion; and much recent literature on the problems of transferring modern technology at this level from advanced economies to developing countries reveals very similar diagnoses.[31] It can be argued, as Nathan Rosenberg has done, that three processes of diffusion of skills are involved. The first can be considered simply as international trade in finished products, which, in the case of consumer goods, does not invoke a very high level of skills. Next is the transfer of capital equipment for making these products, originally the subject of commodity trade. This requires skills of operating the new equipment, and also the surrounding administrative and commercial expertise in running the business, as well as the plant, effectively. But such skills directly involved in operating the equipment have to be supplemented with engineering skills of maintenance and repair, making spare parts and the like. This package is much bigger and involves much wider interrelatedness. Then comes the further package of adaptive and creative skills necessary if the imported technology is to be successfully adapted to local circumstances. Building-in technological creativity, indigenizing inventiveness, carries these adaptive skills to a higher order. This sequence (or attempted sequence) is certainly observable in many instances during the eighteenth and early nineteenth centuries in Europe.

[30] A typical individual comment is that of Arthur Young, when visiting the Wilkinson glass factory at Montcenis, in France: 'I conversed with an Englishman who works in the glass house, in the crystal branch. He complained of the country, saying there was nothing good in it but wine and brandy; of which things I question not but he makes a sufficient use.' *Travels in France*, pp. 199–200. See also J. C. la Force, 'Technological Diffusion in the eighteenth century' (note 3 above).

[31] *The Transfer of Technology to Developing Countries*, ed. D. L. Spencer and A. Woroniak (New York, 1969); *Factors in the Transfer of Technology*, ed. W. H. Gruber and D. G. Marquis (Cambridge, Mass., 1969); G. Jones, *The Role of Science and Technology in Developing Countries* (London, 1971). The latter lists many relevant U.N. and U.N.E.S.C.O. Reports. I think it is still true to say that the problems of 'embodied' skills, and training in skills at this level, have been relatively neglected in shaping policies for economic development in less developed countries since 1945. Doubtless there is some connection between this neglect in contemporary development economics and policy and the fact that economic historians have largely taken developing skills for granted in their explanations of industrialization in Western Europe.

The introduction of the new devices invariably depended upon foreign entrepreneurs and artisans (foremen and steady, skilled men being as important as the entrepreneurs) and the attempts so often failed. New devices and processes were not transplanted for decades; when the single man or the small group left or died, the ventures so often collapsed. They did not progress as technology was growing in the originating country. So often there was an inability to maintain machines or repair them and replace them, even if local artisans had been successfully trained to operate them. Advanced capital equipment very often remained in this state of suspended animation, needing transfusions of skills from fitters sent from Soho or other British workshops, whenever it broke down. The important spare parts also had to be sent. Not accidentally, the successful cotton factory at Avila, established as a royal manu-factory of Spain in 1788 by two Englishmen, had a degree of vertical integration said to be unique in Europe. The plant had workshops for making the tools to make the machinery—even making its own scissors for shearing from special high-grade steel. The whole 'package' of technology and skills had to be 'internalized' within the enterprise.[32]

These symptoms are failures to 'indigenize' innovations and new technology in circumstances where the minimum critical level of demand was absent and also where there was very little institutional-izing of these processes and where 'artizan technology' was the crucial medium for carrying technical change. In particular the failure to import successfully a total 'package' of new technology illustrates how extensive was the 'interdependency' and 'inter-relatedness' of the new technology.[33] It proved quite impossible to hope to take an attractive bit of the new technology and slot it into a matrix of older technology. The techniques which were envied, and exported, were only the visible tip of a submerged mass of relationships. So often it proved impossible to transfer the desired devices successfully without carrying over a portmanteau of new techniques, materials, practices and skills upon which they depended —much more obscure, much less advertised, not localized neces-sarily in the same place or within the same groups as those who produced the final products.

Interdependence was far more widely structured than was usually apparent, as the lack of success in so many of these 'trans-plants' quickly showed. The interrelatedness tracked back from the

[32] J. C. la Force, 'Royal Textile factories in Spain' (note 3 above).

[33] The importance of interrelatedness (more widely considered) is stressed in M. Frankel, 'Obsolescence and Technical Change in a Maturing Economy', *American Econ. Rev.* xxxv, (1955).

final product, the machine, and the skills for operating it, to the nature of its manufacture, maintenance and repair, with the skills, materials and special tools for those auxilliary and prior functions. Particular demands might be made upon its raw materials and their preparation, or the local fuels; all dependent upon different strata of skills and inputs in a context where there were very little exact controls possible beyond those learned in an empirical way. And so many of these came back to mineral fuel technology, large-scale metal technology, and power technology—the new crucial matrix of materials, devices, processes and skills, which stood behind a seemingly discrete, even simple, artifact such as an exactly shaped large cylinder or valve or forged crankshaft, or a large sheet of copper; a casting with the necessary exactness of tolerance or a chemical with a required standard of purity. More generally, such interrelatedness reveals that the advance of technology was not just a Schumpeterian-style process, with major strides forward giving identifiable discontinuities in innovation, and entrepreneurs wrestling with the problems of making the new machines profitable by overcoming intractable workmen, organizing finance and discovering markets. At the back of this sequence lay a much less publicized, less dramatic world of a 'continuum' of piece-meal improvements meshed across a wide span of activities: in Nathan Rosenberg's words: 'a continuous stream of innumerable minor adjustments, modifications and adaptations by skilled personnel . . . the technical vitality of an economy employing a machine tech-nology is critically affected by its capacity to make these adapta-tions.'[34] The process of diffusion of technology thus involved, in eighteenth-century Europe as in twentieth-century transfers be-tween advanced and less developed economies, not just imitative functions but innovative functions. Adaptive, creative skills were required.

These comments raise the question of deliberate secrecy as a further constraint against the diffusion of new technology. Contem-porary literature has much to say about secrecy and what we would now term 'industrial espionage'. Industrialists certainly were hypersensitive about allowing visitors to see secret processes. Much of the delay in diffusing new techniques, such as the coke-smelting

[34] S. C. Gilfillan, *The Sociology of Invention* (Cambridge, Mass., 1970); N. Rosenberg, 'Economic Development and the Transfer of Technology: Some Historical Perspectives'; *Technology and Culture*, xi (1970); *id.*, The Diffusion of Technology', *Explorations in Econ. Hist.*, (1973); *id.*, 'The Direction of Technological Change: inducement Mechanisms and focussing devices', *Economic Development and Cultural Change* (1969); *id.*, 'Science, Technology and Economic Growth, *Econ. Journ.*, lxxxiv (1974). This article has been much influenced by Professor Rosenberg's work.

of iron, has been explained by such secrecy, and this tradition is counter-balanced by a 'heroic' view of the acquisition of secret processes from foreigners or rivals by patriotic artisans disguised as innocent visitors watching the process or smuggling out the device. The importance of much of this has to be discounted: the successful diffusion of technology was a more complex process than the individual transfers of secrets implied by these folk traditions.[35] A blend of less visible, more anonymous, undramatic reasons, which cannot be articulated so succinctly, becomes subsumed in a 'secrecy' explanation which is intellectually satisfying at a certain level of discourse, and may also have elements of the truth in it. Unprofitability is doubtless one of the most common explanations for the failure to diffuse an innovation: but there are other aspects of the secrecy issue which have relevance. The consequence of discounting the importance of formal knowledge as the main 'carrier' of innovations is to discount the 'secrecy' which was associated with formal knowledge as a constraint against diffusion: stopping visitors from seeing 'secret' devices and keeping descriptions and plans confidential. On the other hand preventing one's trained artisans, in whom these skills and learning-by-doing had become established, from moving to another employer or setting up in business elsewhere for themselves could be critically important. Attempts to prevent this, by long-term contracts, could not be legally enforced within Britain when a man was out of his apprenticeship; and the law against the emigration of skilled artisans was scarcely effective, as we have seen. However, the law was sound in intention, if skilled artisans were the key 'carriers' of the technology which their skills embodied; and it was no accident that prohibition of emigration was associated with the prohibition of the export of machinery, and that the questions of repeal were considered jointly in 1824 and 1841–43. Slowly accumulated empirical skills were not amenable to being identified, learned and carried away in a short visit, no matter how aware or experienced the visitor. The need to adapt materials, the design of plant, and the know-how of its operation, to the tricks of local circumstances also meant that creative and adaptive skills were required, not just those of observation and imitation. Even the detailed formal knowledge laid out in a patent specification would not be amenable to this sort of cumulative expertise.

Secrecy also had an important economic aspect, apart from the technical, which is less discussed. The first mode of secrecy is that of the actual process or device (or some critical part of it) remaining

[35] For a typical example in silk and steel see: W. H. Chaloner, *People and Industries* (London, 1963), pp. 12–13; S. Smiles, *Men of Invention and Industry* (London, 1884), pp. 112–13; id. *Industrial Biography* (London, 1886), pp. 107–9.

private knowledge. Its economic counterpart is that the costs involved in making a new process or device, in particular the degree of profitability, remain unknown. If costs and profitability are secret (and it may well prove much easier for an entrepreneur to keep them so than the technology itself), there may well be less incentive to diffusion than if both the economic and the technical aspects are known. Knowledge of the technicalities and the costs of new techniques are both relevant when assuming that information is a critical variable or necessary condition in the process of diffusion. Of course, with experiment, costs are eventually discoverable *ex post facto*, provided the necessary technical information exists to experiment with the innovation: the point is simply that *ex ante*, in the absence of such information, there may be less incentive to experiment.

The intricate links between such rising skills and the emergence of the capital goods industries, as specialized engineering firms emerged for the first time in the Industrial Revolution, are only now being given the general importance they deserve. For too long, in fact, the history of technology was separated from the more general analysis of economic development in the eighteenth and nineteenth centuries; pursued as the antiquarian study of actual techniques in their own right rather than viewed in relation to the dynamics of economic change as a whole.

All Souls College, Oxford.

ENGLAND AND EUROPE:
UTOPIA AND ITS AFTERMATH*

By D. B. Fenlon, M.A., Ph.D., F.R.Hist. S.

READ AT THE SOCIETY'S CONFERENCE
20 SEPTEMBER 1974

THE most celebrated product of the early English Renaissance was composed not in English but in Latin. It was conceived in Antwerp, completed in London, published in Louvain, and re-printed in Paris, Basle and Florence long before it was finally rendered into English, some sixteen years after its author had been executed. He was executed for refusing to adhere to the doctrine that the head of the Church was to be found in England, not in Europe.

More's *Utopia* is the solitary exception to the rule that England, in the first phase of her Renaissance, imported everything from Europe. The humanist traffic between towns, universities and courts was a two-way business, but the intellectual and artistic influence was one-way. England received her inspiration from the mainland of Renaissance Europe; she did not, in the early stages, make reciprocal returns. *Utopia* was the exception: England's best-seller in Renaissance Europe. Why?

Perhaps we may find a clue in the closing sentence of the book: 'there are very many features in the Utopian Commonwealth which it is easier for me to wish for . . . than to have any hope of seeing realized.'[1]

An unattainable world of social harmony, unravelled with a sustained irony which disclosed (to those in the know) its own fantastic unreality; scored in counterpoint to a dialogue which explored the entirely real miseries of the present world: until

---

* I am grateful to the editor of *Historical Studies*, ix (1974), for allowing me to substitute another article in place of an earlier version of this one, originally read as a paper to the ninth congress of Irish historians. Readers who may have searched in vain for an article by the present writer, entitled 'The Counter Reformation and the Realisation of *Utopia*', to which reference is made in my book *Heresy and Obedience in Tridentine Italy: Cardinal Pole and the Counter Reformation* (Cambridge, 1972), are informed that they need search no further.

[1] Thomas More, *Utopia*, ed. Edward Surtz, S. J., and J. H. Hexter, *The Yale Edition of the Complete Works of St Thomas More*, iv (New Haven and London, 1965), p. 247. Hereafter cited as *Utopia*.

fairly recently, this would probably account for *Utopia's* hold on the imagination both of its author and of its readers.[2]

In the course of our own century, *Utopia* has come to be invested with another significance; one which can scarcely have been envisaged by its author. Two contradictory interpretations of the work have arisen upon foundations of tacit agreement about one thing: that the historical bearings in terms of which the Utopian polity achieves its full significance lie to a considerable degree outside the period in which the book was written. Thus the case for the apparent modernity' of *Utopia* (originally prompted, as it seems, by Marx and Engels) has been consistently (and I think convincingly) challenged by the case for its dependence upon a tradition of writing developing from the middle ages and antiquity.[3] In each case, attention is directed away from the significance of the book at the time of its appearance.

I do not mean that nobody has enquired what *Utopia* may have meant in its own day. I merely mean that enquiry has not been carried far enough. Curiosity about the question seems to have become arrested at a certain point, and replaced by a preoccupation with the relation of *Utopia* to the past, or to the future. By one school of opinion, *Utopia* has been held to point towards a future realized only centuries after its inception. Another school has been concerned to demonstrate *Utopia's* literary affinities with a receding past, from which it is (sometimes) deemed to survey, as from a vantage point, the ominous descent into modernity. In the midst of these, occasionally embattled, alternatives, the significance of *Utopia* at the time of its publication has been taken, on the whole, for granted. *Utopia* is agreed to be a political satire.

The purpose of this paper is to suggest that *Utopia* is something more than that. The concern to trace its relation to a receding past, or a long-delayed future, has served, in my opinion, to distract attention from certain other questions no less worthy of attention. In particular, there seems to have occurred, within the existing modes of considering *Utopia*, an unwitting reduction in the scale of historical curiosity about what may have impelled More to write

---

[2] See the excellent analysis in R. S. Johnson, *More's Utopia: Ideal and Illusion* (New Haven and London, 1969).

[3] *The German Ideology*, ed. S. Ryazanskaya (London, 1965), p. 507; K. Kautsky, *Thomas More and his Utopia* (London, 1927); J. H. Hexter, *The Vision of Politics on the Eve of the Reformation* (New York and London, 1973). These interpretations find *Utopia's* full significance in its anticipation of modern conditions. Another view is to be found in R. W. Chambers, *Thomas More* (London, 1935); P. Albert Duhamel, 'Medievalism of More's *Utopia*', *Studies in Philology*, lii (1955), pp. 99–126; Edward Surtz, *The Praise of Wisdom* (Chicago, 1957), *The Praise of Pleasure* (Cambridge, Mass., 1957), and Introduction to *Utopia* (n.1 above), pp. cxxv–cxciv.

the book, and the nature of its appeal to the European reading public of its own day.

It may seem paradoxical to suggest as much, in the wake of Professor Hexter's celebrated Introduction to the Yale *Utopia*.[4] His exemplary reconstruction of the circumstances and preoccupations which surround the composition of the work has justly been greeted as a *tour de force* which must command the respect and gratitude of scholars.[5] Yet his argument that *Utopia* opens 'a window on the future' through which More arrived 'on the margins of modernity' with an egalitarian social theory anticipating the 'modern radicalism' of the late R. H. Tawney,[6] may give rise to the conclusion that what we have here (notwithstanding the historical sensitivity and contrary intentions of the author) is a generic variant of the Marxist view, which perceives in *Utopia* an orientation towards conditions finally realized with the advent of modern socialism.[7]

As between the 'medievalist' and 'modernist' readings of *Utopia*, my own preference lies distinctly with the former, as advanced by the scholarship of Chambers, Duhamel, Surtz and other writers. The fact remains that in recent years nobody has done more than Hexter to advance our understanding of the book in its contemporary setting. Yet one may reasonably suppose, without disrespect to those who have addressed themselves to questions of this kind, that neither the 'medievalist' nor 'modernist' line of investigation utterly exhausts the range of problems which surround *Utopia*. None of these scholars can be charged with holding the contrary; their attention has by no means been confined exclusively to such questions. Yet there remain certain problems which have been obscured or neglected. I cannot pretend that I am about to come forward with definitive solutions to these problems. I do not even suppose that they are the only problems which stand in need of more attention. My purpose is simply to venture a hypothesis about a number of questions which happen to have puzzled me. If my hypothesis should turn out to be incomplete or merely mistaken I shall not complain, since in that case it will have served to elicit a more satisfactory response to these questions, by better minds than mine.

Three questions present themselves for immediate consideration. What was the significance of *Utopia* for More himself? What was its

---

[4] n.1 above, pp. xv–cxxiv. Republished in extended form in *The Vision of Politics*, pp. 19–149.

[5] Quentin Skinner, 'More's *Utopia*', *Past and Present*, 38 (1967), pp. 153–68.

[6] *The Vision of Politics*, pp. 117, 119, 136–37.

[7] n.3 above.

significance for the European reading public which first received it? Was there a connection between the issues which it explored and the issues which helped, within a year of its appearance, to precipitate the Protestant Reformation? Each of these questions might be examined singly, and from a variety of perspectives. I propose in this paper to examine them together, for the light they may cast upon a final question: how are we to explain the transition from More's *Utopia* to his religious polemics?

Perhaps the best place to begin is with the publication of the book itself. The first edition appeared at Louvain at the end of 1516. There followed a Paris edition in 1517. Two editions came out at Basle in 1518. In 1519 the work was published at Florence.[8] Five editions, in four European cities, in a space of little more than two years: what was the particular attraction of *Utopia*?

The standard answer to this question is that *Utopia* is a political satire. It is a society so organized as to subvert property and rank. Property, according to the argument of *Utopia*, promotes pride, which in turn governs the institutions of a nominally Christian Europe. The Utopians have removed the roots of pride. Organized as a society where property is held in common, Utopia enjoys conditions favourable to the promotion of justice, piety and peace. Thus the wars, the avarice and the idleness of Europe's military aristocracy are mirrored adversely and satirized in the reflected virtues of Utopia.[9]

What this account justly conveys is the political immediacy of the work. What it omits is any explanation as to why More should have imagined a society founded upon a community of property and conduct; or why his readers should have found such a community (however ironically conceived) attractive. It is not enough to slip free with the observation that this community was deemed to exist Nowhere. That does not dispense us from enquiring: where did its author's disposition to imagine it proceed from? What answering chord was struck within the minds of those who read it?

I do not think that we shall be able to resolve these questions by appealing to Utopian 'social theory'; the supposed adumbration of a classless society; the unwitting arrival on the threshold of more recent times. We should do better, I think, to suppose that there is no social theory in *Utopia*, and to concentrate upon the fact that it remains a work of fiction.

But behind this fiction there existed a mind with personal preoccupations and a literary memory. What was the literature with which More was most familiar? The imaginary commonwealth

---

8 Surtz, Introduction to *Utopia* (n. 1 above), pp. clxxxiii–cxciv.
9 Hexter, *The Vision of Politics*, pp. 50–107.

of Plato's *Republic*; the two cities of St Augustine; the strictures of the Fathers of the Church against *meum et tuum* (their conception of property as the consequence of sin); not least, the natural law tradition of reflection on the virtues to be found in pagans: we know enough of *Utopia* and its author to be confident that these were not unfamiliar to More's mind.[10] Beyond these, there was the matter of his own personal experience: his experience on embassy; his experience as a lawyer; and his experience as a contemplative seeking an outlet in the world. My own opinion is that this last experience was the most formative of all, in that it preceded and entered into all the others. I should like, therefore, to direct attention to a neglected preoccupation in the life of More, and one which, I I believe, lies behind the composition of the book: a preoccupation shared by Erasmus and, as I happen to suspect, rather more extensively in the cities and city-states of Europe. If I am correct in isolating this preoccupation as one which possessed a peculiar historical momentum, then it may serve to throw into sharper relief those other features of the book which gained for it a repeated circulation throughout Europe in the years coinciding with the outbreak of the Reformation.

To return, then, to our original problem. Why did More imagine a society founded upon a community of property and conduct?

Fully to engage that question, I think we ought to revert to a period in More's life some ten or fifteen years before the composition of *Utopia*.

Between 1500 and 1505 More had three dominant preoccupations. In the first place, there was his career in law.[11] Secondly there was his scholarship: his study of Greek literature, philosophy and patristics—the same combination of interests which Erasmus was later to blend in the formulation of his *philosophia Christi*: that philosophy of public renewal which was to be proclaimed in 1516, the same year which saw the publication of *Utopia*. Finally, there was More's preoccupation with monastic or religious life. According to Roper, More spent a period of years in 'devotion and prayer in the Charterhouse of London, religiously living there without vow'.[12] Erasmus tells us that More as a young man thought of entering upon holy orders, but 'as he found he could not overcome his desire for a wife, he decided to be a chaste husband rather than a licentious

[10] *Utopia*, pp. clii, ff. (Introduction by Surtz) and Surtz's other work (above, n. 3).

[11] William Roper, *The Life of Sir Thomas More*, in *Two Early Tudor Lives*, ed. Richard S. Sylvester and Davis P. Harding (New Haven and London, 1962). Hereafter cited as Roper, *Life*.

[12] *Ibid.*, p. 198.

priest'.[13] Erasmus's account of the matter need not be taken at face value: More had probably weighed quite calmly the choice between consecrated celibacy and chaste marriage.[14]

In 1505 More married. His decision to do so seems to have carried with it a complementary decision to invest his life with practices usually thought of as appropriate to the monastic state, and which in the case of More we might suppose to have been derived from the London Charterhouse. Stapleton's remark that 'he lived almost the life of a monk' is not without its point.[15] We know from More's confessor that he was given to wearing a hair shirt.[16] We are told that he heard Mass every morning and recited the Seven Penitential Psalms and the Litanies.[17] As a family man he lived the life, not of an anchorite, but of one living in community. The domestic arrangements of his household, if we have a reliable account of them, illustrate the continuity of the monastic *motif* in his family: at table, the recitation of a passage from Scripture 'intoned in the ecclesiastical or monastic fashion'; at night, the gathering of his household for the recitation of Psalms and evening prayers; among his retainers, the curtailing of idleness and gossip and, as in *Utopia*, the elimination of dice and cards.[18]

The strictly disciplined regime of More's household might almost be seen as an attempt to transpose the monastic virtues into a domestic setting. In such a setting, everything—from the education of his children to the regulation of the domestic staff—proceeded in a communal frame and according to a devotional rhythm which punctuated and controlled the day's activities.[19] Erasmus described More's family and its educational routine. It prompted him to observe that Christians were to be discovered elsewhere than in monasteries.[20] Erasmus also arrived at a similar conclusion about

13 *Opus Epistolarum Des. Erasmi Roterodami*, ed. P. S. Allen and H. M. Allen, 12 vols (Oxford, 1906–58), IV, no. 999, p. 18. Hereafter cited as Allen.

14 I am grateful to Dr Paul Lawrence Rose and Professor Denys Hay for pointing this out to me.

15 Thomas Stapleton, *The Life and Illustrious Martyrdom of Sir Thomas More*, trans. Philip E. Hallett, ed. E. E. Reynolds (London, 1966), p. 62. Hereafter cited as Stapleton, *Life*. A hagiographical portrait from the Counter-Reformation, but its details of More's family life sufficiently coincide with the observations of Erasmus and others to make it seem reliable in this matter.

16 James Gairdner, 'A Letter Concerning Bishop Fisher and Sir Thomas More', *Eng. Hist. Rev.*, vii (1892), pp. 712–15.

17 Stapleton, *Life*, pp. 62–63.

18 *Ibid.*, pp. 88–89.

19 *Ibid.*, pp. 87–102.

20 'Ac talis Morus etiam in aula. Et postea sunt qui putent Christianos non inueniri nisi in monasteriis'. (Allen, iv, no. 999, p. 21). For More's recurrent preoccupation with monastic life, *cf.* Roper, *Life*, pp. 213 and 239.

cities: in the *Enchiridion* he proffered a comparision between a city and a large monastery.[21] Thus the city and the family might be seen, in the eyes of Erasmus, as fit centres for the realization of those virtues enshrined in the ideal of the monastery: prayer, work, community of property. Conversely, the monastery might be seen simply as one among a number of possible frameworks for the realization of the gospel precepts. '*Monachatus non est pietas*': monasticism, Erasmus concluded, was after all only one road to holiness.[22] This proposition, we may assume, held a particular attraction for Erasmus. For More, it held a fascination scarcely less acute. It was, I wish to argue, precisely this proposition which was explored by More when he came to write *Utopia*, where fifty-four city states live 'like a single family'[23] in a society of prayer, work and community of property. Finally, it seems to be the case that similar preoccupations concerning the monastic state and civic welfare, work and prayer, were by no means unique to Erasmus or to More. They were to be found among the laity and clergy in the cities and city-states of Europe, among the confraternities and humanist reforming groups, whose quasi-monastic features have repeatedly arrested the attention of historians.[24] Yet it has not always been allowed that we may look in this direction for an explanation of *Utopia* or its appeal.

Nevertheless, the possibility is worth ventilating. More's preoccupations found their way into *Utopia* and coincided with those of his readers. *Utopia* was concerned with civic poverty and social welfare. So were its readers.[25] *Utopia* was concerned with war and peace, power politics and Christian ethics. So were its readers: the world which gave rise to Machiavelli's *Prince* was the same world which gave rise to *Utopia*.[26] *Utopia*, finally, was the product of a mind which had pondered the tension between contemplative and active life: More was concerned to enquire whether the monastic virtues could be made to work outside the monastery. So, I would

---

[21] James Kelsey McConica, *English Humanists and Reformation Politics*, (Oxford, 1965), p. 41, comments on the affinity between the *Enchiridion* and *Utopia*.

[22] *Ibid.*, p. 22.

[23] *Utopia*, pp. 113, 149.

[24] B. Pullan, *Rich and Poor in Renaissance Venice* (Oxford, 1972); A. D.'Addario, *Aspetti della controriforma a Firenze* (Rome, 1972); A. Renaudet, *Préréforme et Humanisme à Paris pendant les premières guerres d'Italie* (Paris, 1916).

[25] N. Z. Davis, 'Poor relief, humanism and heresy—the case of Lyon', *Studies in Medieval and Renaissance History*, v (1968), pp. 217–75; R. Kingdon, 'Social Welfare in Calvin's Geneva', *American Historical Review*, lxxvi (1971), pp. 51–69; R. W. Henderson, 'Sixteenth century community benevolence: an attempt to re-sacralize the secular', *Church History*, xxxviii (1969), pp. 421–28; M. U. Chrisman, *Strasbourg and the Reform* (New Haven and London, 1967); and n. 24 above.

[26] Hexter, *The Vision of Politics*, pp. 204–30.

like to suggest, were a number of his readers. One recalls the humanist who remarked of Lyons in 1539 that since the poor had been so
cared for, the city had become 'compared to past times, almost a
true monastery and congregation of good brothers'.[27] The con-
ersion of monastic into lay forms of piety and the elevation of these
to a status of their own, was to be a feature of virtually every
religious movement of the sixteenth century.

As to the biographical point of connection between *Utopia* and
More's religious experience, the late R. W. Chambers put his
finger on it. He described More's household as a 'small, patriarchal
monastic Utopia'; and again, he noticed how *Utopia* referred back
'through More's own experience to the life of a Charterhouse
monk'[28] Chambers unfortunately did little to develop or connect
these insights, and one can only remark that he touched here just in
passing, upon a connection which may well do something to
illuminate more fully the immediacy of *Utopia* to the religious
concerns of Europeans in the years which witnessed its first impact
on the reading public.

It has sometimes been suggested that *Utopia* is based on a
monastic model.[29] The suggestion, however, has been submerged
under the weight of more recent interpretations of the work, which
perceive in *Utopia* a society organized as a patriarchal family.[30] It
seems a pity that these suggestions have been held to exclude each
other. In reality they reinforce each other. *Utopia* arises from an
imaginary fusion of More's family arrangements and his monastic
experience: the two combine to yield the perfect state—a commonwealth of cities.

The union of the monastery, the city and the patriarchal family
lies at the heart of the fiction animating the social arrangements of
Utopia. Seen in this light, Utopia becomes an urbanized extension
of More's household, which, together with the London Charterhouse, was the best model of a Christian society known to him.
Hythloday describes the island as *'uelut una familia'*.[31] The word
familia is not detached from its monastic overtones. The Utopians,
like monks, regulate everything in common: their dress (a garment
of undyed natural cloth); their meals (held at fixed hours in re-
fectories); their work (predominantly agricultural, from which no

[27] Davis, 'Poor relief, humanism and heresy', p. 269.
[28] *Thomas More*, p. 178, and pp. 136–37.
[29] *Ibid.*, and, most persuasively, by Duhamel (n. 3 above).
[30] Hexter, *The Vision of Politics*, pp. 40 ff; Skinner, More's' *Utopia*', p. 157.
Hexter, in the course of criticizing Chambers remarks upon the 'neglected theme
. . . of patriarchal familism' in *Utopia*. One feels that a certain credit is due to
Chambers, if only for neglecting his own insights.
[31] *Utopia*, p. 148.

one is exempt, with six hours of manual labour for all but a minority of scholars, ambassadors and priests).[32]

The combination of monastic and domestic arrangements leaves room for a variety of functions within the community. Worship in Utopia includes learning and scientific pursuits, but there are those who forsake scholarship in order to devote themselves to charitable works. Among these (whose concerns are strikingly reminiscent of More's uncertainties as a young man) a number remain celibate and are regarded as more holy, while others marry and are regarded as more prudent.[33] The Utopians are tolerant about the details of belief, as befits a virtuously heathen people; but as befits a society *en route* to Christianity, they are gradually coming to unite in one religion.[34] They have 'priests of extraordinary holiness, and therefore very few'.[35] These few, as in a monastery, regulate morality and excommunicate the reprobate.[36] They educate children and preside over divine worship.[37] The music of Utopian liturgy, as in monastic plain chant, 'represents the meaning by the form of the melody'; it 'penetrates and inflames the souls of those who hear it'.[38] On learning of Christianity, the Utopians are persuaded to embrace it not least because they find that a 'common way of life' had been practised by Christ's disciples, and that 'it is still in use among the truest societies of Christians'.[39] For More, 'the truest societies of Christians' were those which were either themselves monastic, or alternatively, those which, in the middle of the world, sought to apply monastic principles outside the monastery. It is not an accident that More, imagining himself entrusted with the government of Utopia, saw himself garbed in the habit of a Franciscan friar.[40]

The fusion of the monastic and the patriarchal family systems yields a society of city-states based on a community of property and conduct. The monastic rhythm of Utopian life derives its force from the fact that it pervades the collective life of the community, thereby involving everybody from the rulers to the ruled. Utopia is an imaginary projection into civic life of the virtues of the monastery and the well-ordered family. Hence the significance of its basic axiom: 'where nothing is private, men seriously concern themselves with public business'.[41]

[32] *Utopia*, pp. 127–35, and p. 141.

[33] *Ibid.*, p. 226.

[34] *Ibid.*, p. 217.

[35] *Ibid.*, p. 227.

[36] *Ibid.*, pp. 227–29.

[37] *Ibid.*

[38] *Ibid.*

[39] *Ibid.*, p. 219.

[40] Allen, ii, no. 499, p. 414. Trans. in *St Thomas More: Selected Letters*, ed. E. F. Rogers, (New Haven and London, 1961), p. 73. Hereafter cited as Rogers, *Selected Letters*.

[41] '*Hic ubi nihil priuati est, serio publicum negotium agunt*'. (*Utopia*, p. 238).

This axiom was serious; its impracticability made for satire. Much of the detail of *Utopia* is an elaborate satire within a satire: an exchange between the visionary if impractical Hythloday and his unimaginative interlocutors.[42] But the satire projects outwards with devasting effect, precisely because Utopia is not a Christian society. It is the best form of society imaginable without Christian revelation. More is using the virtues of a non-Christian society to make a point about the vices of a nominally Christian one. Thus through what Hythloday calls the 'very wise and very holy institutions' of Utopia[43] More provides a satirical counterworld to a society whose management of institutions he deems neither wise nor holy.

No doubt the dazzling impossibility of the Commonwealth devised in More's imagination, and the humorously astringent piety which prompted its conception, made *Utopia* an attractive fiction to Budé and Erasmus[44] and to their admirers in Louvain, Paris, Basle and Florence. No doubt it satisfied the Christian humanist *élite* to see their political masters cut down to size. No doubt *Utopia* crystallized something of their own heartfelt aspirations to a *Respublica Christiana* renewed in the spirit of the gospel, according to the maxims so recently enunciated in the *philosophia Christi*.

In that case, some of its readers may have been struck by the reflection that *Utopia* implied that such aspirations might be crystallized *only* in fiction: Nowhere, *Nusquama* (as More originally called the book).[45] *Utopia*, after all, advertised itself as fiction: an imaginative riposte to the contradictions which More found between the demands of Christianity and the political and social world in which he lived. It is the purely fictional character of the work which illustrates the significance of its appearance on the eve of the greatest religious crisis which Europe had experienced in centuries. More was exploring the possibility that Christianity and public life might have become mutually exclusive. The Dialogue of Counsel which introduced the book raised the question whether a philosopher had any place in politics: whether politics had any room for virtuous counsellors. The question remained deadlocked, unresolved on both sides, and was then transmuted into the Nowhere-world of Hythloday. More had arrived at the conclusion that a virtuous counsellor might get nowhere in the world of politics. The significance of that conclusion for More himself should not be considered in historical isolation from its implication for everybody else.

More, like Budé and Erasmus, was a Christian humanist. He

---

[42] Johnson, *More's Utopia*.   [43] *Utopia*, p. 103.
[44] *Ibid.*, pp. 2–15.
[45] Allen, ii, no. 461, p. 339; trans. in Rogers, *Selected Letters*, p. 73.

wanted to see society refashioned in the light of the pure theology drawn from the gospel. Yet by the time he came to write *Utopia* he was prepared to envisage the possibility that European society, at every level above the family, might pose an insuperable hindrance to that objective. What was happening in Italy was an example for all Europe: the city states were being devoured in the scramble of the Leviathans for property and power. What happened there might happen anywhere; all over Europe the lamps were going out, and the Leviathans were not notably susceptible to virtuous counsel.[46]

So much we can deduce from the text alone. But there is one further deduction to be drawn. In publishing *Utopia* More not only called into question the feasibility of extending his own principles as a Christian humanist into the field of politics; he also called into question the possibility of anybody else doing so.

The publication of *Utopia* in 1516 marks the abandonment, by one of the leading Christian humanists, of any firm confidence that the *philosophia Christi* could be invested with political or social content. *Utopia* explored the distinct possibility that Christian humanism might be forced into political insolvency. We should not be slow to appreciate the extent and significance of More's pessimism about the matter, less than a year before the outbreak of the Reformation.

More wrote *Utopia* because he was acutely aware that it was impossible to translate the monastic principle or the domestic principle into public life. Faced with the possibility of a contradiction between Christianity and political power, he pared down political circumstance until it reached the level of his family life, merging it with the communal features of the London Charterhouse.

Conversely, the publication of *Utopia* was an expression of the conviction that even the most perfect monastery or the most well regulated family was no substitute for a well-governed Christian public order. Its appearance signalized the political frailty of the Christian humanist aspiration to a godly society. It underlined the vulnerability attached to the ideals of men like Erasmus, Budé, Lefèvre d'Étaples, Briçonnet and Reuchlin, to mention only the most prominent among the Christian humanists. It envisaged the possible evacuation of Christianity from the political arena, and its relegation to the monastery, the family and the study—the last resting-place for even so public a gesture as a work of satire.

Yet More's mind did not rest in this conclusion. With one side of his mind he explored the possibility that Christian humanism might find itself politically crippled. With another side of his mind

[46] *Utopia*, pp. 86–94.

he allowed the possibility that it might yet succeed in exerting limited influence. This was what the Dialogue of Counsel was about. *Utopia* argued the impossibility of politics; it was a statement of the case against. The case for was argued no less forcefully in the Dialogue of Counsel: More and Hythloday argued each other to a halt. Having argued the matter, More then decided to act on that side of the dilemma which allowed room for limited initiatives: he went on to enter politics as the king's counsellor.[47]

In the first three years which witnessed the outbreak of the Reformation, *Utopia* was sent out like a signal and received in the studies of every major centre of humanist activity between Louvain and Florence. One does not have to suppose that its implications were necessarily seized upon by everyone who read it. But a book about the contradictions between civic poverty and wealth, Christian virtue and political aggression, a book about the infusion of monastic virtues into the body politic, was bound to strike a chord in the minds of those who read it: especially among the humanist readership of the European cities, where the problems of poor relief, power politics and monastic Christianity were highly topical.[48]

More himself was far from confident that *Utopia* would do much good, although he hoped that its cautionary tale would be assimilated by at least some people. He wanted the book to be approved by learned men who, like himself, had entered on the path of power with a view to effecting political improvement. Let them but understand the nature of the devil they were dealing with, then perhaps they might go about their business more effectively; and perhaps not. In a letter to Erasmus, More expressed the hope that *Utopia* might be well received by men like Tunstal, Busleiden and the Chancellor of Brabant, John le Sauvage: men who were personally known to him, statesmen and humanists such as (he now disclosed) he had envisaged ruling the Utopian Commonwealth.[49] But perhaps, as he put it to Erasmus, their approval might be 'more than I could wish for, since they are so fortunate as to be top ranking officials in their own governments'. To anyone familiar with the language of *Utopian* satire this is the familiar idiom of irony, denoting More's awareness that humanists were no more exempt than anybody else from finding power more agreeable than philosophy. Yet even if they retained their principles, they had to

[47] G. R. Elton, 'Thomas More, Councillor', in *Studies in Tudor and Stuart Politics and Government*', (Cambridge, 1974), i, pp. 129–54.

[48] Notes 23–25 above.

[49] More to Erasmus, 31 October 1516 (Allen, ii, no. 481, p. 372; Rogers, *Selected Letters*, pp. 80–81).

work with 'some high and mighty clowns as their equals, if not their superiors in authority and influence'. The influence of good and learned officials would be felt, according to More, only by a small number of people at the best.[50] He wanted the attention of such officials; but he was not sure that he would get it. Perhaps their 'present good fortune' (i.e., power) would cause them to dislike *Utopia*. In the end, More would be content if it won the approval of Erasmus. 'We two are a crowd', he wrote.[51] Perhaps it would be too much to hope for an audience.

At best, *Utopia* would address a small number of good and learned officials, arousing their consciences to the realities of power. At worst, it would be understood by just two people. The publication of *Utopia* in 1516 therefore held three implications for its author: first that the fundamental problem confronting the Christian Commonwealth was a problem which turned on the management of institutions; secondly, that humanist ideals, the concerns of the study, might have only the most slender leverage within those institutions; finally, that the monastery and the family, those visible patterns of a Christian community, might provide an exemplar, but were in themselves no substitute for a well ordered *Respublica Christiana*. *Utopia*, where the city, the monastery, the family and the study were conjoined, was an island. The opening words of the book declared: 'The ancients called me Utopia or Nowhere because of my isolation'.[52] The cities, the monasteries, the Christian households, the humanists and their books were stranded in *Utopia* upon an island. It was an imaginative expression of More's realization that his ideals might be perilously remote from the mainland world of power. The Utopian alphabet at the beginning of the book declares: 'Utopus, my ruler, made me from not being an island into an island'.[53] In writing the book More had come to terms with the possibility of isolation.

Since More's ideals were also those of the international humanist community, the significance of *Utopia*'s repeated publication in the first years of the Reformation may be taken as something more than a striking chronological coincidence. *Utopia* addressed a common sequence of social and political preoccupations; *Utopia* furthermore conveyed the sense that Christianity was imperilled; and this was a conviction that was beginning to assume a novel form in Europe's cities in the years between 1517 and 1520.

Utopia explored the tension between Christianity and public life from a vantage point not unfamiliar to readers of Erasmus: a vantage point chosen to consider the possibility of transferring the

[50] *Ibid.*
[51] *Ibid.*
[52] *Utopia*, p. 21.
[53] *Ibid.*, p. 18.

contemplative virtues into public circulation. We do not have to look to Erasmus alone to observe the striking ubiquity of this concern. It was to be found, in one variant or another, in circles where the influence of Erasmus was either irrelevant or auxiliary to the objectives of reformers: in Venice, within the circle of Gasparo Contarini and his monastic friends, Giustiniani and Quirini;[54] in Florence, among the latter-day adherents of Savonarola;[55] in Paris, among the friends and followers of Lefèvre d'Étaples;[56] throughout the cities of Europe among the confraternities and lay religious groups.[57] Yet it was Erasmus who was the most eloquent exponent of this ideal, and the same year which saw the publication of *Utopia* saw the appearance of his most famous formulation of it: the *philosophia Christi*.[58] It is worth recalling how Erasmus arrived at this statement about what Christianity might mean in civic life: how his concern was monastic before it entered the study and went public through the printing press. Erasmus's '*monachatus non est pietas*' was the verdict of a man who had spent six years in a monastery, and whose first work was a little volume entitled *De contemptu mundi*.[59] The monastic setting of his early contact with humanism[60] is amply informative about the genesis of that aspiration which bore fruit in the *philosophia Christi*, to establish through the printing press a means of engaging Christianity within society, beyond the confines of the cloister.

Utopia came close to pronouncing the inefficacy of that aspiration. The writings of Erasmus were subsidized by the wealthy and educated aristocracy of Church and Court; *Utopia* looked behind the *philosophia Christi* to its source of patronage and found it wanting. Erasmus appealed to an interior conversion of heart among the rulers of Church and Commonwealth in Europe;[61] *Utopia* explored the rapacity of rulers and the collusion of the Church in the 'con-

---

[54] J. B. Ross, 'Gasparo Contarini and his Friends', *Studies in the Renaissance*, xvii (1970), pp. 192–232; H. Jedin, *A History of the Council of Trent*, i (London, 1957), pp. 128–30, for the plan advanced by Giustiniani and Quirini for a root and branch reformation of the Church.

[55] D'Addario, *Aspetti della controriforma a Firenze*. It is worth noticing the influence of Florence on More's mind, through the medium of John Pico della Mirandola, whose *Life* he translated.

[56] Renaudet, *Préréforme et Humanisme à Paris*.

[57] Above, n. 24.

[58] Trans. in *Desiderius Erasmus: Christian Humanism and the Reformation, Selected Writings*, ed. John C. Olin (New York, 1965), pp. 92–106.

[59] R. R. Post, *The Modern Devotion* (Leiden, 1968), pp. 660–70; J. D. Tracy, *Erasmus—The Growth of a Mind* (Geneva, 1972), pp. 31–39.

[60] Allen, i, nos. 21–32, pp. 100–25.

[61] n. 58 above.

spiracy of the rich'.[62] 'Preachers', declares Hythloday, 'crafty men that they are', accommodate Christ's teachings to men's morals, 'as if it were a rule of soft lead'.[63] 'The Sovereign Pontiffs', we are told, with unmistakable irony, keep their promises and 'command all other rulers' to do the same, 'by pastoral censure and severe reproof'.[64] In other words, the activity of the popes is indistinguishable from that of other Renaissance princes. Philosopher statesmen might of course be found within the Church or among the laity: Tunstal, and probably Wolsey, featured in More's hopes as much as Busleiden or his lay associates. But philosopher statesmen were a lonely lot, and *Utopia* argued that the humanist reformers might find their proposals stuck fast on the printed page. It located their dilemma in the intractability of institutions.

It did so, moreover, in terms of a conviction which is perhaps too ubiquitous to be merely a coincidence. '*Monachatus non est pietas*': the conviction that monasticism was not the only road to holiness, looks remarkably like a common point of departure uniting figures so otherwise diverse as Erasmus, More, Contarini, Giustiniani, Quirini, Luther, Calvin and Loyola. The drive from a spirituality of retirement to a spirituality of involvement, the evangelization of the laity, and the sanctification of public life was to be the common objective of the reformations of the sixteenth century. They quarrelled, in this respect, from a starting point of agreement, and one from which *Utopia* surveyed the limited prospects for the improvement of the Christian Commonwealth by humanists.

Within months of the publication of *Utopia*, events were set in motion which altered the character of Europe's institutions. Luther went beyond any consideration of the monastery as an exemplar of Christian public life, to its repudiation, in the name of the gospel which it was designed to exemplify. He unlocked the monasteries and gave the priesthood to the laity. And in challenging the papacy on religious grounds he forced men to consider it on religious grounds. He therefore moved on from and transformed the dilemma which *Utopia* had explored, and he challenged the humanists to move either with him, or against him. In either case, they had to move.

In the course of what followed, a number of European cities, notably Zurich, Basle and Strasbourg, embarked upon the creation of miniature Christian Commonwealths under the aegis of the Protestant reforming humanists: Zwingli at Zurich; Oecolampadius

---

[62] *Utopia*, p. 241. [63] *Ibid.*, p. 101.
[64] *Ibid.*, p. 197.

at Basle; Bucer and his companions in Strasbourg.[65] Within a generation, Geneva and Rome had overtaken these experiments and emerged as the competing capitals of international movements which accorded to each capital the status of a holy city. Geneva and Rome ordered domestic and international politics in the light of a divine imperative, much as Savonarola's Florence, Zwingli's Zurich and Bucer's Strasbourg had attempted to order politics on an urban scale. Geneva and Rome thereby re-established an operational condition which More had considered all but extinguished when he wrote *Utopia*: the sanctification of urban and international politics.

It is in the light of these developments that we must assess the view advanced by Hexter, that 'the nearest men came in the sixteenth century to actualizing More's dream of a sober, disciplined commonwealth . . . was the Calvinist capital at Geneva'.[66] The argument rests on the perception that Geneva's ordinances with respect to dress, leisure, work, privacy, education and the enforcement of morals, bear striking comparison with those obtaining in More's 'best ordered commonwealth'.[67] The case is buttressed by the observation that Geneva provided opportunities for action to men of education and intelligence: the sort of learned readership to which *Utopia* had been addressed.

Geneva, of course, was not alone in its approximation to the conditions obtaining in More's 'best-ordered commonwealth'. It had its predecessors in Savonarola's Florence and in the Swiss and German city states. It had competitors in many monasteries and religious orders in the Catholic world, and in particular, in the Society of Jesus which placed its headquarters in the Rome of the Counter-Reformation, and made the evangelization of secular life its principal objective. It may be that, for many, Geneva provided the most conspicuous exemplar of a theocratic city, but there were others who found in Rome a scarcely less commanding centre of awe and inspiration.[68] If we allow, furthermore, that *Utopia* reflects a pre-existing drive to infuse monastic virtues within the body politic, then Calvin's Geneva and the Society of Jesus may be regarded as competing solutions to that ulterior dilemma.

The case for Geneva as the realization of *Utopia* is the case for

---

[65] B. Moeller, *Imperial Cities and the Reformation*, ed. and trans., H. C. Erik Midelfort and Mark U. Edwards (Philadelphia, 1972); A. G. Dickens, *The German Nation and Martin Luther* (London, 1974); Chrisman, *Strasbourg and the Reform*.

[66] *The Vision of Politics*, p. 111.

[67] *Ibid.*, pp. 107–17.

[68] *Cf.*, for example, Gregory Martin, *Roma Sancta (1581)*, ed. George Bruner Parks (Rome, 1969).

Calvinism originally propounded by Max Weber. Weber proposed a famous antithesis between the 'this worldly asceticism' animating Calvinist activity, and the 'other worldly', monastic asceticism animating medieval piety.[69] Calvinism, he wrote, accomplished 'the transformation of asceticism to activity within the world'.[70] In the Catholic middle ages asceticism had been monastic; in the modern world, Calvinism made it active.

Weber's insight needs to be considered in the light of the pre-existing impulse in the cities of Europe to make monastic virtues work outside the cloister; and in the light of Loyola's conspicuous success in providing a new meaning for the expression *ora et labora*.[71] The achievement of the Jesuits was to translate the motto of the monks beyond the monastery: prayer became a continuous presence within action; work and activity a continuous form of prayer.[72] The *ethic* of monastic communities such as the London Charterhouse, was scarcely different from that of the Genevan academy or the German College at Rome. They used the same language: *ora et labora; ad majorem Dei gloriam*.[73] What distinguished the Protestant and Catholic expressions of this ethic was the institutional setting within which it was brought to bear upon the world: the institutional setting, not so much of the State, but of the Church.

Here then, is the heart of my hypothesis: the urge to transform monastic virtues into virtues appropriate to the lay state, locates the appeal of *Utopia* within a common point of departure leading to the Reformation fashioned at Calvin's Geneva and the Counter Reformation in the Church of Rome. As a conjecture it seems to me to be at least worthy of inspection. Within the Catholic world the constitutions of the Society of Jesus might be thought of as marking a decisive stage in its evolution;[74] and it may even be possible to discern a climax in its development, with the appearance, in 1609, of St Francis de Sales's *Introduction to the Devout Life*. The preface to that highly influential little book declared:

---

[69] *The Protestant Ethic and the Spirit of Capitalism*, trans. Talcott Parsons (London, 1967), pp. 116–25.

[70] *Ibid.*, p. 120.

[71] *Cf.* the discussion by John Bossy in H. O. Evenett, *The Spirit of the Counter-Reformation*, ed. J. Bossy (Cambridge, 1968), pp. 126–32.

[72] *Ibid.*, p. 129 and n.1.

[73] Hexter finds in Beza's admonition to the students of the Genevan Academy to 'work for the glory of God' a 'perfect expression of the religious aspiration which the Utopian commonwealth reflected'. (*The Vision of Politics*, p. 111). It was also a perfect counterpart to the Jesuit ideal of living '*ad majorem Dei gloriam*'.

[74] *Monumenta Historica Societatis Jesu*, lxv: *Monumenta Ignatiana*, ser. 3, S. Ignati de Loyola Constitutiones Societatis Jesu, iii (Rome, 1938). D. Knowles, *From Pachomius to Ignatius: A study in the Constitutional History of the Religious Orders* (Oxford, 1966),

Almost all those who have hitherto written about devotion have been concerned with instructing persons wholly withdrawn from the world or have at least taught a kind of devotion that leads to such complete retirement. My purpose is to instruct those who live in towns, within families, or at court, and by their state of life are obliged to live an ordinary life as to outward appearances.[75]

The *Introduction to the Devout Life* was a remarkably serene expression of an ideal which presented itself as one of the main objectives of the Counter Reformation: the translation of interior prayer into external activity in the families, towns and courts of Europe, and the provision of alternatives to 'retirement' as a means of sanctity.[76] The same ideal had given rise to the composition of *Utopia*. It remains to consider the transition in More's mind from *Utopia* to the Counter Reformation.

Utopia had been concerned with Christianity and politics; Luther was concerned with Christianity and the Church. In the course of his protest he directed the focus of institutional concern from a political to an ecclesiastical setting. He complained, not of the State, but of the Church. In attacking the papacy on religious grounds (as he had done by 1521) he provoked the possibility of a counter-opposition. And in repudiating the monastery, he inadvertently suggested the possibility of reinvesting the monastic virtues in the Church which he had attacked. We can see one example of the consequence in the transition from More's *Utopia* to his religious polemics.

In *Utopia* More's grievance against the Renaissance Church was its collusion in the conspiracy of the rich. But there remained, in the mirror-world of Utopia, a distinction between Church and Court. Utopia had been made an island by its author; it is highly significant that, in the end, he did not allow it to remain an island. It was reconnected with the mainland through the arrival of Christian missionaries.

When the Utopians turn to Christianity, they turn to a religion which is sacramental, sacerdotal, and thought by at least some to be dependent upon the 'dispatch of a Christian bishop.[77] More's disillusionment with the Church of his own day did not extend to

pp. 61 ff. M. Bataillon, 'D'Erasme à la compagnie de Jésus', *Archives de Sociologie des Religions*, xxiv (1967), pp. 57–81.

[75] St Francis de Sales, *Introduction to the Devout Life*, trans. and ed., John K. Ryan (2nd revd. edn., New York, 1966).

[76] The eremitic life nevertheless remained the highest ideal. J. Leclercq, *Alone With God*, trans. E. McCabe (London, 1961), pp. 189–92. Bataillon (n. 74 above) comments on the alignment between Jesuit and monastic spirituality.

[77] *Utopia*, p. 219.

the structure of the Church; it derived from his sense of the recession of its members from the standards and means of salvation implanted in it by its founder.

Hence it was not an impossible step to suppose that the Church might yet advance to the taming of organized egoism within itself and in the world: a task which More, in the Dialogue of Counsel, had assigned to the embattled philosopher statesman. This is exactly the step which we find reflected in the *Responsio ad Lutherum* of 1523; a step impelled by the outbreak of the Reformation.[78] *Utopia* was written in the absence of a regenerate Church. The *Responsio ad Lutherum* was written in the hope of one.

The emergence of Luther prompted More to reconsider his opinion of the papacy. On his own admission, he had been 'sometime not of the mind that the primacy of that see should be begun by the institution of God'[79] Under the impact of the Reformation he found himself moved to a contrary conclusion.[80] In his *Responsio ad Lutherum* he explained the grounds which persuaded him to profess 'obedient submission to that see'.[81] There was one reason which seems to have moved him more than others:

> that if [after Luther's manner] the vices of men be imputed to the offices they hold, not only will the papacy not endure, but royalty, and dictatorship and consulate and every other kind of magistracy, and the people will be without rulers, without law, and without order.[82]

'Royalty', 'Consulate', 'Law': these had been the institutions whose mismanagement had prompted the composition of *Utopia*. Now, however, the spectre of political anarchy seemed 'imminent in some parts of Germany'.[83] Accordingly, More hastened to the defence of political institutions which, however corrupt, were preferable to disorder: it was better, he concluded, 'for men to have bad rulers than no rulers at all'.[84]

The same conclusion was valid in the Church as in the State: it would be a great evil for Christendom to be deprived of the pope.[85] It was far preferable 'for the Popes to be reformed than to be removed'.[86] A significant distinction seems here to be introduced between the popes and other rulers: the popes, in More's view, might 'be reformed'. It was possible to pray to this end, that God

[78] *Responsio ad Lutherum*, ed. John M. Headley, *The Yale Edition of the Complete Works of St Thomas More*, v, (2 parts) (New Haven and London, 1969).
[79] More to Cromwell, 5 March 1534 (Rogers, *Selected Letters*, p. 212).
[80] *Ibid.*, pp. 212–14.   [81] *Responsio*, i, pp. 140–41.
[82] *Ibid.*   [83] *Ibid.*
[84] *Ibid.*   [85] *Ibid.*
[86] *Ibid.*

might raise up 'such Popes as will befit the Christian Commonwealth and the dignity of the apostolic office'. More's specifications for a reformed papacy are highly instructive. The popes for whom he prays are such as will

> spurn riches and earthly honours, promote piety among the people and procure peace, exercise the authority which they have received from God against the satraps and strong hunters of the world, delivering up to Satan anyone who either usurps another's authority or misuses his own.[87]

'Piety', 'Peace', contempt for 'riches': these had been the watchwords of *Utopia*. They would never be those of Europe's military aristocracy, the 'satraps and strong hunters' whose position must be defended because bad rulers were better than no rulers. But it remained possible for Churchmen to adopt the monastic virtues: to spurn riches, promote piety and procure peace; to exercise their authority, like the Utopian priests,[88] 'delivering up to Satan' those who oppressed the Christian Commonwealth through the misuse of power.

By 1523, More looked to Rome for assistance in the task of realizing the virtues of *Utopia*—for the transformation of the Church, in the light of the monastic virtues, into a holy community in the middle of a fallen world, exerting its authority in restraint of organized misrule.

More's religious polemics were not light-hearted. Nor did they make the same impression upon Europeans which those of Fisher made.[89] Nevertheless, they were clear-sighted, however grim. They isolated the essential points of disagreement between the Church of Rome and the Protestant Reformers: Scripture and Tradition, the sacraments and papal primacy. More himself never clarified his understanding of the precise relation between pope and general council; a question which arose towards the end of his life with the conflict between England and Rome, between secular and spiritual jurisdictions. By this time the Christian Commonwealth was broken into national fragments. But More (in common with most of his contemporaries) continued to think of Europe and the Church as one.[90] Thus in 1534 he could envisage a general council deposing the present pope and substituting another 'with whom the King's Highness may be very well content'.[91] But it is striking that he should insist that it would have to be with a pope (however

---

[87] *Responsio*, i, pp. 140–41.   [88] *Utopia*, pp. 226–29.
[89] E. Surtz, *The Works and Days of John Fisher* (Cambridge, Mass., 1967, pp. 390 ff.
[90] Where they differed was in their conception of the Church.
[91] More to Cromwell, 5 March 1534 (n. 79 above).

elected) that the king would ultimately have to come to terms. In other words, More was prepared to die rather than deny the unity of the Church as sustained by papal primacy; a conclusion at which he had arrived under the impact of the Reformation. It was in his prison writings, not in his polemics, that the full depths of his humanity were most clearly manifested.[92] It was from his prison cell that he observed the Carthusians setting out for Tyburn, and made his final reflections on the contrast between the monastic and lay roads to holiness.[93]

The execution of More in 1535 prompted Melanchthon to remark on the tragic loss to 'our order' of a man whom he held in considerable esteem.[94] Melanchthon was speaking as a Christian humanist; the 'order' of which he spoke was that of Europe's men of letters. He was commenting upon the death, not of the man who wrote the *Responsio ad Lutherum*, but of the author of *Utopia*. But by 1535 *Utopia* belonged to a world which was rapidly disappearing, in the name of the *Liberty of a Christian Man*, *The Babylonian Captivity*, the *Responsio ad Lutherum*. England and Europe were far from having resolved that common sequence of predicaments which *Utopia* addressed. But the separation of their Churches meant that these problems were now broached in a spirit modified by the reformations of the sixteenth century. The humanists of Europe were now divided on confessional lines. The aftermath of *Utopia* ensured its survival in a world quite different from that in which it had appeared. But then, a successful extravaganza can always survive the circumstances of its composition; and perhaps *Utopia*'s greatest success lay in being short.

Gonville and Caius College, Cambridge.

[92] Louis L. Martz, 'Thomas More: The Tower Works', in *St Thomas More: Action and Contemplation*, ed. R. S. Sylvester (New Haven, 1972), pp. 57–83.
   [93] Roper, *Life*, pp. 239 and 242, quoted in Chambers, *Thomas More*, p. 325.
   [94] *Corpus Reformatorum*, ed. C. Gottlieb Bretschneider, ii (Halle, 1835), pp. 918, 1027. English abstracts in *Letters and Papers, Foreign and Domestic . . . Henry VIII*, ed. J. S. Brewer and J. Gairdner, ix, nos. 222 and 1013.

IDEALISTS AND REALISTS: BRITISH VIEWS OF GERMANY, 1864–1939

By P. M. Kennedy, B.A., D.Phil., F.R.Hist.S.

READ AT THE SOCIETY'S CONFERENCE
20 SEPTEMBER 1974

YET another survey of the much-traversed field of Anglo-German relations will seem to many historians of modern Europe to border on the realm of superfluity; probably no two countries have had their relationship to each other so frequently examined in the past century as Britain and Germany. Moreover, even if one restricted such a study to the British side alone, the sheer number of publications upon this topic, or upon only a section of it like the age of 'appeasement', is simply too great to allow a compression of existing knowledge into a narrative form that would be anything other than crude and sketchy. The following contribution therefore seeks neither to provide such a general survey, nor, by use of new and detailed archival materials, to concentrate upon a small segment of the history of British policy towards Germany in the period 1864–1939; but instead to consider throughout all these years a particular aspect, namely, the respective arguments of Germanophiles and Germanophobes in Britain and the connection between this dialogue and the more general ideological standpoints of both sides. In so doing, the author has produced a survey which remains embarrassingly summary in detail but does at least attempt to offer a fresh approach to the subject.

The starting point for such a survey seemed to be provided in a letter written by the famous German liberal economist, Lujo Brentano, to a friend in 1915, as the first world war was showing signs of becoming a conflict which would exhaust the participants and shatter European civilisation. A prime reason for the catastrophe, Brentano felt, was the recent dominance of that school of thought which rejected any moral basis in politics, whether it be provided by the churches or by the humanist proponents of a philosophy of ethics. The founder of this school had been Machiavelli, who demonstrated 'what man actually did and not what he should do', and who also taught that 'the essence of the state is power'. Modern German writers, such as Treitschke and Bernhardi, had preached much the same thing and attained great

137

influence, but Brentano was convinced that the phenomenon was not confined to his own country. In Britain, too, there had existed political groups which had had no scruples about the employment of force to defend 'national interests', which had favoured expansion overseas and which had striven to preserve an ordered society at home; the world, they had argued, was a hard, cruel, uneven place and it behoved every state to recognize that fact and to act accordingly. Such amoral views had been contested by others who appealed to ethical principles, who worked for the individuality and liberty of all men, and who opposed the use of immoral means to achieve one's ends; but this school, whose leading figures had been Cobden and Bright, were now as powerless in Britain as their equivalents were in Germany.[1]

Mankind, then, was basically divided into two types, the ethical and the practical, or, as I have chosen to call them, the idealists and the realists. The former preached the gospel of international morality and goodwill, the latter the morality of the state and the need to defend national interests; the former disliked war, the latter defended or even glorified it; the former urged arbitration and conciliation, the latter scorned them as a slight to national honour; the former upheld the freedom of the individual, the latter a sense of duty to the state. Referring more specifically to late-nineteenth and early-twentieth century Europe, as Brentano clearly did, further points of difference appear: free trade versus protectionism; anti-imperialism versus imperialism; egalitarianism versus élitism; social reforms versus large defence budgets; Hague Conferences versus arms races. In every case, the proponents of international goodwill and the advocates of a national *Realpolitik* are on different sides of the fence. In Britain, for example, the radical-Liberals who supported idealist policies were constantly at odds with the imperialists and patriots, who were generally to be found at the other end of the political spectrum. Their antagonism seemed total; each sought the destruction of all that the other represented.

Now it may reasonably be objected here that this is not only a very oblique way of approaching the topic 'British Views of Germany, 1864–1939', but that such a sweeping division of Political Man into these two opposing camps is scarcely valid. After all, most men conform neither to one stereotype nor to the other, but possess instead a mixture of idealism and realism; and statesmen especially

---

[1] Bundesarchiv, Koblenz: *Nachlass Brentano*, vol. 244, Brentano to (? a female friend), 11/4/1915. See also Brentano's thoughts on this topic in his book *Der Wirtschaftende Mensch in der Geschichte* (Leipzig, 1923), pp. 55–76, 370–71; and J. J. Sheehan, *The Career of Lujo Brentano. A Study of Liberalism and Social Reform in Imperial Germany* (London, 1966), pp. 182, 186–87, 191–94.

are aware that doctrinal fundamentals, whether of the right or the left, often need to be watered down to remain in power. Secondly, it would be erroneous to equate the idealists in Britain with the Liberal Party and the realists with Conservatives, not only because so many politicians followed a *via media* which makes them difficult to distinguish, but also because such an assumption ignores the Liberal Imperialists and others who rejected Gladstonian internationalism and *laissez-faire* yet who never joined the Tories. Finally, there is a semantic objection. Many of the people I would describe here as idealists, such as Cobden and E. D. Morel and Lansbury, would argue that in fact it was they who were offering the only truly realistic policy in international relations, for if the advocates of militarism and *Machtpolitik* had their way, endemic warfare would follow; it was rather the supporters of Imperial Federation or national conscription or the ordered, corporate state who were the idealists, for their programme could neither appeal to, nor satisfy, the great mass of the population in the long term.[2] All these points are undoubtedly true; and yet, granted such reservations, there still appears to be some merit in examining British attitudes towards Germany in terms of a dialogue between the two schools of thought delineated above. For, as we shall see, during the greater part of the period under discussion, pro-Germans and anti-Germans corresponded to a very large degree with idealists and realists respectively.

In the first half of the nineteenth century, British views of the German people were generally favourable.[3] As far as the links with Prussia were concerned, the Protestant religion was a unifying force; so, too, was the memory of the *Waffenbrüderschaft* of Wellington and Blücher at Waterloo; and there were the many dynastic connections with the German states, the most recent of which was the marriage of Princess Victoria to Crown Prince Frederick of Prussia. Commercial ties drew Britons into contact with the north German sea-ports and the emerging industrialized parts of Westphalia. The two peoples stood close together racially, an important

[2] The radical paper *Concord* expressed this argument well in December 1910: 'Not we are the dreamers, the utopians, but those who set their alarm clocks to signal the hour that threatens the Island with invasion and the Empire with destruction. They are hibernating in a fool's paradise and dreaming wild dreams of unopposed grab and grind. They are the ones who want awakening to the fact that half their day is past. . . .' Quoted in A. J. Anthony Morris, *Radicalism Against War, 1906–1914. The Advocacy of Peace and Retrenchment* (London, 1972), p. 199, n.1.

[3] J. Mander, *Our German Cousins. Anglo-German Relations in the 19th and 20th Centuries* (London, 1974), pp. 1–187; R. J. Sontag, *Germany and England. Background of Conflict, 1848–1894* (New York, 1969 ed.), pp. 3–66; W. E. Mosse, *The European Powers and the German Question 1848–1871* (Cambridge, 1958), pp. 5–9, 17–18, 36–38, 359–62.

consideration in the nineteenth century. But above all, Germany
was respected in cultural and intellectual terms. In the music of
Bach, Haydn, Mozart, Beethoven, Schubert, Handel, Wagner and
Mendelssohn, the literature of Goethe, Schiller and the other
Romantics, the philosophy of Kant and Hegel, the history of the
Göttingen School and Ranke, in theology, geography, economics,
in fact in almost all branches of knowledge, Britons could respect
the achievement of the German race. Finally, at a political level
they could share with the Germans a common suspicion of France
and Austria and Russia. When one adds to all this the mid-Victorian
belief in national self-determination, it comes as no surprise to learn
that the British political nation on the whole favoured the unification of Germany. There was no reservation about the end, simply
about the means. 'Much would depend', Frederick William IV was
reminded archly by Queen Victoria, 'upon the manner in which
this (new German) power was represented' in European affairs.[4]
For a moral and moralizing nation such as England, this was an
important proviso.

Thus the British reaction to the unification of Germany by means
of Bismarck's cunning diplomacy and the military efficiency of the
Prussian Army led to a division of opinion along ideological lines.
Earlier the Liberals had rejoiced when Bismarck had called
Palmerston's bluff over the Schleswig-Holstein question, for this
defeat, in Bright's words, meant that 'the foul Idol' of the balance-
of-power policy had been overthrown; but even their adoption of
non-intervention abroad and their concentration upon reforms at
home could not conceal Bismarck's politics from Liberal eyes. The
provoked war with Austria, the conquest of northern France, the
treatment of its civilian inhabitants and the seizure of Alsace-
Lorraine offended every sensitive Englishman. The latter step
Gladstone referred to as 'a violent laceration', even though he
could do nothing about it. Even Queen Victoria was appalled—
'Odious people the Prussians are, *that* I *must say*'—and she exchanged
many a letter with her daughter about the evil influence of Bismarck.
The philosopher Frederick Harrison was more inclined to place the
blame upon the militaristic traditions of Prussia, 'the sole European
kingdom which has been built up, province by province, upon the
battlefield, cemented stone by stone in blood', and which had now
debauched the German people. 'Let us embrace the savant, the
artist, the poet of the Fatherland', he concluded, 'But let us keep our
powder dry—and study the birth, the growth, and the future of

[4] A. C. Benson and Viscount Esher, *The Letters of Queen Victoria*, 1st ser., 3 vols.
(London, 1907), ii, p. 164.

Bismarckism.'[5] Already, then, the distinction was appearing between *Prussia*, which was militaristic, reactionary and unscrupulous, and *Germany*, which was basically liberal, bourgeois and cultured, if only it could rid itself of the poisonous influences of the Hohenzollern *Machstaat*. Acton, too, one of the torchbearers of German culture and education in Britain but also the quintessence of English liberal idealism, symbolized this change of mood in the years after 1871 when he attacked repeatedly the glorification of power which Machiavelli had introduced into European thought and pointed to the dangers represented by Treitschke's doctrines and Bismarck's politics.[6]

Conservatives in Britain, being less concerned with moral judgments and more with the country's vital interests, found themselves split over the rise of Germany. In the first place, the Russian rejection in 1870 of the Black Sea clauses of the Treaty of Paris produced more excitement, since it revealed that the old enemy had not given up its ambitions in South-East Europe. This consideration, and the memory of the difficulties caused to Britain by the restless and unpredictable ambitions of Napoleon III, induced satisfaction in those who perceived that the two 'flank' powers would be less inclined to indulge in extra-European adventures now that the political vacuum in the centre of the continent had been filled: as Stanley put it in 1866, 'we regard a strong Prussia as an advantage for us, but Russia fears it'.[7] The restoration of the European equilibrium was worth a few misdeeds, a view which Palmerston, despite Schleswig-Holstein, had shared. Others were not so sure, however. Cowley, the British ambassador in Paris, viewed developments pessimistically: 'I do not think the future will be a pleasant one for England. I have no faith in the friendship of Prussia and if she ever becomes a Naval Power she will give us trouble'—a prescient remark, some thirty years before Tirpitz came into power.[8] Many shared the alarm of Sir Robert Morier at the exposure of Britain's ineffectiveness and the failure of Gladstonian political recipes, and must have agreed with his dislike of the German disposition to use force: 'We must never forget', he wrote

[5] F. Harrison, *National and Social Problems* (London, 1908), pp. xix-xx, 4–70.

[6] G. E. Fasnacht, *Acton's Political Philosophy. An Analysis* (London, 1952), pp. 132–39.

[7] Cited in K. Hildebrand, 'Von der Reichseinigung zur "Krieg-in-Sicht"—Krise. Preussen-Deutschland als Faktor der britischen Aussenpolitik 1866—1875', in *Das kaiserliche Deutschland. Politik und Gesellschaft 1870–1918*, ed. M. Stürmer (Düsseldorf, 1970), p. 216; see also R. Millman, *British Foreign Policy and the Coming of the Franco-Prussian War* (Oxford, 1965), pp. 33–37, 107–8, 215–16.

[8] F. Wellesley, *The Paris Embassy during the Second Empire. From the Papers of Earl Cowley* (London, 1928), p. 314.

in 1875, 'that not only Bismarck . . . but the whole of what might be described as the *Schola Theologiae* of Prussian politicians never cease from working out political combinations and problems only soluble in the last instance by "blood and iron".'[9] And, as a forerunner to later examples of 'German invasion' literature, *Blackwood's Magazine* brought out Chesney's famous tale of 'The Battle of Dorking', so frightening its readers with the prospect of mounted Ulhans laying waste to southern England that Gladstone had publicly to denounce the work as a piece of unjustified and ridiculous alarmism.[10]

For more than two decades following 1871, British views of Germany were to be coloured by these early experiences, although it is less easy to detect the pattern for several reasons. The argument between idealists and realists was transferred to other fields, in particular to the great Eastern Crisis of 1876–78 and to the debate upon British imperial policy which culminated in Gladstone's electoral triumph following his Midlothian campaign; while in the 1880s Ireland and Egypt dominated the headlines. Moreover, apart from the 1875 'war in sight' alarm, Britain and Germany were usually in agreement over European problems, each seeking to preserve peace and suspicious of the designs of France and Russia: since the latter were the 'hungry' powers, Salisbury noted, it was natural for the 'satisfied' ones to lean towards each other.[11] What differences there were between London and Berlin usually occurred under a Liberal administration, for Bismarck made little attempt to conceal his hostility towards all that Gladstone represented, seeing in the latter's policies of greater democratisation at home and an end to power-politics abroad a direct threat to the very foundations of the Prusso-German state. It is in the open animosity of these two statesmen that the ideological dichotomy between the ethical and the practical interpretations of politics is best revealed in this period.[12]

In the background, however, far-reaching changes in British political attitudes were occurring which would shortly transform the debate upon the country's relations with Germany. By the 1880s it had become obvious to many observers that Britain's uniquely favourable mid-century position was slipping away under the pressure of foreign competition: her industrial lead was over-

[9] R. Wemyss, *Memoirs and Letters of the Right Hon. Sir Robert Morier*, (London, 1911), ii, p. 356.

[10] I. F. Clarke, *Voices Prophesying War 1763–1984* (London, 1970 edn.), pp. 30–42.

[11] Quoted in W. R. Louis, *Great Britain and Germany's Lost Colonies 1914–1919* (Oxford, 1967), pp. 20–21.

[12] W. N. Medlicott, *Bismarck, Gladstone and the Concert of Europe* (London, 1956), *passim*.

taken; her commercial preponderance was undermined, both in Europe and overseas; her near-monopoly in the colonial world was eroded; even her maritime supremacy was challenged. Under such circumstances, it was argued, the traditional doctrines of *laissez-faire* liberalism were no longer the most appropriate, no longer corresponded to the realities of the world. In impressively large numbers, late-Victorian politicians, philosophers and writers argued instead for a national regeneration, orchestrated and encouraged by an interventionist state; for the forging of closer ties with the Dominions, to form that Greater Britain which would be able to survive in the twentieth-century world of the super-powers; for the strengthening of the country's naval and military forces to a standard commensurate with its world-wide responsibilities; and for the re-organization of industry, of education, of health, of government, all of which would result in greater national efficiency and power. And as the turn of the century brought with it fresh challenges to Britain's world position and further evidence (especially in the Boer War) of its decline, this campaign became more virulent still. Under the banners of 'Imperialism and Social Reform' and 'National Efficiency', arguments were advanced for a protectionist tariff policy, for the introduction of national conscription, and even for a eugenics programme, to produce a fitter imperial race through scientific, selective breeding. Casting aside the execrable doctrines of Cobdenism, and rejecting with almost equal distaste the moderate Toryism of Salisbury and Balfour, the radical Right propagated a set of ideas intended to preserve and enhance the position of the British Empire in the coming century.[13]

Although this new programme could be represented as being logical and coherent in itself, it produced a most startling contradiction in respect of its followers' attitudes towards Germany. To an extraordinary degree that country provided the concrete examples which the 'national efficiency' movement needed. Its philosophy of state power and action attracted all those who, like Coleridge, Carlyle and the early British Germanophiles, detested the utilitarian and *laissez-faire* concepts which put individualism before a duty to the

---

[13] J. R. Jones, 'England', in *The European Right. A Historical Profile*, ed. H. Rogger and E. Weber (Berkeley and Los Angeles, 1965), pp. 29–54; G. R. Searle, *The Quest for National Efficiency. A Study in British politics and British political thought 1899–1914* (Oxford, 1971); B. Semmel, *Imperialism and Social Reform* (London, 1960); M. Beloff, *Imperial Sunset*, i, *Britain's Liberal Empire 1897–1921* (London, 1969), caps. *II–III*; Sontag, *Germany and England*, pp. 93–224; J. Roach, 'Liberalism and the Victorian Intelligentsia', *Historical Journal*, xiii (1957), pp. 58–81; P. Marshall, 'The Imperial Factor in the Liberal Decline, 1880–1885', in *Perspectives of Empire. Essays presented to Gerald S. Graham* ed. J. E. Flint and G. Williams (London, 1973), pp. 136–47.

whole body politic. Its *Zollverein* and scientifically-calculated tariffs offered an example to British protectionists. Its universities and technical institutes were always cited in the many criticisms of the effete, classics-orientated British equivalents. Its obligatory military service was praised by no less a person than Milner, who sought to introduce a similar system into Britain.[14] And its social insurance scheme, a Bismarckian device to destroy the popularity of socialism and to secure the workers' loyalty to the state, was equally admired, and for the same motive.

Yet to these native preachers of continental-style conservatism Germany was also bound to be regarded as a dangerous enemy. Her colonial expansion had not been taken too seriously at first—indeed, British imperialists could join Bismarck in his criticism of Gladstone and Granville's inept handling of African matters in 1884—but when the roars of protest from the Cape, Australia and New Zealand reached the home country, attitudes began to change. The logic of the Imperial Federation movement dictated that the wishes of the Dominions should be given priority over the need to maintain good wishes with Germany, whose imperial ambitions were looked at with increasing suspicion in Britain, especially after Bismarck's fall.[15] Secondly, avid protectionists were aiming to strengthen imperial links and at the same time to destroy the German commercial challenge through the abandonment of free trade: the 'Made in Germany' agitation and the Tariff Reform movement therefore went hand in hand.[16] Thirdly, the swift and impressive rise of the German fleet alarmed all good navalists, who urged the government to respond to this fresh challenge to the supremacy of the Royal Navy.[17] Finally, their hyper-patriotism was offended, not only by these growing signs of a threat to Britain's *material* interests, but also by the virulent Anglophobia in Germany itself. In the period after 1901, when Joseph Chamberlain's last attempt at an alliance treaty with Berlin had broken down, when the pro-Boer feelings in Germany had been widely reported by *The Times* and others, when Tirpitz's naval programme was first considered by the Admiralty to be directed at Britain, and when the

[14] Lord Milner, *The Nation and the Empire* (London, 1913), p. 124.

[15] Louis, *Great Britain and Germany's Lost Colonies*, cap. I; K. Mackenzie, 'Some British Reactions to German Colonial Methods, 1885–1907', *Historical Journal*, xvii (1974), pp. 165–75; P. M. Kennedy, *The Samoan Tangle. A Study in Anglo-German-American Relations, 1878–1900* (Dublin, 1974), pp. 108 ff.

[16] R. J. S. Hoffman, *Great Britain and the German Trade Rivalry, 1875–1914* (Philadelphia, 1933).

[17] A. J. Marder, *The Anatomy of British Sea Power. A History of British Naval Policy in the Pre-Dreadnought Era 1880–1905* (Hamden, Conn., 1964), pp. 288–301, 456–67.

campaign for tariff reform got fully under way, a torrent of abuse was hurled by the British right-wing press against Germany and the 'invasion scare' literature revived again. So powerful and extreme did this sentiment become that even the cool-headed Lansdowne was forced to abandon cooperation with Berlin over the Venezuelan affair and the Bagdad Railway.[18]

The attitude of the 'idealists', radical-Liberals and socialists, to this development was one of mounting concern. If the political habits of Prussia were introduced into Britain, if free trade was rejected in favour of protection, if national conscription and other forms of militarism were instituted, if an aggressive imperialism produced tensions and wars across the globe, and if the old heresy of the balance of power was revived, then liberalism would be eradicated in their country just as certainly as it had been in Bismarck's. The Prussian system might be a detestable one, but at least it was far away: now they had to face an enemy within. Yet in fighting it, they were placed in the tactically weaker position of denying that a German threat existed. The world was big enough for the two powers to develop colonies without confrontation, Harcourt and other anti-imperialists argued; there was also room for everyone's trade, and it was a mercantilist trick to agitate about the German trade rivalry when each country was the other's best customer; even the German naval programme was excused as a pale imitation of Britain's own bloated naval armaments. And when Grey disappointed them by maintaining an anti-German policy after 1905, their answer was to improve relations between the two peoples by non-official means: the exchange of visits, the use of pamphlets and the radical press, the founding of such bodies as the Anglo-German Conciliation Committee, the Society for Anglo-German Friendship and the Anglo-German Understanding Conference. The leading members of these organizations were predominantly Nonconformists, Quakers and radical-Liberals, who preached Cobden's gospel of international morality and goodwill and who had also been involved earlier in supporting the *entente cordiale* with France for the same reason.[19]

Despite these genuine attempts to better Anglo-German relations, however, the main concern of the idealists was with their domestic opponents, as the tariff reform controversy illustrates. The

---

[18] G. W. Monger, *The End of Isolation. British Foreign Policy 1900–1907* (London, 1963), pp. 104–07, 118–23, 222–24. On the revival of 'invasion scare' literature, see Clarke, *Voices Prophesying War*, pp. 138–61.

[19] The best recent survey of the 'idealists' arguments is Morris, *Radicalism Against War*. Also important is A. J. P. Taylor's stimulating book *The Trouble Makers. Dissent over Foreign Policy 1792–1939* (London, 1969 ed.), pp. 87–119.

descendants of the Manchester School stood firm agains anti-German agitation: 'No free trader', sniffed the *Daily News* in its comment upon William's famous book *Made in Germany*, 'can seriously contend that the importation of German goods into this country is a misfortune. If it were so, all foreign commerce would be in itself an evil. . . .'[20] There was no Anglo-German trade rivalry, added Hobson in a pamphlet called *The German Panic*: it was simply 'some private English firms competing with some private German and American firms'. The whole thing had been got up by Capitalists 'to divert the force of popular demands for drastic social reforms'.[21] The opposition's response to such arguments is perhaps best captured by *The Daily Express's* declaration in 1903: 'who doesn't vote for Chamberlain, votes for the national enemy'.[22] Thus Germanophobia could be used to assist tariff reform; tariff reform to awaken the nation to the German challenge, and to make it more efficient; and both would undermine liberalism. The argument about relations with Germany was but one aspect of the larger struggle between two totally opposed ideologies.

Tactically, as I mentioned above, the idealists were always in a weak position as they swam against the flood-tides of nationalism. In addition, the widespread public suspicions of Germany were shared by the court, the army and the navy, the Foreign Office, the greater part of the press and certain Cabinet members, particularly Grey, and it proved impossible to overcome the combined influence of such forces. Thirdly, they secured little support from Germany itself, for liberal circles there were not strong; and the Berlin government turned cool when it discovered that the aim of the British Germanophiles was not (as Bülow had hoped) to break the *entente cordiale* but to transform it into a loose but harmonious triplice between Britain, France and Germany. Finally, the idealists really knew little about Germany and were unable to assess conditions in that country. The realists, on the other hand, were much more familiar with their declared enemy, even if they imposed a one-sided interpretation upon its motives. The 'German experts' of the Foreign Office, Crowe and Tyrell, had both lived in that country; Austen Chamberlain first began to suspect a future German challenge when he had the dubious pleasure of observing Treitschke's Anglophobic outpourings at Berlin University; Leo Amery underwent a somewhat similar experience as a temporary

---

[20] *Daily News*, 25/7/1896.

[21] Quoted in Semmel, *Imperialism and Social Reform*, p. 137.

[22] Deutsches Zentralarchiv, Potsdam: Auswärtiges Amt (Handelspolitische Abteilung), vol. 9094, Metternich to Bülow, no. 910 of 26/12/1903, citing the paper.

correspondent of *The Times* in Berlin during the Boer War.[23] Garvin, influential editor of *The Observer*, informed a German magazine in 1912 that the bookshelves in his study were loaded with the works of Goethe, Kant, Ranke, Sybel, Mommsen and other sages, which he deeply cherished; but he also recalled that they stood next to the complete issues of the *Marine-Rundschau* and *Nauticus*, 'which remind me daily that the second largest fleet in the world has been created in scarcely more than a decade and hitherto no limit has been set upon its growth'.[24] Against optimism, the realists placed cold, hard facts; against ignorance, they placed a wide knowledge; and against ineffectiveness, they placed immense power and influence. The outcome of the debate was not in doubt, and many pro-Germans must have guessed it long before Britain entered the European conflict on the side of France and Russia.

What the idealists did do in the pre-1914 period was to re-establish the notion that the character of the Hohenzollern regime was quite distinct from that of the German people as a whole. After all, despite the efforts to portray Germany as modern, progressive and parliamentary—in contrast to Britain's reactionary entente partner, Russia—the liberal-Radicals were well aware that, as *The Speaker* put it, the German government was still ruled 'by the traditions of Bismarck'.[25] Recent research reveals that this distinction was more widely shared, for Grey and his circle believed that a small but influential 'war party' had managed to defeat the moderate elements in Berlin in July 1914. Thus Asquith could later proclaim that Britain's major war aim was to free Europe from 'Prussian militarism', while the Foreign Office was prepared to concede that 'the leading people in Germany who are mainly responsible for this war never allowed their countrymen to suspect that their designs were aggressive. . . .'[26] Even *Punch* offered some turgid doggerel on 'The Two Germanies':[27]

---

[23] Z. Steiner, *The Foreign Office and Foreign Policy 1898–1914* (Cambridge, 1969), *passim;* L. S. Amery, *My Political Life*, 3 vols. (London, 1953–55), i, pp. 95–99; Sir Charles Petrie, *Life and Letters of Sir Austen Chamberlain*, 2 vols. (London, 1939), i, pp. 27–29.

[24] *Nord und Süd*, vol. 142 (1912), 'Deutsch-Englische Verständigungsnummer', pp. 64–69.

[25] Quoted in Morris, *Radicalism against War*, p. 45. For some favourable contemporary comparisons of Germany with Russia, see Taylor, *The Trouble Makers*, p. 105.

[26] M. Ekstein, 'Sir Edward Grey and Imperial Germany in 1914', *Journal of Contemporary History*, (1971), pp. 121–31; V. H. Rothwell, *British War Aims and Peace Diplomacy 1914–1918* (Oxford, 1971), pp. 18–19, 43–49, 283–84.

[27] *Mr Punch's History of the Great War* (London, 1919), pp. 5–6.

> Once the land of poets, seers and sages,
> Who enchant us with their deathless pages,
> . . .
>
> Now the Prussian *Junker*, blind with fury,
> Claims to be God's counsel, judge and jury.

The Left could use this fact to reassure itself that the conflict was not one between peoples, but between reactionary and aggressive national elites; while the Right could argue from it that a further increase in the pressure upon Germany would expose and widen that fissure in the enemy's camp.

The inevitable consequence of the outbreak of war was to split the realists and idealists in Britain still further, and to reveal how weak the latter's political position actually was. This may partly be explained by the German invasion of Belgium, which gave to the British decision for war a 'moral' air that convinced wavering Cabinet members and many others of the righteousness of their cause; but the main reason was the simple fact that the country was fighting and that all its animosities could be concentrated upon the hated foe. The irrational campaign against Battenberg, Haldane and even Eyre Crowe for their alleged pro-German sympathies is a measure of the bitterness; *Punch* cartoons, the Northcliffe press and Horatio Bottomley pictured the Kaiser as a demon who tortured women and children; and, as the casualty list lengthened, some views hardened further, so that by 1918 Horace Rumbold was stressing the need to 'kill or put out of action another million or so Germans'.[28] Indeed, the war propaganda against the 'Hun' became so extreme that such a person as George Saunders, the former Berlin correspondent of *The Times* who had played a major role in arousing British suspicions of Germany after 1900, felt compelled to protest at the 'simply disgusting' ragings of the press:

> It is true 'he wrote' that the Germans have been absurdly overbearing about their 'Kultur'. But the attempt to make out that they haven't, or never have had any, is equally monstrous. Beethoven may have been Dutch and Slavonic (though he was born and lived in Germany), but Bach, Mozart, Wagner, Goethe, Kant, Copernicus, Thomas à Kempis, Walther von der Vogelweide, Helmholtz, Bunsen, Wilhelm von Humboldt, Tieck, Schlegel and Winckelmann were all German, and Handel came from Halle. War makes people mad and blind—the Germans as well as us.[29]

[28] M. Gilbert, *Sir Horace Rumbold. Portrait of a Diplomatist 1869–1941* (London' 1973), p. 171.
[29] George Saunders Papers (in private hands), Saunders to his sister Maggie, 22/12/1914.

Yet this extreme atrocity-mongering and Germanophobia was bound sooner or later to produce a reaction and to give the radicals their chance, particularly as the war dragged on and the average soldier and citizen lost his early enthusiasm for combat. In August 1914 the radical paper *The Nation* had admitted defeat, proclaiming woefully: 'Who in the future will pay attention to the *Daily News* . . . the *Manchester Guardian* and other journals of the same stamp? These are idealists . . . who refuse to look reality in the face. . . .'[30] Yet it was precisely at that time that the critics of the war broke their links with the Liberal Party's policy and founded the Union of Democratic Control, which was to disseminate their programme of eradicating secret diplomacy and alliances, instituting democratic control of foreign policy, reviving the Concert of Europe and international arbitration, and abolishing armaments and aggressive wars.[31] For the greater part of the war, of course, the UDC was the voice of one crying in the wilderness, scorned by the patriotic press and watched with suspicion by the War Cabinet and the police, which actually arrested and imprisoned its leader, E. D. Morel, in 1917. However, the movement was to be rescued in its hour of distress; help was coming from the New World to restore the ideological balance of the Old.

The increasing intervention of Woodrow Wilson was naturally regarded with rapture by the radicals in Britain, since the American president embodied, and saw himself as embodying, the ideals of mid-nineteenth century British internationalists which had been abandoned in the country of their origin. It was Gladstone whom Wilson regarded as 'the greatest statesman that ever lived'; Gladstone, whose portrait hung over Wilson's desk; Gladstone, whose career inspired Wilson to become a politician; and Gladstone, whose oratory, moral fervour, and belief in free trade, national self-determination, democracy, international cooperation and arbitration, provided the necessary example for Wilson's own crusade to eradicate the world's wrongs.[32] With British statesmen hardened in their determination to fight a war to the finish, the president appeared as a saviour to the opponents of militarism and imperialism. Even C. P. Scott was forced to admit that the attitude

[30] Quoted in Morris, *Radicalism against War*, p. 419.

[31] Taylor, *The Trouble Makers*, pp. 120–51; A. J. Mayer, *Political Origins of the New Diplomacy 1917–1918* (New Haven, 1959); and especially, M. Swartz, *The Union of Democratic Control in British Politics during the First World War* (Oxford, 1971).

[32] H. Notter, *The Origins of the Foreign Policy of Woodrow Wilson* (New York, 1965), pp. 12, 29–31; J. M. Blum, *Woodrow Wilson and the Politics of Morality* (Boston, 1956), pp. 9–10. It was not surprising that Sir Henry Wilson called the president a 'Super-Gladstone'! C. E. Calwell, *Field Marshall Sir Henry Wilson, His Life and Diaries*, 2 vols. (London, 1927), ii, pp. 136–37.

of his friend and confidant Lloyd George 'savours rather of the "real—politik" of Bismarck than of Wilson's idealism which we are supposed to share'.[33] Moreover, Wilson's appeals, like Gladstone's, struck deep into the hearts and minds of many of the lower-middle and working classes, and were thus more influential than the pamphleteering of the U.D.C.

It would be wrong to argue from this that the relative moderation of the Allied peace terms upon Germany at Versailles was due solely to the ideological impact of this 'new diplomacy'. The great mass of the British people simply wanted an end to the conflict and Lloyd George, having won the 1918 election upon a patriotic appeal, was wise enough to perceive this mood and to force upon Clemenceau less swingeing conditions for the defeated enemy. He was supported in this by many of the die-hard imperialists, Milner and Churchill included, who had become convinced that the prolonged trench warfare in Flanders had been a catastrophe for Britain and that, provided western Europe remained free of German influence, there could be little objection to Berlin's *Drang nach Osten*. After all, such an eastward expansion was likely to be at the expense of Bolshevism, which by 1919 was regarded as a far more dangerous threat to the Allies than the now discredited Prussian militarism. Furthermore, in leaving Europe alone the British government would then be free to concentrate upon the enormous problems of the Empire, which faced the threat of internal disruption in Ireland and India, the demands for a renegotiation of status by the Dominions, the challenges from France and Russia in the Middle East, and the task of picking a middle way between Japan and the United States in the Far East.[34]

Not everyone was in favour of this sudden change of heart towards Germany. Conservative backbenchers, many of them sympathetic to France, still wished to squeeze the beaten foe until the pips squeaked. Eyre Crowe, who had now recovered his influence in the Foreign Office, repeatedly warned that the extent of the German collapse should not be exaggerated, and advocated an Anglo-French alliance such as Clemenceau and Poincaré desired.[35]

---

[33] Quoted in Swartz, *The Union of Democratic Control*, p. 134. And see generally, L. W. Martin, *Peace without Victory. Woodrow Wilson and the English Liberals* (New York, 1973 edn.), for an excellent survey of British radical attitudes towards the president.

[34] See briefly, Beloff, *Imperial Sunset*, i, caps, *V–VI*; C. Barnett, *The Collapse o/ British Power* (London, 1972), pp. 308–21; M. Howard, *The Continental Commitment. The Dilemma of British Defence Policy in the Era of Two World Wars* (Harmondsworth., 1974), pp. 65–73.

[35] M. Laffan, 'The Question of French Security in British Policy towards France and Germany, 1918–1925 (unpubd. Ph.D. thesis, Univ. of Cambridge,

Sir Halford Mackinder, social-imperialist and founder of the school of geopolitics, pleaded for the active support by the West of the small 'buffer' states of eastern Europe, to prevent Germany from ever again seizing the 'Heartland' of the continent. In fact, Mackinder's book *Democratic Ideals and Reality* (1919) was a sustained argument against the 'idealists', those Cobdenite internationalists who ignored strategical and military realities.[36]

Within an astonishingly short period after the cessation of hostilities, however, the influence and acceptability of idealist doctrines had overtaken those of the preachers of *Realpolitik* and it was the turn of the latter to be eclipsed. The League of Nations, the arch-stone of Wilson's system, was generally assumed to contain the machinery for solving future international disputes and to destroy the argument for large-scale defence forces. The UDC programme of open diplomacy, democratic controls, no forced transfers of territories or populations, and the pacific settlement of quarrels was so widely accepted that even Wilson was criticized for having surrendered to the forces of reaction and revanchism in agreeing to certain clauses of the Versailles treaty. The Allied treatment of Germany was particularly deplored: the principle of national self-determination, liberally applied to small ethnic groups in eastern Europe, had been denied to her; the seizure of her colonies under the 'fig-leaf' of League of Nations mandates was further evidence of British, French and Japanese imperialism; the disarmament clauses were blatantly unfair and hypocritical when the Allies preserved their own bloated armaments and armies; the prospect of acceding to French wishes for a post-war alliance against Germany was an abhorrence; the claim (in Article 231 of the treaty) that Germany and her allies had been responsible for the war was an historical absurdity when it was well known that all the capitalist powers had been equally guilty; and the reparations demands were not only immoral but also highly foolish, since they threatened the future economic well-being of Germany and of Britain as well.[37]

The latter argument was, of course, the gist of J. M. Keynes's brilliant work *The Economic Consequences of the Peace;* and its main

---

1973), cap. 2; Z. S. Steiner, 'British Foreign Office Attitudes to Germany, 1905–1919', Paper read to the Anglo-German Group of Historians, London, September 1973, p. 3. The views of the Tory 'die-harders' are captured in R. B. McCallum, *Public Opinion and the Last Peace* (London, 1944), pp. 40–45.

[36] Semmel, *Imperialism and Social Reform*, p. 175; H. J. Mackinder, *Democratic Ideals and Reality* (New York edn., 1962), *passim*.

[37] M. Gilbert, *The Roots of Appeasement* (London, 1966), pp. 52–88; *id.* (ed.), *Britain and Germany between the Wars* (London, 1964), pp. 14–17; Taylor, *The Trouble Makers*, pp. 159–60.

economic point, that only if Germany were prosperous enough to buy from and sell to Britain would both countries recover from the wounds of war, was the same liberal-internationalist logic that Adam Smith and his followers had put forward to destroy the narrow mercantilism of the eighteenth century. But mixed in with Keynes's professional judgments were those of the idealist, who could only wring his hands at the fact that Clemenceau viewed the peace settlement 'in terms of France and Germany, not of humanity and of European civilization struggling forwards to a new order'.[38] Nevertheless, the swiftness with which Keynes's views became the accepted orthodoxy in political circles is an indication of the widespread revulsion against Britain's previous policy and of the guilt felt at the treatment meted out to Germany. The message was the same elsewhere: the key modern history books of the inter-war years were Russell's *Freedom and Organisation*, Gooch's *History of Europe*, and Lowes Dickinson's *The International Anarchy*, all written by U.D.C. members, all favourable to Germany. Even works of literature, which were usually apolitical in the 1920s, made their contribution to pacifism with Graves's *Goodbye to All That*, Blunden's *Undertones of War*, Owen's *Poems* and many others.[39] The 'idealists', in other words, enjoyed the backing of almost the entire intellectual establishment and the only dissenters were a few hard-bitten generals and Tory M.P.s, who were simply noises offstage and who isolated themselves even more by their stance over India, where their dislike of concessions to Gandhi in some ways foreshadowed their attitude towards Hitler. The Conservative Party itself, however, had certainly recognized the need to pare the defence estimates, to avoid foreign commitments and to pay homage to the idea of the League if it was to stay in office.

What changed all this were the ominous signs in the early 1930s, in particular the Manchurian Crisis and the coming into power of Hitler, that the millenium of international peace and goodwill was not yet at hand, indeed, was threatening to fade away altogether. At this, the idealists re-doubled their efforts, believing that a policy of magnanimous concessions would satisfy all grievances and avoid conflict. But as the nature of Nazi-ism became clearer, and as the precious League system was shown to be ineffective, their dilemma grew. Could they remain totally inactive when all their highest ideals were being flouted, when international guarantees and territorial boundaries were being ignored, when civil liberties and

---

[38] Quoted in Barnett, *op. cit.*, p. 391.

[39] *Ibid.*, pp. 428–38; Gilbert, *Roots of Appeasement*, pp. 26–29; Taylor, *The Trouble Makers*, p. 162; P. M. Kennedy, 'The Decline of Nationalistic History in the West', *Journal of Contemporary History*, 8 (1973), pp. 91–92.

democratic rights were being brutally suppressed? On the other hand, could they support a policy of re-armament, military alliances and continental commitments, particularly when this would be undertaken by a Conservative government which they detested? For years the members of the U.D.C., the League of Nations Union, the Labour Party, left-wing Liberals, and the Trade Unions wavered between one evil and the other; but after Abyssinia, after the Spanish Civil War, and especially after Munich, their minds were slowly made up. Fascism had to be defeated, appeasement had to stop, an alliance with Soviet Russia and other 'peace-loving' states had to be negotiated, and all this to be done with as little credit to Chamberlain's government as possible. Not surprisingly, this line still appeared confused and contradictory to many observers.[40]

There was far less uncertainty or self-questioning among the advocates of a vigorous defence of Britain's national interests. Few of these had really abandoned their deep-rooted suspicion of Germany, their inner conviction that Prussian militarism somehow lived on even if the Hohenzollerns had gone. Rumbold, about to retire from his embassy in Berlin, sent the Foreign Office a stream of despatches in 1933 to illustrate that parliamentarism 'had been replaced by a regime of brute force', that 'The spirit of Weimar has yielded to the spirit of Potsdam'.[41] Garvin deeply regretted that Germany had not been overrun in 1919, in order to have broken 'the psychological infatuation of their hereditary militarism'.[42] Vansittart strove to convince his political masters of the German menace; Churchill warned against German rearmament; Austen Chamberlain pointed to the evils of Nazi-ism; Amery, Boothby, Sir Edward Spears, Lord Lloyd, Ronald Cartland, Paul Emrys-Evans and others joined in; but the 'anti-appeasers', as they have been called, were impotent so long as Neville Chamberlain's hold over the Cabinet and Commons remained firm. Even after the defection of Eden in 1938 they could hardly be regarded as a coherent political group.[43] In any case, Chamberlain had usurped the adjective 'realistic' for his own policy, whereas Churchill and Vansittart were always portrayed as congenital Germanophobes who had not yet come to terms with the changed conditions

[40] J. F. Naylor *Labour's International Policy* (London 1969), *passim*.

[41] Gilbert, *Sir Horace Rumbold*, pp. 374, 377.

[42] Quoted in Gilbert, *Britain and Germany between the Wars*, p. 16. Garvin's attitude towards Germany later softened considerably, much to Rumbold's disgust.

[43] N. Thompson, *The Anti-Appeasers. Conservative Opposition to Appeasement in the 1930s* (Oxford, 1971), *passim*. The dissensions among the Right are also covered in J. R. Jones, 'England' (n. 13 above), pp. 57–69.

of the post-1919 world. The anti-German comments of *The Daily Telegraph* and *Morning Post*, organs of this ultra-right, imperialist sentiment, could not match the influence or the readership of *The Times, Daily Mail* and other supporters of appeasement. As for the Chiefs of Staff, their pleas for increased armaments were always successfully held by the Treasury and the Prime Minister's office, whilst even such a proponent of adequate armed forces as Hankey preferred to concentrate upon 'imperial' defence rather than the European balance of power.[44]

What was happening by the time of the Czech crisis, however, was a fascinating new development in British politics. In the middle of the political spectrum the appeasers continued to execute their policy whilst, converging upon them in an uncoordinated 'pincer-attack' from the Right and the Left, marched the followers of *Realpolitik* and the followers of idealism. A brief survey of the British press during that crisis reveals this novel re-alignment very well. Although the *Times, Sunday Times, Observer, Express* and *Mail* continued to support Chamberlain's policy, the *Daily Telegraph* was finding it increasingly difficult to toe the party line and to contain its criticism of appeasement. When the Prime Minister flew to Berchtesgaden, he was encouraged to use 'only the most blunt, plain, even brutal language' with Hitler, a sentiment rather similar to Churchill's wish that the summit negotiations should take place on board a British battleship—a symbol of the country's strength, determination and proud heritage. From the other end of the political spectrum, the *Manchester Guardian* and *News Chronicle* launched repeated attacks upon the government's surrender to Hitler on moral grounds. How was it still possible to believe, asked the *Guardian*, that the 'barbarous' Nazis would 'walk hand in hand with justice, tolerance, and humanity—values which this Government is surely pledged to its people to defend?'[45] The Commons, too, witnessed this criticism from both flanks. Whilst Attlee called Munich a defeat 'for reason and humanity . . . a victory for brute force', Duff Cooper scorned the Prime Minister's use of 'the language of sweet reasonableness' with Hitler: 'I have believed that he was more open to the language of the mailed fist . . .' Other right-wingers, Nicolson, Amery, Cranborne, Churchill, tore into the Munich settlement and twenty-two of them ostentatiously refrained from the vote of confidence at the end of the debate; interestingly

---

[44] Howard, *The Continental Commitment*, pp. 74–139. On the anti-German sentiments of the *Daily Telegraph* and *Morning Post*, see F. R. Gannon, *The British Press and Germany 1936–1939* (Oxford, 1971), pp. 43–50; on Hankey, see S. W. Roskill, *Hankey, Man of Secrets*, iii (London, 1974).

[45] Gannon, *op. cit.*, pp. 136–228.

enough, they were in contact with Dalton to see if their tactics could be coordinated with those of the Labour Party.[46]

In late 1938 and early 1939, this criticism from Right and Left mounted. The Labour Party had already ceased to vote against the defence estimates, and now agreed with the policy of offering military alliances to European states who wanted them; the *News Chronicle* supported Duff Cooper's view that Britain should have stood firm against Hitler, the *Manchester Guardian* recalled Nicolson's scornful dismissal of the Munich pact; the *Guardian* also called for the admission of Eden, Churchill and Duff Cooper into the Cabinet. At the same time, the right-wingers were beginning to abandon their traditional aversion to Soviet Russia. Even during the Czech crisis some minds had been turning to the idea of an Anglo-French-Russian front and by the spring of 1939 they had openly joined the demand of the Labour Party for a vigorous diplomatic initiative. Unlike the Left, their views were based upon military necessity rather than any sympathy for the Soviet system. 'I am not prepared to regard Soviet Russia as a freedom-loving nation, but we cannot do without her now', Commander Bower told the Commons, 'I know they have shot a lot of people but there are some 170,000,000 of them left.'[47] Yet if the motives of the realists and idealists differed, their aims were becoming increasingly similar and there is little doubt that this pressure from the Right as well as the Left pushed a reluctant Chamberlain into the negotiations for a Russian alliance, which began in April 1939. Already, in the preceding month, the government had only just avoided a backbenchers' revolt and had had to suffer many criticisms of its callous reaction to the invasion of Prague. With most of the press and public now swinging into an anti-appeasement line, it behoved Chamberlain to follow suit, however reluctantly.

Further stages in this merger between the two opposing schools of thought came in the summer of 1939, as the war-clouds loomed over Poland. Neither the Labour Party, nor the right-wingers, could agree to the government's wish to adjourn Parliament for the summer; on the evidence of the previous year, they declared, it was not possible to trust Chamberlain, who might easily negotiate with Hitler during the recess.[48] And, when Germany fulfilled their predictions by overrunning Poland in early September, the combined attacks upon the government's indecisiveness broke out again.

---

[46] Thompson, *The Anti-Appeasers*, pp. 182–90; Naylor, *Labour's International Policy*, pp. 252–56; Gilbert, *Roots of Appeasement*, pp. 159–86.

[47] Gannon, *The British Press and Germany*, pp. 213, 246–48; Thompson, *op. cit.*, pp. 175–78, 203–4, 208.

[48] Thompson, *op. cit.*, pp. 215–19.

One of the most famous examples of this fusion under the pressure of events took place in the Commons on September 2nd; as Arthur Greenwood of the Labour Party rose to insist upon war, that arch-imperialist Amery shouted across the chamber: 'Speak for England!'[49] But the crowning symbol doubtless came on 10 May 1940, in the aftermath of the Norwegian fiasco, when the Labour Party leaders resolved that they would serve only under the right-winger Churchill.[50] It is also noticeable that there were no important political objectors in Britain during the Second World War, no equivalent of the U.D.C. One side had gone to war chiefly to protect the nation's interests, to maintain its honour and to preserve the balance of power; the other chiefly to uphold the liberties of small states, to destroy the evils of militarism and aggression, and to restore international harmony and goodwill. They would still quarrel over the means used to win the war, and no doubt the difference between the two camps would break out again after the struggle, for it was an eternal debate, between what man is and what man should be; but for a while at least they were united. Hitler had achieved what no other person had done.[51] The realists and the idealists were in agreement at last.

University of East Anglia

[49] Taylor, *The Trouble-Makers*, pp. 181–82.

[50] Thompson, *The Anti-Appeasers*, p. 232.

[51] My colleague, Dr V. R. Berghahn, has pointed out that Hitler was also the ultimate expression of those fears expressed about Germany by the British 'idealists' and 'realists' in the 1860s, which were, respectively, of the rejection of liberalism and democracy and morality in politics, and of the attempt to dominate the continent. Thus British comments from 1864 to 1939 mirror in their own way the problem of 'continuity' and 'discontinuity' in German history which has been the subject of so much recent debate.

WAR AND PEACE IN THE
EARLIER MIDDLE AGES

The Prothero Lecture

By Professor J. M. Wallace-Hadrill, M.A., D.Litt., F.B.A.,
F.R.Hist.S.

READ AT THE SOCIETY'S CONFERENCE
20 SEPTEMBER 1974

MEN of the earlier Middle Ages knew what they meant by war
and peace. Their definitions are not hard to find, even though,
when found, they prove to be inconsistent. They knew that there
were just and unjust wars, good kinds of peace and bad, and they
could envisage war and peace as two poles of a single concept.
My intention is not to survey this large and ramshackle field but
simply to enquire how far some of the definitions tallied with the
facts of war and peace; and whether, at the end, the pressures
making for peace had affected the nature of war. To ask whether
Western Europe in the days of King Alfred and the later Carolingians
was more or less peaceful than it had been four centuries earlier is
not very meaningful, since an entirely new situation was created by
the attacks of the Vikings, Arabs and Magyars; but it is meaningful
to ask whether four centuries of additional experience had caused
men to look at war and peace in a different way.

As always with medieval attitudes, one starts with contributions
from a remoter past; and of three of these contributions—Roman,
Christian and Germanic—we know enough to identify them in the
medieval context. The Roman attitude, at least under the Empire,
was in theory unambiguous and in derivation Greek: every war
needed justification. The best reason for going to war was defence
of the frontiers, and, almost as good, pacification of barbarians
living beyond the frontiers. Outside these reasons one risked an
unjust war, and emperors had to be careful.[1] This at least was the
theoretical position, though practice could be very different. It may
in part explain why we have no Roman treatise on the theory
of war, as we have, for example, a very enlightening treatise from
the late fourth century on its practical application within the

[1] I have to thank Professor P. A. Brunt and my son Andrew for advice on the
Roman view of warfare.

framework of saving manpower and taxation by means of technical innovations.[2] But even in *De Rebus Bellicis* one encounters a certain ambiguity: the purpose of war may be defence, but the technical innovations to which the author wishes to draw the emperor's attention happen to involve weapons of attack. Cicero, in *De Officiis*,[3] had already been clear about the difference between just and unjust wars; and he was not the only one. The Romans must be given more credit than medievalists usually allow them for their consistent belief that warfare ought not to be waged for offensive purposes; and among these they counted the pursuit of glory unaccompanied by further justification.[4] As for peace, the *Pax Romana* so ardently desired, it was significant that the goddess of peace was iconographically very like the goddess of victory.[5] In other words, peace was something to be sought for and won on the battlefield, something to be constantly defended when won. Peace, then, was not merely absence of war; it was a condition that in practice resulted from war, and which would always demand a warlike stance. In the words of Vegetius, leading writer on military matters, *'qui desiderat pacem, praeparet bellum'*[6].

What for these purposes I call the Christian contribution comprises biblical and patristic strands. In brief, it ranges from the Old Testament to Ambrose and Augustine,[7] and is, on the whole, consistent. Warfare for God's purpose must be waged by God's people, and its justification will be peace. Peace is the supreme realization of divine law. It is not then surprising that the Bible seemed to join with Antiquity in urging the necessity for the military virtues. Indeed, it has rightly been said that the collective fury of God's war, the war of the Chosen People, was something more terrible than any act of individual heroism of Germanic epic. God was present in battle as leader of his people,[8] and his enemies could justly be sacrificed to him. There is more to it than that; but I content myself with isolating the strand in the Christian tradition that was to have significant bearing on early medieval practice: the

[2] The text of *De Rebus Bellicis* is edited and translated by E. A. Thompson, *A Roman reformer and inventor* (Oxford, 1952).

[3] *De Officiis*, ed. C. Atzert (Teubner, 4th edn., 1963), i, 34–40; i, 80–82: ii, 18; iii, 46, 88.

[4] According to Giulio Vismara, 'Problemi storici e istituti giuridici della guerra altomedievale', *Settimane di Studio del Centro Italiano di Studi sull' Alto Medioevo*, xv(2) (Spoleto, 1968), p. 1162, the Eastern Empire clung to an imperial doctrine that all war was legitimate if initiated by the emperor; but this needs qualification.

[5] I here follow Gina Fasoli, 'Pace e guerra nell'alto medioevo', *ibid.*, xv(1), to whose paper I am generally indebted.

[6] *De Re Militari*, ed. N. Schwebel (Strasbourg, 1806), iii, prol.

[7] See *e.g.* Deut. 7:21; 9:1; 20:16; 28:47; Numb. 21:14; 1 Chron. 10:11, 27.

[8] Deut., 20:4.

justification for Christian warfare that overrode all obstacles was the achievement of God's purpose. One may sense in this a driving-force, perhaps also an absence of brakes, that could make Christian warfare something more formidable than its pagan imperial counterpart.

Thirdly, the Germans. It is not easy to distinguish their ancient and traditional views on war and peace from those that came to prevail when they were settled within the Empire. We lump them together, both the Germans and their views, in a way that the Romans did not, and by so doing risk dismissing them as uni-formly and invariably warlike. As they come within the ken of the Romans they certainly look warlike—and inevitably, since war was the context in which the Romans knew them. All of them, so far as we know, had a warrior-class, armed and trained to fight, if not always very formidably; and they had leaders in war, as Tacitus tells us.[9] But they did not live for or by warfare. They were agri-cultural peoples, upon whom the necessity of getting a living was imposed. I am far from regarding the Germanic peoples as harmless farmers who somehow wandered, or were pushed, over the frontier into imperial territory. Indeed, I am not sure that we even yet understand the nature of their migration—supposing it to have been a migration. But they could fight for a place in the sun, successfully enough to be hired as mercenaries and settled as such. To this extent they had their contribution to make to the medieval pool of ideas about war and peace. But when we find them settled in Italy and Spain, Gaul and Britain, they have already in varying degrees absorbed something of the ethos of *Romanitas,* and even of Christianity.

At this point it may be well to distinguish the warfare of which I am thinking from feud, the process by which Germanic kindreds settled their differences. A good deal has been written about feud.[10] If it was private warfare (and it could be) it was conditioned by accepted rules imposed by custom, indeed by necessity. When first encountered in written sources, it is already deeply involved with the business of finding composition. In other words, the feuding process was amenable to settlement on agreed terms that were a substitute for bloodshed. Things did not always work out this way; indeed, we cannot tell what generally happened at any one time or place. But the composition-tariffs of the barbarian law-codes can only mean that composition was an accepted part of feud. A feud may of course be private warfare on a very large scale, as between

[9] *Germania,* ed. J. C. G. Anderson (Oxford, 1938), 7, 1.
[10] *Cf.* my 'The bloodfeud of the Franks', in *The Long-Haired Kings* (London, 1962).

kings. There are cases of this in Frankish and in Anglo-Saxon history, where wars between peoples, though caused by personal differences between kings, are yet waged in a manner indistinguishable from any other wars on the same scale. But when we speak of feuds we generally mean quarrels between families, involving the neighbourhood more or less. Such evidence as we have of these by no means suggests that the Germans took to fighting between families as a desirable occupation and proper outlet for bellicose instincts. Rather the opposite.

Which Germanic peoples can be considered essentially war-like and attuned to warfare as a national occupation? One thinks of the Goths. If we may believe Philostorgius, Wulfila decided not to translate the Books of Kings into Gothic lest the stories of war should inflame their warlike instincts.[11] Certainly he did not translate the Books of Kings. But when we see the Goths settled in Spain, we find a military caste indeed, generally ready for an outing, but the people are peaceably scraping a living out of the Meseta of Castile. Gregory of Tours had a low opinion of the Gothic warrior's courage,[12] but he may not be a reliable witness. I do not think we can call the Goths an exceptionally warlike people. The Lombards may be better candidates. Paul the Deacon, writing in the ninth century but using older material, clearly considered them warlike by nature; for them, war was a great tradition, and an occupation properly associated with ritual and sacrifice. Thus Alboin, besieging Pavia, vows that when it has fallen he will kill 'universum populum', which can reasonably be taken as a mass-sacrifice to his gods.[13] But it is another matter to equate the people with the exercitus. Liutprand indeed admitted that he could not eradicate the Lombard military instinct, though in the special context of the iudicium Dei.[14] Yet the Lombards, like all Germanic peoples of whom anything is known, had a clear concept of peace, or rather of various kinds of peace, some of them capable of steady extension. There is no need here to recapitulate the plentiful evidence for the peace of the Germanic homestead, well-attested as it is in Anglo-Saxon practice, nor yet of the general peace of a people, which, if Brunner is right, reaches back to antique times.[15] As recorded, however, it is already associated with kingly authority, and certainly the special peace of the king's residence, his city, his

[11] Cf. D. H. Green, The Carolingian Lord (Cambridge, 1965), p. 279.

[12] Libri Historiarum, ed. B. Krusch and W. Levison, Mon. Germ. Hist., Script. Rer. Mero. (Hanover, 1951), ii, 27.

[13] Historia Langobardorum, ed. G. Waitz, Script. Rer. Germ. in usum schol. (Hanover, 1890) ii, 35.

[14] Leges, cap. 118, Die Gesetze der Langobarden, ed. F. Beyerle (Weimar, 1947).

[15] Deutsche Rechtsgeschichte (2nd edn., Berlin, repr. 1958), ii, sections 65, 66.

servants and travellers seeking him, seems to owe little to Volksrecht. With the Anglo-Saxons, general recognition of the king as protector of the general peace seems to have been a hesitant growth before the eleventh century. In Maitland's words, 'the time has not yet come when the King's peace will be eternal and cover the whole land. Still we have here an elastic notion'.[16] But wherever we look, peace to the German never looks like an abstraction or a distant political ideal. It is rather a condition of non-hostility that a man or a group of men may grant and enforce, insofar as it affects him or them. Often it seems to imply a normal state of enmity from which, by special dispensation, some person or class of persons is exempted. Even to marry into another kin is to make of that kin a friend where before, as a matter of course, one had an enemy. Hence the procedural caution and care that characterize the Germanic marriage-negotiation and settlement. There are, then, varieties of Germanic peace, all of them implying absence of hostility within a specified context, and sometimes extendable by special arrangement. Obviously it is a concept vital to the conduct of the social life of any people, but it is nonetheless negative, resting as it does on the knowledge that the world at large, and especially the world just beyond one's own experience, is naturally hostile. One of the kinds of peace that are found quite early is the peace accorded to the Church, or to churches, which is not the same as the peace accorded by the Church. Churches and their officials need special protection from kings, and, as we know, they got it. No doubt the pagan shrines had also got it. But it raises the point that the evidence of peace-bestowal and peace-protection in the Volksrechte is already associated, however slightly to begin with, with Christian cultus.

We come thus to the Church that faced the Germans when they settled the Western provinces, and to its own notions of peace and war. St Augustine's view was that war is the price of peace, and the just ruler will not be able to avoid it; it will be forced on him by his enemies. The fact that he will be fighting a just war is small comfort, for the cause of war will be the wickedness of his enemies. Behind warfare there is always wickedness. St Augustine does not elaborate this idea of the regrettable just war, though the canonists were to do so;[17] the regret is his, the justness or unjustness is Roman. Isidore is less certain that warfare is regrettable. His section *De Bello et Ludis* (and it is interesting that he lumps them together, making of both a kind of festival), starts with a good Ciceronian definition of

[16] F. Pollock and F. W. Maitland, *The History of English Law before the time of Edward I* (Cambridge, 1895), ii, p. 452; see also i, pp. 22, 23.
[17] *De Civitate Dei*, ed J. E. C. Welldon (London, 1924), xix, cap. 7.

the just and unjust war.[18] A war, he decides, has four stages: battle, flight, victory, peace. '*Pacis vocabulum videtur a pacto sumptum*'. And *pax* will be followed by a *foedus*. In other words, peace is a technicality dependant on victory in the field. Isidore follows this up with a section *De Triumphis*, a concept dear to the mind of Late Antiquity. A witness of much Gothic warfare, he has not concluded that to fight is incompatible with Catholic doctrine. Nor was there any reason why he should have done so. The community of all men under natural law, even when envisaged as divine law,[19] by no means obviates the need to fight in a just cause. The justness still remained to be determined from the Christian standpoint, and the Fathers had been clear that the profession of war was entirely compatible with Christianity. Lactantius, Origen, Tertullian and Ambrose had no doubt about it. Provided that the purpose of war was just, it could be waged; and peace, itself the justification for war, was the supreme realization of divine law. Thus there was nothing in the Christian tradition that need have caused the churchmen of the Early Middle Ages to look upon the warring Germans as wicked because they fought. A just war was still perfectly acceptable, however saddened one might be by bloodshed and destruction.

But could the Germans be induced to fight just wars? Of their disposition to fight there could be no question. Warrior-classes trained in the mysteries of battle, cut off from their fellows by the exercise of a special craft, were not going to lay down their arms because they had become landowners in a Roman province. A young prince, not of weapon-bearing age, is buried at Cologne in the mid-sixth century. He is furnished with a complete military equipment. Some of it is of the right size for adults and the rest look like miniatures or toys. What they constitute is the symbolic or ritual equipment of the class into which he was born.[20] He was not a warrior; but a warrior was all that he could have become, or desired to become. He belonged to a hereditary fighting caste. For such a one, Frankish life *was* war.[21] And not of course Frankish life only, but the life of every German brought up in the military tradition of his people. Whether we should conclude that a whole people was thus dedicated to war is another matter. If we look at Frankish history over the Merovingian period we might indeed be tempted

[18] *Etymologiarum sive Originum Libb.*, ed. W. M. Lindsay (Oxford, 1911), Bk. 18.

[19] *Cf.* Vismara, 'Problemi storici e istituti giuridici della guerra altomedievale' p. 1152.

[20] J. Werner, *Settimane di Studio*, xv(1), p. 101.

[21] See the discussion by J-P. Bodmer, *Der Krieger der Merowingerzeit und seine Welt* (Zürich, 1957).

to reach just such a conclusion, for the Franks seem not often to have let a campaigning season pass without exercising their skills. However, a closer look will reveal that their campaigns were fought for a variety of reasons and in rather different ways. Gregory of Tours, surveying the scene between the accession of Clovis and his own time (late sixth century) has much to record of fighting, but most of it—*bella civilia* caused by fraternal disputes and feuds—falls outside any definition of warfare as a national occupation. National campaigns are fought outside Francia, against Alamans, Saxons, Goths and Lombards, and though they are often inseparable from booty-raids, Gregory, a bishop, does not see them as unjustly aggressive. Indeed, they are the proper pursuit of Catholic kings, who should be extending the sway of the Church (and thus their own) by attacking the heathen. This is specially the case when attacking the Visigoths of Septimania and Spain, craven Arians who are hardly forgiven when their king Reccared accepts Catholicism for them. Gregory's well-known account of Clovis's campaign against Alaric[22] is an account of a Catholic hero fighting under the aegis of St Martin and St Hilary, with the full approval of the Eastern Emperor. Now, whether this account be fundamentally historical or not, it signifies that this is how a Gallo-Roman bishop of the later sixth century can best represent the matter. The Church has accepted the Franks and taught their kings what to fight for, and in which direction to expand their martial energies. There is no question of taming them. The tragedy is, as Gregory sees it, that the Merovingians of his generation have fallen short of Clovis's ideal and turned their swords upon each other. In other words, Gregory stands at the beginning of that process whereby the Church persuaded the Franks to extend their power by warfare associated with missionary objectives. There is nothing said of peace as a national objective but only of peace as the proper relationship of one Merovingian king with another. Neither in Gregory's History nor subsequently do we find kings going forth to righteous warfare as a matter of course with their people uniformly assembled behind them. Foreign campaigns are fought by armies that differ markedly in personnel, equipment, tactics and objectives. Not all Merovingian armies comprised even a majority of Frankish warriors; there were contingents of Burgundians, Aquitanians, Alans and even Saxons; their best generals were Gallo-Romans; their composition varied, according to the need, in the proportions of cavalry, infantry and siege-experts; and the Franks themselves might be city levies on any scale and also the

[22] *Lib. Hist.*, ii, 37.

followings of kings and magnates.[23] We cannot, then, say that the Franks of Gaul were a people habitually in arms; and it is not even certain that so much can be said of their great men, trained as they were for warfare. Yet the Franks are above all other Germans marked out as a warrior-people. Apart from their normally disastrous campaigns in Spain and Italy, to which Gregory and Fredegar often give a religious complexion, their less well-recorded campaigns in the Rhineland deserve attention for what they tell us of war and peace. The Merovingians stepped into Roman shoes to be defenders of Gaul against eastern pressures on the Rhineland. Whether against Frisians, Saxons, Thuringians, Alamans or Bavarians, the Merovingians saw themselves as defenders, not aggressors. True, defence could carry them fairly deep into Germany, as when Dagobert went for Samo's Wendish kingdom in Bohemia;[24] and the eastern emperors were not always happy about Frankish operations over the Rhine. But the general tenor of these operations was certainly defensive. They were campaigns to repel threats or to bolster up allies; and with them went Frankish settlements along the rivers flowing west into the Rhine; and with the settlements went the establishment of churches on a modest scale. Thus Frankish missionary work in Germany antedates the Anglo-Saxon effort by many years. Such limited aims are very different from those of the early Carolingians.[25] The first Frankish expansionist was Charles Martel, but the Frankish *Reihengräber* that stretch from southern Frisia to the Alaman territory belong to an earlier time and bear witness to piecemeal colonization in the marcher lands and approaches to the Rhine.[26] The Frankish lady who was buried among *Reihengräber* at Wittislingen in the mid-seventh century was a Christian,[27] and this argues at least an oratory. It amounts to this: however practical the motives that led to campaigning and settlement in the Rhineland and its northern and eastern approaches, the Merovingians could be represented quite reasonably as acting defensively and the Church went with them. It was the kind of activity that Gregory of Tours had longed for. The missionary

[23] Bernard S. Bachrach, *Merovingian Military Organization, 481–751* (Minneapolis, 1972), discusses the composition of Frankish armies but makes too much of local levies.

[24] Fredegar, *Chronicorum Libri*, ed. B. Krusch, *Mon. Germ. Hist., Script. Rer. Mero.*, ii (Hanover, 1888), and J. M. Wallace-Hadrill (London, 1960), iv, 68.

[25] On the contrast see Rolf Sprandel, *Der merovingische Adel und die Gebiete östlich des Rheins* (Freiburg im B., 1957).

[26] *Cf.* A. Bergengruen, *Adel und Grundherrschaft im Merowingerreich* (Wiesbaden, 1958).

[27] J. Werner, *Das alamannische Fürstengrab von Wittislingen* (Munich, 1950), pp. 75–77.

work of such a one as St Amand, among Slavs, Gascons and finally
Franks and Frisians of the Lower Rhine, was precisely what he had
had in mind; and it worked, then as later, just so long as Frankish
military power was at hand to assist. St Amand was a professional
missionary: '*docete omnes gentes*' was his maxim.[28] Merovingian
military might, when not turned in upon itself, was habitually
employed in ways that answered fairly well to the Catholic requirements of just war.

I do not know that the Anglo-Saxons were much less militarily
inclined than the Franks. Bede does not depict them as engaged in
continuous campaigning, let alone crusading; but much of what
warfare there was could be seen as Christian warfare, justifiable
warfare. Even so, he can write feelingly of a time of peace in our
own sense of the word, a time when ordinary folk could get on with
their business undisturbed, and a woman and child walk safely
anywhere.[29] This great peace—*tanta pax*—was the outcome of a
good deal of righteous battle. Edwin had to win his crown and
fight to keep it. A believer, his earthly power was increased, as that
of Clovis had been, so that he ruled over Britain '*ut quod nemo
Anglorum ante eum*';[30] and so the prophecy was fulfilled that he
should overcome his enemies and surpass in power all former
English kings.[31] Thus, wars of territorial expansion could be just
wars, Christian wars, just as much as those fought for national
preservation. Equally justifiable was the rebellion, amounting to
war, of those who supported Penda's son in Mercia against the
foreign overlord, Oswiu; their courage won back for them their
lands and their freedom. But, Bede goes on, they rejoiced to serve
'*Christo vero regi*'.[32] In other words, though the rebellion was easily
explicable and justifiable as patriotic revulsion against foreign
dominance, it could also be made to bear a religious overtone. But
there were aggressive wars that bore no semblance of justice. Penda
and Cadwallon could not be forgiven their attacks on Northumbria,
nor Cadwalla for his treatment of the Isle of Wight, nor Ecgfrith
of Northumbria for his unprovoked expedition against the innocent
Irish, for which God exacted proper vengeance at Nechtansmere.[33]
In brief, war was a natural condition for the Anglo-Saxons, as for
the Franks and Lombards and Goths; so natural that it should be
prepared for and anticipated by warriors trained and equipped

[28] See Wolfgang H. Fritze, 'Universalis gentium confessio', *Frühmittelalterliche
Studien*, 3 (1969), pp. 88 ff.

[29] *Ecclesiastical History*, ed. and trs. B. Colgrave and R. A. B. Mynors (Oxford,
1969), ii, 16.

[30] *Ibid.*, ii, 9.

[31] *Ibid.*, ii, 12.

[32] *Ibid.*, iii, 24.

[33] *Ibid.*, iv, 26.

in its service. Hence Bede's evident distress at the condition of affairs in Northumbria, as revealed in his letter to Egbert of York; young warriors, deprived of land for their upkeep by improper monastic foundations, are going abroad or living debauched lives instead of preparing themselves to fight for their country against barbarian aggressors.[34] Northumbria is open to invasion; she cannot fight a defensive war, as she should. Northumbrians both noble and simple ought to be training themselves in the art of war, not taking monastic vows; what the result will be, the next generation will discover.[35] Analysis of this kind one might well expect from a political bishop like Gregory of Tours, but it is remarkable indeed from a monastic schoolmaster, however able. The fact is, Bede was a man of his time: he could see the need for a warrior-class both in the political circumstances of Anglo-Saxon England and in the teaching of the Bible and the Fathers. Not for nothing did he comment on the Books of Kings. It was not difficult for him to see in Oswald the ideal of the Christian warrior, praying before battle for God's protection in a just war to defend his people: '*iusta pro salute gentis nostrae bella.*'[36] What could be more explicit? But successful defence merges without too much difficulty into successful aggression. Oswald's power was extended over all Britain.[37] How this came about we are not told. But the justification in Bede's eyes was clearly his Christian piety, which he owed to the teaching of Aidan. Once again, a pious king will have his reward here on earth, as well as hereafter. Not that worldly success, however justified, need always lead to victory: he died in faith, and he died '*pro patria dimicans*';[38] and he died in battle, no longer the victor. King Sigeberht, too, was dragged to battle from his monastery in order to put heart in the East Anglian warriors whose distinguished commander he had once been. But this saintly king with his *virga* in his hand was no longer the same man. He and his warriors were routed and killed by the 'pagans.'[39] Bede faces facts. But Oswald was right to extend his power by battle; Sigebert was right to join his warriors in the field; Oswiu was right to stand against Penda's larger army and defeat him with God's help, though it was a little awkward that he had first tried to buy the old savage off. Another explanation was called for: '*necessitate cogente*'.[40] It was better to fight, as Bede well knew. And of course there was encouragement for this view from higher quarters. Bede gives his readers Pope

---

[34] *Baedae opera historica*, ed. C. Plummer (Oxford, 1896), i, p. 415.
[35] Colgrave and Mynors, *Eccl. Hist.*, v, 23.
[36] *Ibid.*, iii, 2.   [37] *Ibid.*, iii, 6.
[38] *Ibid.*, iii, 9.   [39] *Ibid.*, iii, 18.
[40] *Ibid.*, iii, 24.

Vitalian's letter to Oswiu, in which he assures the Catholic king that 'all his islands' shall be made subject to him, as both he and the writer desire.[41] To seek the kingdom of God, to add a new people to the faith, is a way to win the apostolic promise: 'all these things shall be added unto you'.[42] Moreover, the Old Testament is cited in support. Isaiah had foreseen the bright future of the root of Jesse and the raising up of the tribes of Jacob.[43] The Pope does not in so many words equate Oswiu's people with the People of Israel; but the idea is surely present in his mind. When were the Christian peoples of England happiest? Bede is in no doubt; it had been during Archbishop Theodore's reign. Then had been the '*feliciora tempora*' of brave Christian kings: '*cunctis barbaris nationibus essent terrori*'.[44] One cannot quite call this aggressive, but it points to the need for a Christian society to be on its toes, armed and alert, ready to do battle. A king can do this and more provided he be sustained, like Wihtred of Kent, '*religione simul et industria*',[45] which in context means piety and soldierly zeal. Perhaps one should add a gloss to what looks like a simplified picture of fighting rightly and fighting wrongly. It might be the case that a Christian king would employ pagans in his forces, and this happened with the Franks, who used the Saxons; or again, that an unjustified attack would bring about a desirable end, as when Cadwallon killed the two apostate Northumbrians; or yet again, that a good man might rightly be required to follow his lord to a bad war, which is the poet's assumption when he makes Beowulf fight for Hygelac in an unjustified attack on the Frisians.[46] In tricky cases excuses could be found. Pope Nicholas I informed the emperor Louis II that there was nothing wrong in making arrangements with pagan peoples if it were for the security of Christendom or tended towards conversion, and he cited the examples of Solomon and Charlemagne.[47] The end generally justified the means, so long as one was clear that the right posture of Christians towards pagans was offensive; and so too towards heretics and all enemies to Christian society's peace. Reservations about war therefore do not amount to much. Old English penitentials might brand killing in war as homicide, but the penance was not heavy, and on the other hand there were prayers in the liturgy for those who fought.[48]

But there is a related problem. Germanic pagan peoples had a

[41] Colgrave and Mynors, iii,29. [42] Matth. 6: 33; Luc. 12: 31.

[43] Isaiah, 11:10. [44] *Eccl. Hist.*, iv, 2.

[45] *Ibid.*, iv, 26.

[46] On which see J. E. Cross, 'The ethic of war in Old English', *England before the Conquest*, ed. Peter Clemoes and Kathleen Hughes (Cambridge, 1971), pp. 277–78.

[47] *Mon. Germ. Hist., Epist.* vii (*Karo. Aev.*, iv), no. 54, p. 351.

[48] *Cf.* Cross, 'The ethic of war in Old English', pp. 280–81.

clear sense that war was a religious undertaking, in which the gods were interested. At once one thinks of Woden as a God peculiarly, though not exclusively, connected with warfare. Goths and Vandals were well aware that victory depended on the gods and called for sacrifice. A disobliging war-god stood some risk of being abandoned, as Clovis abandoned his gods after Tolbiac.[49] But when the Goth Totila addresses his troops and informs them that God only favours the side that fights in a just cause[50] we are surely faced with Christian influence, for only a Christian would have allowed that God's favour was not the property of any one people. Moreover, Totila was chivalrous and mild with his enemies, as Goths went. Pagan and pagan-transitional warfare, then, had its religious facet. Not surprisingly, Christian missionaries found this ineradicable, though not unadaptable to their own purposes.[51] Christian vernacular makes considerable use of the terms of pagan warfare. I am uncertain whether the preferred terms are borrowed exclusively from the vocabulary of the *comitatus*, nor, if they were, whether these terms had no religious significance. But they were borrowed, and notably by the Anglo-Saxons. We are told that the earliest use of *dryhten* as a Christian term in any Germanic language is by Caedmon,[52] and this was not long after the conversion of Northumbria. It was to become the standard Old English literary version of Christian *dominus*. Why, then, did the men who converted the Anglo-Saxons differ so sharply from Wulfila? The Anglo-Saxons were not less bellicose than the Goths. The answer may lie in the prudent spirit of accommodation shown by Gregory the Great. More than that, the pope was an ardent supporter of warfare to spread Christianity and convert the heathen,[53] and this last is, I think, the more important consideration. So far from rejecting the Germanic war-ethos the pope means to harness it to his own ends, and the evidence is that he succeeded. The barbarians may fight to their heart's content in causes blessed by the Church, and this is made clear not only in the matter of vocabulary. It is the position of the Church rather than of the Germans that had undergone modification. As Erdmann showed, the Church subsumed and did not reject the warlike moral qualities of its converts.[54] Who shall say that St Michael of later days was not Woden under fresh colours?

---

[49] Gregory of Tours, *Hist. Libb.*, ii, 30, 31.

[50] Procopius, *Gothic War*, ed. H. B. Dewing, vii, xxi, 7–11.

[51] See Green, *The Carolingian Lord*, esp. pp. 279–97.

[52] A. H. Smith, *Three Northumbrian Poems* (London, 1933), pp. 12 ff.

[53] *Gregorii I Registri*, Mon. Germ. Hist., *Epist.* i, no. 73, p. 93.

[54] *Die Entstehung des Kreuzzugsgedankens* (Stuttgart, 1935), pp. 16 ff.

The Anglo-Saxon fruit of so much teaching and experience was King Alfred, commander in a great war that was at once defensive, patriotic and Christian. In his actions and in his translations he reveals himself as a Gregorian, even an Augustinian, king. Under the high-kingship of God he fights God's battles, and he fights in the name of his *dryhten*, Christ.[55] From Orosius he learns that Christian wars, unlike those of an earlier time, are fought for justice, not for conquest; and he knows that mercy is proper to a king. This is very much how Asser saw him; that it so say, as a leader of *Christiani* against *pagani*, an indefatigable warrior who would rather have spent his reign in peaceful pursuits if he had not been compelled to defend his land and people. If he thus appears as a warrior *malgré lui* it is in part because of his remarkable gifts aside from generalship, in part because Asser leans towards an interpretation of a king's duties that sees fighting rather as a grim necessity than as a desirable occupation. Alfred plainly had a positive idea of the blessings of a state of peace; by which I mean that he knew what he would do if prolonged peace were ever his country's lot. Compare this with Einhard's picture of Charlemagne; as real a man as Asser's Alfred, but a different man. Charlemagne is no less interested in the intellectual life and the teachings of the Church than is Alfred and perhaps not much more of a campaigner. But he has a more positive attitude to Christian warfare. There are always justifications for his campaigns: he is defending a frontier, putting down revolts, carrying Christianity to pagans. But no one could deny that the Saxon wars were aggressive, involving as they did deep penetration in Saxony, mass-deportation and slaughter— some of it, as at Verden, done in cold blood. Alfred did nothing like this. Nor does Einhard think it necessary to justify the attack on Spain: he simply reports that, having garrisoned his Saxon frontier, Charlemagne attacked Spain with every man he could raise.[56] Similarly he went for the disobedient Bretons,[57] and then the Lombards,[58] and so on. Einhard is summarizing what he read in the annals, and all he seems to feel, though he does not even add this is so many words, is that you could do as you pleased with pagans and rebels. The upshot was that these wars of the *rex potentissimus* doubled the dominions that his father had left him.[59] It was plain annexation: '*auxit etiam gloriam regni sui*';[60] his kingdom

---

[55] *Cf. King Alfred's West-Saxon version of Gregory's Pastoral Care.* ed. and trs., Henry Sweet, Early English Text Soc., vols. 45, 50 (London, 1871).

[56] *Vita Karoli Magni*, ed. O. Holder-Egger, *Script. Rer. Germ. in usum schol.* (Hanover, 1911), ch. 9.

[57] *Ibid.*, ch. 10.

[58] *Ibid.*

[59] *Ibid.*, ch. 15.

[60] *Ibid.*, ch. 16.

was extended *'subigendis exteris nationibus'*.[61] As to Viking attacks on Francia, here indeed Charlemagne was on the defensive, even if one cause of the attacks may have been earlier Carolingian offensives. But Einhard shows us a traditional Germanic warrior—*'corpore . . . amplo atque robusto'*[62]—whose perfectly serious Christian aspirations for himself and his people were best realized in conquest. No wonder that the inscription over his tomb at Aachen contained the phrase: *'regnum Francorum nobiliter ampliavit'*.[63] It is in Charlemagne, not in Alfred, in Einhard, not in Asser, that one sees the first real triumph of Catholic teaching on war. It can all be justified and held up as an example to a weaker generation. There is no sighing for peace; the *regnum Christianum* is the *regnum Francorum*. This of course is a one-sided view of a complex and fruitful reign, but it certainly protrudes positively as a reason for wonder and pride. Einhard insists that Charlemagne was a traditional man, liking Frankish dress and food, songs and habits. Traditional too, no doubt, was his training for and pleasure in war. But the ninth century is not the sixth, and Frankish bellicosity was not what it had been— which indeed may help to explain why Einhard shows what it should be. Not every magnate wished to be away in Italy or Spain for long months on his lord's wars. This leads me to suppose that the teaching of churchmen had hardened, that the lesson of the just war was more in need of activation than that of the just peace. Traditional Germanic prowess in war now demanded emphasis; and this is what the writers of the ninth century accorded it. But they were lucky. If it took a little consideration to represent the aggressive wars of the Carolingians as wars of religion, there was no problem at all with their defensive wars. Charles Martel could properly meet and defeat the Arabs on Frankish soil *'Christo auxiliante'*;[64] and when the Carolingians had finished with the Arabs, there were the Vikings. Ninth-century writings on Frankish-Viking encounters were not only naturally couched in terms of Christian defence against pagan aggression, but in my opinion justifiably so.[65] It was as a Christian warrior that Louis III met and defeated the Vikings at Saucourt, and his victory could be celebrated in verse.[66] Whether or not we see the Viking assaults as the principal cause of the disintegration of Carolingian power in Francia, that was how they struck contemporaries: the besieged West was a Christian West, and the wasting wars it was called

[61] *Vita Karoli Magni*, ch. 17.   [62] *Ibid.*, ch. 22.
[63] *Ibid.*, ch. 31.   [64] Fredegar, cont., ch. 13.
[65] I defend this position in 'The Vikings in Francia' (Stenton Lecture, Reading, 1974).
[66] By the poet of the *Ludwigslied*.

upon to fight were just wars of defence. It is all the more remarkable, then, to find that Einhard's barbarically aggressive Charlemagne is accepted as a model and an ideal. He appears in Notker's *Gesta* as the idealized iron warrior, whose deeds should be better known;[67] a Christian ruler indeed, but a Davidic figure of formidable power. So too, his son, Louis the Pious, who as pictured by Notker, loved iron and weapons more than gold.[68] This was the right model for the insufficiently militant Charles the Fat. Equally aggressive is the outlook of Ermoldus Nigellus' poem, *In honorem Hludowici*. He starts by invoking Christ who opens the gates of heaven to good warriors (*militibus dignis*),[69] which indeed was an inducement that popes occasionally held out—as did Leo IV in 848. Anyone, he says, who falls in battle and dies in faith shall by no means be denied entry into heaven. Therefore let battle be joined, '*omni timore ac terrore deposito*'.[70] Ermold goes on to describe the expedition of his hero, Louis the Pious, against Barcelona, which he led as Charlemagne's lieutenant. It is quite simply an expedition of destruction. Barcelona is besieged by the Frankish army, while its Saracen commander bewails the appearance of the besiegers: '*fortis et armigera est duraque sive celer*'.[71] 'These men', he says with a deep sigh, 'pass their lives under arms and are trained to war from boyhood . . . the name of Frank makes me shudder, the very word 'Frank' comes from 'ferus'.[72] Nevertheless he resists, thus putting the garrison beyond the pale of Christian charity: they are not merely pagans and rebels (the original reason for the attack) but resisters. So the siege proceeds, with a great deal of taunting from both sides. When at last Barcelona capitulates, we are not told what fate was meted out to the Saracen rank and file: '*hostibus imperitant*' could cover anything.[73] But the commander is taken back to Charlemagne, together with the spoils, which include buckles and cuirasses, clothing and crested helmets, and a horse with a golden bridle.[74] In brief, Louis has conducted a traditionally barbaric campaign and has returned victorious, laden with booty. If Christ has been with him, so too has Mars. Whatever they obtained, the Saracens had deserved no mercy and no warning. It would have been otherwise had they been Christians. Later on in his poem, Ermold describes

---

[67] Ed. H. F. Haefele, *Mon. Germ. Hist., Script. Rer. Germ.*, n.s. xii (Berlin, 1959).
[68] *Ibid.*, p. 87.
[69] *Ermold le Noir*, ed. Edmond Faral (Paris, 1932), p. 2.
[70] Mansi, *Sacrorum conciliorum nova et amplissima collectio*, xiv, 888.
[71] *Ermold le Noir*, p. 32, line 369.
[72] *Ibid.*, ll. 376–79. The same etymology is in Isidore, *Etymol.*, ix, 11, 101.
[73] *Ibid.*, l. 563, p. 44.
[74] *Ibid.*, l. 572–5, p. 46.

a campaign against a converted king, when Louis sends an ambassador to warn him of what is in store for him, 'for he has received baptism and so we ought to give him due notice'.[75] There was a recognized procedure as between Christian combatants. One could even say that there were already the beginnings of something like an international law of war.[76] Of course it would be idle to suppose that the siege of Barcelona bore much resemblance to Ermold's description of it. But the outlines will have been right and also the sentiments; for the poem was intended for Louis himself, as an attempt to win back favour for the poet. This, then, was how the top echelon of Frankish warriors wished to be commemorated.

But it must not be thought that the Church that urged kings to war had nothing to say about peace and made no effort to secure it: I mean, peace as an immediate goal, as opposed to that distant peace which was the Christian justification for all fighting. For such peace was from time to time possible for the great nations of the West; they were not always denied it, as was the mountain-kingdom of the Asturias, a society that only survived because it was organized for perpetual war.[77] Carolingian campaigning did worry churchmen intermittently. If warfare were a Christian undertaking, its rules could to some extent be prescribed and thus its impact controlled. Charles the Simple found it necessary in 923 to attack the rebellious Robert of Paris on a Sunday. The Church was horrified, and at a subsequent synod at Reims imposed penance on both sides. It was a three-year penance during Lent, and during the first Lent the combatants were all to be treated as virtual excommunicants.[78] This was much severer than the three-day fast ordered by the bishops after the battle of Fontenoy: the combatants of 923 had fought, on a Sunday, what amounted to a civil war, one side employing newly-converted Vikings; and the result had been disastrous. Here then was a case of the Church penalizing warriors, if not preventing war. The more clearly one distinguished between warriors and others, the easier perhaps such penalization became. There was an *ordo* whose work was fighting, the *bellatores*, as opposed to the *oratores* and the *imbelle vulgus*, as the author of the Miracles of St Bertin expresses it.[79] It is not the people who fight, but the professionals whose leaders might be induced to listen to

[75] *Ibid.*, ll. 1322–3, p. 102.

[76] Such is the contention of Vismara, 'Problemi storici e istituti giuridici della guerra altomedievale', p. 1199.

[77] See C. Sánchez-Albornoz, 'El ejército y la guerra en el reino Asturleonés', *Settimane di Studio*, xv(1), pp. 293–428.

[78] See the account in A. Eckel, *Charles le Simple* (Paris, 1899), pp. 123–27.

[79] *Mon. Germ. Hist., Scriptores*, xv, 513.

their brethren the bishops. It was Archbishop Theodore who stopped the war between kings Ecgfrith and Æthelred,[80] and Archbishop Hincmar who saved his master by causing Louis the German to withdraw his army from West Frankish territory.[81] The peace and quiet of his kingdom was indeed the proper concern of any Christian king. As the Fathers at Toledo neatly put it, '*sub[regis] pace pax servatur Ecclesiae*',[82] or, in a piece of earlier legislation, there should be '*una et evidens pax*' for all the king's subjects.[83] But then, of course, the upshot of peace and quiet at home was victory over the enemies of the people abroad.[84] The *bellatores* still had a job to do, and the Church would see that they did it. However, one must give some weight to a steady trickle of peaceful admonitions from churchmen of high standing and real influence; for the ninth century was one in which advice was listened to by men of action. Indeed, the wilder the time, the more insistently the lesson of peace was preached, It was preached by Alcuin and Agobard, by Jonas and Hincmar. by Sedulius and Rather of Verona, and it figures in the *arengae* of several imperial and royal diplomas and papal documents, as for example Gregory the Great to the Emperor Maurice in 595: no one can rule rightly '*nisi noverit divina tractare, pacemque rei publicae ex universalis ecclesiae pace pendere*'.[85] Charles the Bald can be praised by Sedulius as a peace-lover, if in a rather equivocal context: '*Lilia pacis amas, bellorum mixta rosetis*'.[86] In poetry and in liturgy, in history and in letters, war and peace remain linked as a pair.[87] It is the Christian warrior who is most often reminded of the blessings of peace; but it is the same warrior who is encouraged to make war. There should be limitations not only on the reasons for fighting but on its seasons. Thus, Pope Nicholas I warns the Bulgarians that though there should not be fighting in Lent, or indeed at any other time, '*si nulla urgat necessitas*', nevertheless, if necessity does urge it, fighting is not merely permissible but right, even in Lent.[88] A further step is taken by the council of Charroux in about 989 when it proclaims the Peace of God to protect non-combatants; and to

---

[80] Bede, *Eccl. Hist.*, iv, 21.

[81] *Pat. Lat.*, cxxvi, cols. 9–25.

[82] *Concilios Visigóticos e Hispano-Romanos*, ed. José Vives (Barcelona-Madrid, 1963), i, Toledo xiv, xii.

[83] *Mon. Germ. Hist., Leges* i, ed. K. Zeumer (Hanover, 1902), ii, 1, i.

[84] *Ibid.*, i, 2, vi ('*Quod triumphet de hostibus lex*'). Cf. P. D. King, *Law and society in the Visigothic kingdom* (Cambridge, 1972), pp. 33 ff.

[85] *Greg. I Reg.*, pp. 320 ff. See H. Fichtenau, *Arenga* (Graz-Cologne, 1957), pp. 76 ff.

[86] *Mon. Germ. Hist., Poetae Aevi Caro.*, iii, ed. L. Traube (Berlin, 1896), p. 181 (*Ad Karolum regem*, line 41).

[87] Cf. Gina Fasoli, 'Pace e guerra nell'alto medioevo', p. 45.

[88] *Pat. Lat.* 119, col. 998.

this are joined three special interdicts and anathemas, one of which covers '*agricolae ceterive pauperes*'.[89] What is new is not the protective sentiment but that the delimitation of war should be enacted as Church law and sanctioned by ecclesiastical punishment. It is the beginning of a long and complex process of definition and intervention, and really marks the end of the early medieval phase of war and peace.

I would conclude that the chances of a peaceful life in the year 900 were somewhat less than in the year 500. The investment in war was greater, and its reach commonly more extensive. The Church had not exactly let Woden out of the bottle, but it had certainly not secured the stopper. Warfare had been canalized in directions suitable to the Church, but not very efficiently. This in its turn encouraged churchmen to preach peace, to limit the proper occasions of war, and to protect non-belligerents and special places and occasions. One is surprised at the measure of their success.

All Souls College, Oxford.

[89] *Cf.* Erdmann, *Die Entstehung des Kreuzzugsgedankens*, pp. 53 ff.

DOMESDAY BOOK AND
ANGLO–NORMAN GOVERNANCE

By Sally P. J. Harvey, M.A., Ph.D., F.R. Hist. S.

READ 18 OCTOBER 1974

DOMESDAY BOOK stands accused of isolation and its historians stand convicted of isolated devotion to Domesday studies. The isolation is not entirely splendid. 'An inestimable boon to a learned posterity but a vast administrative mistake' was the brief verdict of Mr Richardson and Professor Sayles in their treatment of the governance of England from the Norman Conquest to Magna Carta.[1] Reviewing recent Domesday studies Dr King judged that research 'in so arid a climate' has maintained the gap between Domesday Book and its use in eleventh-and twelfth-century government, and made 'the inquiry into the resources of the tenants-in-chief look rather more lonely than before, and rather less necessary'.[2]

Part of the criticism is justified. Domesday Book's own monumentality is one of its greatest hazards. Though it bulks largest as a source of information for eleventh-century England it is by no means the sole survivor of late Anglo-Saxon and of Anglo-Norman administration. Many of the near-contemporary texts have suffered because all have been turned into Domesday 'satellites', even texts which are known to contain figures and arrangements which are not those of Domesday Book. On the other hand, the effort to avoid the magnetism of Domesday has caused a few historians of administration to evade its ambit altogether. Yet, there is a paucity of sources for administrative governance before the beginnings of the Pipe Rolls and before the proliferation of documents in the late twelfth century. The evidence of Domesday Book must be put into context, first, if we are to understand it, and secondly, if it is to make its contribution to the evolution of administration and policy. We then find that the Domesday survey had motives and objectives; its findings were acted upon instantly; and it remained a reference work for years to come. We gain insight into the administration which produced the survey and understand how Domesday's existence affected the character of subsequent administrative policy, particularly in the following reign.

[1] H. G. Richardson and G. O. Sayles, *The Governance of Medieval England from the Conquest to Magna Carta* (Edinburgh, 1963), p. 28.

[2] E. King, 'Domesday Studies', *History*, lviii (1973), p. 407. V. H. Galbraith, *Domesday Book: its place in administrative history* (Oxford, 1974) was published after this paper was read.

How and why Domesday Book was made has been the focus of long discussion. Round's emphasis on the primary role of county and hundred in the making of the survey led naturally to a fiscal purpose: it was 'a geld book'.[3] Professor Galbraith, on the other hand, concentrates on the logical conclusion of Domesday Book's feudal form: it 'set forth the legal theory of the new feudalism'.[4] Yet the dilemma can be resolved if it is recognized that fiscal documents already in existence were drawn on to help with the compilation of a partly feudal and partly fiscal inquiry.[5] It is now possible to separate what the inquiry set out to do *de novo* from the normal practices which helped to construct it.

Chroniclers and cartulary-makers have long told us explicitly of the earlier treasury documents and how the Domesday survey using them as its *exemplar* sought additional and extraordinary material. Heming writes of the '*exemplar* in the king's own *authentica cartula* preserved along with the descriptions of the whole of England in the royal treasury'.[6] An Abingdon scribe introduces a pre-Domesday list of hides: 'Of the hundreds and hides of the Church of Abingdon in Berkshire, just as contained in the records of the royal treasury, arranged by hundreds'.[7] He removes any possibility of a confused identity with Domesday by following it with an extract from Domesday itself entitled: 'From another book of the royal treasury, of the time of King William, which he ordered to be made when he came to England. It contains an abbreviation of hides (*abbreviatio hidarum*) and a description of them'. One narrative source, the late Crowland chronicler who incorporated 'many mistakes', but also 'some curious points of accuracy', has indeed been pilloried for his pains, the Domesday account being one of the grounds on which he has been condemned.[8] He explains that two sets of documents were known as the Winchester Rolls. One set, laid out by counties and hundreds, goes back with others of the same type a very long way. The other is King William's detailed description called Domesday. This, the chronicler tells us, was also known as the Winchester Roll, because

---

[3] J. H. Round, *Feudal England* (2nd edn, London, 1964), pp. 17–26; F. W. Maitland, *Domesday Book and Beyond* (Fontana edn, 1960), pp. 27–8.

[4] V. H. Galbraith, *The Making of Domesday Book* (Oxford 1961), pp. 2–54, esp. p. 54.

[5] S. Harvey, 'Domesday Book and its Predecessors', *English Historical Review*, lxxxvi (1971), pp. 753–73.

[6] *Cartularium Ecclesiae Wigorniensis*, ed. T. Hearne (Oxford, 1723), p. 288.

[7] Printed in D. C. Douglas, 'Some early surveys from the Abbey of Abingdon', *Eng. Hist. Rev.*, xliv (1929), pp. 623–25.

[8] See W. G. Searle, *Ingulph and the Historia Croylandensis* (Cambridge Antiquarian Soc. Publs., xxvii, 1894), in which the unreliability, and otherwise, of its contents, and its borrowings from sound sources which include Florence of Worcester are analysed, and summarised pp. 206–8.

it was kept at Winchester and because it was modelled on the lines of the others: *exemplar* is again the term used. King William's Domesday survey contained 'not just counties and hundreds, woods, marshes and all villages, but also how many carucates of land on all estates, how many yokes, acres, pasture and meadow, what holdings there were and who held them'.[9] In a few words this maligned compilation has shown the reason for the modern dissension over the nature of the Winchester Rolls, and resolved it.

A few instances of the records of hides (which often appear as *breves* or *brevia*) will draw their character. Many, like Domesday, were tenurial in form within counties. In the abundant Canterbury texts there is the whole of a pre-Domesday assessment list for Kent, and there is also an earlier one for the cathedral priory and archbishopric of Canterbury.[10] Within each fief the estates are usually in a regular order of hundreds, as the Domesday estates are. In Kent, the complete list was the exemplar for the Domesday layout, whilst the earlier list was the exemplar for the different hundredal order of the Domesday Monachorum. The dominating order could be reversed. In the eastern region, where hundredal organization was more important, the arrangement of estates was sometimes under hundreds, and grouped according to landholder within the hundred: the pattern which is reflected in the *Inquest of the County of Cambridge*, the text on which Round based much of his theory.[11] Both patterns are exemplified in the folios of Domesday Book itself, in the assessment lists for substantial parts of Yorkshire.[12] These lists are arranged by ridings, and then, largely, according to wapentake, with the lands of one holder grouped together within the wapentake. Nevertheless, the Richmond honour, Count Alan's fief, has a primarily tenurial arrangement. These Yorkshire lists have been type-cast as post-Domesday 'summaries', but their place-name forms, as well as their record of the carucates of some lands which Domesday dismisses as 'waste', show them to be independent.[13] They were probably temporarily inserted in Domesday Book

---

[9] *Chronicles of Crowland Abbey*, ed. W. de Grey Birch (Wisbech, 1883), pp. 140–41; *Rerum Anglicarum Scriptorum Veterum*, ed. G. Fulman, i (Oxford, 1684), pp. 79–80.

[10] Printed in R. S. Hoyt, 'A Pre-Domesday Kentish Assessment List', *Early Medieval Miscellany* (Pipe Roll Soc., lxxvi, 1960, new ser. xxxvi, 1962), pp. 189–202, and *The Domesday Monachorum of Christchurch, Canterbury*, ed. D. C. Douglas (London, 1944), pp. 99–104; the earlier list, *ibid*, pp. 80–81. For analysis of texts and relationships cited in this paragraph and for other examples, see Harvey, *loc. cit.* (n. 5 above).

[11] *Inquisitio Comitatus Cantabrigiensis subjicitur Inquisitio Eliensis*, ed. N. E. S. A. Hamilton (London, 1886); *cf.* Round, *Feudal England*.

[12] *D(omesday) B(ook)*, i (Record Commission, 1783), fos 379ª–82ᵈ.

[13] Harvey, *op. cit.* (n. 5 above), pp. 761–63.

because of the still unstable state of Yorkshire following the devastat-
ions. That these lists contributed to, but were not intended to
remain part of, the finished text is reinforced by their omission from
the later refined versions of Domesday Book.[14] The lists of hides
were simple, schematic by comparison with Domesday. Under
headings of hundred (or wapentake) or landholder appeared just
the place-name, holder and number of hides (or carucates). Other
shire lists still retain a lay-out according to Anglo-Saxon landholder,
(a feature which recurs in certain sections of Domesday Book, thus
betraying its parentage).[15] Whatever was novel about Domesday
Book it was not the intrusion of great landholder between shire and
hundred. Great landholders were officially in that position already.

In Domesday Book we meet another class of documentation
which was probably kept in the treasury at Winchester: that recording the farms and dues of shires and boroughs. Much information
enshrined under the boroughs is of Edwardian relevance as, for
instance, in the case of Dover, Cambridge and Hereford, and details
for 1086 have relatively little space.[16] It has long been known
that the descriptions of boroughs and royal lands bear every sign
of a different provenance from those of the rest of the shire.[17] They
are usually on separate folios and have their own terminology. It
seems that they are derived in fact from a distinct and earlier
inquiry. It is worthy of note that the terms of reference surviving
in the *Inquest of Ely* include no questions about boroughs or towns.[18]

It seems likely that the class of records concerning fixed charges,
farms, and miscellaneous dues from boroughs and royal estates were
the basis of the royal returns, whilst the county lists of landholders
and estates with their assessments, arranged by hundreds, constituted the basic structure for the inquiry from landholders.

Both the record of hides and the record of farms are mentioned
occasionally in Domesday Book. The Huntingdon account refers
to the list of hides: 'in Hurstingstone Hundred the demesnes are
exempt from the king's tax, but the *villani* and sokemen pay geld
according to the hides in the written record (*in brevi scripta*).'[19] The
royal record of farms makes an appearance when the Worcester-
shire Domesday talks of eighteen hides which, though they pay geld
and plead in Doddingtree Hundred, pay their set charge or farm to

[14] Public Record Office, MS. Museum Case 6; MS. Miscellaneous Books E.164.
[15] British Library, Cotton MS. Vespasian B xxiv, fos 57–62; Harvey, *op. cit.*,
p. 763; *e.g.*, *D.B.* i, fo 180^b–c; *D.B.* ii, fos 191–201.
[16] *E.g.*, *D.B.* i, fos 2^b, 75–76, 154, 246.
[17] R. W. Finn, *The Liber Exoniensis* (London, 1964), pp. 40, 145.
[18] *Op. cit.* (above, n. 11), ed. Hamilton, p. 97; *English Historical Documents*, ii (ed.
D. C. Douglas, London, 1953), p. 882.
[19] *D.B.* i, fo 203^b.

Hereford as it is 'written in the king's record (*scripta in brevi regis*).'[20] Particularly illuminating are the disputes over the lands which Earl Ralf held at his downfall in 1075, for in them Domesday employs *brevis* in its three current senses; as the county hide list arranged by landholders, as the royal record of farms and, more familiar, as the royal writ. After Earl Ralf's fall, Godric Dapifer held the land at farm 'at the king's treasury *in brevi suo* for 20 shillings'. So in the 1070s there was a royal record of farms to which royal officials made account. In 1086 the land was held by William de Warenne, but the men of the hundred said that they had seen neither the king's messenger nor the writ that delivered it to him. The other disputed land was in Roger Bigot's *breve* or record, though Godric Dapifer claimed it along with the land which was in the king's *breve*.[21]

The royal records in use before Domesday were still in use long afterwards. A list of hides for Gloucestershire coexists with a detailed rental of the royal boroughs of Gloucester and Winchcomb from the 1090s.[22] From the early twelfth century a roll of farms contains livestock on royal manors in Herefordshire and the total geld for the county, juxtaposed to a county list of landholders and their hides.[23] Again, in the early years of the twelfth century the *liber de thesauro* was consulted by barons and officials met in session in the treasury at Winchester to determine to which hundred the Abingdon Abbey manor of Lewknor owed obligations. The reference cannot be to Domesday Book, as so often assumed, for information on hundreds is absent from the relevant section.[24] Much later, in the more sophisticated 1180s, Richard fitz Nigel identifies the record of farms as the *breve de firmis* or *rotulus exactorius*, though it corresponds to no surviving text. He defines it: 'the exactor's roll is that in which are most distinctly and clearly enumerated the farms of the king which arise from each county'.[25] The record of farms and the record of hides provided a common foundation for royal administration through much of the eleventh and twelfth century. Such

[20] *D.B.* i, fo. 178[a].

[21] *D.B.* ii, fos 276[b], 176[a-b], 277-78[a]. Other instances are quoted and discussed in my unpublished Ph.D. thesis, *Aspects of Anglo-Norman Governance: the Definition of Data in Domesday Book* (University of Birmingham, 1971), pp. 61-63.

[22] H. E. Ellis, *An Introduction to Domesday Book*, ii (Record Commission, London, 1833), pp. 445-47; British Library, Cotton MS. Vespasian B xxiv, fos 57-62.

[23] *Herefordshire Domesday*, ed. V. H. Galbraith and J. Tait (Pipe Roll Soc., lxiii, 1947-48, new ser., xxv, 1950), pp. xxi-xxii.

[24] *Chronicon Monasterii de Abingdon*, ed. J. Stevenson, ii (Rolls Ser., 1858), pp. 115-16; *cf.* D.B. i, fo 156[d]; *e.g.* Round, *Feudal England*, pp. 120-21; Richardson and Sayles, *The Governance of Medieval England*, p. 29.

[25] *Dialogus de Scaccario*, ed. C. Johnson (London, 1950), pp. 62-65 (my translation).

ordinary, much-used, and often out-dated material had little chance of wholesale survival.

The office of *exactor* too affords an example of continuity of terminology. In Old English laws the king's shire reeves were identified in Latin as *exactores*, especially when connected with toll, public tribute and royal revenue.[26] The Crowland chronicler linked the first Winchester roll with royal *exactiones*.[27] In William Rufus' reign, Rannulf Flambard was several times accorded the title *exactor totius regni*, exactor of the whole kingdom.[28] And more than a hundred years after the Domesday survey a text from St Paul's recalled 'the hide of land which the *exactores* confirmed to them in the description of all England concerning what dues and customs they should pay the king'.[29]

Domesday's evidence on boroughs and farms reveals both the continuity and sophistication of pre-Domesday treasury procedure. Money payments of royal revenues could be required by tale, by weight, or assayed, or at a high rate to allow for changes in the weight of the coins.[30] Payments by weight and assayed were known in Edward's day, which is not surprising as we know that the Anglo-Saxon coinage was highly organized and continued so with few changes in the Norman period. Another principle obtaining in the late twelfth-century Exchequer was observed, though not yet stereotyped, before Domesday was compiled. Richard fitz Nigel explains: 'a farm is paid "blanch" when it is blanched by the taking of an assay . . . we also said that a farm is paid "by tale" when it is merely met by counting coins without an assay; when the king confers an estate on anyone with the hundred or the pleas which arise in the hundred court, that estate is said to be granted "blanch" '.[31] Now, there is in Domesday a large measure of identity between royal estates which made payments in some way surcharged, especially assayed or in commutation of this method, and estates which are connected with a hundred. It could be a causal relationship. When the hundreds were added to a farm, as in the case of Winchcomb, the farm's payment was surcharged. When Wye in Kent was a royal

---

[26] W. A. Morris, *The Medieval English Sheriff to 1300* (Manchester, 1927), pp. 3–5; W. Stubbs, *Constitutional History of Medieval England*, i (Oxford, 1896), p. 348.

[27] *Chronicle of Crowland Abbey*, p. 140 (n. 9 above).

[28] *Florentii Wigorniensis, Chronicon*, ed. B. Thorpe, ii (London, 1849), pp. 44–46; Henry of Huntingdon, *Historia Anglorum*, ed. T. Arnold (Rolls Ser., 1879), p. 232.

[29] *Royal Commission on Historical Manuscripts*, 9th Report, pt. 1 (1833), App. 1, p. 65.

[30] S. Harvey, 'Royal Finance and Domesday Terminology', *Economic History Review*, 2nd ser., xx (1967), pp. 221–28.

[31] *Dialogus de Scaccario*, pp. 85–86.

manor with the suit of 22½ small hundreds attached to it, it paid a surcharged amount; after King William gave it to his new foundation of Battle Abbey it reverted to a normal sum by tale.[32] However, Domesday also shows that additional specifications could be charged for the management of other extraordinary resources, such as extensive woodland or pasture.[33]

We may emphasize the background documentation and treasury practice that enabled the Domesday survey to be taken so quickly. Nevertheless, the enterprise was prodigious and indicates that existing documentation was deemed inadequate. The inquiry was in part a far-seeing governmental response to a particular crisis. In order to see the aims and attainments of the Domesday survey in context we must spend a little time on the political situation of 1084–85.

It was a time of intense preoccupation with the payment of geld, its liability and its evasion. In 1084 a great geld had been levied at the unusually high rate of six shillings on the hide,[34] a levy almost equal to one-third of the annual returns from land, which could be said to average roughly £1 per hide. But it was the husbandmen who usually had to shoulder the geld, the home demesnes of the lords being largely exempt.[35] The geld accounts from Exeter suggest that the tax was so heavy that it was incompletely paid, and that an inquiry into this and its evasions was in progress the following year.[36] In six counties of the south-east liability was re-assessed, as Domesday's own figures and collation with the pre-Domesday list of Kentish assessments show.[37] But the new rating was both unhelpful and ephemeral. Wherever the assessment was changed, it was lowered, the great ecclesiastical estates obtaining considerable reductions. The problem of the short-fall was dramatically highlighted when early in 1085 King William received news that King Cnut of Denmark, having a certain claim to the English throne, had prepared a huge fleet to invade England. The threat was sufficient to cause William to bring from the continent 'a larger force of

---

[32] *D.B.* i, fo 162ᵉ; *D.B.* i, fo 11ᵈ.

[33] *E.g.*, *D.B.* i, fos 172ᵇ, 172ᶜ, 38ᶜ.

[34] *The Anglo-Saxon Chronicle*, ed. D. Whitelock (London, 1961), pp. 160–61.

[35] See for instance, E. Searle, 'Hides and Virgates at Battle Abbey', *Economic History Review*, 2nd ser., xvi (1963), pp. 290–300, for the continued working of this process.

[36] Exon Domesday refers to an *inquisitio gheldi*, *D.B.* iv, p. 493; J. F. A. Mason, 'The Date of the Geld Rolls', *Eng. Hist. Rev.*, lxix (1954), pp. 283–89 shows that land which in Domesday 'never paid geld' appeared in the geld rolls which are to be dated to 1086. Finn suggested that some hundredal reorganisation took place as well, *op. cit.* (above, n. 17), p. 42.

[37] Harvey, 'Domesday Book and its Predecessors', *Eng. Hist. Rev.*, lxxxvi, pp. 755–60.

mounted men and infantry than had ever come to this country before', apportioning them to landholders, 'each in proportion to his land', for which the fiscal rating in hides was the only measure available. Cnut's assassination saved England from invasion, but not before William's military preparations, including a scorched-earth policy along the east coast, had made the possibility of raising revenue even less easy.[38]

The Christmas Council of 1085, therefore, was the occasion for a serious review of the situation and its lessons. Those whose duty it was to counsel William had known their profitable enterprise of conquest to be in jeopardy. The latest high rate of the geld was leading towards diminishing returns and superficial attempts at revision had been unsuccessful. The great landholders' revenues, on the other hand, were being nibbled away in support of soldiers. The king had 'much thought and a very deep discussion' with his council about the country and how it was peopled, and decided upon his course.[39]

Attention was paid first to the existing records of royal revenue. The Anglo-Saxon Chronicler has in fact always distinguished carefully the two compartments of the great project: the royal from the tenurial survey. First, the king 'sent his men all over England into every shire and had them find out how many hundred hides there were in the shire, or what land and cattle the king himself had in the country or what dues he ought to have in twelve months from the shire'. Secondly, and this outraged the Chronicler,

'he also had a record made of how much land his archbishops had, and his bishops and his abbots and his earls—and though I relate it at too great length—what or how much everybody had who was occupying land in England, in land or cattle, and how much money it was worth. So very narrowly did he have it investigated, that there was no single hide nor virgate of land, nor indeed (it is a shame to relate but it seemed no shame to him to do) one ox nor one cow nor one pig which was there left out and not put down in his record'.[40]

All who held directly from the king were questioned about the stock and value of their holdings. Under the surveillance of the most eminent and experienced magnates acting as commissioners in regions of the country where they had no vested interest the answers were attested, or otherwise, by the sheriff and the representatives of the hundreds. The king then ordered that the two

[38] *Anglo-Saxon Chronicle*, ed. Whitelock, p. 161.
[39] *Ibid.*
[40] *Ibid.*, pp. 161–62.

inquiries 'should be written in one volume and . . . placed in his treasury at Winchester.'[41]

Detailed as the resulting returns were, all the information was relevant to one or more of the three purposes of Domesday. They were, first, to record the transfer and possession of land; second, to obtain the annual value of estates: third, to allocate a new fiscal rating system to raise taxation in a more effective manner. Details of assets and of demesne stock were needed to reinforce the figures given; there may also have been a transitory desire to know where stock, especially traction power, lay for the carriage and purveyance of royal armies.

The inquiry supplied the opportunity to find out how far military men and royal officials had over-reached themselves in the chaos of conquest and moved on to lands not rightfully theirs. It was a chance to establish 'the day on which King Edward was alive and dead' as a legal baseline. Disputes over the possession of land had already featured prominently in William's reign. Land pleas had included those of Ely Abbey, the church of Worcester and the abbey of Evesham, and, close to the seat of Anglo-Norman rule, Archbishop Lanfranc *versus* Odo of Bayeux.[42] They had been held before shire assemblies in the presence of reliable magnates. This method of reviewing possession was generalized in the Domesday inquiry. When possession of an estate was disputed, it was usually transferred to the end of the account of the fief or to the end of the shire returns to await action.[43]

In disputes between two Normans, the verdict or opinion of the English men of the hundred was sought and recorded because they were living testimony to the authority of the shire lists. Though their reasoning appears at first sight contorted, they knew who was responsible for the land in Edward's day and who was his successor. Concerning Haconby in Lincolnshire: 'they say that Oger holds nine bovates of land unjustly because Gilbert de Gand ought to have them through Ulf Fenisc his predecessor who had them in the time of King Edward'.[44] In another Lincolnshire dispute between two claimants the hundred resolved: 'the lands shall be rightly divided according to the way they pay geld'.[45] This process explains why in Domesday Book, and beyond, questions of tenure are often

[41] *English Historical Documents*, ii, p. 853, no. 202.

[42] D. C. Douglas argues that Domesday must be regarded as 'a great judicial inquiry', though it does not always 'settle the disputes' as he suggests, in 'Odo, Lanfranc, and the Domesday Survey', *Historical Essays in Honour of James Tait*, ed. J. G. Edwards, V. H. Galbraith, E. F. Jacobs (Manchester, 1933), pp. 47–57, and 'The Domesday Survey', *History*, xxi (1937), pp. 249–57; E. Miller, 'The Ely land pleas in the reign of William I', *Eng. Hist. Rev.*, lxii (1947), pp. 438–56.

[43] E.g. D.B. i, fos 78^d, 373^a–77^d; *D.B.* ii, fos 197^b–201^b.

[44] *D.B.* i, fo 377^b.   [45] *D.B.* i, fo 377^a.

tied up with questions of taxation. The Anglo-Norman régime seems already to have relied on existing tax lists to determine possession. Geoffrey, bishop of Coutances who presided over the land plea between the bishop of Worcester and the abbot of Evesham was instructed to make concord between them 'as it had been on the day when the geld for the building of the ship was last taken in the reign of King Edward'.[46] It was a principle which had obtained early in the eleventh century. A law of Cnut declared: 'He who, with the cognisance of the shire, performed the duties demanded of a landowner . . . shall hold his hand unmolested by litigation during his life and after his death shall have the right of disposing of it'.[47]

Secondly, and without precedent, the Domesday survey set out the annual value of estates, giving a present idea of the wealth of individual magnates and a calculation which could form the basis of future dealings with tenants-in-chief, directly useful in any dispute over what feudal obligations the estate could support. In the practice of feudal relations, a relief, sometimes a year's income from land, was demanded from the heir of a tenant-in-chief just as a year's 'first fruits' were due from an ecclesiastical benefice. Another profitable incident of feudal lordship was the wardship of land if an heir were under age or if it escheated. Domesday supplied the king with the value of the lands he granted or farmed out. In the first part of 1087, the year of William I's death, it was noticed that 'the king sold his lands on very hard terms, as hard as he could' and 'did not care how sinfully the reeves got it back from poor men'.[48] Thanks to the Domesday inquiry, the data was now adequate for a really hard bargain.

Despite few survivals of financial records from William II's reign, some examples of Domesday's use remain. William I had granted Haddenham in Buckinghamshire to St Andrew's, Rochester, for the king's lifetime; later, Lanfranc suggested to William Rufus that the grant should be made permanent. After some haggling Rufus was advised that £40 should be the sum asked, which is in fact just the value of Haddenham in the Buckinghamshire Domesday, to which Rufus added a demand to build a castle at Rochester.[49] There are pointers that calculations of expected returns from vacant bishoprics drew on the data of Domesday Book. One addition of value of the archiepiscopal lands of Canterbury in Domesday Book produces the

[46] *Monasticon Anglicanum*, ed. W. Dugdale, i (edn of J. Caley, H. Ellis, B. Bandinel, 1846), pp. 601–2.

[47] *The Laws of the Kings of England (from Edmund to Henry I)*, ed. A. J. Robertson (Cambridge, 1925), p. 215.

[48] *Anglo-Saxon Chronicle*, p. 163.

[49] *Anglia Sacra*, i (ed. H. Wharton, 1691), pp. 337–38; A. J. Macdonald, *Lanfranc* (1926), p. 244; *D.B.* i, fo 143ᵈ.

figure £1,586. The farm of the land of the archbishopric of Canterbury in the Pipe Rolls of 11 and 12 Henry II is £1,562 15s. 5½d.[50] This nearness in total cannot be due to the stagnation of Canterbury land values, as plentiful records show how much they had risen in the intervening period.[51]

Testimony from William II's reign leaves no doubt as to the use to which he and his minister, Rannulf, could put the Domesday values in cases of vacancy and inheritance. More than one chronicler emphasizes William Rufus's dealings in this field as the most outstanding feature of his rule:

> He kept down God's Church, and all the bishoprics whose incumbents died in his days he sold for money or kept in his own hands and let out for rent, because he had intended to be the heir of everyone, cleric and lay, and so on the day he died he had in his own hands the archbishopric of Canterbury, and the bishopric of Winchester and that of Salisbury, and eleven abbacies all let out for rent.[52]

The Coronation Charter of Henry I's reign paid close attention to the policy as it affected lay estates, the complaints of the Anglo-Norman landholders focusing on the painfully high level of dues demanded.[53] Chief of the unjust *exactiones* was to require the heir of an estate to buy back his father's land before he succeeded. It is hardly surprising that the policy caused them to look back to the customs that obtained in Edward's day. The performance of public obligations to the shire, together with the payment of a heriot, had then permitted many landholders to dispose of their lands as they wished. With the figures for the annual value of wardships and bishoprics before them, William II and his minister could not bear to let lands go lightly from their hands, indeed they could hardly bear to let ecclesiastical benefices go out of their hands at all. Their exactions were so ruthlessly effective because they could now be realistically precise.

It is significant that the governmental document of the twelfth century which most resembles Domesday Book in lay-out and information is that known as the *Rotuli de Dominabus et Pueris et Puellis*, which contains lands temporarily in the king's hands.[54] The roll, which survives for twelve counties, is especially concerned with the

---

[50] *Pipe Roll 11 Henry II* (Pipe Roll Soc., 8, 1887), p. 108; *Pipe Roll 12 Henry II* (Pipe Roll Soc., 9, 1888), p. 114.

[51] *E.g.*, Canterbury Literary MS., B.16.

[52] *Anglo-Saxon Chronicle*, p. 176.

[53] *Select Charters*, ed. W. Stubbs (9th edn, Oxford, 1921), pp. 117–19.

[54] Ed. J. H. Round (Pipe Roll Soc., 35, 1913).

annual value in the context of a certain level of livestock, and whether a higher return would be possible if the estate were better stocked. Nearly a hundred years later than the inquiry, the same type of information in the same sort of detail as the unabbreviated Domesday was needed in the supervision of revenue from vacancies and wardships.

The third, and undoubtedly exercising, task of the Domesday inquiry was the attempt at fiscal re-assessment. The figures are characterized in the so-called Domesday 'ploughland' or 'teamland' (often *terra est x carrucis*), a Domesday item which has not yet found an accepted and satisfactory definition. At first sight the obvious interpretation of the ploughland is that it represents the potential arable land, the number of ploughs that there is scope for.[55] As such, it makes patent sense for five counties of one circuit—Middlesex, Hertfordshire, Buckinghamshire, Cambridgeshire, and Bedfordshire.[56] The difficulty is that elsewhere the ploughland figure is frequently at odds with the actual number of ploughs. Where existing ploughs are fewer than the arable could take there is no problem. But confidence in the definition wilts when these cases are interspersed with others where the ploughs are more in number than the amount of arable land.[57] A crucial drawback to the development of medieval agriculture was the lack of winter feed for stock; the smallest acreages of meadow land were at a premium; and plough beasts constituted the heaviest call on winter feed. It is not possible to subscribe to any theory which suggests that peasants and lords were keeping more traction oxen than they had land to use them on. Alternative suggestions, that the ploughland figure is derived from the ploughs working in Edward's day or that it is an earlier fiscal assessment, fail to explain why the item is consistently given in the present tense, apart from some aberrant Leicestershire cases.[58] Not

[55] Both the obvious definition and its difficulties are recognized in F. M. Stenton, 'Introduction', *The Lincolnshire Domesday and the Lindsey Survey*, ed. C. Foster and T. Longley (Lincoln Record Soc., 19, 1924), p. xv. Lack of an accepted definition has prevented the full use of the ploughland data in the Domesday Geographies edited by H. C. Darby. The problem, the interpretations that have been put forward, and the evidence for the theory which I present here are dealt with much more fully in chapter III of my thesis (above, n. 21) which I hope to publish.

[56] A typical entry runs: 'in Fulham the bishop of London holds 40 hides, there 40 ploughlands. In demesne 4 ploughs, the freemen and *villani* have 26 ploughs, and there could be 10 ploughs more.' *D.B.* i, fo 127c.

[57] *E.g.*, Hartland: 'There 110 ploughlands; in demesne are 15 ploughs and 30 slaves, 60 *villani* and 45 *bordarii* with 30 ploughs', *D.B.* i, fo 100d; *cf.* Otterton: 'There 20 ploughlands; in demesne are 6 ploughs, 1 *villanus* and 20 *bordarii* with 40 ploughs', *D.B.* i, fo. 104b.

[58] In Leicestershire there is sometimes the phrase 'in King Edward's time there was land for *x* ploughs'. Maitland's argument that the phrase is thus synonymous

only for Domesday studies, but in the wider setting of population and agricultural estimates, it is important to know whether we have in this figure almost country-wide data for the amount of arable land in England in 1086, 1066, or not at all.

In fact, in regions other than the Middlesex circuit, the plough-land figure is often in closer correspondence with other items in Domesday Book such as the value of the estate, its population, or its fiscal assessment, rather than its working ploughs. Yet, the varying and regional nature of the ploughland is explicable if we regard it as a new fiscal assessment which took the best basis it could, given the regional character of agriculture and of local administration. In this it does but follow a similar policy to the Roman *iugatio* and *capitatio* which attempted a uniform assessment of widely varying agricultural lands and peoples by measuring in oxen yokes, *iugera*, for uniformity's sake. Twenty *iugera* of first class arable would be rated the same as forty *iugera* of second class land. Small amounts of profitable vineyard were expressed in larger numbers of *iugera*.[59] The variants of the ploughland relationship in Domesday are under-standable in the light of such pragmatic methods. In some counties, quite reasonably, the number of ploughlands follows the value of the estate. A Lincolnshire folio has consecutively estates of 6 plough-lands worth £6, 1 ploughland £1, 5 ploughlands £5, 2 ploughlands £1 10s., 2 ploughlands £2, 2 ploughlands £1 10s.[60] Sometimes the ploughland tallies with the number of peasantry working there: a soundly based principle, as it is they who have to pay. On some Burton Abbey estates the free rent-payers, absent in Domesday Book, are represented only in the ploughland figures.[61] The plough-lands may be put at half the old assessment in the deliberately devastated north.[62] Often it is double the old assessment, particu-larly in the western counties. There is a list of holdings in the March of Wales which add up to 18 hides and which never before paid geld, and these holdings are assessed at 36 ploughlands, though there is no arable there and it is technically 'waste';[63] it is, however,

---

with the ploughland is no more compelling than to suggest that a different phrase is used because something different was intended, *Domesday Book and Beyond*, pp. 484–86. The Leicestershire phrase probably has the same function but it falls back on different criteria, and tells us so.

[59] A. H. M. Jones, '*Capitatio et Iugatio*', *Journal of Roman Studies*, xlvii (1957), pp. 88–94; id, *The Later Roman Empire 282–602*, i (Oxford, 1964), pp. 448–69.

[60] *D.B.* i, fo 356ᵇ.

[61] J. F. Walmsley, 'The *Censarii* of Burton Abbey and the Domesday Popula-tion', *North Staffordshire Journal of Field Studies*, viii (1968), pp. 74–75.

[62] E.g., *D.B.* i, fos 305ᶜ, 306ᵇ, also in the Lincolnshire wolds. In some hundreds there is a consistent ratio of 2:1 or 3:2.

[63] *D.B.* i, fo 186ᵈ; other examples *D.B.* i, fos 187ᵃ, 252ᶜ.

good cattle-raising country. In other regions other ratios are employed. In Lincolnshire, ploughlands frequently correspond to the geld-paying carucates in a 2:1 ratio.[64] The dependence is very occasionally explicit: 'there is land for as many ploughs' as there are geld-paying hides.[65] Very occasionally too the doubling of geld-paying hides is explicit.[66] In some counties the commissioners seem defeated by their task, for the ploughland figure tallies artificially with the old rating, for instance, 'Siward had $7\frac{1}{8}$ carucates to the geld, there is land for $7\frac{1}{8}$ ploughs'.[67] It is this aspect, the fiscal interest in the ploughland, that the chronicler Henry of Huntingdon stressed when he characterized Domesday as first of all an 'inquiry to be made by sworn inquest (as to) how many hides, that is to say ploughlands each sufficient for one plough in the year, there were in each village.'[68]

The important point about the Domesday ploughland is that it achieved what the re-rating of 1085 in the south-east had not: a net doubling of the rateable assessment. The number of hides or carucates in the Domesday counties which offer ploughland data is about 32,000. The ploughlands in the same counties total about 60,000. Nor was this totally unreasonable. Lennard's work on the Domesday peasantry suggests that their recorded virgates and hides greatly underestimate the amount of arable land they held, as evidenced by their plough oxen.[69] Moreover, the assessment in ploughlands was increased significantly in the counties where the value of land averaged higher than £1 per hide. It was raised, too, in Northamptonshire where a lower assessment had been made earlier to allow for deliberate devastation, and where some economic recovery had since occurred. Though the 1086 ploughland figure of about 2,900 is a great increase from the post-devastation concession of 1,250 hides, it is vindicated by the 1086 value being nearer to £2 than £1 per hide; it also lies part-way between the earlier 3,200 of the County Hidage and the 2,500 ploughs actually at work in Northamptonshire in 1086.[70]

The testimony of Domesday Book, in fact, upholds the substance

---

[64] Stenton, *Lincolnshire Domesday*, pp. xvi–vii, where the observation is made in reverse.

[65] *Terra est totidem carrucis*, D.B. i, fo 244ᶜ.

[66] *Terra dupliciter ad arandum*, D.B. i, fo 365ᵃ.

[67] *D.B.* i, fo 275ᵇ.

[68] *Eng. Hist. Docs.*, ii, 853.

[69] R. Lennard, *Rural England* (Oxford, 1959), pp. 351–55; *id.* 'The Economic Position of the Domesday *Villani*', *Economic Journal*, lvi (1946), pp. 244–63.

[70] Maitland, *Domesday Book and Beyond*, pp. 464–65, 525, 536; C. Hart, *The Hidation of Northamptonshire* (Occasional Papers, 2nd ser., no. 3, Dept. of English Local History, Leicester, 1970), p. 25. I have rounded the figures and taken Hart's not Maitland's sum for the current Domesday hidage.

of the story told by Orderic Vitalis when he said that Rannulf Flambard recommended 'the revision of the *descriptio* of all England'. 'With the king's consent, he had all the ploughlands which are called hides in English, measured by the rope and recorded, setting aside the larger measurement which the generous English had apportioned by order of King Edward; to increase the royal taxes, he reduced the size of the fields belonging to the peasants.'[71] Orderic's account has been dismissed by older historians as 'a fabulous tale' and has been but partially rehabilitated as a regional re-assessment.[72] But Orderic, although clumsy in expression, stands vindicated on two points: the Domesday inquiry was in some sense a great revision of existing property lists, and, in estimating fiscal ploughlands anew it did set out to halve the size of the Edwardian hides.

The attempt to base taxation on an agricultural fiscal unit derived from the plough or the ploughland had both predecessors and successors in England. The very terms *bovate* and *carucate* of the Domesday north and *iugum* and *sulung* of Domesday Kent are sufficient to demonstrate the familiarity of the concept. Ethelred's Seventh Code sought a tax based on every plough.[73] And Richard I's assessment of 'carucage' is a well-known successor which, rather like Domesday, had often to fall back on the old hides or on working ploughs as a guide.[74]

The aims of the Domesday inquiry were threefold, precise, and within the limitations of any great questionnaire, almost completely fulfilled. It checked the official schematic lists of possession and brought to light disputes and wrongful take-overs; it set out to recalculate the rateable units on which taxation was levied; it produced a valuation of the annual income of magnates which provided a basis for the assessment of feudal obligations. To these returns were added excerpts from the records of revenues from the royal demesne. The character of some landholders' excerpts from Domesday Book supports the purposes of Domesday suggested here, for they retain for long-term reference simply the Edward's day assessment in hides, the assessment in ploughlands, the values, and nothing else.[75]

---

[71] *The Ecclesiastical History of Orderic Vitalis*, ed. M. Chibnall, iv (Oxford, 1973), p. 172. I have varied the translation somewhat.

[72] F. Pollock, 'A brief survey of Domesday', *Eng. Hist. Rev.*, xi (1896), p. 213; R. W. Southern, 'Ranulf Flambard', in his *Medieval Humanism and Other Studies* (Oxford, 1970), p. 190.

[73] *Laws of the Kings of England*, p. 190.   [74] *Stubbs' Charters*, pp. 249–50, 267.

[75] 'The Burton Cartulary', ed. G. Wrottesley, *Collections for a History of Staffordshire* (William Salt Archaeological Soc., pt. 1, v, 1884), pp. 7–8; G. Fowler, An Early Cambridgeshire Feodary', *Eng. Hist. Rev.*, xlvi (1931), pp. 442–43.

Domesday Book also had an unexpected result. It showed up the importance of the powerful under-tenant, the feudal 'middleman', and revealed something of the scope of the magnates' patronage. It showed, for instance, the extent and the value of the lands held by the disgraced Odo of Bayeux's powerful tenants.[76] Strictly, such men lay beyond the feudal relationship between tenant-in-chief and government. As soon as the extent of this problem was unearthed by the Domesday inquiry action was taken. All landed men of consequence from all over England, as the Anglo-Saxon Chronicler said, 'no matter whose vassals they might be', were summoned to Salisbury at Lammas to take an oath of fealty to William.[77] It was an occasion directed at the under-tenants; the tenants-in-chief, by definition, would have already submitted themselves as William's vassals.

Indeed, the policies which inspired the Domesday inquiry and the actions associated with it are the same policies pursued by William Rufus and Rannulf Flambard in the second William's reign. Rannulf Flambard concentrated on three associated avenues of governance: the incidence of general taxation, the exaction of feudal dues, and the initiation of law suits and land pleas. He also intervened on occasion to extract feudal dues from undertenants, an intervention strictly beyond the rights of feudal lordship.[78] Professor Galbraith has suggested that the Domesday-like text known as the Inquest of Ely be a return demanded by Rannulf Flambard in 1093 when the possessions of the abbey were taken into the king's hands.[79] Besides a full description of the Ely manors, it includes a précis of their extent and value, how much their value had increased in the hands of Abbot Symeon and details of the claimed lands of the abbey. A separate section is devoted to the holdings of the peasants and their ploughs.[80] In other words, despite a unique format, the same three interests of the Domesday survey characterize this text.

The coincidence of the policies practised under the two Williams may even have been complete, in that Rannulf Flambard may have had a hand in the engineering of the Domesday inquiry. Although modern historians have not given Flambard much prominence

[76] *D.B.* i, fo 6ᵃ–11ᵈ.

[77] *Anglo-Saxon Chronicle*, ed. Whitelock, p. 162.

[78] Mr Southern's study (above n. 72) is a version of his earlier and important paper 'Ranulf Flambard and Early Anglo-Norman Administration', *Transactions of the Royal Historical Society*, 4th series, xvi (1933), pp. 95–128, both of which characterize Rannulf's activities in William II's reign; see also H. P. R. Finberg, *Lucerna* (1964), pp. 177–78.

[79] *Making of Domesday Book*, pp. 141–42, 136–37.

[80] Ed. Hamilton, pp. 101–73.

under William I, contemporaries were very firm, though not specific, about his power. The *Liber Eliensis* explains that Rannulf was able to ride rough-shod over Ely 'since he was in the same favour with the second William as he was with the first'.[81] As keeper of the king's seal, which he seems to have carried on his person, he had opportunities to use his initiative and did so.[82] Orderic Vitalis described Rannulf's meteoric rise to power under William I, his inflated ambition *vis-à-vis* the great men, his 'superiors', and how he made major accusations in the king's court. He had already earned the nick-name 'Flambard' for 'like a devouring flame he imposed novel practices on the people by which he cruelly oppressed the country and turned the daily chants of the Church into lamentations'.[83] Indeed, one story goes that by 1085 so odious were his activities to a group of magnates that they tried to assassinate him by disposing of him at sea.[84]

Apart from Orderic's account of the re-assessment in plough-lands, there is the curious, individual, and unexplained character of what seems to be a pilot survey in Domesday Book itself, which needs to be accounted for and which may lead us back to Rannulf. A feature of each county is the primary position of the king's lands, often distinguished on a separate folio as from a separate source. The exception is the opening county of Kent, where first place is given neither to the king nor to the archbishop of Canterbury but, sharing a folio with the royal lands and boroughs, to the Canons of St Martin's, Dover, of which Flambard was Master at some time in the eleventh century.[85] That St Martin's twice breached precedence was acknowledged in the later *Breviate* versions of Domesday, where the canons are assigned to their proper place among the lesser ecclesiastical houses of Kent. Superficially, the St Martin's account resembles much of the Exchequer Domesday. But a closer examination reveals differences which indicate an earlier date for this section. There is no ploughland item, nor any gap left for one. Only the Edwardian assessment is there. The later figure and the self-conscious formula common to the rest of the county and circuit are lacking, indicating that it preceded the 1085 reassessment. There is, besides, a preoccupation with who held soke in King Edward's day. Two other unusual features are pertinent both to Domesday and to Rannulf's career. First, there is the concern with the canons' lands

81 *Liber Eliensis*, ed. E. O. Blake (Camden Soc., 3rd ser., xcii, 1962), p. 219.
82 Southern, *Medieval Humanism*, p. 187.
83 *Ecclesiastical History*, iv, p. 172.
84 Southern, *Medieval Humanism*, p. 187.
85 *D.B.* i, fo 1–2; H. H. E. Craster, 'A Contemporary Record of the Pontificate of Ranulf Flambard', *Archaeologia Aeliana*, 4th ser., vii (1930), p. 47.

lost to Odo of Bayeux; second, the total value of St Martin's lands is given, itself unusual, together with a unique calculation of 'how much all these things should be worth per year if the canons had their true rights'. These features recall the enigmatic questions in the *Inquest of Ely*—the closest to the 'terms of reference' of the Domesday inquiry: 'how much has been added or taken away?' and, 'if it is possible that more can be obtained, how it is to be obtained?'[86] The earlier character of the St Martin's account and its interests constitute significant internal evidence for the functions of Domesday Book.

It is at least possible that Rannulf conducted a survey of the estate of which he had charge; and that on the failure of the 1085 reassessment he suggested that a similar survey be required from tenants-in-chief. Orderic Vitalis attributes just such an advisory role to Rannulf, namely, counselling the king to revise the description of all property in England, to make a new division of the land and find out from his subjects all that exceeded the given amount.[87] William of Malmesbury's comment on Rannulf, 'whenever a royal edict went forth taxing England at a certain sum, it was his custom to double it', is not the hyperbole of a literary source.[88] There are in fact small figures on hundred after hundred in the East Midlands and tracts in the Welsh Marches where the number of ploughlands add up to double that of the old assessment.

It is not difficult to comprehend Rannulf's early unpopularity. After fifteen years of such policies, when the reaction to William Rufus coalesced into demands from his successor Henry for a charter eschewing evil customs, it sufficed to sacrifice Flambard. He was imprisoned in the Tower of London, but escaped, and fled to Normandy. There his political expertise managed not only to encourage Duke Robert's invasion of England, but amazingly, to effect his own reconciliation with Henry and the restoration of his lands.[89] It was characteristic that Rannulf should encourage Duke Robert to land on the Hampshire coast and turn for Winchester. In the Anglo-Norman period aspiring kings headed straight for the treasury at Winchester, not only to secure the silver there held, but also (for it was just as important) to take charge of the documents which were the avenue to that silver and the key to authorized tenure, documents to which Flambard was the accomplished guide.

The documentation at Winchester was greatly enlarged by the results of the Domesday inquiry, and together they provided a com-

---

[86] Ed. Hamilton, p. 97; see Galbraith, *Making of Domesday Book*, pp. 36–37.
[87] *Ecclesiastical History*, p. 172.
[88] *De Gestis Pontificum*, ed. N. E. S. A. Hamilton (Rolls Ser., 1870), p. 274.
[89] Southern, *Medieval Humanism*, pp. 196–98.

bination of data important for the development of practices of government, particularly that of the exchequer. Anglo-Saxon practice knew sophisticated treasury calculations for royal revenues; it knew and linked the fiscal and tenurial aspects of shire administration. The Domesday inquiry added to the fiscal records and those of royal revenue the data for the exaction of feudal incidents. The Winchester documentation tied together questions of royal revenue, taxation, and tenure for some time to come.

An understanding of the purpose and role of Domesday Book gives access to a surprisingly coherent view of the methods of Anglo-Norman governance. The development of the exchequer, its accounting of royal revenue from shires, from geld, and from feudal incidents, and its court on tenurial rights are indeed prominent features of the reign of Henry I. The administrative practices of William II and Flambard have been made accessible to us—'the increasing complication of administrative offices, the appearance of more independent officials, the idea, perhaps the existence of the exchequer'.[90] Yet all these are elements documented under William I. A harsh fiscal and feudal policy was already worked out in the data of Domesday Book, which afforded a firm basis for the fiscal feudalism so characteristic of England.

Even in the context of normal administrative procedures Domesday Book must still stand monumental, an epitome of the administration and policy of Anglo-Norman governance in England, governance functioning at full stretch on all lines simultaneously: the product of an old administration and a new ruling group hard driven by a conqueror king.

University of Leeds.

[90] Southern, 'Ranulf Flambard and Anglo-Norman Administration', p. 127.

PRESIDENTIAL ADDRESS

By Professor G. R. Elton, M.A., Ph.D., Litt.D., F.B.A.

TUDOR GOVERNMENT:
THE POINTS OF CONTACT

II. THE COUNCIL

READ 22 NOVEMBER 1974

THE Tudor Parliament, I suggested to you a year ago, quite properly fulfilled a function of giving legitimate political ambition a chance to achieve its ends, more particularly because from the 1530s onwards, at any rate, experience in the Commons could put a man in the way of entering the royal Council. Of course, this would never be true of more than a few such knights and burgesses, nor was it either a sufficient or a necessary cause of their becoming councillors. Still, the link was there. I now want to turn to the Council itself and ask whether its history and membership similarly reflected a useful function in enabling ambition to be satisfied. Here we enter upon territory far less well known than the Houses of Parliament. The Tudor Council is not now quite so free from the attention of historians as it was even ten years ago;[1] but while we may be really well informed about it here and there, and while indeed we all think that we have a fair idea of its place in constitution and society, it remains true that every time one asks oneself a question touching it one comes up against so far unillumined obscurities. The work of any governing body is always difficult to understand because only those there present actually know what goes on and because so much of what does go on never reaches the record; and the Tudor Privy Council made emphatically certain of preserving itself from scholarly prying by keeping no minutes of discussion at all. However, we do know who the councillors were,

---

[1] In 1964 I enquired 'Why the History of the Early-Tudor Council remains Unwritten' (*Studies in Tudor and Stuart Politics and Government* (Cambridge, 1974), i, pp. 308 ff). Since then we have had two valuable and so far unpublished Cambridge dissertations (whose use I here acknowledge with gratitude), by D. E. Hoak on 'The King's Council in the Reign of Edward VI' (1970), and by G. E. Lemasters on 'The Privy Council in the Reign of Queen Mary I' (1971); Mr M. B. Pulman has discussed *The Elizabethan Privy Council in the 1570s* (Berkeley/Los Angeles/London, 1971); Mr D. B. McDonald is at work on the Council in the latter part of the century; and Dr J. A. Guy is pursuing further researches which have already sorted out the Court of Star Chamber in Wolsey's day. Miss Margaret Condon is writing the history of Henry VII's Council.

though even this statement needs qualifying: we know this with anything like certainty only after 1540 when the body settled down into its reformed state. It is therefore possible to enquire whether those who made the grade were the right men: right in their ability to provide for good government, and right also in the sense that those desirous of exercising influence in the body politic had a sufficient chance to get there.

Parliament, as all agreed, represented the nation; did anyone think that the Council, too, should be representative? We remember the attitudes manifest in the early fifteenth century, and before, when people talked of the rights of 'natural' councillors to advise the king and assist in making policy. Under the Lancastrians, at any rate, the composition of the Council was a matter for contention, a lively political issue in which principles that involved limiting the monarch's choice were liberally pronounced and Parliament was used to give substance to such claims. Of such things, hardly anything appears in the sixteenth century. Those chosen and those omitted seem in general to have recognized the Crown's freedom to appoint whom it wished, while the former also recognized their exclusive duty to the monarch. No dualism here—no sense that service as councillor to king or queen also involved a responsibility to the nation (except in adhering to pious platitudes about the good of the commonweal). Perhaps one may see a touch of an official sense that in a shadowy way some such responsibility did exist in the occasional attempt to associate the Council formally with the Crown in executive action, most conspicuously in the Act of Proclamations which insisted that proclamations could be issued only by the king on the advice of his Council.[2] This has a somewhat 'Lancastrian' ring about it, but there was no substance: notoriously, few Tudor proclamations cite the advice of the Council, and we know of no case in which the Council's refusal to advise prevented the publication of a proclamation. 'Our partes is to counsell,' said Cecil— seemingly no more and no less; what happened to the advice given was the business of the queen.[3] Characteristically, Cromwell's definition of a councillor's function was as monarchical but distinctly more dynamic: he held that the office was 'as an eye to the prince, to foresee and in time provide remedy for such abuses, enormities and inconveniences as might else with a little sufferance engender more evil in his public weal than could be after redubbed with much labour, study, diligence and travail'.[4] The contrast

[2] 31 Henry VIII, c. 8, sect. 1.
[3] Cited Pulman, *Elizabethan Privy Council*, p. 52.
[4] *The Life and Letters of Thomas Cromwell*, ed. R. B. Merriman (Oxford, 1902), ii, pp. 112–13.

between Cecil's cool care and Cromwell's ardent activism helps to explain why one died in bed, full of honours, and the other dishonourably on the scaffold; it also helps to explain why Cecil's commonwealth marked time while Cromwell's went through a rebirth.

For our present purpose, however, it is more important that Cromwell's definition was in fact more accurate. The Tudor Privy Council reverberated with activity. It needs to be remembered that, unlike the Councils of France and Spain (able only to advise action which itself could never occur except on the signified authority of the king), that of England *did* things, had full executive authority, and by its own instruments (those letters signed by councillors for which there seems to have been no equivalent in the other national monarchies of the west) produced administrative results throughout the realm. Of course, it was this special capacity that gave such political weight to the privy councillor's place, and Cecil no more than Cromwell in practice ignored the active function of the body over which he presided. Playing it cool did not to him mean confining oneself to shouting advice from the terraces. And foresight —the quality Cromwell pinpointed—was Cecil's most eminent attribute. Even so, the difference between the sixteenth century's two greatest English statesmen is well illustrated by those comments.

However, one thing they were clearly agreed on: the councillor's sole duty pointed towards his sovereign, as indeed the councillor's oath itself indicated. In turn, the sovereign was supposed to confine his counsel-taking to those whom he had chosen to be his councillors, and on the whole it would seem that Tudor monarchs observed this rule, with the notable exception of Mary, whose intimacy with the emperor's ambassador at the time earned her the sort of anger and anguish that was to erupt again when James I appeared to elevate Gondomar to be his *chef du conseil*. Henry VIII may have gone behind his Council's back to the friends and servants gathered in his Privy Chamber,[5] but there was no public scandal, and his Council rightly believed itself to be the real source of advice. And Elizabeth, who assuredly had plenty of non-conciliar favourites, would for once seem to have observed the constitutional rules quite faithfully.[6] Implied in this relationship, however, was one inescapable fact: the sovereign had a totally free hand in choosing his advisers, and membership of the Council depended

[5] Dr D. R. Starkey, whose completed dissertation (Cambridge, 1974) has investigated the institutional history of the Privy Chamber under the two Henries, is at work on the part it played in administration and politics.

[6] Pulman, *Elizabethan Privy Council*, pp. 53–55.

exclusively on his will. No one had a *claim* to appointment, either social, or political, or philosophical.

Once only in the century was this convention challenged. The Pilgrims of Grace made an issue of the king's Council because they wished to be rid of Cromwell, Cranmer and Audley. True to their oldfashioned poses, they revived the sort of talk common one and two centuries before. Their first demand for the exclusion of the hated councillors was met in the king's *Answer* with some disingenuous stuff about the Council of 1536 being more aristocratic than that of 1509, and with an angry denunciation of their interference with the king's right to choose whom he wished.[7] To this they were advised to reply stoutly.[8] It was 'necessary that virtuous men that loves the commonwealth should be of his Council', and if the king insisted on a Council chosen 'at his pleasure' he should remember the entitlements of those naturally born to that position. The memorialist meant in particular the nobility and, surprisingly, pointed to France where such things were allegedly better ordered. His ideal model even led him to mention princes of the blood: did he have Courtenays and Poles in mind? Perhaps Henry was less blameworthy in the blood-bath of 1538 than we have supposed. And, the paper goes on, before Henry rested content with his deplorable choice he ought to remember that such folly had before this caused kings to be deposed, the examples cited being ominous enough—Rehoboam, Edward II, Richard II. This was one man's opinion (offered to Aske), but the attack on favourites and preference for noble councillors pervaded the whole rebellion. Mind you, the Pilgrims do not seem to have put too extravagant a value on nobility. On one occasion there was some cheering at the thought that 'as long as such noblemen of the true blood may reign or rule about the king all should be well',[9] but this pious sentiment was elicited by the news that those at present of Council with Henry VIII were the duke of Norfolk (third of that creation), the earl of Oxford (the Veres really were an old house), the earl of Sussex (plain Sir Robert Radcliffe only eleven years before), the lord admiral (Sir William Fitzwilliam, a creature of Wolsey's), the comptroller of the Household (Sir William Paulet, another such), and Sir William Kingston (one of Henry's upstart courtiers). By this account, noble blood had got a bit cheap, but even so it still, of course, excluded that 'Lollard and traitor Thomas Cromwell'.

In any case, the Pilgrims lost the fight and Henry continued to

[7] G. R. Elton, *Policy and Police* (Cambridge, 1972), p. 200.
[8] L[etters and] P[apers of Henry VIII], xi, no. 1244 (spelling modernized).
[9] *LP*, xii, pt. i, no. 1013.

choose his own Council, as did his children after him, with no more such open challenges. Our question must therefore now be whether their choice was such as to give the Council the opportunity to bring political stability by accommodating those who, dissatisfied by exclusion as the northern aristocrats had been in 1536, might possibly have upset it. And here some quite surprising conclusions emerge. Above all, it will become apparent that the reform which in the 1530s produced the Privy Council proper profoundly altered the place and function of the Council, and with it its character as a reflection of the distribution of power within the body politic. We must look at Council lists.

The most complete list extant for the unreformed King's Council —the institution built up by Henry VII and maintained in Wolsey's day—belongs to 1526–27. It survives only in a copy made for Sir Julius Caesar who found it in a book now lost.[10] Because the king's serjeants are given simply as a body, unquantified, the total is a little difficult to calculate; if we allow for an average of six of them, that Council numbered fifty-three. A further nine, at least, as we shall see, also deserved inclusion. A Council at least sixty-two strong might seem improbable, but plenty of evidence exists (for instance in the attendance lists transcribed from the lost books) to support the accuracy of Caesar's copy. The list of fifty-three includes the five categories of councillors typically found in the records down to the Council reform: seven prelates (Wolsey, five bishops, the abbot of Westminster), fourteen peers (two dukes, two marquesses, two earls, three viscounts, five barons), fifteen administrators of knightly rank, one civilian (the dean of the Chapel), and sixteen common lawyers (all the judges of King's Bench and Common Pleas, the king's serjeants, the attorney and solicitor general). Caesar, in addition, found one more peer, three knights, and two doctors attending on other occasions who were not in the list; though he thought they had not been sworn they were in fact equally councillors in the full sense—Secretary William Knight, for instance, being thus described by February 1514, and Archdeacon Thomas Magnus by October 1520.[11] Three more names turned up in the record of a sitting on 8 June 1527: another knight, another doctor, and the lord mayor of London. This total of sixty-two is a minimum: other people still surviving bore the councillor's title before this date, and it must be pure accident that they are missing

---

[10] British Library, Lansdowne MS 160, fos 311ᵛ–12ᵛ. The list has a few errors in it: Lords Hussey and Windsor, ennobled in 1529, appear here as lords, while Windsor is listed a second time among the knights. Probably the original was carelessly amended in 1529. I have restored the position of 1526.

[11] LP, i, no. 2684(88); iii, no. 1036(23).

from this gathering.[12] My guess is that the total number of sworn councillors in 1527 ran to something like seventy. On the other hand, that July meeting conveniently indicates the sort of Council that could actually be got to meet: four prelates, three peers, ten knights, one doctor, and all the common lawyers—say, thirty-four heads. The Council met that day for important administrative business—an order against seditious preachers and teachers of heresy (Thomas More was present)—but the possibly surprising attendance of all the judges and lawyers, whom some scholars would already like to treat as not strictly of the Council, as regular members is well supported in other presence lists.

The working members of this Council cannot, however, be identified with any of its sections. The lawyers and civilians were office-holders, by definition, and virtually all the knights held office: these three component parts constituted the top-level civil service of the day (much of it in the Household). Of the fifteen peers named (and such expected names as Oxford and Shrewsbury are absent only because the holders of the title at the time were respectively under age and rather ancient), only four held genuine offices (Norfolk as treasurer, Suffolk as president of the Council, Lisle a deputy at Calais, and Sandys as lord chamberlain); and of the seven prelates only Wolsey (lord chancellor) and Tunstall (lord privy seal) occupied formal places in the administration. Others of these councillors had before this been involved in government office—Bishop Clerk had been dean of the Chapel and Lord Berners deputy at Calais—but the fact remains that most of the socially eminent councillors (the true 'lords of the Council') possessed no such qualification at this date. We should be wrong to assume that they were mere decorative additions to the working parts; such men as Bishops West and Longland, or Viscounts Rochford and Fitz-walter (soon to be the earls of Wiltshire and Sussex) were very active councillors indeed. In fact, the whole body was real, not honorific, though I cannot here pursue that point.

What, then, was the meaning of having so large a Council, so many and divers kinds of councillors? It included the career-men in the Household, the law courts, and the offices of state, plus the leading political figures in Church and nobility, plus such outliers as London's mayor and, it seems, some gentlemen in the shires. There is evidence that the lord mayor was habitually sworn of the Council.[13] Such things underline a striking practice of using Council

[12] *E.g.* John Stokesley (*LP*, iii, no. 2954). Thomas Englefield, called by the title in 1524 (*LP*, iv, no. 1298[8]), had certainly held it by July 1513 (Public Record Office, E 159/292: Brevia, Trinity Term 5 Henry VIII, rot. 7d).

[13] Sir John Alen, lord mayor in 1525, retained the councillor's title, then

places to diffuse central authority on the one hand, and to concentrate scattered authority on the other. If what a man anxious to secure standing and influence required was a place on the Council, this kind of Council offered him excellent opportunities. The large number of peers in particular is worth emphasis: we have here all the court nobility of the day, mixing old families with new. The unreformed Council, in short, was well designed to fulfil the role which I am here investigating.

The line of thought exemplified in this Council finds its ultimate end in a well-known note of Cromwell's in the year 1534: 'to appoint the most assured and substantial gentlemen in every shire to be sworn of the king's Council'.[14] His intention was to provide a nation-wide body of men in charge of internal security, a needless purpose (as it turned out) because the substantial gentry proved active enough without taking the Council oath. Behind this fleeting idea, however, stands a concept of the Council as a body of all men who carried weight and as a means for holding the social order together throughout the realm: a concept to which the unreformed Council in effect aspired. If Cromwell's proposal had been adopted it would have diluted the Council irremediably and absolutely demanded the separate creation of that real governing institution which the large Council of Wolsey's day had, despite its size, still managed to be. But to repeat: apart from being the king's instrument of rule (usable in a flexible and protean fashion, as a court, as an advisory and executive board, by way of committees), that Council was also one of those institutional answers to the need to satisfy individual ambition by permitting widespread participation which any stable system requires.

Though Cromwell did not pursue the idea of creating a nation-wide body of sworn councillors, he still did not regard the existing large Council as sufficiently concentrated and efficient. His fundamental reform, which I once dated into 1534–36 and would now

---

acquired, for the rest of his life, though he took no active part thereafter: *LP*, v, no. 1209; vii, no. 1060; Public Record Office, Sta. Cha. 2/34/19 (1532, 1534, 1540). The last time that I can find a current lord mayor called king's councillor is in March 1536 (*LP, Add.*, no. 1053); it would appear, therefore, that the Cromwellian reconstruction, which prevented later lord mayors from getting the appointment, took place about the middle of that year. In 1532, Sir Thomas Denys (of Devon) is described in an indictment taken before him as 'vnus de Concilio domini Regis ac vnus Iusticiorum dicti domini Regis ad pacem' (Public Record Office, KB 9/517/30).

[14] *LP*, vii, no. 420. Cromwell's idea recurs in (was suggested by?) a general plan for revising the police system (Public Record Office, SP 1/144, fo 211) which *LP*, xiv, pt. i, no. 643 places in 1539, but which probably also belongs to 1534: three to six of the 'head commissioners' there suggested might be admitted 'as of his grace's Council, if it so shall stand with his grace's pleasure'.

venture to place in the middle of 1536,[15] created the institution which remained the government of Tudor and early-Stuart England. A look at the next relevant list of councillors shows how drastically things had changed as a result of his work. The Privy Council of August 1540, initiating its minute book as soon as the great lord privy seal was gone, is familiar enough.[16] Its total of nineteen was made up of eight knights, eight peers and three prelates, and of them all only the last (Cranmer, Tunstall, Gardiner) held no office of significance. They were there because in the age of the early Reformation no government could do without powerful ecclesiastical participation. Perhaps it would be proper to remove also the earl of Hertford, equipped with lesser sinecures but no more, from the office-holders; he was there as the king's ex-brother-in-law. But the remaining fifteen, whether noble or not, occupied the leading positions in state and Household—those positions which, as later developments show, were to become equivalent to Cabinet rank: the lord chancellor, lord treasurer, lord steward, lord privy seal, lord great chamberlain, lord admiral, lord chamberlain of the Household, treasurer and comptroller of the Household, master of the horse, vice-chamberlain, principal secretary, chancellors of Augmentations and First Fruits. The last two disappeared in the Exchequer reforms of 1554, but most of the rest, with occasional additions, turn up again and again. Not all those offices involved specific duties: except on coronation day, the great chamberlain's place was one of high dignity only, and some of the other Household offices were on the way to becoming Council-worthy places rather than desk jobs. But with the judges and lawyers and civilians gone, with the old knightly element reduced to the top few office-holders, and with the peerage drastically pruned to leave only active politicians and administrators, the new Council was manifestly a working instrument of government, and no more. Membership, available now to the few and those professionals at that, could no longer be offered in hopes of satisfying private ambitions among the non-professionals, nor was there now anything remotely representative of the orders of the realm about this Council. Representation had now become exclusively the attribute of Parliament, and the emergence of the 'modern' House of Lords (as demonstrated, for instance, in the precedence act of 1539)[17] goes significantly hand in hand with the disappearance of the non-officed peerage from the king's Council. The Privy Council, as set up by its creator, was

---

[15] On the grounds that most lord mayors before that date, and none thereafter, can be found described as king's councillors (above, n. 13).

[16] G. R. Elton, *The Tudor Constitution* (Cambridge, 1960), p. 95.

[17] 31 Henry VIII, c. 10.

a body of politicians and departmental ministers, without any *consiliarii nati*.

Henry VIII could afford a Council entirely in his control from which he had excluded the bulk of the nobility and those men of influence around the kingdom who did not hold qualifying office. Could the notoriously weak regimes of Edward VI and Mary do as much? Tradition, of course, supposes that the desire for membership—political pressure upon the Crown—quickly restored the pre-Cromwellian situation: large and diffused Councils with factions and subdivisions. Recent research has effectively demonstrated the inaccuracy of these superficial impressions. I am grateful to Drs Hoak and Lemasters for allowing me to use their valuable dissertations,[18] and I do not propose to steal the thunder which will surely be theirs once those typescripts have become books. But a few salient points, resting upon their analyses, need to be made.

The Protector Somerset (probably guided by William Paget) made, in fact, no move away from the principles established in the second half of Henry VIII's reign. The old king bequeathed him a Council of the reformed kind, though in a few particulars it deviated from Cromwell's practice: two bishops, five peers (all office-holders), six knights, one civilian (Nicholas Wotton, dean of both Canterbury and York), and two judges. The last three mark the reintroduction of categories excluded in 1536; Wotton had in fact been sworn of the Council in April 1546,[19] but no judges sat there until Henry died. It may be conjectured that Henry thought it advisable to have legal experts on a Council of regency. The knights, reduced in number to make way for the lawyers, now included leading members of the Privy Chamber, a tipping of the balance against the out-of-Household civil service which reflects the growing influence of the court in Henry's last days. This Council Somerset accepted, adding only his brother Thomas who would not be kept out and who became lord admiral (a qualifying office) when Warwick succeeded to the great chamberlaincy left vacant by Somerset's own elevation.[20]

This situation lasted for only the six weeks that Somerset required to set up his primacy, but even when he had a free hand he made no changes in principle. The Councils he appointed down to his fall fluctuated in numbers but averaged about twenty-one, well within the terms of the recent reform, and in type of membership they remained unchanged. The one civilian disappeared (though his brother Edward, treasurer of Calais, remained an ever-absent

---

[18] *Cf.* n. 1, above.
[19] A[cts of the] P[rivy] C[ouncil], ed. J. R. Dasent, i, p. 371.
[20] Hoak, 'Council of Edward VI', pp. 51–55.

member); Cranmer and the equally absent Tunstall represented the Church; up to eight peers, all of recent creation and all but one holding the usual qualifying offices, constituted the characteristically unaristocratic noble element; the knights included not only the leading departmental officers but also always at least two gentlemen of the Privy Chamber. Lord Chief Justice Montague stayed on for a while, but was taken off when he fell out with the Protector.[21] Only the marquess of Northampton (William Parr), so far office-less, broke the pattern: he owed his appointment to his personal relationships and to his political influence. Evidently, this régime experienced no difficulty in adhering to an essentially 'royal' Council of the new kind. Remembering that Somerset's fall was engineered by his fellow councillors, we may wonder whether he would have been wiser to enlarge the Council with supporters (if he could have found any), but at any rate no such attempt was made. At the same time, it looks as though there were no men ambitious to get on the Council; as in the reign of Henry VIII, the reformed Privy Council, though not a political instrument for assuaging opposition, was also no cause of visible dissatisfaction.

No visible dissatisfaction, but what happened under Northumberland raises a question. That duke did increase the size of the Council, and to some extent his additions suggest the sort of political pressure that Henry and Somerset had not experienced. By March 1552, for instance, the Privy Council numbered thirty-one, an increase which marked a serious dent in the principle of Cromwell's reform.[22] The bulk of the councillors were still holders of the normal offices, a fact which put Thomas Goodrich, bishop of Ely, there when he succeeded Rich in the chancellorship. (Tunstall had gone, now that the Reformation was striding ahead, so that the Church remained represented by two prelates). But the number of the knights had gone up to twelve, with such relatively lesser officers as the master of the Ordnance, the master of the Rolls, and the secretary for the French tongue newly elevated to Cabinet rank. Wotton and the two judges enjoyed restoration: whether there is any special significance in this rather depends on whether councillors sworn could ever be thought of as deprived of the stigma except by death, even when for reasons of politics or personality they ceased to be councillors in anything but name. The real change had come among the fourteen peers who, for the first time since 1536, included noblemen without significant office. The single anomaly

[21] Hoak, 'Council of Edward VI', pp. 66, 70, 72–73.
[22] *Ibid.*, p. 89. Things were virtually unchanged a year later: Elton, *Tudor Constitution*, p. 96.

of Northampton (now regularized as great chamberlain) had blossomed forth into a group of seven, one of whom—the ailing Rich —does not count, while another, Pembroke, had been a councillor since 1547 as Sir William Herbert, gentleman of the Privy Chamber. But what were the earls of Shrewsbury, Westmorland and Huntingdon, Viscount Hereford and Lord Cobham doing on the Council? Supporting Northumberland, is the short answer: that duke, unlike his predecessor, was compelled to find places on the Council for political followers. Francis Talbot, by the way, recalls one of the more curious facts about the Privy Council: for something like 180 years, almost none seems to have been reckoned complete without the current earl of Shrewsbury, very few of whom actually ever attended. Even in 1536, Henry VIII had noted that his Council included the then earl 'when he may come'.[23] One is reminded of the mid-nineteenth-century axiom that no Cabinet could survive without at least one duke in it.

Northumberland's Council thus rather makes my point for me. Having used that body to destroy his rival, he needed to strengthen his hand on it, and in order to do so he had to forsake the fundamental principle of Cromwell's reform. Such freedom as he had in choosing councillors was evidently severely circumscribed by the need for a supporting faction, and this meant that men without the newly established qualifications—lesser officers and unofficial noblemen—reentered the Council. Relaxing the rules meant going back to a Council which could bring peace and temporary stability; sticking to them would have meant leaving out men who wished to join the ranks and, dissatisfied, would have been troublesome.

The Council of Edward VI's last years thus testifies to Northumberland's weakness, not the Crown's or even the boy-king's. Mary's accession brought to the throne at least a person of mature years, capable (if a woman were to turn out capable) of exercising personal rule. Yet, on the face of it, her policy towards the Council looked even more like a return to the old, unreformed institution which had worked only because it had not been a Privy Council at all—not a self-sufficient governing body but a group of governors controlled and guided by single men, Henry VII or Wolsey. Notoriously, Mary's large Council—its numbers fluctuating round about forty—provided the scene for much faction fighting, though I think that Dr Lemasters is right when he calls in question an interpretation which has too trustingly reflected the opinions of the imperial ambassador, concerned to explain his own failures. However, what matters here is the membership of that body, that seemingly very

---

[23] *LP*, xi, no. 957. Shrewsbury sat on the reformed Council as lord steward, the office held in 1540 by the duke of Suffolk.

large membership which calls up memories of the 1520s. Here, too, Dr Lemasters' investigation has altered the picture by defining it more closely.[24] It would appear that Mary's councillors fall readily into three groups. The first, numerically the largest, consists of the men who attended her at Framlingham Castle at the time of Northumberland's rebellion: they were very much her personal following and friends (mostly good Catholics). Of these hardly any ever attended the Council. Secondly, there was a group of Henrician survivals or dug-outs, men who lent respectability to the body but acquired real significance only because Gardiner must be counted among them. And lastly, there were the Edwardian professionals, especially Paget and Winchester, without whom the government could not have been carried on. When one identifies the real working Council one comes up with something much more like the Cromwellian Privy Council than its unreformed predecessor: quite a small group (though, since this was no formally identified body, exact numbers cannot be given) once more consisting of the familiar office-holders. Indeed, at one point Paget (trusty guardian of the Cromwellian tradition) tried to enlist the help of King Philip in repeating his late master's achievement by turning this active sector into an institutional extraction from the swollen nominal Council, but nothing came of this.

Queen Mary's Council thus marks a peculiarly interesting stage. On the one hand it illustrates the endurance of Cromwell's reform: government remained in the hands of the type of institution he had devised for it. On the other however, it also demonstrates how the Council could be used to produce political stability —or, alternatively, how pressure upon the monarch could compel the sort of enlargement which found room for a great number of aspirants to the title who might not even intend to perform any serious conciliar duties. They were not functionless: the Framlingham group, all men of little national standing, exercised notable influence in the counties where their native weight benefited from the addition of the councillor's title. Once more, shire worthies were brought into the Council (by accident rather than policy, I think), so that some of the conciliar potential discarded in 1536 revived for a time, at the cost of weakening the singular eminence of the central body. The Framlingham men were councillors in the main because Mary believed in rewarding loyal followers, but also because she needed loyal followers on her Council: the Henrician group because a Council consisting effectively of her brothers' men would have proved unmanageable, but also because they had claims upon her memory which she could not ignore. The Ed-

24 'Privy Council under Mary I,' ch. 2.

wardians simply could not be spared. Mary, half pushed and half pulling, proved that the principles of the pre-reform Council had visible political advantages, but also that only the post-reform Privy Council could be trusted to govern effectively.

As is well known, Elizabeth read the lesson to mean that the second point was more important than the first. She may well have had Paget's and Cecil's advice to that effect, but she was also free from the pressures which had worked upon her sister. No group of loyalists, demonstrating their stand in a crisis, made calls upon her gratitude (not a quality anyway with which she was over-endowed); no elderly gentlemen existed, or were needed, to form a bridge to a lost past. There need be no doubt at all that throughout her reign she maintained perfect control over the choice of privy councillors; no one ever owed appointment except to her, and no one ever succeeded in forcing himself on the Council against her will. The story of the young earl of Essex's hapless years of knocking at the door of the Council chamber is not only familiar but absolutely descriptive. And so Cromwell's Privy Council, hazardously kept alive in the troubled years by William Paget, returned unequivocally in 1558, with no further change in principle or practice till Elizabeth's death. Her Privy Council was not only small and select, but also throughout that precise instrument for royal government which Cromwell had designed. And this means not only that the body once again regarded itself as 'an eye to the prince' but also that Cromwell's other purpose was again achieved: emanation of monarchic power or not, this was a Council that governed independently, taking decisions and executive action on its own responsibility. I may remark in passing that the true Tudor Privy Council, especially when seen by the side of its French and Spanish counterparts, offers proof not so much of the existence of personal monarchy as of its limitations. There was truth in the Venetian observation that 'these lords of the Council behave like so many kings'.[25] So long as there existed the sort of Privy Council that Cromwell has established, truly monolithic kingship did not prevail in England. Michael Walzer has identified the whisper as the characteristic tone of *ancien régime* royal courts.[26] He may well be right for the monarchies of the early Stuarts and later Bourbons, but in the court of Queen Elizabeth the whisper had to compete, often unsuccessfully, with the audible noises emanating from the institutional Privy Council.

[25] Cited E. P. Cheyney, *History of England from the Defeat of the Armada to the Death of Elizabeth* (London, 1926), i, p. 80.

[26] *Regicide and Revolution: Speeches at the Trial of Louis XVI*, ed. Michael Walzer (Cambridge, 1974), p. 28.

Of course, the composition of the Council did not always adhere perfectly to these principles, but the occasional departures are minimal and insignificant. Take the Privy Council of 1579.[27] Of the eight peers, six held qualifying office: Burghley (lord treasurer), Leicester (master of the horse), Sussex (lord chamberlain), Lincoln (lord admiral), Warwick (master of the Ordnance), Bedford (president of Wales). The list of the nine knights' appointments reads familiar enough: the lord keeper, the treasurer, comptroller and vicechamberlain of the Household, the chancellor of the Duchy, the chancellor of the Exchequer, the lord deputy of Ireland (absent, naturally), the two principal secretaries. In the reign of a female sovereign, the Privy Chamber, for obvious reasons, had again lost its place in the Council. No civilians or lawyers (just as Cromwell had laid down), and Elizabeth, as we know, saw no reasons for burdening her government with prelates. The only two members who do not quite fit were the earl of Arundel and Lord Hunsdon. The first, who as lord steward had been a councillor at the beginning of the reign, was back after a period of disfavour, probably at Leicester's urging who wanted an ally in his perpetual sparring with Burghley; the second, soon regularized when in 1583 he succeeded to the lord chamberlaincy on Sussex's death, was the queen's cousin and the nearest thing on her Council to recall Mary's Framlingham friends. But personally he deserved the place better than those worthy nonentities. The exceptions thus were one ex-officer, already indelibly marked with the councillor's oath, and one friend and future officer—not really exceptions at all.

The last Privy Council of the reign, which was also just about the smallest (thirteen members)—perhaps because Elizabeth found it increasingly difficult to replace the departed old faithfuls by the new, young, untried, pushing men that she found troubling her grey years—really exemplified the stubborn persistence of the pattern.[28] With Whitgift and Sir John Popham, the Church and the law had penetrated into the Council, but there were good reasons of personal choice behind these appointments. Both were hard men, willing to put down disaffection and disorder with a heavy hand, and the ageing monarch, unhappy in that last decade of the century with its undercurrent of unrest produced by war and famine, liked such men. For the rest, we find the lords treasurer, admiral and chamberlain, and the master of the horse (always since Edward VI's reign a noble preserve); we find the lord keeper, the comptroller and vice-chamberlain of the Household, the chancellor of the Exchequer, the two secretaries. Only the earl of Shrewsbury,

[27] From the list of attendances in *APC*, xi.
[28] Elton, *Tudor Constitution*, pp. 100–1.

asserting the Talbot mystique, sat there—or rather, practically never sat there—without qualifying office, the one representative of relatively ancient blood.

Of course, in Elizabeth's long reign ancient blood was not much to the fore. The Percies and Nevilles passed through their last eclipse, and even the Howards (ancient enough in their own estimation) suffered more than they benefited (though in the person of the earl of Nottingham, the victor of 1588, a junior branch made it into the Council). But ambitions and claims to recognition were not necessarily confined to noblemen of lineage, and one may wonder whether a Council of thirteen, some of whom had had quite a struggle to get on, could really serve to accommodate all those who thought themselves possessed of title to be there. Indeed, one may wonder whether this reduction by one third from Cromwell's number did not leave this Council dangerously thin and dangerously cliquey—even isolated in its narrow-based eminence. Elizabeth, we know, created a dearth of honours; did she also prove too penurious in making councillors? She may have felt no need to use councillors to keep the peace in the shires, in which indifference she was right; and she would seem to me to have been right also in denying elevation to such men of ambition as Walter Ralegh and Francis Bacon. But did she not keep out able men of proper weight, anxious to take part in the government of the realm at the highest level? For some reason she acted as though there was not enough talent around and doubled up offices, Sir John Fortescue, for instance, being chancellor of both the Exchequer and the Duchy. One would hardly expect to have any real evidence of disgruntled ambition and behind-the-scenes pressure; while the old queen lived, no one liked to question, in ways that would have left evidence behind, her right to choose as she pleased. Yet the unmistakeable pressures of the next reign, when gossip grew rife, call forth doubts. Of Bacon we do know that he had aspirations before and after 1603, and we can justly suspect the same of Ralegh; thereafter such men as Cobham and even Dudley Carleton gave reasonably clear hints of their ambitions. I suspect that the court, and the country too, of Elizabeth contained more than we know of who resented the small size of the Privy Council and wished to be on it.

More to the point, James I at once recognized the facts with his usual insight, even if with his usual bad luck and bad judgment he spoiled everything by picking the wrong men. He inherited a Council larger by one than that of 1601, Sir William Knollys having obtained the then vacant treasurership of the Household and having been succeeded as comptroller by Sir Edward Wotton. In the two weeks after 25 April 1603, James added no fewer than thirteen councillors, effectively doubling the size of the body.[29] Six of them were Scotsmen—a first step towards uniting the two kingdoms, but a step which, while it cost the king immediately some popularity, had neither administrative nor political significance for the Council itself which never saw those North Britons. As for the rest, whom do we find? The earl of Northumberland, 'the wizard earl', thought likely to reconcile the Catholic minority to the new regime; the earl of Cumberland, a tried and elderly courtier, remarkable only for the fact that he personally went off on the privateering expeditions which he fitted out; Lord Mountjoy, conqueror of Ireland (and of Penelope Rich); Lord Thomas Howard, another naval man in his past, but now a courtier who was to achieve the earldom of Suffolk, the lord treasurership, and prison for embezzlement; Lord Henry Howard, soon earl of Northampton, according to the *DNB* the most learned noble of the reign but more familiar as its most malicious intriguer; Lord Zouche whom James remembered as an ambassador to Scotland years before but who since 1602 had been president of the Council in the Marches; and Lord Burghley, the great Burghley's elder and stupid son, now president of the Council in the North. The last two at least held offices which before this had qualified men for the Council, but by the standards of the previous reign they were flotsam. Mountjoy, indeed, was the only man among them to have a touch of real distinction, though in the three years remaining to him he did nothing noteworthy. Still, he was only forty-three when he died, and his appointment may be thought suitable. Northumberland and Cumberland represented court nobility, though not its most useful members; the Howards did so too, but added insatiable ambition and the ability to corrupt a whole fifteen years of government.

A strange crew, *more Jacobeano*, but not without its significance in our present discussion. None, we may believe, answered the call with the reluctance (not as great as he made out) of a Thomas More; these men were looking for a place in the sun. Some—the Howards, Northumberland, possibly Zouche—were probably James's own choice, but it is hard to think that of his own free will he would have called in Burghley, Cumberland or even Mountjoy. In manner this spate of appointments suggests not only that ambition, unsatisfied, to become a privy councillor existed in sufficient magnitude at the court of Queen Elizabeth, but also once more that the strict reformed Privy Council was unsuitable for the role of creating political stability by satisfying ambition. The potential—indeed, the active principle—had been there in the unreformed Council. Its abandonment in 1636 had not then mattered much because the first task

29 *APC*, xxxii, pp. 495, 496, 498.

of the Privy Council was to govern the modernized state, a thing which the reformed Council was much better constructed to do; because Henry VIII and Elizabeth knew how to control unsatisfied men; and because other means existed for giving such ambition outlets, from advancement at court through employment in war to election to Parliament. It is arguable that the expansion of the House of Commons together with the contraction of the Council set up one strand in that tension which was to become so manifest in the reign of James: the increasing number of politically able and ambitious men in the House of Commons were only too likely to start resenting the narrow gate that led to the place of ultimate rule. James did wisely when he enlarged his Council; if only he had continued to look to proven ability when making his choice, he might have used both institutions to promote stability.

In the sixteenth century, every moment of monarchic weakness demonstrated the political disadvantages of a small Council as well as the administrative disadvantages of a large one. It had not mattered so much under Northumberland because his rule lasted so short a time, nor under Mary because her leading ministers managed to preserve efficiency in the melée. Elizabeth's determination to adhere to the principles of a lifetime was, by the 1590s, adding to the general malaise by leaving up-and-coming men frustrated. The dilemma was inescapable: either a Council which will give satisfaction to sufficient individuals and interests, or a Council which will and can govern. On balance, it is impossible to feel that Cromwell, choosing at a time when the pressures of ambition were minimal, made the wrong choice: the Tudor Privy Council was nearly always an impressive and remarkable body of men, discharging very difficult tasks with genuine competence. But their contribution to continued stability could only come from outside— could only consist in their being the prince's vigilant eye, foreseeing and forestalling trouble. They could never create stability by inviting those capable of disturbing it into the charmed circle. There were just too few places.

THE ROYAL HISTORICAL SOCIETY

REPORT OF COUNCIL, SESSION 1973-74

THE Council of the Royal Historical Society has the honour to present the following report to the Anniversary Meeting.

A conference on 'Government, Propaganda and Public Opinion' was held at Derwent College, University of York, from 17 to 19 September 1973. The papers read were:

'New Sources of Power in the Twentieth-Century State'. By Professor Samuel H. Beer.
'Soviet Film: Image, Object and Message' (a lecture illustrated with film). By Mr. M. G. V. Glenny.
'Games People Played: Drama and Ritual as Propaganda in Medieval Europe'. By Professor D. A. Bullough.
'The Theory and Practice of Censorship in Sixteenth-Century England'. By Dr. D. M. Loades.
' "Parnellism and Crime", 1887-1890'. By Professor F. S. L. Lyons.

Fifty-eight members of the Society and twelve guests attended. The University held a reception for them on 18 September. It was decided to hold the fifth annual conference at the University of Exeter from 19 to 21 September 1974, on the topic 'Britain and Europe'.

An evening party was held for Fellows and guests at University College London on 4 July 1973 for which 196 acceptances were received.

Considerable uncertainty now surrounds the plans of University College London to rebuild which were mentioned in the last Report because of a changed financial climate. Council has the problem of the Society's accommodation under review.

At the end of March 1974, Mr. A. G. Watson resigned from being Secretary of the Society, a position he had held for four years. Council wishes to record its gratitude to him for his work. Dr. C. J. Holdsworth took over from him on 1 April.

The representation of the Society upon various bodies was as follows: Professor G. E. Aylmer and Mr. A. T. Milne on the Joint Anglo-American Committee exercising a general supervision over the production of the *Bibliographies of British History*; the President, Professor C. N. L. Brooke, Professor Sir Goronwy Edwards, Professor J. C. Holt and Professor the Rev. M. D. Knowles on the Advisory Committee of the new edition of Gross, *Sources and Litera-*

ture of English History; Professor G. W. S. Barrow, Dr. P. Chaplais and Professor P. H. Sawyer on the Joint Committee of the Society and the British Academy established to prepare an edition of Anglo-Saxon charters; Dr. E. B. Fryde on a committee to regulate British co-operation in the preparation of a new repertory of medieval sources to replace Potthast's *Bibliotheca Historica Medii Aevi*; Professor P. Grierson on a committee to promote the publication of photographic records of the more significant collections of British coins; Professor A. G. Dickens on the Advisory Council on the Export of Works of Art; the President and Professor C. H. Wilson on the British National Committee of the International Historical Congress; Professor G. H. Martin on the Council of the British Records Association; Professor A. M. Everitt on the Standing Conference for Local History; Mr. M. R. D. Foot on the Committee to advise the publishers of *The Annual Register*; Professor D. A. Bullough on the Ordnance Survey Archaeological Advisory Committee, and Miss K. Major on the Lincolnshire Archaeological Trust. Council received reports from these representatives.

The President is *ex officio* a Trustee of the *Spectator*. Professor Medlicott represents the Society on the Court of the University of Exeter.

The Vice-Presidents retiring under By-law XVI were Professor A. G. Dickens, C.M.G. and Professor C. H. Wilson. Professor G. E. Aylmer and Professor R. H. C. Davis were elected to replace them. Professor F. J. Fisher was appointed by Council to act as a Vice-President upon the retirement of Professor M. Roberts to South Africa. The members of Council retiring under By-law XIX were Professor G. E. Aylmer, Miss B. F. Harvey, Professor J. A. S. Grenville and Dr. N. J. Williams. Professor T. C. Barker, Dr. R. F. Hunnisett, Professor D. W. J. Johnson and Professor D. C. Watt were elected to fill the vacancies. Messrs. Beeby, Harmer and Co. were appointed auditors for the year 1973-74 under By-law XXXVIII.

Publications, and Papers Read

Council has undertaken a review of publications policy and has agreed on the broad lines to be followed once the backlog of works already accepted for the *Camden Series* has been cleared. One volume of *Transactions* and *Camden* will appear each year, but the latter will have longer introductions and more complete indexes where the material edited demands such treatment. A series of annual volumes to assist research is also planned and less regular series of short monographs of 25,000–30,000 words. The Literary Directors have been encouraged actively to seek out and commission work for *Camden* and the two new series.

During the year Council has been actively engaged in exploring the possibility of producing an *Annual Bibliography of British and Irish History* to appear in the autumn of the year next after that covered. A trial run has been produced by a body of collaborators working under the editorship of the President and it is hoped to complete negotiations with a publisher in the near future.

The following works were published during the session: *Transactions*, Fifth Series, volume 24; *Camden Miscellany XXV*, Fourth Series, and *A Guide to the Papers of British Cabinet Ministers, 1900–1951*.

At the ordinary meetings of the Society the following papers were read:

'The Progressive Movement in England, 1880–1930'. By Dr. P. F. Clarke. (19 October 1973.)
'Élie Halévy and the Birth of Methodism'. By Dr. J. D. Walsh. (8 February 1974.)
'The Social History of Confession in the Age of the Reformation'. By Dr. J. A. Bossy. (8 March 1974.)
'Reflections on the Government of England, 900–1200. By J. Campbell. (10 May 1974.)

At the Anniversary Meeting on 23 November 1973 the President, Professor G. R. Elton, delivered an address on 'Tudor Politics—Points of Contact: 1. Parliament'.

The David Berry Prize was won by Dr. J. Kirk for his essay on 'Who were the Melvillians: A Study in the Personnel and Background of the Presbyterian Movement in late Sixteenth-century Scotland'.

The Alexander Prize was awarded to Mr. H. Tomlinson for his essay on 'Place and Profit: An Examination of the Ordnance Office, 1660–1714'.

Membership

At a special meeting of the Society on 23 November 1973, it was agreed that Council could elect Fellows into a new category of Retired Fellows, open to Fellows who have reached the age of 70, at a reduced rate of subscription and with a reduced entitlement to publications. By 30 June 1974 23 Fellows had opted to be elected to this new category.

Council records with regret the death of 25 Fellows since 30 June 1973. Among these Council would mention especially Lt. Col. C. Graham Botha, Professor A. Gouber and Professor Virginia Rau,

Corresponding Fellows; Mr. H. C. Johnson, C.B., C.B.E. and Mr. W. A. Pantin, former Vice-Presidents; Sir Denis Brogan, Professor A. V. Judges and Miss Joan Wake, C.B.E. The resignation of 13 Fellows, 5 Associates and 9 Subscribing Libraries was received.

111 Fellows and 7 Associates were elected, and 13 Libraries were admitted. The membership of the Society on 30 June 1974 comprised 1252 Fellows (including 116 Life Fellows), 32 Corresponding Fellows, 153 Associates and 751 Subscribing Libraries (1179, 35, 154 and 747 respectively on 30 June 1973). The Society exchanged publications with 15 Societies, British and foreign.

Finance

On Income and Expenditure Account, the changes in the subscription rates for Fellows and Associates, and the creation of a new class of Retired Fellow, led to many difficulties with bankers' orders and covenants. Estimated arrears of uncollected subscriptions and covenant repayments amounted at the end of the year to the unusually high figure of £1,795. These arrears explain the small deficit of £101.

The Society's Balance Sheet takes into account for the first time the bequest by Professor Andrew Browning of his residuary estate, reported last year. The book value of its assets has consequently risen from £64,149 to £139,951. The market value, however, of the Society's investments, and of those received under the Andrew Browning Bequest, fell very substantially during the course of the year and increased only from £102,672 to £109,474, with an additional £14,500 on seven day deposit. The income derived from the Society's investments continues to make an extremely important and growing contribution to its revenue.

The cost of printing and distributing the Society's publications has continued to rise at an inordinate pace. After a careful review of the position, Council has decided that it is necessary to increase the subscription of subscribing libraries, last raised in 1972, from £5 to £7 with effect from 1st July 1974.

THE ROYAL HISTORICAL SOCIETY
Balance Sheet as at 30 June 1974

30.6.73 £				
	ACCUMULATED FUNDS			
	General Fund			
44,158	As at 1 July 1973			44,297
	Royalties from reprints of the Society's publications			
2,020	received in the year and treated as capital . .		1,469	
	Royalties from *Essays in Medieval and Modern History*			
3	(Macmillan, 1968)		7	
2,235	212 Donations from Life Members		43	
				1,519
46,393				46,816
—	*Add* Profit on Sale of Investments in year . .			608
46,393				47,424
	Less Excess of Expenditure and Provisions over Income			
1,096	for year			101
45,297				47,323
	Sir George W. Prothero Bequest			
13,852	As at 1 July 1973			13,852
5,000	Reddaway Fund			5,000
	Andrew Browning Fund			
	Investments received from the Executors as valued			
	at 15 May 1973		76,225	
	Less Net Loss on changes in Investments in the			
	year		5,041	
			71,184	
	Add Income from Investments and tax recovered			
	to date		2,592	
				73,776
64,149				£139,951
	REPRESENTED BY:			
64,401	Quoted Investments—at cost		121,684	
	Market Value £109,471 (1973: £102,672)			
	Money on 7-day Deposit		14,500	
	Due from Stockbrokers		71	
				136,255
	Sum Due on Surrender of Lease of 96 Cheyne Walk			
3,750	As at 1 July 1973		2,500	
1,250	Paid in year		1,250	
	(Payable in annual instalments of £1,250)			
2,500				1,250
	Current Assets			
	Balances at Bank:			
794	Current Accounts		1,425	
4,909	Deposit Account		10,654	
29	Cash in Hand.		16	
135	Payments in Advance		139	
5,867			12,234	
	Less Current Liabilities			
896	Subscriptions received in advance .	1,305		
219	Conference Fees received in advance .	187		
204	Sundry Creditors	996		
7,300	Provision for Publications in Hand .	7,300		
8,619			9,788	
(2,752)				2,446
64,149				£139,951

NOTE: The cost of the Society's Library, Furniture and Office Equipment, and the Stock of its own publications, has been written off to Income and Expenditure Account as and when acquired.

30.6.73	£					
		INCOME				
	219	Subscriptions for 1973/74: Associates	357			
	3,121	Libraries	2,849			
	4,227	Fellows	6,960			
7,567				10,16		
		(The Society also had 116 Life Fellows at 30 June 1974)				
	850	Tax recovered on Covenanted Subscriptions . .	63			
	433	Arrears of Subscriptions recovered in year . . .	59			
	4,492	Interest and Dividends received and Income Tax recovered	4,70			
	40	Prothero Royalties and Reproduction Fees . .	27			
	46	Donations and Sundry Receipts	6			
£13,428			£16,45			

		EXPENDITURE			
		SECRETARIAL & ADMINISTRATIVE EXPENSES			
	4,541	Salaries, Pension Contributions and National Insurance	5,184		
	506	General Printing and Stationery	701		
	384	Postage, Telephone and Sundries	556		
	243	Accountancy and Audit	291		
	50	Office Equipment	48		
	118	Insurance	136		
	183	Meeting and Conference Expenses	377		
6,025				7,29	
		PUBLICATIONS			
	200	Directors' Expenses	200		
		Publishing Costs in the year:			
		Transactions, Fifth Series, Vol. 23 (total cost)	3,163		
		Camden, Fourth Series, Vol. 12 (total cost)	3,227		
		Guide to Cabinet Ministers' Papers (total cost)	3,341		
			9,731		
		Less Provision made 30 June 1973 .	7,300		
	1,751			2,431	
		Provision for Publications in Progress:			
		Transactions, Fifth Series, Vol. 24 . .	3,800		
		Camden, Fourth Series, Vol. 13 .	3,500		
	7,300			7,300	
		Purchase of *Essays in Medieval History* . .	63		
		Preparation expenses *Annual Bibliography* . .	135		
		Carriage of Stock	12		
	9,251			10,141	
	1,368	*Less* Sales of Publications	1,775		
7,883				8,36	
£13,908		*Carried forward*		£15,65	

EXPENDITURE (contd.)

0.6.73	£							£
3,908		*Brought forward*						15,659
		LIBRARY AND ARCHIVES						
	290	Purchase of Books and Publications .	.	.	.	212		
	243	Library Assistance and Equipment .	.	.	.	535		
533								747
		OTHER CHARGES						
	15	Alexander Prize and expenses .	.	.	.	19		
	18	Subscriptions to other bodies .	.	.	.	18		
	50	Prothero Lecture fee and expenses .	.	.	.	108		
83								145
4,524		TOTAL EXPENDITURE .	.	.	.	.	.	16,551
3,428		INCOME AS ABOVE	.	.	.	.	.	16,450
1,096		EXCESS OF EXPENDITURE AND PROVISIONS OVER INCOME FOR THE YEAR						£101

. R. ELTON, *President.*

. R. C. DAVIS, *Treasurer.*

We have examined the foregoing Balance Sheet and Income and Expenditure Account with
ne books and vouchers of the Society. We have verified the Investments and Bank Balances
ppearing in the Balance Sheet. In our opinion the above Balance Sheet and annexed Income
nd Expenditure Account are properly drawn up so as to exhibit a true and fair view of the
tate of the affairs of the Society according to the best of our information and the explanations
iven to us and as shown by the Books of the Society.

BEEBY, HARMAR & CO.,
Chartered Accountants, Auditors

INSBURY COURT,
INSBURY PAVEMENT,
ONDON EC2A 1HH
3th August 1974

THE DAVID BERRY TRUST

Receipts and Payments Account for the Year Ended 30 June 1974

30.6.73	£	Receipts		£	
		BALANCE IN HAND 1 July 1973:			
		Cash at Bank:			
	6	Current Account	.	6	
	38	Deposit Account	.	115	
574	530	483.63 Shares Charities Official Investment Fund .	.	530	651
72		DIVIDEND ON INVESTMENT per Charity Commissioners	.		76
5		INTEREST RECEIVED ON DEPOSIT ACCOUNT . .	.		11
£651					£738

Payments

	—	DAVID BERRY PRIZE	.	50	
	—	DAVID BERRY MEDAL	.	48	
	—	EXAMINERS' FEES	.	30	
		BALANCE IN HAND 30 June 1974:		—	128
		Cash at Bank:			
	6	Current Account	.	14	
	115	Deposit Account	.	66	
		483.63 Shares Charities Official Investment			
651	530	Fund (Market Value 30.6.74 £419) . . .	.	530	610
£651					£738

We have examined the above account with the books and vouchers of the Trust and find it to ' in accordance therewith.

BEEBY, HARMAR & CO.,
Chartered Accountants, Auditors

FINSBURY COURT,
FINSBURY PAVEMENT,
LONDON EC2A 1HH
13th August 1974

The late David Berry, by his Will dated 23rd day of April, 1926, left £1,000 to provide in eve three years a gold medal and prize money for the best essay on the Earl of Bothwell or, at t discretion of the Trustees, on Scottish History of the James Stuarts I to VI in memory of l father, the late Rev. David Berry.

The Trust is regulated by a scheme sanctioned by the Chancery Division of the High Court Justice dated 23rd day of January, 1930, and made in an action 1927 A.1233 David Anders Berry Deceased, Hunter and another v. Robertson and another.

The Royal Historical Society is now the Trustee. The Investment held on Capital Accou consists of 634 Charities Official Investment Fund Shares (Market Value £549).

The Trustee will in every second year of the three year period advertise in *The Tim* inviting essays.

ALEXANDER PRIZE

The Alexander Prize was established in 1897 by L. C. Alexander, F.R.Hist.S. It consists of a silver medal awarded annually for an essay upon some historical subject. Candidates may select their own subject provided such subject has been previously submitted to and approved by the Literary Director. The essay must be a genuine work of original research, not hitherto published, and one which has not been awarded any other prize. It must not exceed 6,000 words in length and must be sent in on or before 1 November 1975. The detailed regulations should be obtained in advance from the Secretary.

LIST OF ALEXANDER PRIZE ESSAYISTS (1898–1974)[1]

1898. F. Hermia Durham ('The relations of the Crown to trade under James I').
1899. W. F. Lord, B.A. ('The development of political parties in the reign of Queen Anne').
1901. Laura M. Roberts ('The Peace of Lunéville').
1902. V. B. Redstone ('The social condition of England during the Wars of the Roses').
1903. Rose Graham ('The intellectual influence of English monasticism between the tenth and twelfth centuries').
1904. Enid W. G. Routh ('The balance of power in the seventeenth century').
1905. W. A. P. Mason, M.A. ('The beginnings of the Cistercian Order').
1906. Rachel R. Reid, M.A. ('The Rebellion of the Earls, 1569').
1908. Kate Hotblack ('The Peace of Paris, 1763').
1909. Nellie Nield, M.A. ('The social and economic condition of the unfree classes in England in the twelfth and thirteenth centuries').
1912. H. G. Richardson ('The parish clergy of the thirteenth and fourteenth centuries').
1917. Isobel D. Thornley, B.A. ('The treason legislation of 1531–1534').
1918. T. F. T. Plucknett, B.A. ('The place of the Council in the fifteenth century').
1919. Edna F. White, M.A. ('The jurisdiction of the Privy Council under the Tudors').
1920. J. E. Neale, M.A. ('The Commons Journals of the Tudor Period')
1922. Eveline C. Martin ('The English establishments on the Gold Coast in the second half of the eighteenth century').
1923. E. W. Hensman, M.A. ('The Civil War of 1648 in the east midlands').
1924. Grace Stretton, B.A. ('Some aspects of mediæval travel').
1925. F. A. Mace, M.A. ('Devonshire ports in the fourteenth and fifteenth centuries').
1926. Marian J. Tooley, M.A. ('The authorship of the *Defensor Pacis*').

[1] No award was made in 1900, 1907, 1910, 1911, 1913, 1914, 1921, 1946, 1948, 1956, 1969. The prize Essays for 1909 and 1919 were not published in the *Transactions*. No Essays were submitted in 1915, 1916 and 1943.

1927. W. A. Pantin, B.A. ('Chapters of the English Black Monks, 1215–1540').

1928. Gladys A. Thornton, B.A., Ph.D. ('A study in the history of Clare, Suffolk, with special reference to its development as a borough').

1929. F. S. Rodkey, A.M., Ph.D. ('Lord Palmerston's policy for the rejuvenation of Turkey, 1839–47').

1930. A. A. Ettinger, D.Phil. ('The proposed Anglo-Franco-American Treaty of 1852 to guarantee Cuba to Spain').

1931. Kathleen A. Walpole, M.A. ('The humanitarian movement of the early nineteenth century to remedy abuses on emigrant vessels to America').

1932. Dorothy M. Brodie, B.A. ('Edmund Dudley, minister of Henry VII').

1933. R. W. Southern, B.A. ('Ranulf Flambard and early Anglo-Norman administration').

1934. S. B. Chrimes, M.A., Ph.D. ('Sir John Fortescue and his theory of dominion').

1935. S. T. Bindoff, M.A. ('The unreformed diplomatic service, 1812–60').

1936. Rosamund J. Mitchell, M.A., B.Litt. ('English students at Padua, 1460–1475').

1937. C. H. Philips, B.A. ('The East India Company "Interest", and the English Government, 1783–4').

1938. H. E. I. Phillips, B.A. ('The last years of the Court of Star Chamber, 1630–41').

1939. Hilda P. Grieve, B.A. ('The deprived married clergy in Essex, 1553–61').

1940. R. Somerville, M.A. ('The Duchy of Lancaster Council and Court of Duchy Chamber').

1941. R. A. L. Smith, M.A., Ph.D. ('The *Regimen Scaccarii* in English monasteries').

1942. F. L. Carsten, D.Phil. ('Medieval democracy in the Brandenburg towns and its defeat in the fifteenth century').

1944. Rev. E. W. Kemp, B.D. ('Pope Alexander III and the canonization of saints').

1945. Helen Suggett, B.Litt. ('The use of French in England in the later middle ages').

1947. June Milne, B.A. ('The diplomacy of Dr John Robinson at the court of Charles XII of Sweden, 1697–1709').

1949. Ethel Drus, M.A. ('The attitude of the Colonial Office to the annexation of Fiji').

1950. Doreen J. Milne, M.A., Ph.D. ('The results of the Rye House Plot, and their influence upon the Revolution of 1688').

1951. K. G. Davies, B.A. ('The origins of the commission system in the West India trade').

1952. G. W. S. Barrow, B.Litt. ('Scottish rulers and the religious orders, 1070–1153').

1953. W. E. Minchinton, B.Sc.(Econ.) ('Bristol—metropolis of the west in the eighteenth century').

1954. Rev. L. Boyle, O.P. ('The *Oculus Sacerdotis* and some other works of William of Pagula').

1955. G. F. E. Rudé, M.A., Ph.D. ('The Gordon riots: a study of the rioters and their victims').

1957. R. F. Hunnisett, M.A., D.Phil. ('The origins of the office of Coroner').

1958. Thomas G. Barnes, A.B., D.Phil. ('County politics and a puritan *cause célèbre*: Somerset churchales, 1633').

1959. Alan Harding, B.Litt. ('The origins and early history of the Keeper of the Peace').

1960. Gwyn A. Williams, M.A., Ph.D. ('London and Edward I').

1961. M. H. Keen, B.A. ('Treason trials under the law of arms').

1962. G. W. Monger, M.A., Ph.D. ('The end of isolation: Britain, Germany and Japan, 1900–1902').

1963. J. S. Moore, B.A. ('The Domesday teamland: a reconsideration').

1964. M. Kelly, Ph.D. ('The submission of the clergy').

1965. J. J. N. Palmer, B.Litt. ('Anglo-French negotiations, 1390–1396').

1966. M. T. Clanchy, M.A., Ph.D. ('The Franchise of Return of Writs').

1967. R. Lovatt, M.A., D.Phil., Ph.D. ('The *Imitation of Christ* in late medieval England').

1968. M. G. A. Vale, M.A., D.Phil. ('The last years of English Gascony, 1451–1453').

1970. Mrs Margaret Bowker, M.A., B.Litt. ('The Commons Supplication against the Ordinaries in the light of some Archidiaconal Acta').

1971. C. Thompson, M.A. ('The origins of the politics of the Parliamentary middle group 1625–1629').

1972. I. d'Alton, B.A., ('Southern Irish Unionism: A study of Cork City and County Unionists, 1884–1914').

1973. C. J. Kitching, B.A., Ph.D. ('The quest for concealed lands in the reign of Elizabeth I').

1974. H. Tomlinson, B.A. ('Place and Profit: an Examination of the Ordnance Office, 1660–1714').

DAVID BERRY PRIZE

The David Berry Prize was established in 1929 by David Anderson-Berry in memory of his father, the Reverend David Berry. It consists of a gold medal and money prize awarded every three years for Scottish history. Candidates may select any subject dealing with Scottish history within the reigns of James I to James VI inclusive, provided such subject has been previously submitted to and approved by the Council of the Royal Historical Society. The essay must be a genuine work of original research not hitherto published, and one which has not been awarded any other prize. The essay must not exceed 50,000 words. It must be sent in on or before 31 October 1976.

LIST OF DAVID BERRY PRIZE ESSAYISTS (1937–73)[1]

1937. G. Donaldson, M.A. ('The polity of the Scottish Reformed Church c. 1560–1580, and the rise of the Presbyterian movement').

1943. Rev. Prof. A. F. Scott Pearson, D.Th., D.Litt. ('Anglo-Scottish religious relations, 1400–1600').

1949. T. Bedford Franklin, M.A., F.R.S.E. ('Monastic agriculture in Scotland, 1440–1600').

1955. W. A. McNeill, M.A. (' "Estaytt" of the king's rents and pensions, 1621').

1958 Prof. Maurice Lee, Ph.D. ('Maitland of Thirlestane and the foundation of the Stewart despotism in Scotland').

1964. M. H. Merriman ('Scottish collaborators with England during the Anglo-Scottish war, 1543–1550').

1967. Miss M. H. B. Sanderson ('Catholic recusancy in Scotland in the sixteenth century').

1970. Dr Athol Murray, M.A., LL.B., Ph.D. ('The Comptroller, 1425–1610').

1973. Dr J. Kirk ('Who were the Melvillians: A study in the Personnel and Background of the Presbyterian Movement in late Sixteenth-century Scotland').

[1] No Essays were submitted in 1940. No award was made in 1946, 1952 and 1961.

THE ROYAL HISTORICAL SOCIETY

(INCORPORATED BY ROYAL CHARTER)

OFFICERS AND COUNCIL—1974

Patron
HER MAJESTY THE QUEEN

President
PROFESSOR G. R. ELTON, MA, PhD, LittD, FBA

Honorary Vice-Presidents

PROFESSOR SIR HERBERT BUTTERFIELD, MA, LLD, DLitt, DLit, LittD, FBA.
PROFESSOR C. R. CHENEY, MA, DLitt, FBA.
SIR CHARLES CLAY, CB, MA, LittD, FBA, FSA.
PROFESSOR SIR GORONWY EDWARDS, MA, DLitt, LittD, FBA, FSA.
PROFESSOR V. H. GALBRAITH, MA, DLitt, LittD, FBA.
PROFESSOR R. A. HUMPHREYS, OBE, MA, PhD, DLitt, LittD, DUniv.
PROFESSOR SIR JOHN NEALE, MA, DLitt, LittD, LHD, FBA.
THE HON SIR STEVEN RUNCIMAN, MA, DPhil, LLD, LittD, DLitt, LitD, DD, DHL, FBA, FSA.
SIR RICHARD SOUTHERN, MA, DLitt, LittD, DLitt, FBA.
DAME LUCY SUTHERLAND, DBE, MA, DLitt, LittD, DCL, FBA.

Vice-Presidents

PROFESSOR C. N. L. BROOKE, MA, LittD, FBA, FSA.
PROFESSOR A. Goodwin, MA.
P. CHAPLAIS, PhD, FBA, FSA.
PROFESSOR D. HAY, MA, DLitt, FBA.
PROFESSOR M. ROBERTS, MA, DPhil, FilDr, FBA.
Professor J. M. WALLACE-HADRILL, MA, DLitt, FBA
PROFESSOR G. E. AYLMER, MA, DPhil.
PROFESSOR R. H. C. DAVIS, MA, FSA.
PROFESSOR F. J. FISHER, MA.

STANDING COMMITTEES—1974

Finance Committee
PROFESSOR T. C. BARKER.
C. E. BLUNT, OBE, FBA, FSA.
R. F. HUNNISETT.
N. J. WILLIAMS, MA, DPhil, FSA.
PROFESSOR C. H. WILSON, MA, FBA.
And the Officers.

Publications Committee
PROFESSOR G. E. AYLMER.
P. CHAPLAIS.
PROFESSOR I. R. CHRISTIE.
PROFESSOR F. J. FISHER.
M. R. D. FOOT.
B. H. HARRISON.
MRS A. E. B. OWEN.
PROFESSOR P. H. SAWYER.
PROFESSOR D. C. WATT.
And the Officers.

Library Committee
T. H. ASTON.
PROFESSOR G. E. AYLMER.
PROFESSOR F. J. FISHER.
M. R. D. FOOT.
And the Officers.

LIST OF FELLOWS OF THE
ROYAL HISTORICAL SOCIETY

(CORRECTED TO 31 DECEMBER 1974)

*Names of Officers and Honorary Vice-Presidents are printed in capitals.
Those marked* have compounded for their annual subscriptions.*

Abbott, A. W., CMG, CBE, Frithys Orchard, West Clandon, Surrey.
Adair, J. E., MA, PhD, 1 Crockford Park Road, Addlestone, Surrey.
Adam, R. J., MA, Cromalt, Lade Braes, St Andrews, Fife.
*Addleshaw, G. W. O., The Very Rev. the Dean of Chester, MA, BD, FSA,
The Deanery, Chester.
Ainsworth, Sir John, Bt, MA, c/o National Library, Kildare Street,
Dublin 2, Eire.
Akrigg, Professor G. P. V., BA, PhD, Dept of English, University of
British Columbia, Vancouver 8, B.C., Canada.
Albion, Rev. Canon Gordon, DSc (Louvain), Sutton Park, Guildford.
Alcock, L., MA, FSA, 29 Hamilton Drive, Glasgow G12 8DN.
Alder, G. J., PhD, Childs Hall, Upper Redlands Road, Reading RG1 5JW.
Alderman, G., MA, DPhil, 172 Colindeep Lane, London, NW9 6EA.
Alexandrowicz, Professor C. H., LLD, DrJur, 8 Rochester Gardens,
Croydon, Surrey.
Allan, D. G. C., MSc(Econ), FSA, Hambalt Road, London SW4 9EQ.
Allen, D. H., BA, PhD, 105 Tuddenham Avenue, Ipswich, Suffolk
IP4 2HG.
Allen, Professor, H. C., MC, MA, School of English and American
Studies, University of East Anglia, University Plain, Norwich NOR
88C.
ALLMAND, C. T., MA, DPhil, *(Assistant Literary Director)*, 59 Menlove
Avenue, Liverpool L18 2EH.
Altholz, Professor J., PhD, Dept of History, University of Minnesota,
614 Social Sciences Building, Minneapolis, Minn. 55455, USA.
Altschul, Professor M., PhD, Case Western Reserve University, Cleveland,
Ohio 44106, USA.
Anderson, Professor M. S., MA, PhD, London School of Economics,
Houghton Street, WC2 2AE.
Anderson, Mrs O. R., MA, BLitt, Westfield College, NW3.
*Anderson, R. C., MA, LittD, FSA, 9 Grove Place, Lymington, Hants.
Andrews, K. R., BA, PhD, Dept of History, University of Hull, Cotting-
ham Road, Hull HU6 7RX.
Anglo, S., BA, PhD, FSA, Dept of History of Ideas, University College,
Swansea.
Annan, Lord, OBE, MA, DLitt, DUniv, University College, Gower
Street, WC1E 6BT.
Appleby, J. S., Little Pitchbury, Brick Kiln Lane, Great Horkseley,
Colchester, Essex CO6 4EU.
Armstrong, Miss A. M., BA, 7 Vale Court, Mallord Street, SW3.
Armstrong, C. A. J., MA, FSA, Hertford College, Oxford.
Armstrong Professor F. H., PhD, University of Western Ontario, London
72, Ontario.

Armstrong, W. A., BA, PhD, Eliot College, The University, Canterbury, Kent.

Arnstein, Professor W. L., PhD, Dept of History, University of Illinois at Urbana–Champaign, 309 Gregory Hall, Urbana, Ill. 61801, U.S.A.

Ashton, Professor R., PhD, The Manor House, Brundall, near Norwich NOR 86Z

Ashworth, Professor W., BSc(Econ), PhD, Dept of Econ. and Soc. History, The University, Bristol.

Aston, Mrs M. E., MA, DPhil, Castle House, Chipping Ongar, Essex.

Aston, T. H., MA, FSA, Corpus Christi College, Oxford, OX1 4JF.

Auchmuty, Professor J. J., MA, PhD, MRIA, University of Newcastle, N.S.W., Australia.

Avery, D. J., MA, BLitt, 6 St James's Square, London, SW1.

Axelson, Professor E. V., DLitt, University of Cape Town, Rondebosch, S. Africa.

*Aydelotte, Professor W. O., PhD, State University of Iowa, Iowa City, Iowa, U.S.A.

Aylmer, Professor G. E. MA, DPhill, University of York, Heslington York YO1 5DD.

Bagley, J. J., MA, 10 Beach Priory Gardens, Southport, Lancs.

Bagshawe, T. W., FSA, c/o Luton Museum, Wardown Park, Luton. Bedfordshire.

Bahlman, Dudley W. R., PhD, Dept of History, Williams College, Williamstown, Mass., U.S.A.

Baillie, H. M. G., MBE, MA, FSA, 12B Stanford Road, W8 3QJ.

Baily, L. W. A., 29 Saxon Way, Saffron Walden, Essex.

Bailyn, Professor B., MA, PhD, LittD, LHD, Widener J. Harvard University, Cambridge, Mass. 02138, U.S.A.

Baker, L. G. D., MA, BLitt, Dept of Medieval Hist., The University, Edinburgh.

Baker, T. F. T., BA, Camden Lodge, 50 Hastings Road, Pembury, Kent.

Balfour, Professor M. L. G., CBE, MA, Waine's Cottage, Swan Lane, Burford, Oxon.

Ballhatchet, Professor K. A., MA, PhD, 35 Rudall Crescent, Hampstead London, NW3 6UE.

Banks, Professor J. A., MA, Dept of Sociology, The University, Leicester LE1 7RH.

Barker, E. E., MA, PhD 60 Marina Road, Little Altcar, Formby, via Liverpool, Lancs. L37 6BP

Barker, Professor T. C., MA, PhD, Minsen Dane, Brogdale Road, Faversham, Kent.

Barkley, Professor the Rev. J. M. MA, DD 2 College Park, Belfast, N. Ireland.

*Barlow, Professor F. MA, DPhil, FBA, Middle Court Hall, Kenton, Exeter.

*Barnes, Professor D. G. MA, PhD, 2300 Overlook Road, Cleveland, Ohio 44106, U.S.A.

Barnes, Miss P. M., PhD, Public Record Office, Chancery Lane, WC2.

Barnes, Professor T. G. AB, DPhil, University of California, Berkeley, Calif., 94720, U.S.A.

*Barnes, Professor Viola F., MA, PhD, LLD, 16 North Sycamore Street, South Hadley, Mass. 01075, U.S.A.

Barratt, Miss D. M., DPhil, The Corner House, Hampton Poyle, Kidling-
ton, Oxford.

Barron, Mrs C. M., MA, PhD, 35 Rochester Road, NW1.

Barrow, Professor G. W. S., MA, DLitt The Old Manse, 19 Westfield
Road, Cupar, Fife KY15 5AP.

Bartlett, C. J., PhD, 5 Strathspey Place, West Ferry, Dundee DD5 1QB.

Batho, G. R., MA, The University, Sheffield 10.

Baugh, Professor Daniel A., PhD, Dept of History, McGraw Hall, Cornell
University, Ithaca, N.Y. 14850, U.S.A.

Baxter, Professor S. B., PhD, 608 Morgan Creek Road, Chapel Hill, N.C.
27514 U.S.A.

Baylen, Professor J. O., MA, PhD, Georgia State University, 33 Gilmer
Street S.E., Atlanta, Georgia, U.S.A.

Beales, D. E. D. MA, PhD, Sidney Sussex College, Cambridge.

Beales, H. L., DLitt, 16 Denman Drive, London, NW11.

Bealey, Professor F., BSc(Econ), Dept of Politics, Taylor Building, Old
Aberdeen AB9 2UB.

Bean, Professor J. M. W., MA, DPhil, 622 Fayerweather Hall, Columbia
University, New York, N.Y. 10027, U.S.A.

Beardwood, Miss Alice, BA, BLitt, DPhil, 415 Miller's Lane, Wynnewood,
Pa. U.S.A.

Beasley, Professor W. G. PhD, FBA, 172 Hampton Road, Twickenham,
Middlesex TW2 5NJ.

Beattie, Professor J. M., PhD Dept of History, University of Toronto,
Toronto M5S 1A1, Canada.

Beaumont, H., MA, Silverdale, Severn Bank, Shrewsbury.

Beckett, Professor J. C., MA, 19 Wellington Park Terrace, Belfast 9, N.
Ireland.

Beckingsale, B. W., MA, 8 Highbury, Newcastle upon Tyne.

Beddard, R. A., MA, DPhil, Oriel College, Oxford.

Beeler, Professor J. H., PhD, 1302 New Garden Road, Greensboro, N.C.
27410, U.S.A.

*Beer, E. S. de, CBE, MA, DLitt, FBA, FSA, 31 Brompton Square, SW3
2AE.

Beer, Professor Samuel H., PhD, Faculty of Arts & Sciences, Harvard
University, Littauer Center G-15, Cambridge, Mass, 02138, U.S.A.

Begley, W. W., 17 St Mary's Gardens, SE11.

Behrens, Miss C. B. A., MA, Dales Barn, Barton, Cambridge.

Bell, P. M. H., BA, BLitt, The School of History, The University, P.O.
Box 147, Liverpool.

Beller, E. A., DPhil, Dept of History, Princeton University, N.J., 08540,
U.S.A.

Beloff, Professor M., MA, BLitt, All Souls College, Oxford.

Bennett, Capt. G. M., RN(ret.), DSC, Stage Coach Cottage, 57 Broad
Street, Ludlow, Salop, SY8 1NH.

Bennett, Rev. Canon G. V., MA, DPhil, FSA, New College, Oxford.

Bennett, R. F., MA, Magdalene College, Cambridge.

Bethell, D. L. T., MA, Dept of Medieval History, University College,
Belfield, Dublin 4, Ireland.

Bethell, L. M., PhD, University College, Gower Street, WC1 E6BT.

Biddiss, M. D., MA, PhD, The University, Leicester LE1 7RH.

Biddle, M, MA, FSA, Winchester Research Unit, 13 Parchment Street,
Winchester.

Bidwell, Brig. R. G. S., OBE, Royal United Services Institute, Whitehall SW1A 2ET.

Bindoff, Professor S. T., MA, 2 Sylvan Gardens, Woodlands Road, Surbiton, Surrey.

*Bing, H. F., MA, 45 Rempstone Road, East Leake, nr Loughborough, Leics.

Binney, J. E. D., DPhil, 6 Pageant Drive, Sherborne, Dorset.

Birch, A., MA, PhD, University of Hong Kong, Hong Kong.

Bishop, A. S., BA, PhD, 254 Leigham Court Road, Streatham, SW16 2RP.

Bishop, T. A. M., MA, The Annexe, Manor House, Hemingford Grey, Hunts.

Black, Professor Eugene C., PhD, Dept of History, Brandeis University, Waltham, Mass. 02154 U.S.A.

Blair, P. Hunter, MA, Emmanuel College, Cambridge.

Blake, E. O., MA, PhD, Roselands, Moorhill Road, Westend, Southampton.

Blake, Professor J. W., CBE, MA, DLitt, Willow Cottage, Mynoe, Limavady, Co. Londonderry, N. Ireland.

Blake, Lord, MA, FBA, The Provost's Lodgings, The Queen's College, Oxford OX1 4AW.

Blakemore, H., PhD, 43 Fitzjohn Avenue, Barnet, Herts.

*Blakey, Professor R. G., PhD, c/o Mr Raymond Shove, Order Dept, Library, University of Minnesota, Minneapolis, Minn., U.S.A.

Blakiston, H. N., BA, 6 Markham Square, SW3.

Blaxland, Major W. G., Lower Heppington, Street End, Canterbury, Kent, CT4 7AN.

Blomfield, Mrs K., 8 Elmdene Court, Constitution Hill, Woking, Surrey GU22 7SA.

Blunt, C. E., OBE, FBA, FSA, Ramsbury Hill, Ramsbury, Marlborough, Wilts.

*Bolsover, G. H., OBE, MA, PhD, 7 Devonshire Road, Hatch End, Middlesex.

Bolton, Miss Brenda, BA, 21 Steeles Road, London, NW3.

Bolton, Professor G. C., MA, DPhil, 6 Melvista Avenue, Claremont, Western Australia.

Bolton, Professor W. F., AM, PhD, FSA, Douglass College, Rutgers University, New Brunswick, N.J. 08903, U.S.A.

Bond, M. F., OBE, MA, FSA, 19 Bolton Crescent, Windsor, Berks.

Borrie, M. A. F., BA, 14 Lancaster Gate, W2.

Bossy, J. A., MA, PhD, The University, Belfast.

Bottigheimer, Professor Karl S., Dept of History, State University of New York at Stony Brook, Long Island, N.Y., U.S.A.

Boulton, Professor J. T., BLitt, PhD, School of English Studies, The University, Nottingham.

Bowker, Mrs M., MA, BLitt, 5 Spens Avenue, Cambridge.

Bowyer, M. J. F., 32, Netherhall Way, Cambridge.

*Boxer, Professor C. R., DLitt, FBA, Ringshall End, Little Gaddesden, Berkhamsted, Herts.

Boyce, D. G., BA, PhD, Dept of Political Theory and Government, University College, Swansea, SA2 8PP.

Boyle, Professor the Rev. L. E., DPhil, STL, Pontifical Institute of Mediaeval Studies, 59 Queen's Park, Toronto 181, Canada.

Boynton, L. O. J., MA, DPhil, FSA, Westfield College, NW3.

Bramsted, E. K., PhD, DPhil, Woodpeckers, Brooklands Lane, Weybridge, Surrey KT13 8UX.

Breck, Professor A. D., MA, PhD, LittD, DLitt, University of Denver, Denver, Colorado 80210, U.S.A.

Brentano, Professor R., DPhil, University of California, Berkeley, Calif., U.S.A.

Brett-James, E. A., MA, Royal Military Academy, Sandhurst, Camberley, Surrey.

Bridge, F. R., PhD, The Poplars, Radley Lane, Radley, Leeds.

Briers, Miss P. M., BLitt, 58 Fassett Road, Kingston-on-Thames, Surrey.

Briggs, Professor A., BSc(Econ), MA, DLitt, University of Sussex, Stanmer House, Stanmer, Brighton.

Briggs, J. H. Y., University of Keele, Staffs ST5 5BG.

Briggs, R., MA, All Souls College, Oxford OX1 4AL.

Brock, M. G., MA, 31 Linton Road, Oxford OX1 6UL.

Brock, Professor W. R., MA, PhD, Department of History, University of Glasgow, Glasgow 2.

Brodie, Miss D. M., PhD, 137 Roberts Road, Pietermaritzburg, Natal, South Africa.

Brogan, D. H. V., MA, St John's College, Cambridge.

*Bromley, Professor J. S., MA, Merrow, Dene Close, Upper Bassett, Southampton.

*Brooke, Professor C. N. L., MA, LittD, FBA, FSA, 28 Wood Lane, Highgate N6 5UB.

Brooke, J., BA, 63 Hurst Avenue, Chingford E4 8DL.

Brooke, Mrs R. B., MA, PhD, 28 Wood Lane, Highgate N6 5UB.

Brooks, F. W., MA, FSA, The University, Hull.

Brooks, N. P., MA, DPhil, The University, St Andrews, Fife.

Brown, A. L., MA, DPhil, The University, Glasgow G12 8QQ.

Brown, G. S., PhD, 1720 Hanover Road, Ann Arbor, Mich., 48103, U.S.A.

Brown, Judith M., MA, PhD, Dept of History, The University, Manchester M13 9PL.

Brown, Miss L. M., MA, PhD, 93 Church Road, Hanwell, W7.

Brown, Professor M. J., MA, PhD, 333 South Candler Street, Decatur, Georgia 30030, U.S.A.

Brown, P. R. Lamont, MA, FBA, Hillslope, Pullen's Lane, Oxford.

Brown, R. A., MA, DPhil, FSA, King's College, Strand, WC2.

Bruce, J. M., MA, 6 Albany Close, Bushey Heath, Herts, WD2 3SG.

Bruce, Professor M., BA, 22 Chorley Drive, Sheffield, S10 3RR.

Bryant, Sir Arthur W. M., CH, CBE, LLD, 18 Rutland Gate, SW7.

Buckland, P. J., MA, PhD, 6 Rosefield Road, Liverpool L25 8TF.

Bueno de Mesquita, D. M., MA, PhD, Christ Church, Oxford.

Bullock, Sir Alan (L.C.), MA, DLitt, FBA, St Catherine's College, Oxford.

Bullough, Professor D. A., MA, FSA, Dept of Mediaeval History, 71 South Street, St Andrews, Fife.

Burke, U. P., MA, 15 Lower Market Street, Hove, Sussex, BN3 1AT.

Burleigh, The Rev. Principal J. H. S., BD, 4 Braid Avenue, Edinburgh.

Burns, Professor J. H., MA, PhD, 39 Amherst Road, W.13.

Burroughs, P., PhD, Dalhousie University, Halifax, Nova Scotia, Canada.

Burrow, J. W., MA, PhD, Sussex University, Falmer, Brighton.

Bury, J. P. T., MA, Corpus Christi College, Cambridge.

*Butler, Professor Sir James R. M., MVO, OBE, MA, Trinity College, Cambridge CB2 1TQ.

Butler, Professor L. H., MA, DPhil, Principal, Royal Holloway College, Englefield Green, Surrey.

Butler, R. D'O, CMG, MA, All Souls College, Oxford.

BUTTERFIELD, Professor Sir Herbert, MA, LLD, DLitt, DLit, LittD, FBA, 28 High Street, Sawston, Cambridge CB2 4BG.

Bythell, D., MA, DPhil, University College, The Castle, Durham.

Cabaniss, Professor J. A., PhD, University of Mississippi, Box No. 153, University, Mississippi, U.S.A.

Calvert, Brig. J. M. (ret.) MA, Flat 9, Station Parade, East Horsley, Sussex.

Calvert, P. A. R., MA, PhD, AM, Dept of Politics, University of Southampton, Highfield, Southampton SO9 5NH.

Cameron, Professor K., PhD, The University, Nottingham.

Campbell, Professor A. E., MA, PhD, School of History, University of Birmingham, P.O. Box 363, Birmingham B15 2TT.

*Campbell, Miss A. M., AM, PhD, 190 George Street, Brunswick, N.J., U.S.A.

Campbell, Major D. A., FSAScot, An Cladach, Achnacree Bay, Connel, Argyll PA37 1RD.

Campbell, J., MA, FSA, Worcester College, Oxford.

*Campbell, Professor Mildred L., PhD, Vassar College, Poughkeepsie, N.Y., U.S.A.

Campbell, Professor R. H., MA, PhD, University of Stirling, Scotland.

Campbell, Miss Sybil, OBE, MA, Drim-na-Vulun, Lochgilphead, Argyll.

Cant, R. G., MA, 2 Kilburn Place, St Andrews, Fife.

Cantor, Professor Norman F., PhD, Dept of History, State University of New York at Binghampton, N.Y. 13901, U.S.A.

Capp, B. S., MA, DPhil, Dept of History, University of Warwick, Coventry, Warwickshire CV4 7AL.

Cargill-Thompson, W. D. J., MA, PhD, Dept of Ecclesiastical History, King's College, Strand, WC2.

*Carlson, Professor L. H., PhD, Southern California School of Theology, 1325 College Avenue, Claremont, Calif., U.S.A.

Carman, W. Y., FSA, 94 Mulgrave Road, Sutton, Surrey.

Carr, A. R. M., MA, St Antony's College, Oxford.

Carr, W., PhD, 16 Old Hay Close, Dore, Sheffield.

Carrington, Miss Dorothy, 3 Rue Emmanuel Arene, 20 Ajaccio, Corsica.

Carter, Mrs A. C., MA, 12 Garbrand Walk, Ewell, Epsom, Surrey.

Cartlidge, Rev. J. E. G., Sunnyside House, Snowhill, St George's, Oakengates, Salop.

*Carus-Wilson, Professor E. M., MA, FBA, FSA, 14 Lansdowne Road, W11.

Catto, R. J. A. I., MA, Oriel College, Oxford.

Chadwick, Professor W. O., DD, DLitt, FBA, Selwyn Lodge, Cambridge.

Challis, C. E., MA, PhD, 14 Ashwood Villas, Headingley, Leeds 6.

Chambers, D. S., MA, DPhil, Warburg Institute, Woburn Square, WC1.

Chandaman, Professor C. D., BA, PhD, St David's University College, Lampeter, Cardiganshire.

Chandler, D. G., MA, Hindford, Monteagle Lane, Yately, Camberley, Surrey.

Chaplais, P., PhD, FBA, FSA, Wintles Farm House, 36 Mill Street, Eynsham, Oxford.

Charles-Edwards, T. M., DPhil, Corpus Christi College, Oxford.

*CHENEY, Professor C. R., MA, DLitt, FBA, 236 Hills Road, Cambridge CB2 2QE.
Chew, Miss H. M., MA, PhD, Seven Hills Nursing Home, St Margaret's Road, St Marychurch, Torquay.
Chibnall, Mrs Marjorie, MA, DPhil, 6 Millington Road, Cambridge.
Child, C. J., OBE, MA, PhM, 94 Westhall Road, Warlingham, Surrey CR3 9HB.
Chorley, The Hon. G. P. H., BA, 40 Castelnau Mansions, London SW13.
Chrimes, Professor S. B., MA, PhD, LittD, 24 Cwrt-y-Vil Road, Penarth, Glam. CF6 2HP.
Christie, Professor I. R., MA, 10 Green Lane, Croxley Green, Herts., WD3 3HR.
Church, Professor R. A., BA, PhD, University of East Anglia, Norwich NOR 88C.
Cirket, A. F., 71 Curlew Crescent, Bedford.
Clanchy, M. T., MA, The University, Glasgow W2.
Clark, A. E., MA, 32 Durham Avenue, Thornton Cleveleys, Blackpool.
Clark, Professor Dora Mae, PhD, 134 Pennsylvania Ave., Chambersburg, Pa. 17201, U.S.A.
Clark, G. S. R. Kitson, MA, LittD, DLitt, Trinity College, Cambridge CB2 1TQ.
Clarke, P. F., MA, PhD, Dept of History, University College, Gower Street, WC1E 6BT.
*CLAY, Sir Charles (T.), CB, MA, LittD, FBA, FSA, 30 Queen's Gate Gardens, SW7.
Clementi, Miss D., MA, DPhil, Flat 7, 43 Rutland Gate, SW7.
Clemoes, Professor P. A. M., BA, PhD, Emmanuel College, Cambridge.
Cliffe, J. T., BA, PhD, 263 Staines Road, Twickenham, Middx.
Clive, Professor J. L., PhD, 38 Fernald Drive, Cambridge, Mass. 02138, U.S.A.
Clough, C. H., MA, DPhil, School of History, The University, 8 Abercromby Square, Liverpool 7.
Cobb, H. S., MA, FSA, 1 Child's Way, Hampstead Garden Suburb, NW11.
Cobb, Professor R. C., MA, FBA, Worcester College, Oxford.
Cobban, A. B., MA, PhD, School of History, The University, 8 Abercromby Square, Liverpool 7.
Cockburn, J. S., LLB, LIM, PhD, c/o Public Record Office, Chancery Lane, London WC2A 1LR.
Cocks, E. J., MA, Middle Lodge, Ardingly, Haywards Heath, Sussex.
*Code, Rt Rev. Monsignor Joseph B., MA, STB, ScHistD, DLitt, The Executive House 21E, 4466 West Pine Blvd., St Louis, MO 63108, U.S.A.
Cohn, H. J., MA, DPhil, University of Warwick, Coventry CV4 7AL.
Cohn, Professor N., MA, DLitt, 61 New End, NW3.
Cole, Lieut-Colonel H. N., OBE, TD, DL, FRSA, 4 Summer Cottages, Guildford Road, Ash, nr Aldershot, Hants.
Coleman, B. I., MA, PhD, Dept of History, The University, Exeter.
Coleman, Professor D. C., BSc, PhD, FBA, Over Hall, Cavendish, Sudbury, Suffolk.
Collier, W. O., MA, FSA, 34 Berwyn Road, Richmond, Surrey.
Collieu, E. G., MA, BLitt, Brasenose College, Oxford.
Collins, Mrs I., MA, BLitt, School of History, 8 Abercromby Square, Liverpool 7.

Collinson, Professor P., MA, PhD, Department of History, University of Sydney, N.S.W. 2006 Australia.

Colvin, H. M., CBE, MA, FBA, St John's College, Oxford.

Conacher, Professor J. B., MA, PhD, 151 Welland Avenue, Toronto 290, Ontario, Canada.

Congreve, A. L., MA, FSA, Orchard Cottage, Cranbrook, Kent.

Connell-Smith, Professor G. E., PhD, 7 Braids Walk, Kirkella, Hull, Yorks. HU10 7PA.

Constable, G., PhD, 25 Mount Pleasant Street, Cambridge, Mass, U.S.A.

Conway, Professor A. A., MA, University of Canterbury, Christchurch 1, New Zealand.

Cooke, Professor J. J., PhD, Dept of History, College of Liberal Arts, University of Mississippi, University, Miss. 38677, U.S.A.

Coolidge, Professor R. T., MA, BLitt, 27 Rosemount Avenue, Westmount, Quebec, Canada.

Cooper, J. P., MA, Trinity College, Oxford.

Copeland, Professor, T. W., PhD, 32 Granville Court, Cheney Lane, Headington, Oxford OX3 OH5.

Cornford, Professor J. P., Dept of Politics, University of Edinburgh, William Robertson Bldg., George Sq., Edinburgh EH8 9JY.

Cornwall, J. C. K., MA, 1 Orchard Close, Copford Green, Colchester, Essex.

Corson, J. C., MA, PhD, Mossrig, Lilliesleaf, Melrose, Roxburghshire.

Costeloe, M. P., BA, PhD, The University, Bristol.

Cowan, I. B., MA, PhD, University of Glasgow, Glasgow, G12 8QH.

Cowdrey, Rev. H. E. J., MA, St Edmund Hall, Oxford OX1 4AR.

Cowie, Rev. L. W., MA, PhD, 38 Stratton Road, Merton Park, S.W.19.

Cowley, F. G., PhD, 17 Brookvale Road, West Cross, Swansea.

Cowling, M. J., MA Peterhouse, Cambridge CB2 1RD.

Cragg, Professor G. R., PhD, Andover Newton Theological School, Newton Center, Mass. 02159 U.S.A.

Craig, R. S., BSc(Econ), 99 Muswell Avenue, N10.

Cramp, Professor Rosemary, MA, BLitt, FSA, Department of Archaeology, The Old Fulling Mill, The Banks, Durham.

Cranfield, L. R., 31a Clara Street, South Yarra, Victoria, Australia.

*Crawley, C. W., MA, 1 Madingley Road, Cambridge.

Cremona, The Hon. Mr Justice Professor J. J., DLitt, PhD, LLD, 5 Victoria Gardens, Sliema, Malta.

Crittall, Miss E., MA, FSA, 16 Downside Crescent, NW3.

Crombie, A. C., BSc, MA, PhD, Trinity College, Oxford OX1 3BH.

Crompton, J., MA, BLitt, FSA, Digby Hall, Stoughton Drive South, Leicester LE2 2NB.

Cromwell, Miss V., MA, University of Sussex, Falmer, Brighton, Sussex.

Cross, Miss M. C., MA, PhD, University of York, York YO1 5DD.

Crowder, C. M. D., MA, DPhil, Queen's University, Kingston, Ontario, Canada.

Crowe, Miss S. E., MA, PhD, St Hilda's College, Oxford.

Cruickshank, C. G., MA, DPhil, 15 McKay Road, Wimbledon Common, SW20.

Cumming, Professor I., MEd, PhD, The University, Auckland, New Zealand.

Cummins, J. S., PhD, University College, Gower Street, WC1E 6BT.

Cumpston, Miss I. M., MA, DPhil, Birkbeck College, Malet Street, WC1.

Cunliffe, Professor M. F., MA, BLitt, Dept of American Studies, University of Sussex, Falmer, Brighton.

Cunningham, Professor A. B., MA, PhD, Simon Fraser University, Burnaby 2, B.C., Canada.

Curtis, Professor L. Perry, PhD, Dept of History, Brown University, Providence, R.I. 02912, U.S.A.

Curtis, M. H., PhD, Scripps College, Claremont, Calif., U.S.A.

Cushner, Rev. N. P., SJ, MA, Canisius College, Buffalo, New York 14208, U.S.A.

*Cuttino, Professor G. P., DPhil, Department of History, Emory University, Atlanta, Ga., U.S.A.

Dakin, D., MA, PhD, 7 Langside Avenue, SW15.

Darlington, Professor R. R., BA, PhD, FBA, FSA, Warrenhurst, Twyford, Reading.

Davies, Professor Alun, MA, 46 Eaton Crescent, Swansea.

Davies, C. S. L., MA, DPhil, Wadham College, Oxford.

Davies, I. N. R., MA, DPhil, 22 Rowland Close, Wolvercote, Oxford.

Davies, R. R., DPhil, University College, Gower Street, WC1E 6BT.

*Davis, G. R. C., MA, DPhil, FSA 214 Somerset Road, SW19 5JE.

Davis, Professor R. H. C., MA, FSA, 56 Fitzroy Avenue, Harborne, Birmingham B17 8RJ.

*Dawe, D. A., 46 Green Lane, Purley, Surrey.

*Day, P. W., MA, 2 Rectory Terrace, Gosforth, Newcastle upon Tyne.

Deane, Miss Phyllis M., MA, Newnham College, Cambridge.

*Deanesly, Professor Margaret, MA, FSA, 196 Clarence Gate Gardens, NW1.

*Deeley, Miss A. P., MA, 41 Linden Road, Bicester, Oxford.

de la Mare, Miss A. C., MA, PhD, Bodleian Library, Oxford.

Denham, E. W., MA, 27 The Drive, Northwood, Middx, HA6 1HW.

Dennis, Professor P. J., MA, PhD, Dept of History, The Royal Military College of Canada, Kingston, Ont. K7L 2W3. Canada.

Denton, J. H., BA, PhD, The University Manchester M13 9PL.

Dickens, Professor A. G., CMG, MA, DLit, FBA, FSA, Institute of Historical Research, University of London, Senate House, WC1E 7HU.

Dickinson, H. T., MA, PhD, Dept of Modern History, The University, Edinburgh.

Dickinson, Rev. J. C., MA, FSA, The University, Birmingham 15.

Dickson, P. G. M., MA, DPhil, St Catherine's College, Oxford.

Diké, Professor K. O., MA, PhD, Dept of History, Harvard University, Cambridge, Mass, 02138, U.S.A.

Dilks, Professor D. N., BA, Dept. of International History, The University, Leeds.

Dilworth, Rev. G. M., OSB, PhD, The Abbey, Fort Augustus, Inverness-shire.

Dobson, R. B., MA, DPhil, Department of History, The University, Heslington, York.

*Dodwell, Miss B., MA, The University, Reading.

Dodwell, Professor C. R., MA, PhD, FSA, History of Art Department, The University, Manchester M13 9PL.

Dolley, R. H. M., BA, MRIA, FSA, 48 Malone Avenue, Belfast 9.

Don Peter, The Very Rev. W. L. A., MA, PhD, Aquinas College, Colombo 8, Sri Lanka.

Donald, Professor M. B., MSc, Rabbit Shaw, Stagbury Avenue, Chipstead, Surrey.

*Donaldson, Professor G., MA, PhD, DLitt, Preston Tower Nursery Cottage, Prestonpans, East Lothian EH32 9EN.

*Donaldson-Hudson, Miss R., BA, (address unknown).

Donoughue, B., MA, DPhil, London School of Economics, Houghton Street, London, WC1.

Dore, R. N., MA, Holmrook, 19 Chapel Lane, Hale Barns, Altrincham, Cheshire WA15 0AB.

Douglas, Professor D. C., MA, DLitt, FBA, 4 Henleaze Gardens, Bristol.

Douie, Miss D. L., BA, PhD, FSA, Flat A, 2 Charlbury Road, Oxford.

Doyle, A. I., MA, PhD, University College, The Castle, Durham.

*Drus, Miss E., MA, The University, Southampton.

Du Boulay, Professor F. R. H., MA, Broadmead, Riverhead, Sevenoaks, Kent.

Duckham, B. F., MA, Hillhead Cottage, Balfron, Stirlingshire.

Duggan, C., PhD, King's College, Strand, WC2.

Dugmore, The Rev. Professor C. W., DD, King's College, Strand, WC2.

Duly, Professor L. C., PhD, Dept of History, University of Nebraska, Lincoln, Neb. 68508, U.S.A.

Dunbabin, J. P. D., MA, St Edmund Hall, Oxford.

Duncan, Professor A. A. M., MA, University of Glasgow, 9 University Gardens, Glasgow G12 8QH.

Dunham, Professor W. H., PhD, 200 Everit Street, New Haven, Conn. 06511, U.S.A.

Dunn, Professor R. S., PhD, Dept of History, The College, University of Pennsylvania, Philadelphia 19104, U.S.A.

Dunning, Rev. P. J., CM, MA, PhD, St. Vincent's, 293 Waldegrave Road, Strawberry Hill, Twickenham, Middx. TW1 4SO.

Dunning, R. W., BA, PhD, FSA, 16 Comeytrowe Rise, Taunton, Somerset.

Durack, Mrs I. A., MA, PhD, University of Western Australia, Crawley, Western Australia.

Dykes, D. W., MA, Cherry Grove, Welsh St Donats, nr Cowbridge, Glam. CF7 7SS.

Dyos, Professor H. J., BSc(Econ), PhD, 16 Kingsway Road, Leicester.

Eastwood, Rev. C. C., PhD, Heathview, Monks Lane, Audlem, Cheshire.

Eckles, Professor R. B., PhD, P.O. Box 3035, West Lafayette, Indiana, 47906, U.S.A.

Ede, J. R., MA, Public Record Office, Chancery Lane, WC2.

Edmonds, Professor E. L., MA, PhD, Dean of Education, Univ. of Prince Edward Island, Charlottetown, Prince Edward Island, Canada.

Edwards, F. O., SJ, BA, FSA, 114 Mount Street, W1Y 6AH.

EDWARDS, Professor Sir (J.) Goronwy, MA, DLitt, LittD, FBA, FSA, 35 Westmorland Road, SW13.

Edwards, Miss K., MA, PhD, FSA, Dunbar Cottage, 10 Dunbar Street, Old Aberdeen.

Edwards, Professor R. W. D., MA, PhD, DLitt, 21 Brindon Road, Donnybrook, Dublin 4.

Ehrman, J. P. W., MA, FBA, FSA, Sloane House, 149 Old Church Street, SW3 6EB.

Elliott, Professor J. H., MA, PhD, FBA, King's College, Strand, WC2.

Ellis, R. H., MA, FSA, Cloth Hill, 6 The Mount, NW3.

Ellul, M., BArch, DipArch, 'Pauline', 55 Old Railway Road, Birkirkara, Malta.

Elrington, C. R., MA, FSA, Institute of Historical Research, Senate House, WC1E 7HU.

ELTON, Professor G. R., MA, PhD, LittD, FBA (*President*), 30 Millington Road, Cambridge CB3 9HP.

Elvin, L., 10 Almond Avenue, Swanpool, Lincoln.

*Emmison, F. G., MBE, PhD, DUniv, FSA, Bibury, Links Drive, Chelmsford.

d'Entrèves, Professor A. P., DPhil, Strada Ai Ronchi 48, Cavoretto, Torino, Italy.

Erickson, Charlotte J., PhD, London School of Economics, Houghton Street, WC2.

*Erith, E. J., Shurlock House, Shurlock Row, Berkshire.

Erskine, Mrs A. M., MA, BLitt, FSA, 44 Birchy Barton Hill, Exeter EX1 3EX.

Evans, Mrs A. K. B., PhD, FSA, White Lodge, 25 Knighton Grange Road, Leicester.

Evans, Sir David (L.), OBE, BA, DLitt, 2 Bay Court, Doctors Commons Road, Berkhamsted, Herts.

Evans, Miss Joan, DLitt, DLit, LLD, LittD, FSA, Thousand Acres, Wootton-under-Edge, Glos.

Evans, R. J. W., MA, PhD, Brasenose College, Oxford.

Evans, The Very Rev. S. J. A., CBE, MA, FSA, The Old Manor, Fulbourne, Cambs.

Everitt, Professor A. M., MA, PhD, The University, Leicester.

Eyck, Professor U. F. J., MA, BLitt, Dept of History, University of Calgary, Alberta T2N IN4, Canada.

Fage, Professor J. D., MA, PhD, Centre of West African Studies, The University, Birmingham B15 2TT.

Fagg, J. E., MA, 47 The Avenue, Durham DH1 4ED.

Farmer, D. F. H., BLitt, FSA, The University, Reading.

Farr, M. W., MA, FSA, 12 Emscote Road, Warwick.

Fearn, Rev. H., MA, PhD, Holy Trinity Vicarage, 6 Wildwood, Northwood, Middlesex.

Fenlon, D. B., BA, PhD, Gonville and Caius College, Cambridge.

Fenn, Rev. R. W. D., MA, BD, FSAScot, Glascwm Vicarage, Llandrindod Wells, Radnorshire.

Ferguson, Professor A. B., PhD, Dept of History, 6727 College Station, Duke University, Durham, N.C. 27708, U.S.A.

Feuchtwanger, E., MA, PhD, Highfield House, Dean, Sparsholt, nr Winchester, Hants.

Fieldhouse, D. K., MA, Nuffield College, Oxford.

Finer, Professor S. E., MA, All Souls College, Oxford OX1 4AL.

Fink, Professor Z. S., PhD, 6880 Hawthorne Circle, Tucson, Arizona 85710, U.S.A.

Finlayson, G. B. A. M., MA, BLitt, 11 Burnhead Road, Glasgow G43 2SU.

Finley, Professor M. I., MA, PhD, 12 Adams Road, Cambridge.

Fisher, D. J. V., MA, Jesus College, Cambridge CB3 9AD.

Fisher, Professor F. J., MA, London School of Economics, Houghton Street, WC2.

Fisher, F. N., Duckpool, Ashleyhay, Wirksworth, Derby DE4 4AJ.

Fisher, Professor S. N., PhD, Box 162, Worthington, Ohio 43085, U.S.A.

Fitch, M. F. B., FSA, c/o Phillimore & Co. Ltd, Shopwyke Hall, Chichester, Sussex.

*Fletcher, The Rt Hon. The Lord, PC, BA, LLD, FSA, 9 Robin Grove, N6 6PA.

Flint, Professor J. E., MA, PhD, Dalhousie University, Halifax, Nova Scotia, Canada.

Fogel, Professor R. W., PhD, Dept of Economics, University of Chicago, Chicago, Ill., U.S.A.

Foot, M. R. D., MA, BLitt, Orchard Cottage, Thakeham, Pulborough, Sussex.

Forbes, D., MA, 89, Gilbert Road, Cambridge.

Ford, W. K., 48 Harlands Road, Haywards Heath, Sussex RH16 1LS.

Forrester, E. G., MA, BLitt, Spring Cottage, Pebble Lane, Brackley, Northants.

Forster, G. C. F., BA, FSA, The University, Leeds 2.

Foster, Professor Elizabeth R., AM, PhD, 205 Stafford Avenue, Wayne, Pa. 19087, U.S.A.

Fowler, K. A., BA,PhD, 2 Nelson Street, Edinburgh 3.

Fox, L., OBE, DL, LHD, MA, FSA, FRSL, Silver Birches, 27 Welcombe Road, Stratford-upon-Avon.

Fox, R., MA, DPhil, The University, Bailrigg, Lancaster LA1 4YG.

Francis, A. D., CBE, MVO, MA, 21 Cadogan Street, SW3.

Franklin, R. M., BA, Baldwins End, Eton College, Windsor, Berks.

*Fraser, Miss C. M., PhD, 39 King Edward Road, Tynemouth, North Shields NE30 2RW.

Fraser, Miss Maxwell, MA, Crowthorne, 21 Dolphin Road, Slough, Berks SL1 1TF.

Fraser, P., BA, PhD, Dept of History, Dalhousie University, Halifax, 8 Nova Scotia, Canada.

Frend, Professor W. H. C., TD, MA, DPhil, DD, FSA, Marbrae, Balmaha, Stirlingshire.

Fryde, Professor E. B., DPhil, 1 Plas Danycoed, Aberystwyth, Cards.

*Fryer, Professor C. E., MA, PhD, (address unknown).

Fryer, Professor W. R., BLitt, MA, 68 Grove Avenue, Chilwell, Beeston, Notts.

Frykenberg, Professor R. E., MA, PhD, 1840 Chadbourne Avenue, Madison, Wis. 53705, U.S.A.

*Furber, Professor H., MA, PhD, History Department, University of Pennsylvania, Philadelphia, Pa., U.S.A.

Fussell, G. E., DLitt, 55 York Road, Sudbury, Suffolk, CO10 6NF.

Fyrth, H., BSc(Econ.), Dept of Extra Mural Studies, University of London, 7 Ridgemount Street, WC1.

Gabriel, Professor A. L., PhD, FMAA, CFIF, CFBA, Box 578, University of Notre Dame, Notre Dame, Indiana 46556, U.S.A.

*Galbraith, Professor J. S., BS, MA, PhD, University of California, Los Angeles, Calif. 90024, U.S.A.

GALBRAITH, Professor V. H., MA, DLitt, LittD, FBA, 20A Bradmore Road, Oxford.

Gale, Professor H. P. P., OBE, PhD, 6 Nassau Road, London SW13 9QE.

Gale, W. K. V., 19 Ednam Road, Goldthorn Park, Wolverhampton WV4 5BL.

Gann, L. H., MA, BLitt, DPhil, Hoover Institution, Stanford University, Stanford, Calif., U.S.A.

Ganshof, Professor F. L., 12 Rue Jacques Jordaens, Brussels, Belgium.
Gash, Professor N., MA, BLitt, FBA, Gowrie Cottage, 73 Hepburn Gardens, St Andrews.
Gee, E. A., MA, DPhil, FSA, 28 Trentholme Drive, The Mount, York YO2 2DG.
Gerlach, Professor D. R., MA, PhD, University of Akron, Akron, Ohio 44325, U.S.A.
Gibbs, G. C., MA, Birkbeck College, Malet Street, WC1.
Gibbs, Professor N. H., MA, DPhil, All Souls College, Oxford.
Gibson, Margaret T., MA, DPhil, School of History, The University, Liverpool L69 3BX.
Gifford, Miss D. H., PhD, FSA, Public Record Office, Chancery Lane, WC2.
Gilbert, Professor Bentley B., PhD, Dept of History, University of Ill. at Chicago Circle, Box 4348, Chicago, Ill. 60680, U.S.A.
Gilbert, M., MA, The Map House, Harcourt Hill, Oxford.
Gilley, S., BA, DPhil, Dept of Ecclesiastical History, St Mary's College, University of St Andrew's, St Andrew's, Fife.
Ginter, D. E., AM, PhD, Dept of History, Sir George Williams University, Montreal 107, Canada.
Girtin, T., MA, Butter Field House, Church Street, Old Isleworth, Mddx.
Gleave, Group Capt. T. P., CBE, RAF(Ret.), Willow Bank, River Gardens, Bray-on-Thames, Berks.
*Glover, Professor R. G., MA, PhD, Carleton University, Ottawa 1, Canada.
*Godber, Miss A. J., MA, FSA, Mill Lane Cottage, Willington, Bedford.
Godfrey, Professor J. L., MA, PhD, 231 Hillcrest Circle, Chapel Hill, N.C., U.S.A.
Goldthorp, L. M., MA, Wilcroft House, Pecket Well, Hebden Bridge, Yorks.
Gollancz, Miss M., MA, 41 Crescent Court, Surbiton, Surrey, KT6 4BW.
Goodman, A. E., MA, BLitt, Dept of Medieval History, The University, Edinburgh.
Goodspeed, Professor D. J., BA, 164 Victoria Street, Niagara-on-the-Lake, Ontario, Canada.
Goodwin, Professor A., MA, Windsor Court, 12 Hound Street, Sherborne, Dorset DT9 3AA.
*Gopal, S., MA, DPhil, 30 Edward Elliot Road, Mylapore, Madras, India.
Gordon, Professor D. J., MA, PhD, Wantage Hall, Upper Redlands Road, Reading.
Gordon-Brown, A., Velden, Alexandra Road, Wynberg, C.P., South Africa.
Goring, J. J., MA, PhD, Little Iwood, Rushlake Green, Heathfield, Sussex TW21 9QS.
Gorton, L. J., MA, 41 West Hill Avenue, Epsom, Surrey.
Gosden, P. H. J. H., MA, PhD, The University, Leeds.
Gough, J. W., MA, DLitt, Oriel College, Oxford.
Gowing, Professor Margaret M., BSc(Econ), Linacre College, Oxford.
*Graham, Professor G. S., MA, PhD, Hobbs Cottage, Beckley, Sussex.
Gransden, Mrs A., MA, PhD, FSA, 51 Burlington Road, Sherwood, Nottingham.
Grassby, R. B., MA, Jesus College, Oxford.
Grattan-Kane, P., 12 St John's Close, Helston, Cornwall.

Graves, Professor Edgar B., PhD, LLD, 318 College Hill Road, Clinton, New York 13323, U.S.A.

Gray, J. W., MA, Dept of Medieval History, Queens University, Belfast BT7 1NN.

Greaves, Mrs R. L., PhD, 1920 Hillview Road, Lawrence, Kansas, U.S.A.

Greaves, Professor R. W., MA, DPhil, 1920 Hillview Road, Lawrence, Kansas, U.S.A.

Green, H., BA, Rhinog, Brands Hill Avenue, High Wycombe, Bucks.

Green, Rev. V. H. H., MA, DD, Lincoln College, Oxford.

Greenhill, B. J., CMG, BA, FSA, National Maritime Museum, Greenwich, SE10 9FN.

Greenleaf, Professor W. H., BSc(Econ), PhD, University College, Singleton Park, Swansea, Glam.

Grenville, Professor J. A. S., PhD, University of Birmingham, P.O. Box 363, Birmingham 15.

Gresham, C. A., BA, DLitt, FSA, Bryn-y-deryn, Criccieth, Caerns. LL5 0HR.

Grierson, Professor P., MA, LittD, FBA, FSA, Gonville and Caius College, Cambridge.

Grieve, Miss H. E. P., BA, 153, New London Road, Chelmsford, Essex.

Griffiths, J., MA, Springwood, Stanley Road, New Ferry, Cheshire.

Griffiths, R. A., PhD, University College, Singleton Park, Swansea.

Grimble, I., PhD, 13 Saville Road, Twickenham, Mddx.

Grimm, Professor H. J., PhD, Department of History, 216 North Oval Drive, The Ohio State University, Columbus, Ohio, U.S.A.

Grisbrooke, W. J., MA, 1 Whetstone Close, Farquhar Road, Birmingham B15 2QL.

*Griscom, Rev. Acton, MA, (address unknown).

Gum, Professor E. J., PhD, 5116 Grant Street, Omaha, Nebraska 68104. U.S.A.

Gundersheimer, Professor W. L., MA, PhD, 507 Roumfort Road, Philadelphia, Pa. 19119, U.S.A.

Habakkuk, H. J., MA, FBA, Jesus College, Oxford OX1 3DW.

Haber, Professor F. C., PhD, 3026 2R Street NW, Washington, DC 20007, U.S.A.

*Hadcock, R. N., DLitt, FSA, Winchcombe Farm, Briff Lane, Bucklebury, Reading.

Haffenden, P. S., PhD, 36 The Parkway, Bassett, Southampton.

Haigh, C. A., BA, PhD, Dept of History, The University, Manchester M13 9PL.

Haight, Mrs M. Jackson, PhD, 8 Chemin des Clochettes, Geneva, Switzerland.

Haines, Professor R. M., MA, MLitt, DPhil, FSA, Dalhousie University, Halifax, N.S., Canada.

Hair, P. E. H, MA, DPhil, The School of History, The University, P.O. Box 147, Liverpool.

Halcrow, Miss E. M., MA, BLitt, Achimota School, Achimota, P.B.11, Ghana, West Africa.

Hale, Professor, J. R., MA, FSA, University College, Gower Street, WC1E 6BT.

Haley, Professor K. H. D., MA, BLitt, 15 Haugh Lane, Sheffield 11.

Hall Professor A. R., MA, PhD, 23 Chiswick Staithe, W.4.

Hall, Professor B., MA, PhD, FSA, University of Manchester, M13 9PL.

*Hall, C. S., MA, Flat 16, Petersgath, Moorhead Lane, Shipley, Yorks.
Hall, Professor D. G. E., MA, DLit, 4 Chiltern Road, Hitchin, Herts.
Hall, G. D. G., MA, The President's Lodgings, Corpus Christi College, Oxford OX1 4JF.
Hallam, Professor H. E., MA, PhD, University of Western Australia, Nedlands, Western Australia.
Haller, Professor W., PhD, Rte 2, Southbridge, Holland, Mass. 01550, U.S.A.
Hamer, Professor D., MA, DPhil, History Dept, Victoria University of Wellington, P.O. Box 196, Wellington, New Zealand.
Hamilton, B., BA, PhD, The University, Nottingham NG7 2RD.
Hammersley, G. F., BA, University of Edinburgh, William Robertson Building, George Square, Edinburgh EH8 9JY.
Hampson, Professor N., MA, Ddel'u, The University, Heslington, York YO1 5DD.
Hand, G. J., MA, DPhil, Woodburn, Sydney Avenue, Blackrock, Co. Dublin, Ireland.
Hanham, H. J., MA, PhD, The Dean, School of Humanities and Social Science, Massachusetts Institute of Technology, Cambridge, Mass. 02139, USA.
Hanke, Professor L. U., PhD, University of Massachusetts, Amherst, Mass. 01002, U.S.A.
Harding, A., MA, BLitt, 3 Tantallon Place, Edinburgh.
Harding, F. J. W., MA, BLitt, FSA, Brynrhos, 187 Mayals Road, Swansea SA3 5HQ.
Harding, H. W., BA, LLD, 39 Annunciation Street, Sliema, Malta.
Hargreaves, Professor J. D., MA, 146 Hamilton Place, Aberdeen.
Hargreaves-Mawdsley, Professor W. N., MA, DPhil, FSA, The University, Brandon, Manitoba, Canada.
Harman, Rev. L. W., Hardingstone Vicarage, Northampton.
Harris, Mrs J. F., BA, PhD, Dept of Social Science and Administration, London School of Economics, London WC2.
Harris, Professor J. R., MA, PhD, The University, P.O. Box 363, Birmingham.
Harrison, B. H., MA, DPhil, Corpus Christi College, Oxford OX1 4JF.
Harrison, C. J., BA, St John's College, Oxford OX1 3JP.
Harrison, Professor Royden, MA, DPhil, 4 Wilton Place, Sheffield S10 2BT.
Harriss, G. L., MA, DPhil, Magdalen College, Oxford.
Hart, C. J. R., MA, MB, BS, Goldthorns, Stilton, Peterborough.
Hart, Mrs J. M., MA, St Anne's College, Oxford.
Harte, N. B., BSc(Econ), University College, Gower Street, London WC1E 6BT.
Hartwell, R. M., MA, DPhil, Nuffield College, Oxford.
Harvey, Miss B. F., MA, BLitt, Somerville College, Oxford OX2 6HD.
Harvey, Margaret M., MA, DPhil, St Aidan's College, Durham DH1 3LJ.
Harvey, P. D. A., MA, DPhil, FSA, 9 Glen Eyre Close, Bassett, Southampton.
Harvey, Sally P. J., MA, PhD, School of History, The University, Leeds LS2 9JT.
Haskell, Professor F. J., MA, FBA, Trinity College, Oxford.
Haskins, Professor G. L., AB, LLB, JD, MA, University of Pennsylvania, The Law School, 3400 Chestnut Street, Philadelphia, Pa. 19104 U.S.A.
Haslam, E. B., MA, 5 Pymers Mead, Dulwich SE21 8NQ.

Hassall, W. O., MA, DPhil, FSA, The Manor House, 26 High Street, Wheatley, Oxford OX9 1XX.

Hastings, Professor Margaret, PhD, Douglass College, Rutgers University, New Brunswick, N.J. 08903, U.S.A.

Hatcher, M. J., BSc(Econ), PhD, Eliot College, The University, Canterbury, Kent.

Hattersley, Professor A. F., MA, DLitt, 1 Sanders Road, Pietermaritzburg, S. Africa.

Hatton, Professor Ragnhild M., PhD, London School of Economics, Houghton Street, WC2.

Havighurst, Professor A. F., PhD, Blake Field, Amherst, Mass. 01002, U.S.A.

Havran, Professor M. J., PhD, Corcoran Dept of History, Randall Hall, University of Virginia, Charlottesville, Va. 22903, U.S.A.

Hay, Professor D., MA, DLitt, FBA, Dept of History, The University, Edinburgh EH8 9JY.

Hayes, P. M., PhD, Keble College, Oxford OX1 3PG.

Hazlehurst, G. C. L., BA, DPhil, FRSL, Inst. of Advanced Studies, R.S.S.S., Australian National University, Box 4, P.O. Canberra, ACT, Australia.

Headlam-Morley, Miss A., BLitt, MA, 29 St Mary's Road, Wimbledon SW19.

Hearder, Professor H., PhD, University College, Cathays Park, Cardiff.

Hembry, Mrs P. M., PhD, Flat 24, Thorncliffe, Lansdown Road, Cheltenham GL51 6PZ.

Hemleben, S. J., MA, DPhil, (address unknown).

Henderson, A. J., AB, AM, PhD, 247 North Webster, Jacksonville, Ill. 62650, U.S.A.

Hendy, M. F., MA, The Manor House, Bristol Road, Northfield, Birmingham 31.

Henning, Professor B. D., PhD, Saybrook College, Yale University, New Haven, Conn., U.S.A.

Hennock, P., MA, PhD, School of Cultural and Community Studies, University of Sussex, Falmer, Brighton, Sussex BN1 9QN.

Hexter, Professor J. H., PhD, Dept of History, 237 Hall of Graduate Studies, Yale University, New Haven, Conn. 06520, U.S.A.

Highfield, J. R. L., MA, DPhil, Merton College, Oxford.

HILL, Sir (J. W.) Francis, CBE, MA, LLD, LittD, FSA (Hon Solicitor), The Priory, Lincoln.

Hill, J. E. C., MA, DLitt, FBA, The Master's Lodgings, Balliol College, Oxford.

Hill, Professor L. M., MA, PhD, 5066 Berean Lane, Irvine, Calif. 92664, U.S.A.

*Hill, Miss M. C., MA, County Record Office, Shirehall, Shrewsbury.

*Hill, Professor Rosalind M. T., MA, BLitt, FSA, Westfield College, Hampstead NW3.

Hilton, Professor R. H., DPhil, University of Birmingham, P.O. Box 363, Birmingham 15.

Himmelfarb, Professor Gertrude, PhD, The City University of New York Graduate Center, 33 West 42 St, New York, N.Y. 10036.

*Hinsley, Professor F. H., MA, St John's College, Cambridge.

*Hodgett, G. A. J., MA, FSA, King's College, Strand, WC2.

*Hogg, Brigadier O. F. G., CBE, FSA, 1 Hardy Road, Blackheath SE3.

HOLDSWORTH, C. J., (*Hon. Secretary*), MA, PhD, West End House, Totteridge Lane, N20.

Hollaender, A. E. J., PhD, FSA, 110 Narbonne Avenue, South Side, Clapham Common SW4 9LQ.

*Hollingsworth, L. W., PhD, Flat 27, Mayfair, 74 Westcliff Road, Bournemouth.

Hollis, Patricia, MA, DPhil, 30 Park Lane, Norwich.

Hollister, Professor C. Warren, MA, PhD, University of California, Santa Barbara, Calif. 93106, U.S.A.

Holmes, G. A., MA, PhD, 431 Banbury Road, Oxford.

Holmes, Professor G. S., MA, BLitt, Tatham House, Burton-in-Lonsdale, Carnforth, Lancs.

Holt, Miss A. D., Fasga-na-Coille, Nethy Bridge, Inverness-shire.

Holt, Professor J. C., MA, DPhil, FSA, University of Reading, Whiteknights Park, Reading, Berks RG6 2AA.

Holt, Professor P. M., MA, DLitt, School of Oriental and African Studies, Malet Street, London WC1E 7HP.

Hook, Mrs Judith, MA, PhD, Dept of History, Taylor Building, King's College, Old Aberdeen AB9 2UB.

Hope, R. S. H., 25 Hengistbury Road, Southbourne, Bournemouth, Hants.

Horwitz, Professor H. G., BA, DPhil, Dept of History, University of Iowa, Iowa City, Iowa 52240, U.S.A.

*Howard, C. H. D., MA, 15 Sunnydale Gardens, NW7.

*Howard, M. E., MC, MA, FBA, The Homestead, Eastbury, Newbury, Berks.

Howarth, Mrs J. H., MA, St Hilda's College, Oxford.

Howat, G. M. D., MA, BLitt, Old School House, North Moreton, Berks.

Howell, Miss M. E., MA, PhD, 10 Highland Road, Charlton Kings, Cheltenham, Glos. GL53 9LT.

Howell, Professor R., MA, DPhil, Bowdoin College, Brunswick, Maine 04011, U.S.A.

Huehns, Miss G., PhD, 35A Sterling Avenue, Edgware, Mddx. HA8 8BP.

Hufton, Miss O. H., PhD, 40 Shinfield Road, Reading, Berks.

Hughes, Professor J. Q., BArch, PhD, Loma Linda, Criccieth, Caerns.

Hughes, Miss K. W., MA, PhD, FSA, Newnham College, Cambridge.

Hull, F., BA, PhD, Roundwell Cottage, Bearsted, Maidstone, Kent ME14 4EU.

Hulton, P. H., BA, FSA, 46 St Paul's Road, N1.

HUMPHREYS, Professor R. A., OBE, MA, PhD, DLitt, LittD, DUniv, 13 St Paul's Place, Canonbury N1 2QE.

Hunnisett, R. F., MA, DPhil, 54 Longdon Wood, Keston, Kent BR2 6EW.

Hurst, M. C., MA, St John's College, Oxford.

Hurstfield, Professor J., DLit, 7 Glenilla Road, NW3.

Hurt, J. S., BA, BSc(Econ), PhD, 66 Oxford Road, Moseley, Birmingham B13 9SQ.

*Hussey, Professor Joan M., MA, BLitt, PhD, FSA, Royal Holloway College, Englefield Green, Surrey.

Hyams, P. R., MA, DPhil, Pembroke College, Oxford.

Hyde, Professor F. E., MA, PhD, Heather Cottage, 41 Village Road, West Kirby, Wirral, Cheshire.

*Hyde, H. Montgomery, MA, DLit, Westwell, Tenterden, Kent.

Hyde, J. K., MA, PhD, The University, Manchester.

Ingham, Professor K., MA, DPhil, The Woodlands, 94 West Town Lane, Bristol 4.
Ives, E. W., PhD, 214 Myton Road, Warwick.

Jack, Professor R. I., MA, PhD, University of Sydney, Sydney, N.S.W., Australia.
Jack, Mrs Sybil M., MA, BLitt, University of Sydney, N.S.W., Australia.
Jackman, Professor S. W., PhD, FSA, 1065 Deal Street, Victoria, British Columbia, Canada.
Jackson, E. D. C., FSA, (address unknown).
Jaffar, Professor S. M., BA, Khudadad Street, Peshawar City, N.W.F. Province, W. Pakistan.
James, M. E., MA, University of Durham, 43–45 North Bailey, Durham.
James, Professor Robert R., MA, FRSL, United Nations, N.Y. 10017, U.S.A.
Jarvis, R. C., ISO, FSA, Shelley, Station Road, Hockley, Essex.
Jasper, Rev. Canon R. C. D., MA, DD, 1 Little Cloister, Westminster Abbey, SW1.
Jeffs, R. M., MA, DPhil, 25 Lawson Road, Sheffield S10 5BU.
Jenkins, D., MA, LLM, Dept of Law, University College of Wales, Aberystwyth, Cards. SY23 2DB.
Jeremy, D. J., BA, MLitt, 16 Britannia Gardens, Westcliff-on-Sea, Essex SS0 8BN.
John, Professor A. H., BSc(Econ), PhD, London School of Economics, Houghton Street, WC2.
John, E., MA, The University, Manchester 13.
Johnson, D. J., BA, 41 Cranes Park Avenue, Surbiton, Surrey.
Johnson, Professor D. W. J., BA, BLitt, University College, Gower Street, WC1E 6BT.
*Johnson, J. H., MA, Whitehorns, Cedar Avenue, Chelmsford.
Johnson, W. Branch, FSA, Hope Cottage, 22 Mimram Road, Welwyn, Herts.
Johnston, Miss E. M., MA, PhD, The University, Sheffield S10 2NT.
Johnston, Lieut-Colonel G. R., RA, FRSA, Wood Corner, Lankhills Road, Winchester.
Johnston, Professor S. H. F., MA, Fronhyfryd, Llanbadarn Road, Aberystwyth.
Jones, Dwyryd W., MA, DPhil, The University, Heslington, York YO1 5DD.
Jones, G. A., MA, PhD, Dept of History, Faculty of Letters, University of Reading, Whiteknights, Reading, Berks.
Jones, Professor G. Hilton, PhD, Dept of History, Eastern Ill. University, Charleston, Ill. 61920, U.S.A.
Jones, G. J., The Croft, Litchard Bungalows, Bridgend, Glam.
*Jones, Professor G. P., MA, 16 Priory Lane, Grange-over-Sands, Cumbria.
Jones, H. W., MA, PhD, 32 Leylands Terrace, Bradford BD9 5QR.
Jones, Professor I. G., MA, 12 Laura Place, Aberystwyth, Cards.
Jones, Professor J. R., MA, PhD, School of English and American Studies University Plain, Norwich.
Jones, Professor M. A., MA, DPhil, Dept of History, University College, Gower Street, WC1E 6BT.
Jones, M. C. E., MA, DPhil, The University, Nottingham.
Jones, The Rev. Canon O. W., MA, The Vicarage, Builth Wells, Breconshire.

Jones, P. J., DPhil, Brasenose College, Oxford.
Jones, Professor W. J., PhD, Dept of History, The University of Alberta, Edmonton T6G 2E1, Canada.
Jordan, Professor P. D., PhD, LLD, 26 Cascade Terrace, Burlington, Iowa 52601, U.S.A.
Jordan, Professor W. K., PhD, 3 Conrad Avenue, Cambridge, Mass. 02138, U.S.A.
Judson, Professor Margaret A., PhD, 8 Redcliffe Avenue, Highland Park, N.J. 08904, U.S.A.
Jukes, Rev. H. A. Ll, MA, The Vicarage, Tilney All Saints, nr King's Lynn, Norfolk.

Kamen, H. A. F., MA, DPhil, The University, Warwick, Coventry CV4 7AL.
*Kay, H., MA, 16 Bourton Drive, Poynton, Stockport, Cheshire.
Kearney, Professor H. F., MA, PhD, Edinburgh University, Old College, South Bridge, Edinburgh 8.
Keeler, Mrs Mary F., PhD, Yale University, Box 1603A, Yale Station, Conn. 06520, U.S.A.
Keen, M. H., MA, Balliol College, Oxford.
Kellaway, C. W., MA, FSA, 2 Grove Terrace, NW5.
Kellett, J. R., MA, PhD, Dept of Economic History, University of Glasgow, G12 8QQ.
Kelly, Professor T., MA, PhD, 55 Freshfield Road, Formby, nr Liverpool.
Kemp, Miss B., MA, FSA, St Hugh's College, Oxford.
Kemp, B. R., BA, PhD, 12 Redhatch Drive, Earley, Reading, Berks.
Kemp, The Very Rev. E. W., DD, The Deanery, Worcester WR1 2LH.
Kemp, Lt-Commander P. K., RN, Malcolm's, 51 Market Hill, Maldon. Essex.
Kendall, Professor P. M., PhD, 928 Holiday Drive, Lawrence, Kansas 66044, U.S.A.
Kennedy, J., MA, 14 Poolfield Avenue, Newcastle-under-Lyme, Staffs. ST5 2NL.
Kennedy, P. M., BA, DPhil, University of East Anglia, Norwich NOR 88C.
Kent, Rev. J. H. S., MA, PhD, Dept of Theology, University of Bristol, Senate House, Bristol BS8 1TH.
Kenyon, Professor J. P., PhD, Nicholson Hall, Cottingham, Yorks.
Ker, N. R., MA, DLitt, FBA, FSA, Slievemore, Foss, by Pitlochry, Perthshire.
Kerling, Miss N. J. M., PhD, 26 Upper Park Road, NW3.
Kerridge, E. W. J., PhD, Llys Tudur, Myddleton Park, Denbigh LL16 4AL.
Kershaw, Ian, BA, DPhil, 6 Cranston Drive, Sale, Cheshire.
Ketelbey, Miss D. M., MA, 18 Queen's Gardens, St Andrews, Fife.
Khan, M. Siddiq, MA, LLB, The Bougainvilleas, No. 64 North Dhanmondi, Kalabagan, Dacca-5, Bangladesh.
Khanna, Kahan Chand, MA, PhD, 3-B Mathura Road, New Delhi 14, India.
Kiernan, Professor V. G., MA, University of Edinburgh, William Robertson Building, George Square, Edinburgh.
*Kimball, Miss E. G., BLitt, PhD, Drake's Corner Road, Princeton, N.J., U.S.A.
King, E. J., MA, PhD, Dept of History, The University, Sheffield S10 2TN.
King, P. D., BA, PhD, Lancaster View, Bailrigg, Lancaster.

Kinsley, Professor J., MA, PhD, DLitt, FBA, University of Nottingham, Nottingham NG7 2RD.
Kirby, D. P., MA, PhD, Manoraven, Llanon, Cards.
Kirby, J. L., MA, FSA, 209 Covington Way, Streatham, London SW19 3BY.
Klibansky, Professor R., MA, PhD, DPhil, FRSC, McGill University, Dept of Philosophy, Montreal, Canada.
Knecht, R. J., MA, 22 Warwick New Road, Leamington Spa, Warwickshire.
*Knight, L. Stanley, MA, Little Claregate, 1 The Drive, Malthouse Lane, Tettenhall, Wolverhampton.
Knowles, C. H., PhD, University College, Cathays Park, Cardiff CF1 1XL.
Kochan, L. E., BA, PhD, 237 Woodstock Road, Oxford.
Koenigsberger, Professor H. G., PhD, Dept of History, Kings College, Strand, London WC2.
Koeppler, Professor H., CBE, DPhil, Wilton Park, Wiston House, Steyning, Sussex.
Kossmann, Professor E. H., DLitt, Rijksuniversiteit te Groningen, Groningen, The Netherlands.

Lambert, M. D., MA, 17 Oakwood Road, Henleaze, Bristol BS9 4NP.
Lamont, W. M., PhD, 9 Bramleys, Kingston, Lewes, Sussex.
Lancaster, Miss J. C., MA, FSA, 43 Craigmair Road, Tulse Hill, SW2.
Lander, J. R., MA, MLitt, Middlesex College, University of Western Ontario, London, Ont., Canada.
Landes, Professor D. S., PhD, Widener 97, Harvard University, Cambridge, Mass., 02138, U.S.A.
Landon, Professor M. de L., MA, PhD, The University, Mississippi 38677 U.S.A.
La Page, J., FSA, Craig Lea, 44, Bank Crest, Baildon, Yorkshire.
Laprade, Professor W. T., PhD, 1108 Monmouth Avenue, Durham, N. Carolina, U.S.A.
Larkin, Professor the Rev. J. F., CSV, PhD, University College, De Paul University, 25E Jackson Blvd., Chicago, Ill. 60604, U.S.A.
Larner, J. P., MA, The University, Glasgow W2.
Latham, Professor R. C., MA, Magdalene College, Cambridge.
Lawrence, Professor C. H., MA, DPhil, Bedford College, Regent's Park, NW1.
*Laws, Lieut-Colonel M. E. S., OBE, MC, Bank Top Cottage, Seal Chart, Sevenoaks, Kent.
Leddy, J. F., MA, BLitt, DPhil, University of Windsor, Windsor, Ontario, Canada.
Lee, J. M., BA, PhD, Birkbeck College, Malet Street, London WC1.
Lees, R. McLachlan, MA, Kent Cottage, Harbridge, Ringwood, Hants.
Legge, Professor M. Dominica, MA, DLitt, 191A Woodstock Road, Oxford OX2 7AB.
Lehmann, Professor J. H., PhD, De Paul University, 25E Jackson Blvd., Chicago, Ill. 60604, U.S.A.
Lehmberg, Professor S. E., PhD, Dept of History, University of Minnesota, Minneapolis, Minn. 55455, U.S.A.
Lenanton, Lady, CBE, MA, FSA, Bride Hall, nr Welwyn, Herts.
Le Patourel, Professor J. H., MA, DPhil, Ddel'U, Westcote, Hebers Ghyll Drive, Ilkley, Yorks. LS29 9QH.
Leslie, Professor R. F., BA, PhD, 23 Grove Park Road, W4.

Levine, Professor Mortimer, PhD, 529 Woodhaven Drive, Morgantown, West Va. 26505, U.S.A.

Levy, Professor F. J., PhD, University of Washington, Seattle, Wash. 98195, U.S.A.

Lewis, Professor A. R., MA, PhD, History Dept, University of Massachusetts, Amherst, Mass, 01003, U.S.A.

Lewis, Professor B., PhD, FBA, 55 Springfield Road, NW8.

Lewis, C. W., BA, FSA, University College, Cathays Park, Cardiff.

Lewis, E. D., MA, DSc, Glamorgan College of Education, Buttrils Road Barry, Glam.

Lewis, P. S., MA, All Souls College, Oxford.

Lewis, R. A., PhD, University College of North Wales, Bangor.

Leyser, K., MA, Magdalen College, Oxford.

Lhoyd-Owen, Commander J. H., RN, 37 Marlings Park Avenue, Chislehurst, Kent.

Liebeschütz, H., MA, DPhil, Dockenhuden, Marines Road, Liverpool 23.

*Lindsay, Mrs H., MA, PhD, Girton College, Cambridge.

Linehan, P. A., MA, PhD, St John's College, Cambridge.

Lipman, V. D., DPhil, FSA, Flat 14, 33 Kensington Court, W8.

Livermore, Professor H. V., MA, Sandycombe Lodge, Sandycombe Road, St Margarets, Twickenham.

Lloyd, H. A., BA, DPhil, The University, Hull, HU6 7RX.

Loades, D. M., MA, PhD, Oatlands, Farnley Mount, Durham.

Lobel, Mrs M. D., BA, FSA, 16 Merton Street, Oxford.

Lockhart, L., MA, PhD, LittD, Cedarwood House, West Green, Barrington, Cambridge CB2 5SA.

Lockie, D. McN., MA, Chemin de la Panouche, Saint-Anne, Grasse, Alpes Maritimes, France.

Logan, Rev. F. D., MA, MSD, Emmanuel College, 400 The Fenway, Boston, Mass, 02115, U.S.A.

London, Miss Vera C. M., MA, Underholt, Westwood Road, Bidston, Birkenhead, Cheshire.

Longford, The Right Honble The Countess of, MA, DLitt, Bernhurst, Hurst Green, Sussex.

Longley, D. A., BA, 13 Bournbrook Road, Birmingham 29.

Longrais, Professor F. Joüon des, D-en-droit, LèsL, 4 rue de la Terrasse, Paris XVII, France.

Loomie, Rev. A. J., SJ, MA, PhD, Fordham University, New York, N.Y. 10458, U.S.A.

Lourie, Elena, MA, DPhil, 66 Brandeis Street, Tel-Aviv, Israel.

Lovatt, R. W., MA, DPhil, Peterhouse, Cambridge.

Lovell, J. C., BA, PhD, Eliot College, University of Kent, Canterbury.

Lowe, P. C., BA, PhD, The University, Manchester.

Loyn, H. R., MA, FSA, 196 Fidlas Road, Llanishen, Cardiff.

Lucas, C. R., MA, DPhil, Balliol College, Oxford OX1 3BJ.

Lucas, P. J., MA, PhD, University College, Belfield, Dublin 4, Ireland.

Luft, The Rev. H. M., MA, MLitt, Merchant Taylor's School, Crosby, Liverpool.

Lumb, Miss S. V., MA, Torr-Collin House, 106 Ridgway, Wimbledon, London SW19.

Luscombe, Professor D. E., MA, PhD, 129 Prospect Road, Totley Rise, Sheffield.

Luttrell, A. T., MA, DPhil, Dept of History, The Royal University of Malta, Msida, Malta.

Lyman, Professor R. W., PhD, Office of the President, Stanford University, Stanford, Calif. 94305, U.S.A.

Lynch, Professor J., MA, PhD, University College, Gower Street, London WC1E 6BT.

Lyon, Professor Bryce D., PhD, Dept of History, Brown University Providence, Rhode Island 02912, U.S.A.

Lyons, Professor F. S. L., MA, PhD, LittD, The Provost, Trinity College, Dublin.

Lyttelton, The Hon, N. A. O., BA, St Antony's College, Oxford.

Mabbs, A. W., Public Record Office, Chancery Lane, WC2.

MacCaffrey, Professor W. T., PhD, 745 Hollyoke Center, Harvard University, Cambridge, Mass. 02138, U.S.A.

McConica, Professor J. K., OSB, MA, DPhil, Pontifical Institute of Medieval Studies, 59 Queen's Park Crescent, Toronto 181, Ont., Canada.

McCord, N., PhD, 7 Hatherton Avenue, Cullercoats, North Shields, Northumberland.

McCracken, Professor J. L., MA, PhD, New University of Ulster, Coleraine, Co. Londonderry, N. Ireland.

McCulloch, Professor S. C., MA, PhD, 2121 Windward Lane, Newport Beach, Calif. 92660, U.S.A.

MacDonagh, Professor O., MA, PhD, RSSS, Australian National University, Box 4 GPO, Canberra, ACT, Australia.

Macdonald, Professor D. F., MA, DPhil, Queen's College, Dundee.

McDonald, Professor T. H., MA, PhD, T.H. McDonald Enterprises, Fort Sumner, New Mexico 88119, U.S.A.

McDowell, Professor R. B., PhD, LittD, Trinity College, Dublin.

Macfarlane, A., MA, DPhil, PhD, King's College, Cambridge CB2 1ST.

Macfarlane, L. J., PhD, FSA, King's College, University of Aberdeen, Aberdeen.

McGrath, P. V., MA, University of Bristol, Bristol.

MacGregor, D. R., BA, 99 Lonsdale Road, SW13.

McGregor, Professor O. R., BSc(Econ), MA, Far End, Wyldes Close, London N.W.11.

McGurk, J. J. N., BA, MPhil, Conway House, Stanley Avenue, Birkdale, Southport, Lancs.

McGurk, P. M., PhD, Birkbeck College, Malet Street, London WC1E 7HX.

Machin, G. I. T., MA, DPhil, Dept of Modern History, University of Dundee, DD1 4HN.

MacIntyre, A. D., MA, DPhil, Magdalen College, Oxford.

McKendrick, N., MA, Gonville and Caius College, Cambridge.

McKenna, Professor J. W., MA, PhD, Haverford College, Haverford, Pa. 19041, U.S.A.

Mackesy, P. G., MA, Pembroke College, Oxford.

*Mackie, Professor J. D., CBE, MC, MA, LLD, FSAScot, 67 Dowanside Road, Glasgow W2.

McKinley, R. A., MA, 42 Boyers Walk, Leicester Forest East, Leics.

Mackintosh, Professor J. P., MA, MP, House of Commons, London SW1A 0AA.

McKisack, Professor May, MA, BLitt, FSA, 59 Parktown, Oxford.

Maclagan, M., MA, FSA, Trinity College, Oxford.

Maclean, J. N. M., BLitt, PhD, 61 Learmouth Court, Edinburgh 4.

MacLeod, R. M., AB, PhD, Dept of History and Social Studies of Science, Physics Bldg, University of Sussex, Falmer, Brighton BN1 9QH.
McManners, Professor J., MA, Christ Church, Oxford OX1 1DP.
MacMichael, N. H., FSA, 2B Little Cloister, Westminster Abbey, SW1.
MacNiocaill, G., PhD, Dept of History, University College, Galway, Ireland.
McNulty, Miss P. A., BA, St George's Hall, Elmhurst Road, Reading.
MacNutt, Professor W. S., MA, University of New Brunswick, Fredericton, N.B., Canada.
Macpherson, C. B., BA, MSc(Econ), DSc(Econ), DLitt, LLD, FRSC, University of Toronto, 100 George Street, Toronto, Canada M55 1A1.
McRoberts, Rt Rev. Monsignor David, STL, DLitt, FSA, 16 Drummond Place, Edinburgh EH3 6PL.
Madariaga, Miss Isabel de, PhD, 27 Southwood Lawn Road, N6.
Madden, A. F. McC., DPhil, Nuffield College, Oxford.
Maddicott, J. R., MA, DPhil, Exeter College, Oxford.
Maehl, Professor W. H., PhD, University of Oklahoma, Norman, Oklahoma 73069, U.S.A.
Magnus-Allcroft, Sir Phillip, Bt. CBE, FRSL, Stokesay Court, Craven Arms, Shropshire SY7 9BD.
Mahoney, Professor T. H. D., AM, PhD, MPA, Massachusetts Institute of Technology, Cambridge, Mass. 02138, U.S.A.
Major, Miss K., MA, BLitt, LittD, 21 Queensway, Lincoln.
Mallett, M. E., MA, DPhil, University of Warwick, Coventry CV4 7AL.
Malone, Professor J. J., PhD, 629 St James Street, Pittsburgh, Pa. 15232, U.S.A.
Mann, Miss J. de L., MA, The Cottage, Bowerhill, Melksham, Wilts.
Manning, B. S., MA, DPhil, The University, Manchester.
Manning, Professor R. B., PhD, 2848 Coleridge Road, Cleveland Heights, Ohio 44118, U.S.A.
Mansergh, Professor P. N. S., OBE, DPhil, DLitt, LittD, FBA, The Master's Lodge, St John's College, Cambridge.
Marchant, Rev. R. A., PhD, BD, Laxfield Vicarage, Woodbridge, Suffolk.
Marder, Professor A. J., PhD, University of California, Irvine, Calif. 92664, U.S.A.
Marett, W. P., BSc(Econ), BCom, MA, PhD, Rutherford Lodge, The University, Loughborough, Leics.
Margetts, J., MA, DipEd, DrPhil, 5 Glenluce Road, Liverpool LI9 9BX.
Markham, F. M. H., MA, Hertford College, Oxford.
Markus, R. A., MA, PhD, The University, Nottingham NG7 2RD.
Marriner, Sheila, MA, PhD, Social Studies Building, Bedford Street South, Liverpool.
Marsden, A., BA, PhD, 9 Fort Street, Dundee DD2 1BS.
Marshall, J. D., PhD, 16 Westgate, Morecambe, Lancs.
Marshall, P. J., MA, DPhil, King's College, Strand, WC2.
Martin, Professor G. H., MA, DPhil, 21 Central Avenue, Leicester LE2 1TB.
Marwick, Professor, A. J. B., MA, BLitt, Dept of History, The Open University, Walton Hall, Walton, Bletchley, Bucks.
Mason, F. K., 147 London Road, St Albans, Hertfordshire.
Mason, J. F. A., MA, DPhil, FSA, Christ Church, Oxford OX1 1DP.
Mason, T. W., MA, DPhil, St Peter's College, Oxford OX1 2DL.
Mather, F. C., MA, 69 Ethelburg Avenue, Swaything, Southampton.

McManners, Professor J., MA, Christ Church, Oxford OX1 1DP.

MacMichael, N. H., FSA, 2B Little Cloister, Westminster Abbey, SW1.

MacNiocaill, G., PhD, Dept of History, University College, Galway, Ireland.

McNulty, Miss P. A., BA, St George's Hall, Elmhurst Road, Reading.

MacNutt, Professor W. S., MA, University of New Brunswick, Fredericton, N.B., Canada.

Macpherson, C. B., BA, MSc(Econ), DSc(Econ), DLitt, LLD, FRSC, University of Toronto, 100 George Street, Toronto, Canada M55 1A1.

McRoberts, Rt Rev. Monsignor David, STL, DLitt, FSA, 16 Drummond Place, Edinburgh EH3 6PL.

Madariaga, Miss Isabel de, PhD, 27 Southwood Lawn Road, N6.

Madden, A. F. McC., DPhil, Nuffield College, Oxford.

Maddicott, J. R., MA, DPhil, Exeter College, Oxford.

Maehl, Professor W. H., PhD, University of Oklahoma, Norman, Oklahoma 73069, U.S.A.

Magnus-Allcroft, Sir Phillip, Bt. CBE, FRSL, Stokesay Court, Craven Arms, Shropshire SY7 9BD.

Mahoney, Professor T. H. D., AM, PhD, MPA, Massachusetts Institute of Technology, Cambridge, Mass. 02138, U.S.A.

Major, Miss K., MA, BLitt, LittD, 21 Queensway, Lincoln.

Mallett, M. E., MA, DPhil, University of Warwick, Coventry CV4 7AL.

Malone, Professor J. J., PhD, 629 St James Street, Pittsburgh, Pa. 15232, U.S.A.

Mann, Miss J. de L., MA, The Cottage, Bowerhill, Melksham, Wilts.

Manning, B. S., MA, DPhil, The University, Manchester.

Manning, Professor R. B., PhD, 2848 Coleridge Road, Cleveland Heights, Ohio 44118, U.S.A.

Mansergh, Professor P. N. S., OBE, DPhil, DLitt, LittD, FBA, The Master's Lodge, St John's College, Cambridge.

Marchant, Rev. R. A., PhD, BD, Laxfield Vicarage, Woodbridge, Suffolk.

Marder, Professor A. J., PhD, University of California, Irvine, Calif. 92664, U.S.A.

Marett, W. P., BSc(Econ), BCom, MA, PhD, Rutherford Lodge, The University, Loughborough, Leics.

Margetts, J., MA, DipEd, DrPhil, 5 Glenluce Road, Liverpool L19 9BX.

Markham, F. M. H., MA, Hertford College, Oxford.

Markus, R. A., MA, PhD, The University, Nottingham NG7 2RD.

Marriner, Sheila, MA, PhD, Social Studies Building, Bedford Street South, Liverpool.

Marsden, A., BA, PhD, 9 Fort Street, Dundee DD2 1BS.

Marshall, J. D., PhD, 16 Westgate, Morecambe, Lancs.

Marshall, P. J., MA, DPhil, King's College, Strand, WC2.

Martin, Professor G. H., MA, DPhil, 21 Central Avenue, Leicester LE2 1TB.

Marwick, Professor, A. J. B., MA, BLitt, Dept of History, The Open University, Walton Hall, Walton, Bletchley, Bucks.

Mason, J. F. K., 147 London Road, St Albans, Hertfordshire.

Mason, J. F. A., MA, DPhil, FSA, Christ Church, Oxford OX1 1DP.

Mason, T. W., MA, DPhil, St Peter's College, Oxford OX1 2DL.

Mather, F. C., MA, 69 Ethelburg Avenue, Swaythling, Southampton.

*Mathew, The Most Rev. Archbishop D. J., MA, LittD, FSA, Stonor Park, Henley-on-Thames, Oxon.

Mathias, Professor P., MA, All Souls College, Oxford.

*Mathur-Sherry, Tikait Narain, BA, LLB, 17/254 Chili-Int-Road, Agra (U.P.), India.

Matthew, D. J. A., MA, DPhil, The University, Durham.

Mattingly, Professor H. B., MA, Dept of Ancient History, The University, Leeds.

Mayr-Harting, H. M. R. E., MA, DPhil, St Peter's College, Oxford.

Medlicott, Professor W. N., MA, DLit, DLitt, 2 Cartref, Ellesmere Road, Weybridge, Surrey.

Meekings, C. A. F., OBE, MA, 42 Chipstead Street, SW6.

Merson, A. L., MA, The University, Southampton.

Micklewright, F. H. A., MA, 228 South Norwood Hill, SE25.

Midgley, Miss L. M., MA, 84 Wolverhampton Road, Stafford ST17 4AW

Miller, E., MA, LittD, 36 Almoners Avenue, Cambridge CB1 4PA.

Miller, E. J., BA, 37 Aldbourne Road, W.12.

Miller, Miss H., MA, 32 Abbey Gardens, NW8.

Milne, A. T., MA, 9 Dixon Close, SE21 7BD.

Milne, Miss D. J., MA, PhD, King's College, Aberdeen.

Milsom, Professor S. F. C., MA, FBA, London School of Economics, Houghton Street, WC2.

Milward, Professor A. S., MA, PhD, Inst. of Science and Technology, University of Manchester, PO Box 88, Sackville Street, Manchester M60 1QD.

Minshinton, Professor W. E., BSc(Econ), The University, Exeter EX4 4PU.

Mingay, Professor G. E., PhD, Mill Field House, Selling Court, Selling, nr Faversham, Kent.

Mitchell, C., MA, BLitt, LittD, Woodhouse Farmhouse, Fyfield, Abingdon, Berks.

Mitchell, L. G., MA, DPhil, University College, Oxford.

Mitchison, Mrs R. M., MA, 6 Dovecot Road, Edinburgh 12.

*Moir, Rev. Prebendary A. L., MA, 55 Mill Street, Hereford.

Momigliano, Professor A. D., DLitt, FBA, University College, Gower Street, WC1E 6BT.

Moody, Professor T. W., MA, PhD, Trinity College, Dublin.

Moore, B. J. S., BA, University of Bristol, 67 Woodland Road, Bristol.

*Moorman, Mrs, MA, Bishop Mount, Ripon, Yorks.

Morey, Rev. Dom R. Adrian, OSB, MA, DPhil, LittD, Benet House, Mount Pleasant, Cambridge.

Morgan, B. G., BArch, PhD, ARIBA, 29 Gerard Road, Wallasey, Cheshire.

Morgan, K. O., MA, DPhil, The Queen's College, Oxford OX1 4BH.

Morgan, Miss P. E., 1A The Cloisters, Hereford, HR1 2NG.

*Morrell, Professor W. P., MA, DPhil, 20 Bedford Street, St Clair, Dunedin SW1, New Zealand.

Morris, The Rev. Professor C., MA, 53 Cobbett Road, Bitterne Park, Southampton SO2 4HJ.

Morris, G. C., MA, King's College, Cambridge.

Morris, J. R., BA, PhD, Little Garth, Ashwell, nr Baldock, Herts.

Morris, Professor R. B., PhD, Dept of History, Colombia University in the City of New York, 605 Fayerweather Hall, New York, N.Y. 10552 U.S.A.

Morton, Miss C. E., MA, MLS, FSA, Fairview Cottage, Buckland St. Mary, Chard, Somerset TA20 3LE.
Morton, Professor W. L., MA, BLitt, LLD, DLitt, Champlain College, Peterborough, Ont., Canada.
Mosse, Professor G. L., PhD, Dept of History, The University of Wisconsin, 3211 Humanities Bldg., 435 N. Park Street, Madison, Wis. 53706 U.S.A.
Mosse, Professor W. E. E., MA, PhD, Dawn Cottage, Ashwellthorpe, Norwich, Norfolk.
MULLINS, E. L. C., OBE, MA (*Librarian*), Institute of Historical Research, University of London, Senate House, WC1E 7HU.
Muntz, Miss I. Hope, FSA, Fairview Cottage, Buckland St. Mary, Chard, Somerset TA20 3LE.
Murray, A., BA, BPhil, The University, Newcastle upon Tyne.
Murray, Athol L., MA, LLB, PhD, 33 Inverleith Gardens, Edinburgh EH3 5PR.
Myers, Professor A. R., MA, PhD, FSA, Rosemount, 3 Cholmondeley Road, West Kirby, Wirral, Cheshire.
Myres, J. N. L., CBE, MA, LLD, DLitt, DLit, FBA, PSA, The Manor House, Kennington, Oxford OX1 5PH.

Naidis, Professor M., PhD, 10847 Canby Avenue, Northbridge, California 91324.
Nath, Dwarka, MBE, 30 Crowther Road, South Norwood, SE25.
*NEALE, Professor Sir John (E), MA, DLitt, LittD, LHD, FBA, Adare, Penn Road, Beaconsfield, Bucks.
Nef, Professor J. U., PhD, 2726 N Street NW, Washington DC 20007, U.S.A.
New, Professor J. F. H., Dept of History, Waterloo University, Waterloo, Ontario, Canada.
Newman, A. N., MA, DPhil, 33 Stanley Road, Leicester.
Newsome, D. H., MA, Christ's Hospital, Horsham, Sussex.
Newton, K. C., MA, 82 Dorset Road, Maldon, Essex.
Nicholas, Professor H. G., MA, FBA, New College, Oxford.
Nicholl, Professor D., MA, Rosthene, Common Lane, Betley, nr Crewe, Cheshire.
Nicol, Professor D. M., MA, PhD, King's College, London WC2R 2LS.
Noakes, J. D., MA, DPhil, The University, Exeter EX4 4OJ.
Norman, E. R., MA, PhD, Jesus College, Cambridge.

Oakeshott, W. F., MA, LLD, FBA, FSA, Lincoln College, Oxford.
Obolensky, Prince Dimitri, MA, PhD, FSA, Christ Church, Oxford.
O'Connell, Professor D. P., BA, LLM, PhD, LLD, All Souls College, Oxford.
*Offler, Professor H. S., MA, 28 Old Elvet, Durham.
O'Gorman, F., BA, PhD, The University, Manchester M13 9PL.
Orme, N. I., MA, DPhil, The University, Exeter EX4 4OJ.
*Orr, J. E., MA, ThD, DPhil, 11451 Berwick Street, Los Angeles, Cal. 90049, U.S.A.
Osborn, Professor, J. M., PhD, FSA, Beinecke Library, 1603A Yale Station, New Haven, Conn. 06520, U.S.A.
Oschinsky, Dorothea, DPhil, PhD, The University, Liverpool L69 3BX.
Otway-Ruthven, Professor A. J., MA, PhD, 7 Trinity College, Dublin, Eire.
Outhwaite, R. B., BA, PhD, The University, Leicester.

Owen, A. E. B., MA, 79 Whitwell Way, Coton, Cambridge CB3 7PW.
Owen, Mrs D. M., MA, FSA, 79 Whitwell Way, Coton, Cambridge CB3 7PW.
Owen, G. D., MA, PhD, Casa Alba, Wray Lane, Reigate, Surrey.
Owen, J. B., BSc, MA, DPhil, The University, Calgary 44, Alberta, Canada.

Pace, G. G., CVO, MA(Lambeth), FSA, FRIBA, 18 Clifton Green, York YO3 6LW.
*Packard, Professor S. R., PhD, 126 Vernon Street, Northampton, Mass, U.S.A.
Pakeman, Professor S. A., MC, MA, 45 Kensington Mansions, Trebovir Road, London SW5 9TE.
Palliser, D. M., MA, DPhil, 14 Verstone Croft, Birmingham B31 2QE.
Pallister, Miss Anne, BA, PhD, The University, Reading RG6 2AA.
Palmer, J. J. N., BA, BLitt, PhD, 59 Marlborough Avenue, Hull.
Parker, N. G., MA, PhD, Dept of Modern History, St Salvator's College, The University, St Andrew's, Fife.
Parker, R. A. C., MA, DPhil, The Queen's College, Oxford OX1 4BH.
Parker, The Rev. Dr T. M., MA, DD, FSA, 36 Chalfont Road, Oxford OX2 6TH.
*Parkinson, Professor C. N., MA, PhD, Les Caches House, St Martins, Guernsey, C.I.
Parris, H., MA, Civil Service College, Sunningdale Park, Ascot, Berks. SL5 0QE.
Parry, E. Jones, MA, PhD, 3 Sussex Mansions, Old Brompton Road, SW7.
Parry, Professor J. H., MA, PhD, Pinnacle Road, Harvard, Mass. 01451, U.S.A.
Parsloe, C. G., BA, 1 Leopold Avenue, SW19.
Patterson, Professor A. T., MA, The Sele, Stoughton, Chichester, Sussex.
PEARL, Mrs V. L., MA, DPhil, (*Literary Director*), 11 Church Row, Hampstead, NW3.
Pearn, B. R., OBE, MA, The White House, Beechwood Avenue, Aylmerton, Norfolk NOR 25Y.
Peaston, Rev. A. E., MA, BLitt, The Manse, Dromore, Co. Down, N. Ireland.
Peek, Miss H. E., MA, FSA, FSAScot, Taintona, Moretonhampstead, Newton Abbot, Devon TQ13 8LG.
Pegues, Professor F. J., PhD, 71 Acton Road, Columbus, Ohio 43214, U.S.A.
Pelham, R. A., MA, PhD, The Court House, West Meon, Hants.
Pennington, D. H., MA, Balliol College, Oxford.
*Percy-Smith, Lt Col H. K., 14 Elmcroft, Fairview Avenue, Woking, Surrey GU22 7NX.
Perkin, Professor H. J., MA, Borwicks, Caton, Lancaster.
Petrie, Sir Charles, Bt, CBE, MA, 190 Coleherne Court, SW5.
Philip, I. G., MA, FSA, 28 Portland Road, Oxford.
Philips, Professor Sir Cyril (H.), MA, PhD, DLitt, 3 Winterstoke Gardens, London NW7.
Phillips, Sir Henry (E. I.), CMG, MBE, MA, 34 Ross Court, Putney Hill, SW15.
Phillips, J. R. S., BA, PhD, Dept of Medieval History, University College, Dublin 4, Ireland.
Pitt, H. G., MA, Worcester College, Oxford.

Platt, C. P. S., MA, PhD, FSA, 24 Oakmount Avenue, Highfield, South-ampton.

Platt, Professor D. C. St M., MA, DPhil, St Antony's College, Oxford.

Plumb, Professor J. H., PhD, LittD, FBA, FSA, Christ's College, Cam-bridge.

Pocock, Professor J. G. A., PhD, Johns Hopkins University, Baltimore, Md. 21218, U.S.A.

Poirer, Professor Philip P., PhD, Dept of History, The Ohio State Univer-sity, 216 North Oval Drive, Columbus, Ohio 43210, U.S.A.

Pole, J. R., MA, PhD, 6 Cavendish Avenue, Cambridge.

Pollard, Professor S., BSc(Econ), PhD, Dept of Economic History, The University, Sheffield S10 2TN.

Porter, B. E., BSc(Econ), PhD, Dept of International Politics, University College of Wales, Aberystwyth SY23 3DB.

Porter, H. C., MA, PhD, Selwyn College, Cambridge.

Postan, Professor M. M., MA, FBA, Peterhouse, Cambridge CB2 1RD.

*Potter, Professor G. R., MA, PhD, FSA, Herongate, Derwent Lane, Hathersage, Sheffield S30 1AS.

Powell, W. R., BLitt, MA, FSA, 2 Glanmead, Shenfield Road, Brentwood, Essex.

Powicke, Professor M. R., MA, University of Toronto, Toronto 5, Ont., Canada.

Prest, J. M., MA, Balliol College, Oxford.

Prest, W. R., MA, DPhil, Dept of History, University of Adelaide, Ade-laide, S. Australia 5001.

Preston, Professor A. W., PhD, R.R.3, Bath, Ontario, Canada.

*Preston, Professor R. A., MA, PhD, Duke University, Durham, N.C., U.S.A.

Prestwich, J. O., MA, The Queen's College, Oxford.

Prestwich, Mrs M., MA, St Hilda's College, Oxford.

Prestwich, M. C., MA, DPhil, Dept of Medieval History, The University, St Andrews, Fife.

Price, A. W., 19 Bayley Close, Uppingham, Rutland, LE15 9TG.

Price, F. D., MA, BLitt, FSA, Keble College, Oxford.

Price, Professor Jacob, M., AM, PhD, University of Michigan, Ann Arbor, Michigan 48104, U.S.A.

Pritchard, Professor D. G., PhD, 11 Coedmor, Sketty, Swansea, Glam. SA2 8BQ.

Proctor, Miss Evelyn E. S., MA, Little Newland, Eynsham, Oxford.

Pronay, N., BA, School of History, The University, Leeds.

Prothero, I. J., BA, PhD, The University, Manchester.

*Pugh, Professor R. B., MA, DLitt, FSA, 67 Southwood Park, N.6.

Pugh, T. B., MA, BLit, 28 Bassett Wood Drive, Southampton.

Pullan, Professor B. S., MA, PhD, The University, Manchester M13 9PL.

Pulman, M. B., MA, PhD, University of Denver, Colorado 80210, U.S.A.

Pulzer, P. G. J., MA, PhD, Christ Church, Oxford OX1 1DP.

Quinn, Professor D. B., MA, PhD, DLit, DLitt, 9 Knowsley Road, Cres-sington Park, Liverpool 19.

Rabb, Professor T. K., MA, PhD, Princeton University, Princeton, N.J. 08540, U.S.A.

Radford, C. A. Ralegh, MA, DLitt, FBA, FSA, Culmcott, Uffculme, Cullompton, Devon EX15 3AT.

*Ramm, Miss A., MA, Somerville College, Oxford.
*Ramsay, G. D., MA, DPhil, St Edmund Hall, Oxford OX1 4AR.
Ramsey, Professor P. H., MA, DPhil, Taylor Building, King's College, Old Aberdeen.
Ranft, Professor B. McL., MA, DPhil, 16 Eliot Vale, SE3.
Ransome, Miss M. E., MA, 16 Downside Crescent, NW3.
Rathbone, Eleanor, PhD, Flat 5, 24 Morden Road, SE3.
Rawley, Professor J. A., PhD, University of Nebraska, Lincoln, Nebraska 68508, U.S.A.
Read, D., BLitt, MA, Darwin College, University of Kent, Westgate House, Canterbury, Kent.
Reader, W. J., BA, PhD, 67 Wood Vale, N10 3DL.
Rees, Professor W., MA, DSc, DLitt, FSA, 2 Park Road, Penarth, Glam. CF6 2BD.
Reese, T. R., PhD, Institute of Commonwealth Studies, 27 Russell Square, WC1B 5DS.
Reeves, Miss M. E., MA, PhD, 38 Norham Road, Oxford.
Reid, Professor L. D., MA, PhD, College of Arts and Science, 127 Switzler Hall, University of Missouri, Columbia, Mo. 65201, U.S.A.
Reid, Professor W. S., MA, PhD, University of Guelph, Guelph, Ontario, Canada.
Renold, Miss P., MA, 6 Forest Side, Worcester Park, Surrey.
Reynolds, Miss S. M. G., MA, 26 Lennox Gardens, SW1.
Rich, Professor E. E., MA, St Catharine's College, Cambridge.
Richards, Rev. J. M., MA, BLitt, STL, Heythrop College, 11–13 Cavendish Square, W1M 0AN.
*Richards, R., MA, FSA, Gawsworth Hall, Gawsworth, Macclesfield, Cheshire.
Richardson, K. E., MA, PhD, Lanchester Polytechnic, Priory Street, Coventry.
Richardson, R. C., BA, PhD, Thames Polytechnic, London SE18.
Richardson, Professor W. C., MA, PhD, Louisiana State University, Baton Rouge, Louisiana, U.S.A.
Richter, M., DrPhil. Institut f. mittelalterliche Geschichte, D355 Marburg, Am Krummbogen 28-CW, West Germany.
Rigold, S. E., MA, FSA, 2 Royal Crescent, W11.
Riley, P. W. J., BA, PhD, The University, Manchester.
Riley-Smith, J. S. C., MA, PhD, 53, Hartinton Grove, Cambridge.
Rimmer, Professor, W. G., MA, PhD, University of New South Wales, P.O. Box 1, Kensington, N.S.W. 2033, Australia.
Ritcheson, Professor C. R., DPhil, 47 Chelsea Square, London SW3 6LH.
Roach, Professor J. P. C., MA, PhD, 1 Park Crescent, Sheffield S10 2DY.
Robbins, Professor Caroline, PhD, 815 The Chetwynd, Rosemont, Pa. 19010, U.S.A.
Robbins, Professor K. G., MA, DPhil, University College of North Wales, Bangor.
Roberts, J. M., MA, DPhil, Merton College, Oxford.
Roberts, Professor M., MA, DPhil, FilDr, FBA, 38 Somerset Street, Grahamstown, C.P., South Africa.
Roberts, Brig. M. R., DSO, Swallowfield Park, Swallowfield, Reading, Berks. RG7 1TG.
Roberts, P. R., MA, PhD, FSA, Keynes College, The University, Canterbury, Kent.

Roberts, Professor R. C., PhD, 284 Blenheim Road, Columbus, Ohio 43214, U.S.A.

Roberts, Professor R. S., PhD, University of Rhodesia, Salisbury, P.B. 167H, Rhodesia.

*Robinson, Professor Howard, MA, PhD, LLD, 75 Elmwood Place, Oberlin, Ohio, U.S.A.

Robinson, K. E., CBE, MA, DLitt, LLD, The Old Rectory, Church Westcote, Kingham, Oxford OX7 6SF.

Robinson, R. A. H., BA, PhD, School of History, The University, Birmingham B15 2TT.

Robinton, Professor Madeline R., MA, PhD, 210 Columbia Heights, Brooklyn, New York, U.S.A.

*Rodkey, F. S., AM, PhD, 152 Bradley Drive, Santa Cruz, Calif., U.S.A.

Rodney, Professor W., MA, PhD, 14 Royal Roads Military College, Victoria, B.C., Canada.

Roe, F. Gordon, FSA, 19 Vallance Road, London N22 4UD.

Rogers, A., MA, PhD, FSA, The Firs, 227 Plains Road, Mapperley, Nottingham.

Rolo, Professor P. J. V., MA, The University, Keele, Staffordshire.

Roots, Professor I. A., MA, University of Exeter, Exeter.

ROPER, M., MA (Hon. Treasurer), Public Record Office, Chancery Lane, London WC2A 1LR.

Rose, P. L., MA, DenHist (Sorbonne), University of Cambridge, Free School Lane, Cambridge CB2 3RH.

Roseveare, H. G., PhD, King's College, Strand, WC2.

Roskell, Professor J. S., MA, DPhil, FBA, The University, Manchester M13 9PL.

Roskill, Captain S. W., CBE, DSC, RN(ret), Frostlake Cottage, Malting Lane, Cambridge CB3 9HF.

Ross, C. D., MA, DPhil, Wills Memorial Building, Queens Road, Bristol.

Rothney, Professor G. O., PhD, University of Manitoba, Winnipeg R3T 2N2, Canada.

Rothrock, Professor G. A., MA, PhD, University of Alberta, Edmonton, Alberta T6G 2E1, Canada.

Rothwell, Professor H., PhD, Hill House, Knapp, Ampfield, nr Romsey, Hants.

*Rowe, Miss B. J. H., MA, BLitt, St Anne's Cottage, Winkton, Christchurch, Hants.

Rowe, W. J., DPhil, 20 Seaview Avenue, Irby, Wirral, Cheshire.

Rowland, Rev. E. C., 8 Fay Street, Frankston, Victoria 3200, Australia.

Rowse, A. L., MA, DLitt, DCL, FBA, All Souls College, Oxford.

Roy, I., MA, DPhil, Dept of History, King's College, Strand, London WC2.

Roy, Professor R. H., MA, PhD, 2841 Tudor Avenue, Victoria, B.C., Canada.

Rubens, A., FRICS, FSA, 16 Grosvenor Place, SW1.

Rubini, D. A., DPhil, Temple University, Philadelphia, Penn., U.S.A.

Rubinstein, N., PhD, Westfield College, Hampstead NW3.

Ruddock, Miss A. A., PhD, FSA, Birkbeck College, Malet Street, WC1.

Rudé, Professor G. F. E., MA, PhD, Sir George Williams University, Montreal 107, P.Q., Canada.

*RUNCIMAN, The Hon. Sir Steven, MA, DPhil, LLD, LittD, DLitt, LitD, DD, DHL, FBA, FSA, Elshiesfields, Lockerbie, Dumfriesshire.

Rupp, Rev. E. G., MA, DD, FBA, 580 Newmarket Road, Cambridge CB5 8LL.
Russell, C. S. R., MA, Bedford College, NW1.
Russell, Mrs J. G., MA DPhil, St Hugh's College, Oxford.
Russell, Professor P. E., MA, 23 Belsyre Court, Woodstock Road, Oxford.
Ryan, A. N., MA, University of Liverpool, 8 Abercromby Square, Liverpool 7.
Ryder, A. F. C., MA, DPhil, University of Ibadan, Nigeria.

Sachse, Professor W. L., PhD, Dept of History, University of Wisconsin, Madison, Wis. 53706 U.S.A.
Sainty, J. S., MA, 22 Kelso Place, W8.
*Salmon, Professor E. T., MA PhD, McMaster University, Hamilton, Ontario, Canada L8S 4L9.
Salmon, Professor J. H. M., PhD, Bryn Mawr College, Bryn Mawr, Pa. 19101, U.S.A.
*Saltman, Professor A., MA, PhD, Bar Ilan University, Ramat Gan, Israel.
Saltmarsh, J., MA, FSA, King's College, Cambridge CB2 1ST.
Samaha, Professor Joel, PhD, University of Minnesota, Minneapolis, U.S.A.
Sammut, E., LLD, 4 Don Rue Street, Sliema, Malta.
Samuel, E. R., 8 Steynings Way, N12 7LN.
Sanders, I. J., MA, DPhil, Ceri, St Davids Road, Aberystwyth.
Sanderson, Professor G. N., MA, PhD, Dept of Modern History, Royal Holloway College, Englefield Green, Surrey.
Saville, Professor J., BSc(Econ), Dept of Economic and Social History, The University, Hull HU6 7RX.
Sawyer, Professor P. H., MA, The University, Leeds LS2 9JT.
Sayers, Miss J. E., MA, BLitt, FSA, 17 Sheffield Terrace, Campden Hill, W8
Scammell, G. V., MA, Pembroke College, Cambridge.
Scammell, Mrs J. M., BA, 137 Huntingdon Road, Cambridge.
Scarisbrick, Professor J. J., MA, PhD, 35 Kenilworth Road, Leamington Spa, Warwickshire.
Schenck, H. G., MA, DPhil, Dr Jur, University College, Oxford.
Schoeck, Professor R. J., PhD, Folger Shakespeare Library, Washington, D.C. 20003, U.S.A.
Schofield, A. N. E. D., PhD, 15 Westergate, Corfton Road, W5.
Schofield, R. S., MA, PhD, Cambridge Group for History of Population, 20 Silver Street, Cambridge.
Scouloudi, Miss I. C., MSc(Econ), FSA, 67 Victoria Road, W8.
Seaborne, M. V. J., MA, Chester College, Cheyney Road, Chester CH1 4BJ.
Seary, Professor E. R., MA, PhD, LittD, DLitt, FSA, Memorial University of Newfoundland, St John's, Newfoundland, Canada.
Semmel, Professor Bernard, PhD, Dept of History, State University of New York at Stony Brook, Stony Brook, N.Y. 11790, U.S.A.
Seton-Watson, C. I. W., MC, MA, Oriel College, Oxford.
Seton-Watson, Professor G. H. N., MA, FBA, Dept of Russian History, School of Slavonic Studies, London WC1.
Shackleton, R., MA, DLitt, LittD, FBA, FSA, Brasenose College, Oxford.
Shannon, R. T., MA, PhD, 84 Newmarket Road, Norwich, Norfolk.
Sharp, Mrs M., PhD, 59 Southway, NW11 6SB.

Shaw, I. P., MA, 3 Oaks Lane, Shirley, Croydon, Surrey CR0 5HP.
*Shaw, R. C., MSc, FRCS, FSA, Orry's Mount, Kirk Bride, nr Ramsey, Isle of Man.
Shead, N. F., MA, BLitt, 16 Burnside Gardens, Clarkston, Glasgow.
Shennan, J. H., PhD, Glenair, Moorside Road, Brookehouse, Caton, nr Lancaster.
Sheppard, F. H. W., MA, PhD, FSA, 55 New Street, Henley-on-Thames, Oxon.
Sherborne, J. W., MA, 26 Hanbury Road, Bristol.
Sigsworth, Professor E. M., BA, PhD, The University, Heslington, York.
Sillery, A., MA, DPhil, 24 Walton Street, Oxford.
Simmons, Professor J., MA, The University, Leicester.
Simpson, G. G., MA, PhD, FSA, Taylor Building, King's College, Old Aberdeen.
Sinar, Miss J. C., MA, 60 Wellington Street, Matlock, Derbyshire DE4 3GS.
Siney, Professor Marion C., MA, PhD, 2676 Mayfield Road, Cleveland Heights, Ohio 44106, U.S.A.
Singhal, Professor D. P., MA, PhD, University of Queensland, St Lucia, Brisbane, Queensland, Australia 4067.
Skidelsky, Professor R., BA, PhD, Flat 1, 166 Cromwell Road, London SW5 0TJ.
Skinner, Q. R. D., MA, Christ's College, Cambridge.
Slack, P. A., MA, DPhil, Exeter College, Oxford OX1 3DP.
Slade, C. F., PhD, FSA, 28 Holmes Road, Reading.
Slater, A. W., MSc(Econ), 146 Castelnau, SW13 9ET.
Slatter, Miss M. D., MA, 5 Inglewood Court, Liebenrood Road, Bath Road, Reading.
Slavin, Professor A. J., PhD, University of California, Los Angeles, Calif., U.S.A.
Smail, R. C., MBE, MA, PhD, FSA, Sidney Sussex College, Cambridge.
*Smalley, Miss B., MA, PhD, FBA, 5c Rawlinson Road, Oxford OX2 6UE.
Smith, A. G. R., MA, PhD, 40 Stanley Avenue, Paisley, Renfrewshire.
Smith, A. Hassell, BA, PhD, Inst. of East Anglian Studies, University of East Anglia, University Village, Norwich.
Smith, E. A., MA, Faculty of Letters, The University, Whiteknights, Reading RG6 2AA.
Smith, Professor F. B., MA, PhD, Dept of History, Australian National University, Canberra, A.C.T., Australia 2600.
Smith, Professor Goldwin A., MA, PhD, DLitt, Wayne State University, Detroit, Michigan 48202, U.S.A.
Smith, J. Beverley, M.A., University College, Aberystwyth SY23 2AX.
Smith, Professor L. Baldwin, PhD, Northwestern University, Evanston, Ill. 60201, U.S.A.
Smith, P., MA, DPhil, 81 St. Stephen's Road, West Ealing, London W13 8JA.
Smith, S., BA, PhD, Les Haies, Oatlands Road, Shinfield, Berks.
Smith, W. J., MA, 5 Gravel Hill, Emmer Green, Reading, Berks.
*Smyth, Rev. Canon C. H. E., MA, 12 Manor Court, Pinehurst, Cambridge.
Snell, L. S., MA, FSA, Newman College, Bartley Green, Birmingham 32.
Snow, Professor V. F., MA, PhD, University of Nebraska, Lincoln, Nebraska, U.S.A.

Snyder, Professor H. L., MA, PhD, 1324 Strong Avenue, Lawrence, Kansas 66044, U.S.A.

Soden, G. I., MA, DD, Buck Brigg, Hanworth, Norfolk.

Somers, Rev. H. J., JCB, MA, PhD, St Francis Xavier University, Antigonish, Nova Scotia.

Somerville, Sir Robert, KCVO, MA, FSA, 15 Foxes Dale, Blackheath, London SE3.

Sosin, Professor J. M., PhD, History Dept, University of Nebraska, Lincoln, Nebraska 68508, U.S.A.

SOUTHERN, Sir Richard (W.), MA, DLitt, LittD, DLitt, FBA, The President's Lodgings, St John's College, Oxford OX1 3JP.

Southgate, D. G., BA, DPhil, 40 Camphill Road, Broughty Ferry, Dundee, Scotland.

Speck, W. A., MA, DPhil, The University, Newcastle upon Tyne.

Spencer, B. W., BA, FSA, 6 Carpenters Wood Drive, Chorleywood, Herts.

Spooner, Professor F. C., MA, PhD, The University, 23 Old Elvet, Durham.

Spufford, Mrs H. Margaret, MA, PhD, 101 Horwood, The University, Keele, Staffs.

Spufford, P., MA, PhD, The University, Keele, Staffs ST5 5BG.

Stanley, Professor G. F. G., MA, BLitt, DPhil, Library, Mount Alison University, Sackville, New Brunswick, Canada.

Stansky, Professor Peter, PhD, Dept of History, Stanford University, Stanford, Calif. 94305, U.S.A.

Steefel, Professor L. D., MA, PhD, 3549 Irving Avenue South, Minneapolis, Minn. 55408 U.S.A.

Steele, E. D., MA, PhD, The University, Leeds.

Steer, F. W., MA, FSA, 63 Orchard Street, Chichester, Sussex.

Steinberg, J., MA, PhD, Trinity Hall, Cambridge.

Steiner, Mrs Zara S., MA, PhD, New Hall, Cambridge.

Stéphan, Rev. Dom John, OSB, FSA, St Mary's Abbey, Buckfast, Buckfastleigh, Devon.

Stephens, W. B., MA, PhD, FSA, 37 Batcliffe Drive, Leeds 6.

Steven, Miss M. J. E., PhD, University of Western Australia, Perth, W. Australia 6009.

Stone, E., MA, DPhil, FSA, Keble College, Oxford.

Stone, Professor L., MA, Princeton Univesrity, Princeton, N.J., U.S.A.

*Stones, Professor E. L. G., PhD, FSA, Dept. of History, The University, Glasgow G12 8QH.

Storey, Professor R. L., MA, PhD, 19 Elm Avenue, Beeston, Nottingham NG9 1BU.

*Stoye, J. W., MA, DPhil, Magdalen College, Oxford.

Street, J., MA, PhD, 6 Thulborn Close, Teversham, Cambridge.

Strong, Mrs F., MA, South Cloister, Eton College, Windsor SL4 6DB.

Strong, R., BA, PhD, FSA, Victoria & Albert Museum, London SW7.

Stuart, C. H., MA, Christ Church, Oxford.

Styles, P., MA, FSA, 21 Castle Lane, Warwick.

Supple, Professor B. E., BSc(Econ), PhD, Dept of Econ. and Social History, The University of Sussex, Falmer, Brighton BN1 9QQ.

Surman, Rev. C. E., MA, 352 Myton Road, Leamington Spa CV31 3NY.

Sutherland, Professor D. W., DPhil, State University of Iowa, Iowa City, Iowa 52240, U.S.A.

SUTHERLAND, Dame Lucy, DBE, MA, DLitt, LittD, DCL, FBA, 59 Park Town, Oxford.

Sutherland, N. M., MA, PhD, St John's Hall, Bedford College, NW1.

Swanton, M. J., BA, PhD, The University, Exeter EX4 4QH.

Swart, Professor K. W., PhD, LittD, University College, Gower Street, WC1E 6BT.

Sydenham, M. J., PhD, Carleton University, Ottawa 1, Canada.

Sylvester, Professor R. S., PhD, The Yale Edition of the works of St Thomas More, 1986 Yale Station, New Haven, Conn. U.S.A.

Syrett, Professor D., PhD, 46 Hawthorne Terrace, Leonia, N.J. 07605, U.S.A.

Talbot, C. H., PhD, BD, FSA, 47 Hazlewell Road, SW15.

Tanner, J. I., MA, PhD, Flat One, 57 Drayton Gardens, SW10 9RU.

Tanner, L. E., CVO, MA, DLitt, FSA, 32 Westminster Mansions, Great Smith Street, Westminster SW1P 3BP.

Tarling, Professor P. N., MA, PhD, LittD, University of Auckland, Private Bag, Auckland, New Zealand.

Taylor, Arnold J., CBE, MA, DLitt, FBA, FSA, 56 Langham Road, Teddington, Middlesex.

Taylor, Professor Arthur J., MA, The University, Leeds LS2 9JT.

Taylor, J., MA, The University, Leeds LS2 9JT.

Taylor, J. W. R., 36 Alexandra Drive, Surbiton, Surrey KT5 9AF.

Taylor, W., MA, PhD, FSAScot, 25 Bingham Terrace, Dundee.

Temple, Nora C., BA, PhD, University College, Cardiff.

Templeman, G., MA, PhD, FSA, 22 Ethelbert Road, Canterbury, Kent.

Thirsk, Mrs I. J., PhD, St Hilda's College, Oxford OX4 1DY.

Thistlethwaite, F., MA, University of East Anglia, Earlham Hall, Norwich NOR 88C.

Thomas, Professor H. S., MA, University of Reading, Reading.

Thomas, Rev. J. A., MA, PhD, 164 Northfield Lane, Brixham, Devon.

Thomas, K. V., MA, St John's College, Oxford OX1 3JP.

Thomas, P. G. D., MA, PhD, University College, Aberystwyth SY23 2AU.

Thomas, W. E. S., MA, Christ Church, Oxford OX1 1DP.

Thomis, M. I., MA, PhD, 28 Keir Street, Bridge of Allan, Stirlingshire.

Thompson, A. F., MA, Wadham College, Oxford OX1 3PN.

Thompson, Mrs D. K. G., MA, School of History, The University, Birmingham.

Thompson, E. P., MA, Warwick University, Coventry.

Thompson, Professor F. M. L., MA, DPhil, Bedford College, Regent's Park NW1 4NS.

Thompson, P., MA, DPhil, Dept of Sociology, University of Essex, Wivenhoe Park, Colchester, Essex, CO4 3SQ.

Thomson, J. A. F., MA, DPhil, The University, Glasgow W2.

*Thomson, T. R. F., MA, MD, FSA, Cricklade, Wilts.

Thorne, C., BA, School of European Studies, University of Sussex, Brighton.

Thorne, Professor S. E., MA, LLB, FSA, Harvard Law School, Cambridge, Mass., U.S.A.

Thornton, Professor A. P., MA, DPhil, 11 Highbourne Road, Toronto 7, Canada.

Thorpe, Prof. Lewis, BA, LèsL, PhD, Ddel'U, 26 Parkside, Wollaton Vale, Nottingham.

*Thrupp, Professor S. L., MA, PhD, University of Michigan, Ann Arbor, Mich., 48104, U.S.A.

Thurlow, The Very Rev. A. G. G., MA, FSA, Dean of Gloucester, The Deanery, Gloucester.

Tibbutt, H. G., FSA, 12 Birchdale Avenue, Kempston, Bedford.

Titow, J. Z., PhD, Dept of Economic History, The University, Nottingham.

Titterton, Commander G. A., RN(ret), Flat 4, Clarence House, 8 Granville Road, Eastbourne, Sussex.

Tomkeieff, Mrs O. G., MA, LLB, 88 Moorside North, Newcastle upon Tyne NE4 9DU.

Toynbee, Miss M. R., MA, PhD, FSA, 22 Park Town, Oxford OX2 6SH.

Trebilcock, R. C., MA, Pembroke College, Cambridge CB2 1RF.

*Trevor-Roper, Professor H. R., MA, FBA, Oriel College, Oxford.

Trickett, Professor The Rev. A. Stanley, MA, PhD, 236 South Lake Drive, Lehigh Acres, Florida, 33936, U.S.A.

Tyacke, N. R. N., MA, DPhil, 1a Spencer Rise, London NW5.

Tyler, P., BLitt, MA, DPhil, University of Western Australia, Nedlands, Western Australia 6009.

Ugawa, Professor K., BA, MA, PhD, 1008 Ikebukuro, 2 Chome, Tokyo 171, Japan.

Ullmann, Professor W., MA, LittD, Trinity College, Cambridge.

Underdown, Professor David, PhD, Dept of History, Brown University, Providence, Rhode Island 02912, U.S.A.

Underhill, C. H., The Lodge, Needwood, Burton-upon-Trent, Staffs.

Upton, A. F., MA, 5 West Acres, St Andrews, Fife.

Urry, W. G., PhD, FSA, St Edmund Hall, Oxford.

Vaisey, D. G., MA, FSA, 52 Mill Street, Eynsham, nr Oxford.

Vale, M. G. A., MA, DPhil, Dept of History, The University, Heslington York.

Van Caenegem, Professor R. C., LLD, Veurestraat 18, 9821 Afsnee, Belgium.

Van Cleve, Professor T. C., MA, PhD, DLitt, Bowdoin College, Brunswick, Maine, U.S.A.

Vann, Professor Richard T., PhD, Dept of History, Wesleyan University, Middletown, Conn. 06457, U.S.A.

*Varley, Mrs J., MA, FSA, 164 Nettleham Road, Lincoln.

Vaughan, Sir (G.) Edgar, KBE, MA, 29 Birch Grove, West Acton, London W3 9SP.

Veale, Elspeth M., BA, PhD, Goldsmith's College, New Cross, London SE14 6NW.

Véliz, Professor C., BSc, PhD, Dept of Sociology, La Trobe University, Melbourne, Victoria, Australia.

Vessey, D. W. T. C., MA, PhD, 10 Uphill Grove, Mill Hill, London NW7.

Villiers, Lady de, MA, BLitt, 4 Church Street, Beckley, Oxford.

Virgoe, R., BA, PhD, University of East Anglia, Norwich.

Waddell, Professor D. A. G., MA, DPhil, University of Stirling, Stirling FK9 4LA.

*Wagner, Sir Anthony R., KCVO, MA, DLitt, FSA, College of Arms, Queen Victoria Street, EC4.

Waites, B. F., MA, 6 Chater Road, Oakham, Rutland.

Walcott, Professor R., MA, PhD, The College of Wooster, Wooster, Ohio 44691 U.S.A.

Waley, D. P., MA, PhD, Dept of Manuscripts, British Museum, WC1B 3DG.

Walford, A. J., MA, PhD, FLA, 45 Parkside Drive, Watford, Herts.

Walker, Rev. Canon D. G., DPhil, FSA, University College, Swansea.

Wallace, Professor W. V., MA, New University of Ulster, Coleraine, N. Ireland.

Wallace-Hadrill, Professor J. M., MA, DLitt, FBA, All Souls College, Oxford OX1 4AL.

Wallis, Miss H. M., MA, DPhil, FSA, 96 Lord's View, St John's Wood Road, NW8 7HG.

Wallis, P. J., MA, 27 Westfield Drive, Newcastle upon Tyne 3.

Walne, P., MA, FSA, County Record Office, County Hall, Hertford.

Walsh, T. J., MB, BCh, PhD, MA, LC, 5 Lower George Street, Wexford, Ireland.

Walters, (W.) E., MA, Burrator, 355 Topsham Road, Exeter.

Wangermann, E., MA, DPhil, The University, Leeds.

*Ward, Mrs G. A., PhD, FSA, Unsted, 51 Hartswood Road, Brentwood, Essex.

Ward, J. T., MA, PhD, Dept of Economic History, McCance Bldg., 16 Richmond Street, Glasgow C1 1XQ.

Ward, Professor W. R., DPhil, University of Durham, 43 North Bailey, Durham.

*Warmington, Professor E. H., MA, 48 Flower Lane, NW7.

Warren, Professor W. L., MA, DPhil, The Queen's University, Belfast, N. Ireland BT7 1NN.

*Waterhouse, Professor E. K., CBE, MA, AM, FBA, Overshot, Badger Lane, Hinksey Hill, Oxford.

*Waters, Lt-Commander D. W., RN, FSA, Jolyons, Bury, nr Pulborough, West Sussex.

Watkin, Rev. Dom Aelred, OSB, MA, FSA, Downside Abbey, Stratton-on-the-Fosse, nr Bath BA3 4RJ.

Watson, A. G., MA, BLitt, FSA, University College, Gower Street, WC1E 6BT.

Watson, D. R., MA, BPhil, Department of Modern History, The University, Dundee.

Watson, J. S., MA, The University, College Gate, North Street, St Andrews, Fife, Scotland.

Watt, Professor D. C., MA, London School of Economics, Houghton Street, WC2.

Watt, D. E. R., MA, DPhil, Dept of Mediaeval History, St Salvator's College, St Andrews, Fife, Scotland.

Watt, J. A., BA, PhD, The University, Hull.

Webb, J. G., MA, 11 Blount Road, Pembroke Park, Old Portsmouth, Hampshire PO1 2TD.

Webb, Professor R. K., PhD, 3307 Highland Place N.W., Washington DC 20008, U.S.A.

Webster (A.) Bruce, MA, FSA, 5 The Terrace, St Stephens, Canterbury.

Webster, C., MA, DSc, Corpus Christi College, Oxford.

Wedgwood, Dame Veronica, OM, DBE, MA, LittD, DLitt, LLD, 22 St Ann's Terrace, St John's Wood, NW8.

Weinbaum, Professor M., PhD, 133–33 Sanford Avenue, Flushing, N.Y. 11355, U.S.A.

Weinstock, Miss M. B., MA, 26 Wey View Crescent, Broadway, Weymouth, Dorset.

Wernham, Professor R. B., MA, Worcester College, Oxford.

*Weske, Mrs Dorothy B., AM, PhD, Oakwood, Sandy Spring, Maryland 20860, U.S.A.

West, Professor F. J., PhD, Dept of History, The University College at Buckingham, Old Bank Building, 2 Bridge Street, Buckingham.

Weston, Professor Corinne C, PhD, 200 Central Park South, New York N.Y. 10019, U.S.A.

*Whatmore, Rev. L. E., MA, St Wilfred's South Road, Hailsham, Sussex.

Whelan, Rev. C. B., OSB, MA, Belmont Abbey, Hereford.

White, Professor B. M. I., MA, DLit, FSA, 3 Upper Duke's Drive, Eastbourne, Sussex BN20 7XT.

White, Rev. B. R., MA, DPhil, 55 St Giles', Regent's Park College, Oxford.

*Whitelock, Professor D., CBE, MA, LittD, FBA, FSA, 30 Thornton Close, Cambridge.

Whiteman, Miss E. A. O., MA, DPhil, FSA, Lady Margaret Hall, Oxford OX2 6QA.

Wiener, Professor J. H., BA, PhD, City College of New York, Convent Avenue at 138 Street, New York, 10031 U.S.A.

Wigmore-Beddoes, Rev. D. G., MA, DLitt, 26 Cadogan Park, Belfast BT9 6HH.

Wilkinson, Rev. J. T., MA, DD, Brantwood, Farrington Lane, Knighton, Radnorshire.

Wilks, M. J., MA, PhD, Dept of History, Birkbeck College, Malet Street, WC1E 7HX.

*Willan, Professor T. S., MA, DPhil, 3 Raynham Avenue, Didsbury, Manchester M20 0BW.

Williams, Professor C. H., MA, 6 Blackfriars, Canterbury.

Williams, D., MA, PhD, DPhil, University of Calgary, Calgary, Alberta T2N 1N4, Canada.

Williams, Sir Edgar (T.), CB, CBE, DSO, MA, Rhodes House, Oxford.

Williams, Professor Glanmor, MA, DLitt, University College, Swansea,

Williams, Glyndwr, BA, PhD, Queen Mary College, Mile End Road, E1.

Williams, Professor G. A., MA, PhD, University of Wales, Cathay's Park, Cardiff CF1 3NS.

Williams, J. A., BSc(Econ), MA, 44 Pearson Park, Hull, E. Yorks HU5 2TG.

Williams, N. J., MA, DPhil, FSA, 57 Rotherwick Road, NW11 7DD.

Williams, P. H., MA, DPhil, New College, Oxford OX1 3BN.

*Williams, T. G., MA, 63 Eardley Crescent, SW5.

*Wilson, Professor A., McC, MA, PhD, 1 Brookside, Norwich, Vermont 05055, U.S.A.

Wilson, Professor C. H., MA, FBA, Jesus College, Cambridge.

Wilson, Professor D. M., MA, FSA, Department of Scandinavian Studies, University College, Gower Street, London WC1E 6BT.

Wilson, H. S., BA, BLitt, The University, Heslington, York YO1 5DD.

Wilson, Professor T., MA, DPhil, Dept of History, University of Adelaide, Adelaide, South Australia.

Winks, Professor R. W. E., MA, PhD, 648 Berkeley College, Yale University, New Haven, Conn. 06520, U.S.A.

Wiswall, F. L., PhD, 23 Richmond Drive, Darien, Conn. 06820, U.S.A.

Withrington, D. J., MA, BEd, Inst. of Scottish Studies, King's College, Aberdeen, Scotland.

Wolffe, B. P., MA, BLitt, DPhil, Highview, 19 Rosebarn Avenue, Exeter EX4 6DY.

*Wood, Rev. A. Skevington, PhD, Ridgeway, Curbar, Sheffield.

Wood, Mrs S. M., MA, BLitt, St Hugh's College, Oxford.

Woodfill, Professor W. L., PhD, University of California, Davis, Calif. 95616, U.S.A.

Wood-Legh, Miss K. L., BLitt, PhD, DLitt, 49 Owlstone Road, Cambridge.

Woods, J. A., MA, PhD, The University, Leeds 2.

Woolf, S. J., MA, DPhil, The University, Whiteknights, Reading.

Woolrych, Professor A. H., BLitt, MA, Patchetts, Caton, nr Lancaster.

Worden, A. B., MA, DPhil, St Edmund Hall, Oxford OX1 4AR.

Wormald, B. H. G., MA, Peterhouse, Cambridge CB2 1RD.

Wortley, The Rev. J. T., MA, PhD, History Dept, University of Manitoba, Winnipeg, Manitoba R3T 2N2, Canada.

Wright, Professor E., MA, Institute of United States Studies, 31 Tavistock Square, London WC1H 9EZ.

Wright, L. B., PhD, 3702 Leland Street, Chevy Chase, Md. 20015, U.S.A.

Wright, Maurice, BA, Dept of Government, Dover Street, Manchester M13 9PL.

Wroughton, J. P., MA, 11 Powlett Court, Bath, Somerset BA2 6QJ.

Yates, W. N., MA, 81 Aldwych Drive, North Shields, Tyne and Wear NE29 8SY.

Youings, Professor Joyce A., PhD, The University, Exeter EX4 4OJ.

Young, Brigadier P., DSO, MC, MA, FSA, Bank House, Ripple, Tewkesbury, Glos. GL20 6EP.

Zagorin, Professor P., PhD, 4927 River Road, Scottsville, N.Y. 14546.

Zeeveld, Professor W. Gordon, PhD, Deep Meadow, Woodbine, Md. 21797, U.S.A.

Zeldin, T., MA, DPhil, St Antony's College, Oxford OX2 6JF.

ASSOCIATES OF THE
ROYAL HISTORICAL SOCIETY

Addy, J., MA, PhD, 66 Long Lane, Clayton West, Huddersfield HD8 9PR.

Baird, Rev. E. S., BD, The Vicarage, Harrington, Workington, Cumberland.
Begley, M. R., 119 Tennyson Avenue, King's Lynn, Norfolk.
Bird, E. A., 29 King Edward Avenue, Rainham, Essex RNL3 9RH.
Bratt, C., 65 Moreton Road, Upton, Wirral, Cheshire.
Brigg, Mrs M., The Hollies, Whalley Road, Wilpshire, Blackburn, Lancs.
Brocklesby, R., BA, The Elms, North Eastern Road, Thorne, nr Doncaster, York.
Bryant, W. N., MA, PhD, College of S. Mark and S. John, King's Road, SW10.
Bullivant, C. H., FSA, Sedgemoor House, Warden Road, Minehead, Somerset.
Burton, Commander R. C., RN(ret), Great Streele Oasthouse, Framfield, Sussex.
Butler, Mrs M. C., MA, 4 Castle Street, Warkworth, Morpeth, Northumberland NE65 0UW.

Cairns, Mrs W. N., MA, Alderton House, New Ross, Co. Wexford, Eire.
Carter, F. E. L., CBE, MA, 8 The Leys, London N2 0HE.
Cary, R. H., BA, 23 Bath Road, W4.
Chandra, Shri Suresh, MA, MPhil, 90–36, 155th Street, Jamaica, New York 11432.
Condon, Miss M. M., BA, 56 Bernard Shaw House, Knatchbull Road, London NW10.
Cook, Rev. E. T., 116 Westwood Park, SE23 3QH.
Cooper, Miss J. M., MA, 203B Woodstock Road, Oxford.
Cox, A. H., Winsley, 11A Bagley Close, West Drayton, Middlesex.
Creighton-Williamson, Lt.-Col D., Foxhills, 25 Salisbury Road, Farnborough, Hants.

d'Alton I, BA, 5 Cosin Court, Peterhouse, Cambridge.
Dawson, Mrs S. L., 5 Sinclair Street, Nkana/Kitwe, Zambia.
Dowse, Rev. I. R., Y Caplandy (The Cathedral Chaplain's House), Glanrafon, Bangor, Caerns. LL57 1LH.
Draffen of Newington, George, MBE, KLJ, MA, Meadowside, Balmullo, Leuchars, Fife KY16 0AW.
Drew, J. H., 19 Forge Road, Kenilworth, Warwickshire.
Driver, J. T., MA, BLitt, 25 Abbott's Grange, Off Liverpool Road, Chester.

Emberton, W. J., Firs Lodge, 13 Park Lane, Old Basing, Basingstoke Hants.
Emsden, N., Strathspey, Lansdown, Bourton-on-the-Water, Cheltenham, Glos. GL54 2AR.

Fawcett, Rev. T. J., BD, PhD, 4 The College, Durham DH1 3EH.
Ferguson, J. T., MA, Fayerweather Hall, Columbia University, New York N Y., U.S.A.

Field, C. W., FSG, The Twenty-Sixth House, Robertsbridge, Sussex TN32 5AQ.

Fitzwilliam, B. R., ACP, ThA, Rockhampton Grammar School, Archer Street, Rockhampton, Queensland 4700, Australia.

Fryer, J., BA, Greenfields, Whitemore, nr Congleton, Cheshire.

Gardner, W. M., Chequertree, Wittersham, nr Tenterden, Kent.

Granger, E. R., Bluefield, Blofield, Norfolk.

Greatrex, Mrs J. G., MA, Dept of History, St Patrick's College, Carleton University, Colonel By Drive, Ottawa K1S 1N4, Canada.

Green, P. L., MA, 9 Faulkner Street, Gate Pa, Tauranga, New Zealand.

Griffiths, Rev. G. Ll., MA, BD, Rhiwlas, 10 Brewis Road, Rhos-on-Sea, Colwyn Bay, Denbighs.

Haines, F. D., PhD, Southern Oregon College, Ashland, Oregon, U.S.A.

Hall, P. T., Accrington College of Further Education, Sandy Lane, Accrington, Lancs.

Hanawalt, Mrs B. A., MA, PhD, Indiana University, Bloomington, Ind. 47401, U.S.A.

Hannah, L., BA, St John's College, Oxford OX1 3JP.

Harding, Rev. F. A. J., BSc(Econ), 74 Beechwood Avenue, St Albans.

Hardy, Rev. P. E., The Manse, 20 Victoria Road, Hanham, Bristol.

Hawtin, Miss G., BA, PhD, FSAScot, Honey Cottage, 5 Clifton Road, London SW19.

Heal, Mrs F., PhD, 13 Friar Road, Brighton, Sussex.

Heath, P., BA, Dept of History, The University, Hull HU6 7RX.

Henderson-Howat, Mrs A. M. D., 7 Lansdown Crescent, Edinburgh EH12 5EQ.

Henriques, Miss U. R. Q., BA, BLitt, 4 Campden Hill Square, W11.

Hoare, E. T., 70 Addison Road, Enfield, Middx.

Hodge, Mrs G., 85 Hadlow Road, Tonbridge, Kent.

Hope, R. B., MA, MEd, PhD, 5 Partis Way, Newbridge Hill, Bath, Somerset.

Hopewell, S., MA, Headmaster's House, Royal Russell School, Addington, Croydon, Surrey CR9 5BX.

Hughes, R. G., 'Hafod', 92 Main Road, Smalley, Derby DE7 6DS.

Hunt, J. L., 90 Woodside, Leigh-on-Sea, Essex SS9 4RB.

Hunt, J. W., MA, 123 Park Road, Chiswick W4.

Jarvis, L. D., Middlesex Cottage, 86 Mill Road, Stock, Ingatestone, Essex.

Jermy, K. E., MA, 8 Thelwall New Road, Thelwall, Warrington, Lancs WA4 2JF.

Jerram-Burrows, Mrs L. E., Parkanaur House, 88 Sutton Road, Rochford, Essex.

Johnston, F. R., MA, 20 Russell Street, Eccles, Manchester.

Johnstone, H. F. V., 96 Wimborne Road, Poole, Dorset.

Joy, E. T., MA, BSc(Econ), The Rotunda, Ickworth, Bury St Edmunds, Suffolk IP29 5QE.

Keen, L. J., 14 Fairfield's Close, Roe Green NW9.

Keir, Mrs G. I., BA, 21 Raleigh Road, Richmond, Surrey.

Kennedy, M. J., BA, Dept of Medieval History, The University, Glasgow W2.

Kitching, C. J., BA, PhD, 54 Compayne Gardens, NW6.

Knight, G. A., BA, 46 Bold Street, Pemberton, Wigan, Lancs. WN5 9E2.
Knowlson, Rev. G. C. V., St John's Vicarage, Knutsford Road, Wilmslow, Cheshire.

Laws, Captain W. F., MLitt, University of Otago, P.O. Box 56 Dunedin, New Zealand.
Lea, R. S., MA, 29 Crestway, SW15.
Lee, Professor M. duP, PhD, Douglass College, Rutgers University, NB, NJ 08903, U.S.A.
Lewin, Mrs J., MA, 3 Sunnydale Gardens, Mill Hill NW7.
Lewis, F., 23 Berwick Road, Rainham, Essex.
Lewis, J. B., MA, CertEd, FRSA, 11 Hawkesbury Road, Buckley, Clwyd CH7 3HR.
Lewis, Professor N. B., MA, PhD, 8 Westcombe Park Road SE3 7RB.
Loach, Mrs J., MA, Somerville College, Oxford.

McIntyre, Miss S. C., BA, Lady Margaret Hall, Oxford.
McLeod, D. H., BA, PhD, School of History, Warwick University, Coventry CV4 7AL.
Mansfield, Major A. D., 38 Churchfields, West Mersea, Essex.
Mathews, E. F. J., BSc(Econ), PhD, 2 Park Lake Road, Poole, Dorset.
Meatyard, E., BA, DipEd, Guston, Illtyd Avenue, Llantwit Major, Glam. CF6 9TG.
Metcalf, D. M., MA, DPhil, Ashmolean Museum, Oxford.
Mills, H. J., BSc, MA, Old Timbers, The Square, Wickham, Hants.
Morgan, D. A. L., MA, Dept of History, University College, Gower Street, London WC1E 6BT.

Newman, L. T., LRIC, CEng, MIGasE, AMInstF, 12 Gay Bowers, Hockley, Essex.
Nicholls, R. E., MA, PhD, Glenholm, Hook Road, Surbiton, Surrey.

Obelkevich, J., MA, (address unknown).
O'Day, Mrs M. R., BA, PhD, 16 The Vale, Edgbaston Park Road, Birmingham B15 2RP.
Oggins, R. S., PhD, c/o Dept of History SM, State University of New York, Binghampton 13901, U.S.A.
Oldham, C.R., MA, Te Whare, Walkhampton, Yelverton, Devon.

Parsons, Mrs M. A., MA, 24 Purleybury Close, Purley, Surrey.
Partridge, Miss F. L., BA, 17 Spencer Gardens, SW14 7AH.
Pasmore, H. S., MB, BS, 21 Edwardes Square, W8.
Paton, L. R., 49 Lillian Road, Barnes, SW13.
Paulson, E., BSc(Econ), 11 Darley Avenue, Darley Dale, Matlock, Derbys.
Perry, E., FSAScot, 28 Forest Street, Hathershaw, Oldham, OL8 3ER.
Pitt, B. W. E., Flat 4, Red Roofs, Bath Road, Taplow, Maidenhead, Berks.
Priestley, E. J., MA, MPhil, 10 Kent Close, Bromborough, Wirral, Cheshire L63 0EF.

Raban, Mrs S. G., MA, PhD, Homerton College, Cambridge.
Rankin, Colonel R. H., 6203 Beachway Drive, Falls Church, Va. 22041, U.S.A.

Rendall, Miss J., BA, Alcuin College, University of York, Heslington, York.

Richards, N. F., PhD, 376 Maple Avenue, St Lambert, Prov. of Quebec, Canada.

Richmond, C. F., DPhil, 59 The Covert, The University, Keele, Staffs.

Rosenfield, M. C., AM, PhD, Box 395, Mattapoisett, Mass. 02739, U.S.A.

Sabben-Clare, E. E., MA, c/o The University Registry, Clarendon Building, Broad Street, Oxford.

Sainsbury, F., 16 Crownfield Avenue, Newbury Park, Ilford, Essex.

Saksena, D. N., First Secretary (Education), Embassy of India, Moscow U.S.S.R.

Sandell, Miss E. M., 12 Avenue Court, 2 Westwood Road, Southampton. SO2 1TX.

Scannura, C. G., 1/11 St. Dominic Street, Valetta, Malta.

Scott, The Rev. A. R., MA, BD, PhD, Ahorey Manse, Portadown, Co. Armagh, N. Ireland.

Seddon, P. R., BA, PhD, The University, Nottingham.

Sellers, J. M., MA, 9 Vere Road, Pietermaritzburg, Natal, S. Africa.

Sharpe, F., FSA, Derwen, Launton, Bicester, Oxfordshire OX6 0DP.

Shores, C. F., ARICS, 40 St Mary's Crescent, Hendon NW4 4LH.

Sibley, Major R. J., 8 Ways End, Beech Avenue, Camberley, Surrey.

Sloan, K., BEd, MPhil, 13 Fernwood, Park Villas, Roundhay, Leeds 8.

Smith, Professor C. D., MA, PhD, 416 Hall of Languages, Syracuse University, Syracuse, N.Y., 13210, U.S.A.

Smith, D. M., Borthwick Institute, St Anthony's Hall, York.

Sorensen, Mrs M. O., MA, 8 Layer Gardens, W3 9PR.

Sparkes, I. G., FLA, 124 Green Hill, High Wycombe, Bucks.

Stafford, D. S., BA, 10 Highfield Close, Wokingham, Berks.

Stitt, F. B., BLitt, William Salt Library, Stafford.

Taylor, R. T., MA, Dept of Political Theory and Government, University College, Swansea SA2 8PP.

Thewlis, J. C., BA, The University, Hull HU6 7RX.

Thomas, Miss E. J. M., 8 Ravenscroft Road, Northfield End, Henley-on-Thames, Oxon.

Thompson, C. L. F., MA, Orchard House, Stanford Road, Orsett, nr. Grays, Essex, RM16 3BX.

Thompson, L. F., Orchard House, Stanford Road, Orsett, nr Grays, Essex RM16 3BX.

Thorold, M. B., 20 Silsoe House, Park Village East, London NW1 4AS.

Tomlinson, H. C., Flat 2, 40 Leverton Street, London NW5.

Tracy, J. N., BA, MPhil, Phd, c/o P. Huth Esq, 6 Chaucer Court, 28 New Dover Road, Canterbury, Kent.

Tristram, B., DipEd, (address unknown).

Tuffs, J. E., 360 Monega Road, Manor Park E12.

Waldman, T. G., MA, 131 Riverside Drive, New York, N.Y., 10024, U.S.A.

Wall, Rev. J., BD, MA, Ashfield, 45 Middleton Lane, Middleton St George, nr Darlington, Co. Durham.

Wallis, K. W., BA, 48 Berkeley Square, W1.

Warrillow, E. J. D., MBE, FSA, Hill-Cote, Lancaster Road, Newcastle, Staffs.

Whiting, J. R. S., MA, DLitt, 15 Lansdown Parade, Cheltenham, Glos.
Wilkinson, F. J., 40 Great James Street, Holborn, London WC1N 3HB.
Williams, A. R., MA, 5 Swanswell Drive, Granley Fields, Cheltenham, Glos.
Williams, H., (address unknown).
Williams, Miss J. M., MA, History Dept, University of Auckland, Private Bag, Auckland, New Zealand.
Windrow, M. C., 40 Zodiac Court, 165 London Road, Croydon, Surrey.
Wood, A. W., 11 Blessington Close, SE13.
Wood, J. O., BA, MEd, Fountains, Monument Gardens, St Peter Port, Guernsey, C.I.
Woodall, R. D., BA, Bethel, 7 Wynthorpe Road, Horbury, nr Wakefield, Yorks WF4 5BB.
Woodfield, R., BD, MTh, 43 Playfield Crescent, SE22.
Worsley, Miss A. V., BA, 17 Essex Street, Forest Gate, London E7 0HL.
Wright, J. B., BA, White Shutters, Braunston, Rutland LE15 8QT.

Zerafa, Rev. M. J., St Dominic's Priory, Valletta, Malta.

CORRESPONDING FELLOWS

Andersson, Ingvar, FilDr, Engelbrektsgatan 6A IV, Stockholm, Sweden.

Bartoš, Professor F. M., PhDr, II, Jihozápadní 7, Praha-Spořilov, Czecho-slovakia.
Bischoff, Professor B., DLitt, 8033 Planegg C. München, Ruffini-Allee 27, Germany.
Braudel, Professor F., École Pratique des Hautes Études, 20 rue de la Baume, Paris VIIIᵉ, France.

Cárcano, M. A., Centeno 3131, Buenos Aires, Argentina.
Coolhaas, Professor W. P., Gezichtslaan 71, Bilthoven, Holland.
Creighton, Professor D. G., MA, DLitt, LLD, Princess Street, Brooklin, Ontario, Canada.

Donoso, R., Presidente de la Sociedad Chilena de Historia y Geografía, Casilla, 1386, Santiago, Chile.
Dvornik, Professor the Rev. F., DD, D-ès-Lettres, DLit, Harvard University, Dumbarton Oaks, 1703 32nd Street, Washington, D.C., U.S.A.

Ganshof, Professor F. L., 12 rue Jacques Jordaens, Brussels, Belgium.
Giusti Rt Rev. Mgr M., JCD, Prefect Archivio Segreto Vaticano, Vatican City, Italy.
Glamann, Professor K., DrPhil, Frederiksberg, Bredegade 13A, 2000 Copenhagen, Denmark.
Gwynn, Professor the Rev. A., SJ, MA, DLitt, Milltown Park, Dublin 6, Eire.

Halicki, Professor O., DrPhil, 35 Baker Avenue, White Plains, New York, U.S.A.
Hancock, Professor Sir Keith, KBE, MA, DLitt, FBA, Australian National University, Box 4, P.O., Canberra, ACT, Australia.
Hanke, Professor L. U., PhD, University of Massachusetts, Amherst, Mass. 01002, U.S.A.
Heimpel, Professor Dr H., DrPhil, Direktor des Max Planck-Instituts für Geschichte, Gottingen, Düstere Eichenweg 28, Germany.

Inalcik, Professor Halil, PhD, The University of Ankara, Ankara, Turkey.

Kuttner, Professor S., MA, JUD, SJD LLD, Institute of Medieval Canon Law, University of California, Berkeley, Calif. 94720, U.S.A.

Langer, Professor W. L., PhD, LLD, DPhil, LHD, LittD, 1 Berkeley Street, Cambridge, Mass. 02138, U.S.A.

Morison, Professor S. E., PhD, LittD, Harvard College Library, 417 Cam-bridge, Mass., U.S.A.

Ostrogorsky, Professor G., The University, Belgrade, Yugoslavia.

Peña y Cámara, J. M. de la, Juan del Castillo, 5, 2°, Seville, Spain.

Perkins, Professor D., MA, PhD, LLD, University of Rochester, Rochester, N.Y., U.S.A.

Perroy, Professor E. M. J., D-ès-L, 5 rue Monticelli, Paris XIVe, France.

Renouvin, Professor P., D-ès-L, 2 Boulevard Saint Germain, Paris, France.

Rodrígues, Professor José Honório, Rua Paul Redfern, 23, ap. C.O.1, Rio de Janeiro, Gb. ZC—37, Brasil.

Sapori, Professor A., Università Commerciale Luigi Bocconi, Via Sabbatini 8, Milan, Italy.

Van Houtte, Professor J. A., PhD, FBA, Termunkveld, Groeneweg 51, Egenhoven, Heverlee, Belgium.

Verlinden, Professor C., PhD, 8 Via Omero (Valle Giulia), Rome, Italy.

Zavala, S., LLD, Mexican Embassy, 9 rue de Longchamp, Paris XVIe, France.

TRANSACTIONS AND PUBLICATIONS
OF THE
ROYAL HISTORICAL SOCIETY

The annual publications of the Society issued to Fellows and Sub-scribing Libraries include the *Transactions*, supplemented since 1897 by a continuation of the publications of the Camden Society (1838-97) as the *Camden Series*, and since 1937 by a series of *Guides and handbooks*. The Society also began in 1937 an annual bibliography of *Writings on British History*, for the continuation of which the Institute of Historical Research accepted responsibility in 1965; it publishes, in conjunction with the American Historical Association, a series of *Bibliographies of British History*; and from time to time it issues miscellaneous publications. Additional copies of the *Transactions*, the *Camden Series*, the *Guides and handbooks*, and the 'Miscellaneous publications' may be obtained by Fellows and Sub-scribing Libraries at the prices stated below. The series of annual biblio-graphies of *Writings on British History* and the *Bibliographies of British history* are not included among the volumes issued to subscribers, but may be obtained by them at the special prices stated below by ordering from a book-seller or from the publishers. Associates, while receiving only the *Transactions* in return for their subscription, are entitled to purchase at a reduction of 25 per cent one copy of other volumes issued to Fellows and Subscribing Libraries and one copy of each of the volumes of the *Writings on British history* and the *Bibliographies of British history* at the special price.

N.B. Current volumes of the *Transactions* and *Camden Series* (*i.e.* those for the current year and two years preceding) are not sold by the Society to the public, but are available only to members on application to the Society.

Back issues of both series are obtainable from Wm. Dawson & Sons Ltd, Cannon House, Folkstone, Kent, and *Guides and handbooks* from Dawsons of Pall Mall at the same address.

TRANSACTIONS

Additional copies of *Transactions* may be had for £3·00 (Special price to members, who should order from the Society, £2·25).

Volumes out of print in *Transactions*, *Old*, *New and Third Series* may be obtained from Kraus-Thomson Organisation Ltd.

Old series, 1872–82. Vols. I to X.
New series, 1884–1906. Vols. I to XX.
Third series, 1907–17. Vols. I to XI.
Fourth series, 1918–50. Vols. I to XXXII.
Fifth series, 1951–   . Vols. I to XXIV.

MISCELLANEOUS PUBLICATIONS

Copies of the following, which are still in print, may be obtained from the Society, with the exception of *The Domesday Monachorum of Christ Church, Canterbury* and *The Royal Historical Society, 1868–1968*, which can be ordered from Dawsons of Pall Mall, Cannon House, Folkestone, Kent, and *Essays in Modern History*, which is obtainable from Macmillan and Co., Ltd.

Domesday studies. 2 vols. Edited by P. E. Dove. 1886. £3·50. (Vol. 1 out of print.)

German opinion and German policy before the War. By G. W. Prothero. 1916. 75p.

The *Domesday monachorum* of Christ Church, Canterbury. 1944. £15.

Essays in Medieval History, selected from the Transactions of the Royal Historical Society. Edited by R. W. Southern. 1968. London, Macmillan. *p.b.*, 50p.

Essays in Modern History, selected from the Transactions of the Royal Historical Society. Edited by Ian R. Christie. 1968. London, Macmillan. 2·75, *p.b.*, £1·50.

The Royal Historical Society, 1868–1968. By R. A. Humphreys. 1969. £1·25.

BIBLIOGRAPHIES ISSUED IN CONJUNCTION WITH THE AMERICAN HISTORICAL ASSOCIATION

Copies of the following cannot be supplied by the Society, but may be ordered through a bookseller.

Bibliography of British history: Tudor Period, 1485–1603. Edited by Conyers Read. 1st ed. 1933; 2nd ed. 1959. Oxford Univ. Press £3·75. (Special price, £2·80.)

Bibliography of British history: Stuart period, 1603–1714. 2nd ed. Edited by Mary F. Keeler, 1970. Oxford Univ. Press. £5. (Special price, £3·75.)

Bibliography of |British history: 1714–89. Edited by S. M. Pargellis and D. J. Medley. 1951. Oxford Univ. Press. (Out of print.) Supplement, edited by A. T. Milne and A. N. Newman, *in preparation.*

Bibliography of British history: 1789–1851. Edited by Ian R. Christie and Lucy M. Brown, *in preparation.*

Bibliography of British history: 1851–1914. Edited by H. J. Hanham, *in preparation.*

Bibliography of English History to 1485. Based on The Sources and Literature of English History from earliest times by Charles Gross. Revised and expanded by Edgar B. Graves, *in the press.*

ANNUAL BIBLIOGRAPHIES

Copies of the following cannot be supplied by the Society, but may be ordered from a bookseller or the Institute of Historical Research.

Writings on British history, 1901–33 (5 vols. in 7); Vol. 1–3, 1968, Vol. 4, 1969, Vol. 5, 1970. London, Jonathan Cape. Vol. 1, £5·25 (special price £4·58); Vol. 2, £3·15 (special price £2·75); Vol. 3, £5·25 (special price £4·58); Vol. 4 (in two parts), £7·35 (special price £6·40); Vol. 5 (in two parts), £8·40 (special price £7·35).

Writings on British history, 1934. Compiled by A. T. Milne, 1937. London, Jonathan Cape, (out of print).

Writings on British history, 1935. Compiled by A. T. Milne. 1939. London, Jonathan Cape (out of print).

Writings on British history, 1936. Compiled by A. T. Milne. 1940. London, Jonathan Cape (out of print).

Writings on British history, 1937. Compiled by A. T. Milne. 1949. London, Jonathan Cape (out of print).

Writings on British history, 1938. Compiled by A. T. Milne. 1951. London, Jonathan Cape (out of print).

Writings on British history, 1939. Compiled by A. T. Milne. 1953. London, Jonathan Cape (out of print).

Writings on British history, 1940–45. 2 vols. Compiled by A. T. Milne. 1960. London, Jonathan Cape (out of print).

Writings on British history, 1946–48. Compiled by D. J. Munro. 1973. University of London Inst. of Historical Research, £12·00. (Special price £9·00.)

GUIDES AND HANDBOOKS

Main series

1. Guide to English commercial statistics, 1696–1782. By G. N. Clar k with a catalogue of materials by Barbara M. Franks. 1938. £1·50.
2. Handbook of British chronology. Edited by F. M. Powicke and E. B. Fryde, 1st ed. 1939; 2nd ed. 1961. £4·50.
3. Medieval libraries of Great Britain, a list of surviving books. Edited by N. R. Ker, 1st ed. 1941; 2nd ed. 1964. £4·50.
4. Handbook of dates for students of English history. By C. R. Cheney. 1970. £1·50.
5. Guide to the national and provincial directories of England and Wales, excluding London, published before 1856. By Jane E. Norton. 1950. £2·00.
6. Handbook of Oriental history. Edited by C. H. Philips. 1963. £2·25.
7. Texts and calendars: an analytical guide to serial publications. Edited by E. L. C. Mullins. 1958. £4·50.
8. Anglo-Saxon charters. An annotated list and bibliography. Edited by P. H. Sawyer. 1968. £5·25.
9. A Centenary Guide to the Publications of the Royal Historical Society, 1868–1968. Edited by A. T. Milne. 1968. £3·00.

Supplementary series

1. A Guide to Cabinet Ministers' papers, 1900–51. Edited by Cameron Hazlehurst and Christine Woodland. 1974. £3·00.

Provisionally accepted for future publication:

A Handbook of British Currency. Edited by P. Grierson and C. E. Blunt.

Texts and calendars: an analytical guide to serial publications. Supplement, 1958–68. By E. L. C. Mullins.

A Guide to the Local Administrative Units of England and Wales. Edited by F. A. Youngs.

A Register of Parliamentary Poll Books, c. 1700–1870. Edited by E. L. C. Mullins.

A Guide to Bishops' Register to 1640. Edited by D. M. Smith.

A Guide to the Records and Archives of Mass Communications. Edited by Nicholas Pronay.

A Guide to the Maps of the British Isles. Edited by Helen Wallis.

THE CAMDEN SERIES

Camdens published before the *Fourth Series* are listed in A. T. Milne's *A Centenary Guide to the Publications of the Royal Historical Society.*

Additional copies of volumes in the *Camden Series* may be had for £3·50 (Special price to members £2·63.)
Volumes out of print in the *Camden Old* and *New Series* may be obtained from Johnson Reprint Co. Ltd. Orders for out-of-print volumes in *Camden Third* and *Fourth Series* should be placed with Wm. Dawson & Sons, Ltd., Cannon House, Folkestone, Kent.

FOURTH SERIES

1. Camden Miscellany, Vol. XXII: 1. Charters of the Earldom of Hereford, 1095–1201. Edited by David Walker. 2. Indentures of Retinue with John of Gaunt, Duke of Lancaster, enrolled in Chancery, 1367–99. Edited by N. B. Lewis. 3. Autobiographical memoir of Joseph Jewell, 1763–1846. Edited by A. W. Slater. 1964.
2. Documents illustrating the rule of Walter de Wenlock, Abbot of Westminster, 1283–1307. Edited by Barbara Harvey. 1965.
3. The early correspondence of Richard Wood, 1831–41. Edited by A. B. Cunningham. 1966. (Out of print.)
4. Letters from the English abbots to the chapter at Cîteaux, 1442–1521. Edited by C. H. Talbot. 1967.
5. Select writings of George Wyatt. Edited by D. M. Loades. 1968.
6. Records of the trial of Walter Langeton. Bishop of Lichfield and Coventry (1307–1312). Edited by Miss A. Beardwood. 1969.
7. Camden Miscellany, Vol. XXIII: 1. The Account Book of John Balsall of Bristol for a trading voyage to Spain, 1480. Edited by T. F. Reddaway and A. A. Ruddock. 2. A parliamentary diary of Queen Anne's reign. Edited by W. A. Speck. 3. Leicester House politics, 1750–60, from the papers of John, second Earl of Egmont. Edited by A. N. Newman. 4. The Parliamentary diary of Nathaniel Ryder, 1764–67. Edited by P. D. G. Thomas. 1969.
8. Documents illustrating the British Conquest of Manila, 1762–63. Edited by Nicholas P. Cushner. 1971.
9. Camden Miscellany, Vol. XXIV: 1. Documents relating to the Breton succession dispute of 1341. Edited by M. Jones. 2. Documents relating to Anglo-French negotiations, 1439. Edited by C. T. Allmand. 3. A 'Fifteenth century chronicle' at Trinity College, Dublin. Edited by G. L. Harriss. 1972.
10. Herefordshire Militia Assessments of 1663. Edited by M. A. Faraday. 1972.
11. The early correspondence of Jabez Bunting, 1820–29. Edited by W. R. Ward. 1972.
12. Wentworth Papers, 1597–1628. Edited by J. P. Cooper. 1973.
13. Camden Miscellany, Vol. XXV: 1. The Letters of William, Lord Paget. Edited by Barrett L. Beer and Sybil Jack. 2. The Parliamentary Diary of John Clementson, 1770–1802. Edited by P. D. G. Thomas. 3. J. B. Pentland's Report on Bolivia, 1827. Edited by J. V. Fifer. 1974.
14. Camden Miscellany, Vol. XXVI: 1. Duchy of Lancaster Ordinances, 1483. Edited by Sir Robert Somerville. 2. A Breviat of the Effectes devised for Wales. Edited by P. R. Roberts. 3. Gervase Markham, The Muster-Master. Edited by Charles L. Hamilton. 4. Lawrence Squibb, A Booke of all the Severall Officers of the Court of the Exchequer (1642). Edited by W. H. Brysom. 5. Letters of Henry St John to Charles, Earl of Orrery, 1709–11. Edited by H. T. Dickinson. 1975.

15. Sidney Ironworks Accounts, 1541–73. Edited by D. W. Crossley (*in the press*).

Provisionally accepted for future publication:

The Account Book of Beaulieu Abbey. Edited by S. F. Hockey.

Select documents illustrating the internal crisis of 1296–98 in England. Edited by Michael Prestwich.

The *Acta* of Archbishop Hugh of Rouen (1130–64). Edited by T. Waldman.

Cartularies of Reading Abbey. Edited by B. R. Kemp.

A calendar of Western Circuit Assize Orders, 1629–49. Edited by J. S. Cockburn.

The Letter Book of Thomas Bentham, Bishop of Coventry and Lichfield. Edited by M. Rosemary O'Day and J. A. Berlatsky.

Correspondence of Henry Cromwell, 1655–59. Edited by Clyve Jones.

Correspondence of William Camden. Edited by Richard DeMolen.

Fifteenth-Century Treatises on English Political Ideas. Edited by J.-Ph. Genet.

Heresy Trials in the Diocese of Norwich, 1428–31. Edited by N. P. Tanner.

Proceedings of the Short Parliament of 1640. Edited by Esther S. Cope in collaboration with Willson H. Coates.

George Rainsford's *Ritratto d'Ingliterra*, 1556. Edited by Peter S. Donaldson.

Early Paget Correspondence. Edited by C. J. Harrison and A. C. Jones.